Mae West

Empress of Sex

MAE WEST

Empress of Sex

✧

MAURICE LEONARD

121 4274.

A BIRCH LANE PRESS BOOK
Published by Carol Publishing Group

FOR NELLIE AND TONY LIDDELL

First Carol Publishing Group Edition 1992

Copyright © 1991 by Maurice Leonard

A Birch Lane Press Book
Published by Carol Publishing Group
Birch Lane Press is a registered trademark of
Carol Communications, Inc.

Editorial Offices	Sales & Distribution Offices
600 Madison Avenue	120 Enterprise Avenue
New York, NY 10022	Secaucus, NJ 07094

In Canada: Canadian Manda Group
P.O. Box 920, Station U
Toronto, Ontario M8Z 5P9

First published in Great Britain in 1991
by HarperCollins Publishers, London

Manufactured in the United States of America
10 9 8 7 6 5 4 3 2 1

Carol Publishing Group books are available at special discounts
for bulk purchases, for sales promotions, fund raising, or
educational purposes. Special editions can also be created to
specifications. For details contact: Special Sales Department,
Carol Publishing Group, 120 Enterprise Ave., Secaucus, NJ 07094

Library of Congress Cataloging-in-Publication Data

Leonard, Maurice.
    Mae West : empress of sex / Maurice Leonard.
        p.   cm.
    "A Birch Lane Press book."
    ISBN 1-55972-151-0
    Includes index.
        1. West, Mae. 2. Motion picture actors and actresses—United
States—Biography. 3. Entertainers—United States—Biography.
I. Title.
PN2287.W4566L46   1992   92-20877
791.43'028'092—dc20   [B]   CIP

Contents

Contents

ACKNOWLEDGEMENTS

The idea for a biography of Mae West came from Marilyn Gaunt. Special mention must be made of Christina Hatt whose assistance has been enormous and invaluable, as indeed has that of William R. Fitts of West Hollywood. The book would never have come together without my editor JoAnne Robertson. Robert Duran of Los Angeles has also been extremely helpful. In addition to these people I must also thank John Alarimo of Hollywood, Barbara F. Baird, Tom Baker, Chris Basinger of Los Angeles, Caroline Blackadder, The British Film Institute, Mrs V. M. Bayliss, Bruno Barnabe, Donald S. Brady of Los Angeles, Joe Cohen of *Variety* (New York), Orion Crawford of California, Tony Curtis, Victor Davis, Louise Dennis, Malcolm Dodds, Marion S. Donaldson of Scotland, Yolande Donlan, Angela Doyle, Roy Fewins, Leslie Flint, Zsa Zsa Gabor, Deborah Gaunt, Milton Goldman, John Graham, Larry Grayson, Joyce Haber of Beverly Hills, Bill Hall, Dr Geoffrey Handley-Taylor, Lee Harrington, Ken Hughes, John Jamieson of Dundee, Sue Jerrard, the late Christine Jorgensen, Kathryn J. Kay of Harris County (Texas), Brian Klein, The Kobal Collection, Kenneth R. Cobb of the Municipal Archives (City of New York), David N. Mason, Joe Mitchenson, Fred Otash of Hollywood, Alvista Perkins of Los Angeles, *Psychic News*, Harry Ransom of the Humanities Research Center at the University of Texas at Austin, Anne Rea of California, Scott Richards of Kentucky, Dr William Russell, Ann Rutherford, Mr Salt of Dunlop Tyres, Santa Monica Superior Court, Michael Sarne, Margaret Stallard, Hy Steirman, Raymond Strait, Dorothy L. Swerdlove at New York Public Library, W. E. Townsend, Jon Tuska, Vanderbilt and Bergdolf, Alexander Walker, Marc Wanamaker, Micky Webber, Colin Williams, Mayla Woolf.

MAE WEST
EMPRESS OF SEX

Safe upon the solid rock the ugly houses stand:
Come and see my shining palace built upon the sand!
EDNA ST VINCENT MILLAY

'Mae West . . . that sweet apostle of studied lewdery.'
GEOFFREY HANDLEY-TAYLOR

chapter one

BIRTH OF THE LEGEND

The legend of Mae West, as the vulgar, wisecracking whore with a heart of gold, began on 19 April 1927 in New York. Five years before she made her first movie, Judge George E. Donnellan sentenced her to jail for ten days after finding her guilty of 'corrupting the morals of youth, or others'. The charge was made after a performance of her own play, the blatantly titled *SEX*, in which she had starred.

The account of her spectacular arrest – she had been bundled into the paddy wagon straight from the stage door – amused the public as much as her trial. Her stint in Welfare Island prison catapulted her into newspaper headlines. Nice people did not include Mae West's name on their social lists.

Crowds gathered to watch her make her entrance into the court during her trial. She always arrived with the same coterie, a colourful trio who consisted of her portly, but well-corseted mother, Tillie; Beverly, her glamorous, blonde sister; and James A. Timony, a heavy man with a tough manner, wearing a pin-striped suit and Homburg hat. Timony was Mae's lover and lawyer, elsewhere described as a mouthpiece of the mobsters.

But Timony did not act as Mae's representative at the trial. He was not speaking for anyone apart from himself since he, too, faced similar charges to Mae because he had helped finance her play. And, like her, he was sent to prison.

Strangely, both Beverly and Timony limped and it was said that Timony's limp was the result of a gangster's bullet. The West family gave out that Beverly's limp was caused by a riding accident, but this was not true. Beverly had had polio as a child and this left her with a withered leg. For some reason the Wests

1

considered polio something of a disgrace and did not want it known.

There was a father, too, a rumbustious, hard-drinking former boxer, now turned bouncer, but he did not appear at the trial, which was just as well, for when angered John West was quick to use his fists. He was fiercely proud of his little girl, Mae, and she was already in enough trouble. A punch on the jaw of someone giving evidence would have delighted the public, but it would have done nothing to help her plea of not guilty.

Part of the public interest lay in the fact that Mae was so eyecatching. She was thirty-four years old and petite, standing just five feet two inches in her bare feet. Always a stylish dresser, she wore a coat with a fox collar, high-heeled shoes which showed off her ankles, and a cloche hat, pulled low on her brow as was the fashion of the day. Her pretty, rounded face told of her German ancestry as did her eyes, which were of that penetrating blue found in Teutonic people.

Her arrest had taken place ten weeks earlier on 9 February. Before that Mae had earned a precarious living as a soubrette and vaudeville turn. When times were hard her income had been augmented by Timony.

She had been writing her own plays, or 'sex-dramas' as she called them, for years, but *SEX* was the first to receive any success. Its subject matter concerned blackmail, drugs and prostitution, themes which fascinated her, and to which she constantly returned.

Mae had always rubbed shoulders with gangsters, as the world of club life, which she inhabited, was porous with corruption. More so in the prohibition-shackled New York of the Twenties than at any other time in history. Booze was illegal, yet the punters wanted it, so someone had to supply it. Many of the venues in which Mae performed were backed by bootleg money. Her father, in his capacity as bodyguard, protected the bootleggers. Her boyfriend represented them in court.

Some of New York's hoodlums turned up in court to see how she would fare, but one who could not be present was Owney Madden, owner of Harlem's Cotton Club. He was a business partner of Mae's and had a financial stake in *SEX*, but was prevented from witnessing how the verdict went – as he was in Sing Sing at the time.

There were no tears from Mae when she heard her sentence, instead a strutting insouciance to disguise her nerves. After all, it was only a short sentence and some of her best friends had made the trip to city jail before her.

She was driven to prison in a paddy wagon. She did ask if she could go in her limousine or even a taxi, but the official needed to grant such a dispensation could not be found, so she settled herself in the wagon, waved to her cheering onlookers, and was speedily dispatched on her way.

She received a warm welcome at the jail. The newspaper coverage had ensured she was a celebrity of the calibre approved by the other prisoners in that she had cocked a snook at authority. She was cooperative with the prison authorities; the governor introduced himself and took her to lunch before detailing her to work in the library.

Mae was a model prisoner and given three days off her sentence for good behaviour. When she came to take her farewell, Warden Schleth, under whose supervision she had been, pronounced her 'A fine woman, a great character'.

Her imprisonment was the highlight of her life. She was fiercely proud of it, and even fifty years on rarely let a press interview of any depth pass without mentioning it. As an old lady, she would forget her more recent triumphs and steer the conversation round to the days she had spent in the 'slammer' in her 'youth'. During the production of her last film, made when she was eighty-four, Tony Curtis recalls her telling him all about it. It had established her as a personality, a racy sex revolutionary.

After the sentence, her box office took an upward swing, her gangster friends considered her one of the boys, and without the publicity she would never have attracted the attention of Hollywood.

Mae was eternally grateful.

chapter two

CHILDHOOD

Mary Jane West, better known to the world as Mae, was born on 17 August 1893, the very month and year that the famous strong man, 'The Great Sandow', under the direction of the impresario Florenz Ziegfeld, was enjoying his huge success at the Chicago Trocadero. He had achieved national fame after posing for a series of photographic 'art' studies which enjoyed wide sales as postcards. It was an appropriate omen as musclemen were to feature prominently in Mae's life. She loved them. She was also to have dealings with Flo Ziegfeld.

In 1893 births were not registered with the same diligence as they are today, and John and Tillie West did not register Mae's birth. This oversight led to speculation about the true year of her birth, with estimates varying from 1887 to 1893, the latter date provided by Mae herself in 1932 when, to her annoyance, documents were discovered proving that she must be at least that old. Previously, when cornered, she had lopped seven years off her age.

1887 was put forward as a possible date, owing to a story told by Jules Stein, former musician and founder of the mighty MCA, one of America's foremost theatrical agencies. Stein claimed he had worked with Mae in 1913, when he was a lad of eighteen and playing in vaudeville orchestras. He professed he had propositioned her, but she had declined, protesting that at twenty-six she was too old for him. His claim is absurd as Mae never in her entire life turned down a man on the grounds she thought she was too old for him; sometimes she declined because she thought they were too old for her. If the incident did, indeed, take place, probably her rejection of

Stein was her kindly way of giving him the brush-off. But her kindness backfired and the legend circulated that she was born in 1887 – which would have made her twenty-six in 1913.

Mae was the second child of John and Tillie West. Her elder sister, Katie, had died in infancy from respiratory complications. Although there is no record of Mae's birth, there reposes at New York's Municipal Archives, in the Department of Records and Information, the birth certificate of Katie West, daughter of Tillie and John, of 152 Varet Street, Brooklyn. The return had been made by the midwife, Miss C. Genenda. Tillie was twenty at the time and John twenty-five.

Tillie West gave birth to Katie on 23 August 1891. As Kenneth R. Cobb, Deputy Director of the City of New York Municipal Archives, states, 'According to the certificate, Katie was the first child, so Mae West could be no older than this one . . . Given that she admitted to being born in at least 1893 . . . there wouldn't have been much point in shaving off one year if she had been born in 1892.' Therefore, it seems Mae began telling the truth about her age in 1932, but no one really believed her.

By the time of Mae's birth, the family had moved to Bushwick Avenue, Brooklyn. She was delivered at home with no medical attendant present, merely a relative acting as midwife. The house stood two blocks from where Clara Bow was born and a few streets distant from the birthplace of Marion Davies. The area contained so many churches it was known as the City of Churches, and the sound of church bells became part of her childhood. The house has now been demolished and yet another church built on the site.

Mae wrote of the Brooklyn of her childhood as a place that was leafy and green. Carriages bowled through sunlit lanes and families took picnics in dappled groves; for her it was a version of Arcadia, in which lovers might be glimpsed, through the trees, strolling hand in hand. As L. P. Hartley says, 'The past is a foreign country: they do things differently there.'* In adult

---

* *The Go-Between*, Hamish Hamilton, 1953.

life, childhood environments can sometimes seem rosier than they were.

Certain parts of turn-of-the-century Brooklyn may have fit Mae's description, but it was also a cosmopolitan sorting house containing a rough dockland area and tenements of teeming slums. Immigrants came to New York in their thousands and discovered, as immigrants often do, that there was little awaiting them but poverty and squalor. The only way to make money was to turn to crime. There were areas of Mae's Brooklyn where even strong men never dared walk alone and where respectable women never walked at all.

Katie's birth certificate states that her father's occupation was a bridle maker. Yet, in press interviews Mae gave over the years his occupation gradually became grander, and there was a period when she forsook the world of horses altogether and announced that John West had been a doctor. But this notion was dropped as abruptly as it made its appearance, and she reverted to horses. In 1970 she told Denis Hart of the *Daily Telegraph* that her father 'owned ten carriages before he married my mother. He used to hire them out. I remember when I was a child we always had our own carriage . . .' By the time she reached Hollywood she was claiming kinship with the French aristocracy.

Tillie had been distraught at the death of Katie and when Mae arrived two years later no child could have been more welcome. Her twenty-two-year-old mother, fiercely over-protective, spoiled her hopelessly.

Tillie would proudly ride out in one of the carriages, showing off her rudely healthy, pink and plump baby, nicknamed 'Peaches' because of her lovely complexion. Mae had an abundance of frilled and laced clothes, many in Tillie's favourite colour of lilac. It became Mae's favourite colour, too.

John West was almost a local celebrity. A slight, wiry man, in his youth he had been a featherweight prizefighter who fought under the name of 'Battling Jack'. The soubriquet stuck and he remained Battling Jack throughout Brooklyn. Mae described him in the following manner for the *Sunday Dispatch* in 1935: 'Papa was a fighting man. Mind you, I wouldn't pretend he could have given Dempsey five yards in the hundred. Or taken Tunney for a ride over points. Pa was the good old prizefighter who fought a nifty battle, loved the game, and made a nice little reputation for himself.'

When Battling Jack became too old to battle any more for money, he started a detective agency, which Mae described as a 'private police force'. He seems principally to have acted as a bodyguard to Brooklyn racketeers.

He thoroughly enjoyed this work, particularly when the going got rough, for there was nothing Battling Jack liked so much as a good punch-up. He would think nothing of taking on opponents two, or even three, stones heavier than himself. He liked to keep his hand, or rather, his fist, in.

Mae proudly relates in her autobiography, *Goodness Had Nothing To Do With It,** how Battling Jack would wade into a fight on the slightest provocation. It was a quality she admired. Battling Jack kept fast company. Just as his daughter was to do.

Although born in New York, Battling Jack was of English and Irish descent, the English side of his family originating from the Buckinghamshire town of Long Crendon. His father's family had come to America in the eighteenth century, but Mae claimed the family tree could be traced back to the twelfth. To illustrate the point, she had a coat of arms, which she claimed was rightfully the Wests', hanging in her Hollywood apartment. Another crest, which delineated Tillie's purported French ancestry, hung in her bedroom.

Battling Jack's mother, Mary Jane Copley, had been born in Ireland but had come to America while still a baby.

His father, another John West, had been a whaler and he would visit the Wests, delighting baby Mae with tales of his adventures on the high seas. He was a doughty old man who lived to be over ninety. He had never visited a dentist and would proudly show off his teeth if given the least encouragement. Mae, too, was to retain a near perfect set of teeth and, like her grandfather, would invite inspection of them when in her old age.

* Published by W. H. Allen, 1960.

Her grandfather was deeply religious: Mae told Denis Hart that he 'always got down on his knees and prayed before dinner when he'd visit us, and he'd pray again before he'd leave the house'. His piety seems extreme even by nineteenth-century standards, but Mae responded to it and, in addition to his good teeth, inherited his need to worship. There was a spiritual side to her nature which craved submission to some higher authority.

When Battling Jack married Tillie Doelger, grandfather West presented him with the family bible. As used to be the fashion, this ancient and commodious volume recorded all the births, deaths and weddings of the West family, and the record went back, according to Mae, hundreds of years. She treasured it, but alas it was stolen. In her interview with Denis Hart she bemoaned its loss: ' "I have my suspicions who took it . . ." For a moment (she) contemplates her loss and is troubled by it and is silent.'

Tillie was born in Bavaria, but had relatives who owned a brewery in New York (no mean attraction in itself in Battling Jack's eyes); these comfortably-off people enabled her to emigrate to America. She never lost her German accent.

Before marrying Battling Jack, Tillie lived with her relatives and helped support herself by putting her fine figure to use modelling corsets. Mae often described her as a 'modiste'. She was buxom, fair-complexioned and bore a resemblance to the celebrated Broadway beauty, Lillian Russell.

Miss Russell was Tillie's idea of the perfect woman. Tillie herself was infatuated with the theatre and had dreamed of becoming an actress. Marriage put paid to that, but she determined her daughter should be pointed firmly in the right direction. She was a strong-willed woman.

John was Catholic and Tillie claimed to be the same. Mae, however, said she had been christened Protestant, in tribute to Grandpa West – who was Church of England. If this was true then the Wests were unusual Catholics. Most priests take it as their duty to ensure that the children of their congregation are also brought up Catholic. In all probability, just as her birth was not registered, neither was she christened.

8

Research, however, does not bear out Mae's claim of Pro-
testantism. She was Jewish. Mae's friend, journalist Ruth
Biery, endorsed this as does Mike Sarne, who was later to
direct Mae in *Myra Breckinridge*. Sarne, who is also Jewish,
claims that Mae confided to him that Tillie was Jewish and
had taught her Yiddish, which she spoke to Sarne. If Mae's
mother was Jewish then, according to the Jewish faith, her
children were also Jewish. There is no doubt Mae could speak
Yiddish as many years later, during one of her performances
of *Diamond Lil* which was given to a predominantly Jewish
audience, she sprinkled some of her dialogue with Yiddish
phrases to gain a few laughs (which she got). But she further
confessed to Sarne that Tillie, for reasons known only to herself, made her promise never to reveal her Jewishness. Mae
mostly respected her mother's wish but did admit sometimes
to being Jewish, just as she also said she was Protestant or
Catholic on other occasions.

Tillie practised life as a Christian and took an active part in
the social activities of the church. This had the double advantage of enabling her to get out of the house and to take Mae
with her, away from arguments, as her marriage to Battling
Jack had more than its share of ups and downs. He was quick to
lose his temper and shout, particularly when drunk, and from
an early age Mae could see that married life was not uninterrupted bliss.

Tillie and Battling Jack always ran a free-wheeling household with relatives and friends constantly popping in and out.
Mae was fascinated by the tales they told of a great aunt who
had possessed three breasts. It was believed the additional
breast gave the aunt supernatural powers, and Mae was drawn
to the supernatural from babyhood.

There were quite a few theatrical types in Mae's family (Tillie
and Battling Jack themselves virtually came into that category,
what with Tillie's former modelling days and Battling Jack's
appearances in the square ring). One, a cousin, was a Ziegfeld
girl who later featured in an advertisement for hair shampoo.

The Wests were a good-looking bunch. In one photograph
Battling Jack has a smiling face and is wearing full evening

9

dress. His eyes are fine, set wide apart in a squarish face, and he has a head of thick, neatly groomed hair.

Tillie, who by all accounts was a true beauty, appears rather blowsy in certain photographs. One, in particular, shows her wearing make-up which might have been applied with a trowel. Her eyes have black rings painted around them and the amount of lipstick she is wearing would not have been unsuitable on the lips of Bette Davis in her celebrated portrayal of Baby Jane. Her hair appears to have been bleached white. Neither the hair colour nor the make-up in this photo belong to the era of Tillie's youth, but rather to the Forties and Fifties, and the eyes are straight from the Sixties. The photograph is doctored to such an extent that much of the original has been hidden. The lips, eyes and hair colour were all added later by Mae's inexpert hand. Mae wished to present her beloved mother as ageless, glamorous, and as timeless in her beauty as Mae believed herself to be.

Mae's sister, Mildred, who renamed herself Beverly, was born nearly six years after Mae, and her brother John two years after that. Mae was very much the elder sister and kept an eye on both of them, something which lasted until her death. 'Being the only child for six years I had all the attention,' she told Denis Hart, 'then, by the time my sister and brother arrived, I had my own personality.'

She told the *News of the World*, 'I started my stage life early . . . even before I was five I convinced my parents it would be all right to let me stay up long enough to let me see shows with them.'* And she saw plenty of shows, for when Tillie was not in church she was at the theatre. Usually just she and Mae went, but sometimes, Tillie could persuade Battling Jack to accompany them. The times were rough and the streets harboured thieves, rapists and even murderers. Vice was abroad and baby Mae, decked out in her organdie dresses, would peep from the carriage and see the prostitutes openly plying their trade. Brooklyn was colourful and exciting, and Mae had nothing to fear sitting between her pretty mother and warrior father.

* 7 October 1934.

The Wests did not favour drama, but preferred the extravaganzas that played to packed Broadway houses. They sat in the stalls (Battling Jack was making a good living) and the impressionable Mae watched what was happening and was as absorbent as blotting paper.

Broadway, at that time, consisted of approximately forty theatres, clustered between 23rd and 40th Street. Among the more prominent were the Weber and Fields Music Hall, Palmer's, Wallack's, Hammerstein's, and the Knickerbocker.

By the turn of the century, under the aegis of the powerful Keith Circuit and William Hammerstein, vaudeville was approaching its peak in popularity. Literally thousands of theatres were built, mostly concentrated in the big cities but spreading across small town America.

The public could not see enough vaudeville. Top theatres played twice daily; but the lowliest could run up to seven shows in a day. Among the most popular acts were dancers, comedians, impressionists, acrobats, performing animals – including the ever-popular singing duck – and magicians. Monologuists enjoyed a vogue as did the diseuse, and dialect comedians were constantly updating their acts of mimicking the shifting patois of the immigrants. Freaks were popular, the more bizarre the better, as were acquitted murderers. Mae tells in her autobiography of one particular murderess who, after a fruitful theatrical run, found she could no longer draw audiences. 'What should I do?' she asked her agent. 'Kill someone else,' he told her.

Successful vaudevillians could be spotted immediately. They arrived at venues in the new horseless carriages, sporting extravagant clothes and flashy jewellery. The more successful a vaudevillian the bigger the diamonds. The women had their earrings, necklaces and brooches, the men tiepins, lapel badges, and jewelled watches. Their manners were as flamboyant as their clothes, and the women were discovering the delights of modern cosmetics. Tinted face-powder came in in 1903.

Longacre Square, later Times Square, contained many restaurants into which wealthy patrons and the stars, with their entourages, would spill after the show. Rector's was the most popular restaurant, its Louis XIV décor glittering with mirrors and chandeliers, its frontage boasting the only revolving door in New York. Inside there were a hundred tables and, upon entry, brocade, feathers, gems, fans, perfume, cigar smoke and the odours of rich food and wines assailed the senses. When Battling Jack was in funds he and Tillie, with Mae, sometimes went to Rector's. It became Mae's favourite restaurant.

Mae was naturally left-handed but, as this was considered a stigma, she was encouraged to use her right hand as much as possible. She always used her right hand to eat when in public, and later mastered signing her name with her right hand, but in private she was predominantly left-handed.

The theatre was Mae's kindergarten and she had the opportunity to see the finest entertainers of her day, including Eddie Foy, George M. Cohan, Bert Williams and Nora Bayes. Above all, she thrilled to the fabulous Follies of Florenz Ziegfeld – the beauty of his chorus girls was legendary.

Aside from Lillian Russell, Tillie worshipped Eva Tanguay. It was not for nothing Miss Tanguay was labelled the Belle of Broadway. She was the uncontested Queen of the Circuit, a position she fiercely guarded. She made an immediate impression upon her audiences by her strident delivery, her magnificent clothes and her pungent dialogue. A hint of wickedness enveloped her, epitomized by her theme song 'I Don't Care'. It seemed that Miss Tanguay really did not care, at least not much about public opinion, as she quickly got through four husbands and squandered a fortune estimated at two million dollars.

This was the model upon whom Tillie based Mae's career. Often, when they returned from their theatre trips, Tillie would dress up Mae, and encourage her to mimic the artists they had seen. But after an Eva Tanguay performance the routine was intensified until every mannerism and trick of speech had been faithfully copied by Mae.

Neighbours were invited to watch the finished performance, as were callers to the house. Mae was happy to perform her routines and, accustomed to being doted upon by Tillie, she came to expect similar treatment from everyone else. Among those who saw her act was the parish priest who invited Tillie to put her into a show he was staging at the church. It is ironic that it should be a priest who unleashed Mae West upon the world. Had he glanced at Tillie's face, its determination might have frightened him. For her this was no jape but a foretaste of things to come. Tillie was determined Mae should become a Broadway star.

By the time Mae was six, Tillie had already put her into several amateur shows, mostly organized by the church. Mae unselfconsciously charmed the audiences with her impressions. She had by now learned a 'skip-dance' and a few acrobatic movements taught her by Battling Jack.

He may not have shared Tillie's theatrical ambitions for Mae, but he enjoyed taking her to the gym where the boxers trained to show her off to his cronies. Some of her warmest childhood memories were of boxers. She later told a friend, 'When I was a little girl, I would sit on the floor and watch all the beautiful men, their magnificent muscles rippling, and their foreheads dripping with sweat. I felt I learned a lot about men, a little tyke just sitting on the floor.'

The boxers made a fuss of her and she enjoyed doing the exercises they taught her. She became fascinated by muscular men, associating muscles with her father and security.

Battling Jack made no concessions to her femininity and determined she should be able to take care of herself – the Wests did not go in for weaklings. He did the best he could to toughen her up with a system of keep-fit exercises and taught her some rudimentary punches and self-defence moves. Mae proved a willing pupil. She stated several times in her life that she had never had any interest in dolls, but did like her dumbbells, and toned-up with them regularly. She also enjoyed going to boxing matches and was thrilled when taken to the circus at Coney Island. The lions particularly fascinated her.

Tillie continued to groom her for more important things. Always fussy about Mae's clothes – she went through a period of attaching cloth rosebuds to her dresses – she now took care to give her a balanced diet. Mae had the constitution of an ox, but Tillie nevertheless insisted she eat fresh foods and forbade tinned goods. She ensured Mae had plenty of rest, drumming into her head the importance of a good night's sleep, believing this restored energy, made the eyes sparkle and kept the skin clear.

When Denis Hart asked Mae if she remembered herself as a child, she replied, 'Sure I do. And I like what I remember. I'd turn on you. I wouldn't do anything unless you used the right tone of voice. Mother knew how to get me to do anything by using the right tone of voice.' This portrait of a wilful but sensitive child constantly crops up in any commentary about Mae's extraordinary life.

chapter three

MARRIAGE

It was the era of the child star, and its formidable champion, the stage mother – that pushy individual who was determined to secure baby a career whether or not baby wanted it. The slightest trace of talent was pampered or tortured into an act. When baby basked in the spotlight it was mother who was thrilled. Tillie was the apotheosis of the stage mother.

When Mae was seven Tillie enrolled her for dancing lessons with 'Professor' Watts who ran a dancing school in nearby Fulton Street. Watts's title owed nothing to his professional status; at that time anyone who set themselves up as a teacher could adopt the designation. Mae showed such promise that Watts put her into a Sunday vaudeville concert organized to raise funds for the Elks, a charitable body. This took place at the Theater Royal, a fair-sized house on Fulton Street.

The bill consisted of professional acts but there was a talent spot for amateurs. The audience decided the winner by the strength of its applause. Mae was to take part: she would have the opportunity to dance and sing to the accompaniment of a twelve-piece orchestra.

Tillie chose a song for her called 'Movin' Day' and bought her a pink and green dress with gold spangles. After Tillie had dressed her, she escorted Mae to the wings to await her cue. Mae was calm, not the least intimidated by the size of the auditorium. Tillie clutched her daughter's shoulders, only letting go when Mae walked out on stage.

But something went wrong. The orchestra struck up her introduction but Mae did not sing. Instead, to Tillie's horror, she stamped her foot and bawled. The orchestra fell silent and

Mae's indecipherable yells began to make sense. She was shouting for a spotlight. The professionals had had one, but it was not being used for the amateurs. Mae demanded it. The audience was tickled by the spectacle and, good-naturedly, shouted for the stage manager to do as she asked. He had no option other than to oblige. Only then, to encouraging shouts, did Mae sing 'Movin' Day' and it certainly moved the audience. She received the loudest round of applause and won a gold medal.

Tillie had persuaded Battling Jack to attend the performance and he sat in the stalls, puffing his cigar, surrounded by chums who told him they thought Mae was great.

Mae's success inspired Tillie: armed with the gold medal to persuade any possible doubters of her daughter's ability, she entered Mae for further amateur nights. Mae proved that the Elks concert was no flash in the pan, and often won a first prize of $10 or more. Her repertoire swelled to include such songs as 'My Marioocha Maka da Hoochy-macooch', performed in dialect, and 'Doin' the Grizzly Bear'. She improved her impressions, too, impersonating George M. Cohan (which brought down the house) and Eddie Foy. Weight-lifting – using the dumbbells – was thrown in.

By the time she was eight she was making regular amateur appearances at the Gotham Theater, Brooklyn. Amateur actors were popular with producers as they did not have to be paid. For just a few dollars' prize money, a dozen or so acts could be included.

The Gotham was run by Hal Clarendon who was owner, producer, director and star of the Hal Clarendon Stock Company. When not performing, Handsome Hal, as he was known, watched the shows from his box. He noticed the enthusiastic applause Mae received after performing her Grizzly Bear routine and sent for her.

When Tillie brought her round to his box Mae took to him at once. After a short conversation, it was agreed that Mae should join his company as a juvenile.

Although she did not work exclusively for Clarendon, she stayed with his company, on and off, for three years. He started her on a salary of $18 a week, an amount which suddenly made Battling Jack take an interest, and this eventually rose to $30. During this time she played a variety of roles including Little Lord Fauntleroy, Little Willie in *East Lynne*, Little Mother in *The Fatal Wedding*, and Little Eva in *Uncle Tom's Cabin*. She was also Lovey Mary in *Mrs Wiggs of the Cabbage Patch*.

Mrs Wiggs of the Cabbage Patch, the story of a poverty-stricken shanty-town family, was produced on Broadway in 1904 when Mae would have been eleven. It is conceivable that Mae was in this production. She often mentioned that she had played Broadway as a child. 'I danced my way across the Brooklyn Bridge to Broadway when most girls of my age were playing with dolls,' she told the *News of the World* in the Thirties.

But the first role Handsome Hal gave Mae was in *Ten Nights in a Bar Room*. The play warned against the evils of drink – a pertinent topic as drunkenness was rampant because alcohol was cheap. Mae was required to run on stage, grab the coat tails of her drunken stage father, and wail, 'Father, dear father, come home with me now, the clock on the steeple strikes one.' Prophetic sentiments, considering her future dislike of excessive alcohol consumption.

While with Clarendon she had the opportunity to watch other acts at work. 'Song and dance men were the wittiest, best dressed and most amusing people on earth,' she enthuses in her autobiography. She spent hours in the wings analysing their skills and learning the importance of timing. It was a great school for a budding star.

She liked Clarendon and even played tricks on him. Handsome Hal, although basically kind could, in keeping with his status as actor-manager, be grand at times. Mae told Paramount publicity executive Tom Baily of an occasion when she had stolen the key to Hal's dressing room and, armed with her make-up box, painted his nose red, and given him a beard, moustache and 'a few other artistic touches' while he was asleep. He was furious when he awoke, but eventually saw the funny side. The story of her escapade spread round the company like wildfire.

17

When Clarendon had no work for her she appeared with other stock companies, including the Alvin Reynolds Company. Tillie was her chief chaperone but with increasing frequency Battling Jack accompanied them. He had developed a taste for the theatre.

Her relationship with her father was ambivalent, although it relaxed towards the end of his life. Her feelings towards him veered between love and revulsion. As an adult she told one interviewer, 'Father always had a long, black cigar in his mouth, and I hated to have him kiss me. Even now, the smell of cigars makes me uncomfortable.'

She later added, in another interview, 'My father was cruel, you know, and I took a dislike to him.' Elsewhere she confessed that she did not like her father because of his violent temper, his rages that terrorized the family, and, above all, the way he made her mother suffer.

Mae developed a hatred of cigar and cigarette smoke long before it was fashionable to do so. When she was young everyone with any style smoked. She, too, smoked in her films, because women of the sort she portrayed did. Off screen, however, she not only abstained, but forbade others to smoke in her presence.

She was equally uncompromising in her dislike of alcohol. In adulthood she was known to take the occasional glass of wine or beer but she was almost a teetotaller and detested heavy drinkers. Battling Jack's rages happened after drinking binges.

Yet, Mae hero-worshipped her father and every man she later took up with seriously had something of Battling Jack in him. It is not unusual for women to seek relationships with men who resemble their fathers, but Mae's feelings towards Battling Jack ran deeper. She was fascinated all her life by the prizefighters he symbolized and would regularly attend boxing matches, the more violent the better, which she watched with the avidity of a zealot. Her fascination developed into an obsession.

She stated that, as an adolescent, she had been revolted when her father tried to kiss her. Could it be that Battling Jack's kisses had been a shade too warm, particularly after a night on the tiles, when he would have reeked of drink and cigar smoke?

Did something more intimate take place and if so, did Mae discover her body involuntarily responding despite her dislike of his behaviour? Such feelings could have developed into a guilt complex and by rejecting symbols of her father such as smoking and drinking she assuaged her guilt.

Mae never could resist muscular men. Was she, subconsciously, trying to recapture that first thrill of sexual awakening brought on by her father? Her earliest memories were of him training in a gym and Mae was later to visit gyms herself in her search for sex partners.

Although surrounded by musclemen in later life, Mae still liked to dominate them. She would bed them as quickly as possible and if she wanted them to pay a return call she would let them know. If not, she made it clear they were to hasten on their way. She was unsentimental about the union but sometimes gave the men a little present to smooth any ruffled feelings. Her behaviour suggests a form of revenge: she could not resist the sexual urge but punished men for inspiring it. Mae West never cried over a man in her films, and refused to do so if it was suggested.

Mae also had a sexual preoccupation with grizzly bears. She writes in the sequel to her autobiography, *On Sex, Health and ESP*,* of how as a child she had a vivid, yet comforting, dream of having sex with a bear. She wrote the book when an old lady but mentions the dream many times elsewhere. One of her songs, as a child performer, was 'Doin' the Grizzly Bear'. Battling Jack was a rough diamond who could pack a hefty punch, yet was capable of a gruff kindness. If he had been metamorphosed into an animal, he would have most resembled a grizzly bear.

'I first heard about sex at nine,' Mae told an interviewer from *Premier* magazine. 'Through a medical book, you know. Suddenly my parents weren't Gods any more. I never told them that, you know. Just had this feeling from reading this book and realizing how we happened. I'd have been better had I not seen that book till twelve or thirteen when I had my first period and

* Published by W. H. Allen, 1975.

needed to know. Then it should have been told by a doctor not your parents. Something goes away when they tell you...' Even Mae West was disillusioned by the facts of life, but she did not let on for years. Instead, she chose to weave a legend that maintained she had been a Lolita long before Nabokov invented his precocious twelve-year-old. She wanted the world to believe that her actions had been consciously motivated by sex since babyhood, and proudly reported that she had been billed as 'the Baby Vamp' aged eight. Not much evidence, however, exists for this boast.

Mae reached her eighth birthday in the first year of the twentieth century. The term 'vamp', in its application to a woman who seduces men, was not in popular circulation until around 1916, when it was coined to describe the film star Theda Bara, now best remembered for *A Fool There Was* and its famous catchphrase, 'Kiss me, my fool'. Before this, Rudyard Kipling wrote a poem called 'The Vampire', but his heroine is a female of a repellent aspect, described as 'a rag, a bone, a hank of hair' – a description inapplicable to either Mae or Miss Bara.

Miss Bara, as the original vamp, was the subject of one of the most bizarre publicity campaigns even Hollywood has known. It was claimed her name was an anagram of 'Arab Death'. Her publicity stated she was 'a half-Arabian embodiment of wicked delight'. She was called 'The Devil's Maidservant' and 'Purgatory's Evil Angel', and wore white make-up with mascaraed eyes, which rolled frighteningly when she meant business. In reality she was a quiet Jewish girl from Ohio, the daughter of a poor tailor.

Her macabre image could not have been more at variance with Mae's hearty appeal. The 'vamp' was sinister, Mae was fun.

But fun was not uppermost in Tillie's mind, as she steered Mae around the various theatrical companies. Although she was single-minded in her purpose, Mae's schooling nonetheless had to be considered. Not that Tillie considered it for too long, or too deeply. Neither she nor Battling Jack had received much education and they had managed well enough, and what use had schooling been to Eva Tanguay or Lillian Russell?

Mae received little formal education. Tom Baily tells us, 'Her life as a child actress and later in vaudeville prevented her from going to school regularly.' Journalist Ben Maddox elaborated, 'Her schooling was evidently fragmentary.' When queried about it she answered, 'Oh, you mean where did I learn to write? Well, I had a tutor to teach me writing and reading, and I studied German, too.' It was Tillie who taught her German, of course, and she also taught her some French. Mae was proud of this and liked to flaunt her 'languages'. Several of her films are decorated with a few French phrases.

Most of her formal education took place in the single year when she was aged between twelve and thirteen. During that year she had, virtually, to retire for a while as she became difficult to cast. 'I'd gotten too mature to get away with playing child roles any more,' she told *Premier* magazine; she had earlier told Ruth Biery, 'I was neither one thing nor the other, there's no place on stage for that inbetween age.' As work petered out she was allowed to go to school.

Tillie did not encourage Mae to help her around the house. She never taught her even the rudiments of cooking and when Mae undressed she left her clothes where they fell for Tillie to pick up. Mae had her own dressing table, and this was permanently cluttered until Tillie eventually cleared it.

While still a child she developed her love of precious gems. She would pass a jeweller's on her way to school and, with face flattened to the window, longed for the time when she could be ablaze with diamonds. Tillie assured her such a day would come.

Mae attended school in Brooklyn for a short while. Long enough, however, to develop a crush on her young male teacher. She later claimed he was her first lover, and that she had seduced him by arranging things so that she could stay behind at school. The consummation had taken place in the classroom after hours. He had had no chance, she claimed, because she overwhelmed him.

This seduction scene was not the intoxicating stuff she sometimes made it out to be. She gave a modified version of what happened to Ruth Biery: 'In school there had been a school teacher. He was awful handsome. He got me to stay after school. I helped to correct papers and things. I was too young to feel anything, you know. But I liked it because he was paying me attention. I always wanted attention.' This account probably contained more of the truth than her other lurid versions. 'Seduction' probably meant no more than a kiss and cuddle, but to a twelve-year-old a kiss can be overwhelming.

Mae still had to keep up her theatrical studies even though she was attending school. To this end Tillie found her another teacher, Ned Wayburn, who was also an agent; he later represented several well-known artists including Marion Davies and Broadway star Marilyn Miller. Wayburn had been a noted tap dancer in his day and under his tutelage she learned, in addition to tap, acrobatic dancing, the backbend and the splits.

Mae was not a brilliant dancer, neither had she the ideal build, being too heavy and too short, but she had an inborn sense of rhythm and Wayburn gave her the skills to perform certain basic routines efficiently. Wayburn's bread and butter was supplying dancers for the 'pony-line' – hoofers who performed in front of the tabs while scenery was being changed. Although Mae was at school, Wayburn managed to secure a few such engagements for her. But by the time she was thirteen she had blossomed into a young lady, and Wayburn was able to provide consistent work for her on the vaudeville circuit. Tillie, or a relative, travelled with her as chaperone.

She added a fan dance to her repertoire. Fan dancing, whose origins lie in burlesque, is now, alas, a dying art. Traditionally, it is performed by a dancer, naked but for a G-string, expertly manoeuvring two large feathered fans, so that her nudity is never revealed, until she holds the fans aloft a split second before the spotlight blacks out. At its best, when performed by an artist like Gypsy Rose Lee, the fan dance is balletic and tasteful; in less skilled hands it degenerates into a crude striptease. It's doubtful Mae's performance was 'balletic', but according to one contemporary account it was certainly suggestive.

By now Beverly was developing into a good-looking girl even prettier, if anything, than Mae, to whom she bore a striking resemblance. But the poor child was pushed into the background as Mae seemed so promising. No one seemed particularly interested in Beverly while Mae received the lion's share of her mother's attention.

John was a happier child. As the baby, and the only boy, he was spoiled by both parents and sisters. Already he was showing signs of developing into a bruiser like his father, and he seemed to have the same happy-go-lucky temperament as Battling Jack.

In later life Mae lost all interest in children but as a teenager, she was on firm ground with John, Beverly and the neighbourhood kids with whom she grew up. According to a Mrs Theodore Weigland, a Brooklyn neighbour of the Wests', her children positively adored Mae. Buried in the archives of the British Film Institute is an uncredited and undated article about Mae's adolescence written by Mrs Weigland.

'I've never seen a girl who was so crazy about children,' Mrs Weigland recalls. She tells how her nephews, Jack and Girard, both under two, regularly played with Mae. 'If they toddled across the street into Mae's house, they were sure of the warmest welcome of their lives. Before long, the only time they spent at home was for eating and going to bed. At Christmas that year Mae decided the boys were old enough to learn the manly art of boxing. Her father ... agreed. So when the big morning arrived, Jack and Girard found huge boxing gloves under their tree, with a card of warning from Mae that the gloves were to be used.'

Mrs Weigland adds that Mae was determined to turn the lads into boxers, and tells how Mae good-naturedly put up with the toddlers' intrusion even when they bundled into her bedroom first thing in the morning.

Mae's interest in the boys was not confined to boxing. Their uncle owned a Model T Ford and Mae would borrow this, bundle the boys into it and drive them to Long Island. 'Mae at the wheel urging old Nellie on to greater speeds,' recalls Mrs Weigland.

Mae never lost contact with Jack and Girard and whenever she was in Brooklyn the lads would call on her. She bought them cowboy suits, but this did not go down too well with some of the other residents of Bushwick Avenue. 'The neighbors objected a little at first to the blood-curdling war-whoops, that suddenly burst out behind garage doors,' Mrs Weigland explains, 'but Mae took the boys' side. As far as she was concerned it was just another way for them to grow into strong and active young men.'

Aside from playing with the kids, Mae kept herself to herself. The article continues, 'Mae, at this time, was being showered under by floods of invitations for parties, dinners, dances.' She declined most of these. Even in those early Brooklyn years her need for privacy was taking root.

A 'close friend' takes up the Brooklyn story: 'It always seemed strange to me that such a vivacious and beautiful girl would prefer to stay at home with her mother. In all the years I knew her, I can't remember a single wild party that Mae ever attended, and in this neighborhood it's pretty hard to do anything like that without having someone know about it.'

Mae never attended a wild party in her life, and if any gathering she attended threatened to become wild she would leave.

Baby Jack, the co-subject of Mrs Weigland's article, was an adult by the time the piece was published, and he endorsed the picture of the reclusive Mae: 'Sure, she was popular, but she stayed home.'

These Brooklyn neighbours reveal more about Mae's character than Mae ever consciously revealed herself. Neighbours can be enlightening; the truth can blurt out.

At the turn of the century performing acts were governed by 'The Syndicate', a conglomerate comprised of such impresarios as 'Dishonest' Abe Erlanger, Marc Klaw and Charles 'Mr Theater' Frohman. 'The Syndicate' had systematically bought up theatres until it owned a monopoly; artists who did not knuckle under were thrown out of work.

'The Syndicate' was bought out around 1906 by a trio of brothers called Szemanski. In keeping with the tradition established by immigrant Europeans of the time, the Szemanskis changed their name to Shubert. They held majority control over the American theatre until 1956 and the Shubert Theaters still bear their name. Their control was only reluctantly relinquished after the federal government intervened.

In the days before actors formed unions small-time artists, such as Mae, had no redress if an engagement did not meet specification. Contracts were rarely issued and it was not uncommon for an artist to travel to a venue only to find the engagement for which they had been booked filled by someone else. No reimbursement was made for inconvenience. Fees were frequently not met, or an amount less than the agreed sum offered.

For all the Shuberts' power their monopoly was not absolute. Times changed and rival circuits mounted some stiff competition, among them the Keith-Orpheum circuit, which handled first-rate artists. It was the ambition of every performer to become attached to a circuit, since coast-to-coast tours were sometimes offered which provided up to a year's work.

Keith-Orpheum managed to secure the services of the great French tragedienne Sarah Bernhardt, and organized her American Farewell Tour. True, the Divine Sarah was past her best: her wiry hair an uncompromising red, her face caked in make-up and a wooden leg having replaced one which had been amputated. In impatience she would hop about from spot to spot, a skill at which she became adept. For all this Bernhardt's appearances ensured packed houses. Mae saw Madame Sarah in a programme of 'dramatic excerpts' but was unimpressed. Mae came from a younger generation and had no time for this idol of yesteryear; she mocked the Divine Sarah for continuing to perform when but a shadow of her former self – a charge that would rebound against her.

However shabbily some small-time acts were treated, the dispossession of the Shuberts was not greeted with unmitigated joy because under their administration the glory of vaudeville had been at its height. The roster of artists who appeared in their theatres at the heyday of vaudeville bears names which are now part of theatrical history, such as Bojangles Robinson, Sophie Tucker, Fanny Brice, the Marx Brothers and W. C. Fields.

In 1909, at the age of sixteen, Mae toured as a double act with comedian Willie Hogan. They performed a 'Huckleberry Finn' routine in which Mae played a hillbilly girl, replete with drawers, gingham frock and plaits. While playing this act in New York she found herself on the bill with a nineteen-year-old song-and-dance-man called Frank Wallace. Wallace was a brilliant eccentric dancer and Mae would stand in the wings and watch him, fascinated by his skill. Although slightly built there was something about his lean frame that attracted Mae.

She struck up a friendship and brought him home to meet the family. His personality, in a face-to-face situation, was less than that promised by his stage performance, but Tillie deemed this no bad thing. He was not forceful enough to captivate Mae for long and, in the meantime, could serve as a buffer to ward off the attentions of other would-be suitors. For it was clear to both Tillie and Battling Jack that Mae had a more than average sex drive. It was the only sore point between Mae and her mother. Mae was candid with her about everything except her sex life which she kept to herself. For her part Tillie did not want Mae falling in love and forming a relationship which might divert her from her career.

As an old lady of seventy-seven, decrying the permissiveness of an age that had passed her by, Mae told *Premier* magazine that she had been a virgin until she had married. She claimed that all she and her pre-marital partners had done was 'neck and hug and kiss and play with each other'. But if her early sex life in any way resembled her sex life after she hit Hollywood then this was not the truth. Sexual voracity is inveterate, it does not suddenly appear out of the blue. Freud contends that the sexual pattern is set from birth. In Ruth Biery's opinion Mae was 'over-emotionalized', her euphemism for 'over-sexed'. When Ruth asked her if she had ever found the right man, Mae answered 'Plenty of times', a line she was later to use in *She Done Him Wrong*. People are either highly sexed or not.

Mae had to gain her own sex education since her parents told her nothing. Apart from the information contained in the medical textbook she had discovered at nine, she would have had to pick up additional knowledge from her colleagues. The penalty for an unmarried pregnancy was dire in Edwardian times and a girl needed to be knowing, particularly a girl like Mae.

She knew about condoms from an early age. Men had shown them to her and explained their use. These were crude, pre-latex inventions made from unyielding rubber and it is difficult to imagine how any man could attain satisfaction when so con-strained. Yet, Mae developed quite a fetish for them and wrote enthusiastically about them in her books. She also revealed how she practised the 'sponge' method of birth control, and recom-mended it to Fanny Brice (this was an unreliable technique which necessitated inserting a water-soaked sponge into the vagina before intercourse).

Battling Jack, now and then, in his pugilistic fashion, tried to keep Mae on the straight and narrow; he let it be known that he would soon sort out any man who might lead his daughter astray.

Frank Wallace did not seem such a threat.

During the next couple of years Mae continued to see Frank, but she heeded her mother's advice and had many other boy-friends as well. Inevitably she fell in love and Tillie's worst fears were realized when Mae told her she wanted to get married. At Tillie's instigation Battling Jack forbade Mae to see the boy but this only had the effect of making Mae more determined than ever. Tillie realized a more subtle approach was necessary.

'Mother was awful kind,' Mae told Ruth Biery. 'She didn't come right out. We had long talks. She explained that I was young and awful full of emotions. She said that was natural, but that I could use them to help me be very famous or I could waste them on the first man. It was an awful struggle.'

Tillie continued her brainwashing. 'Mother pointed out other married couples to me,' Mae continued. 'Showed me how their lives were wasted. She didn't nag me. She never did. But when I saw her face – how unhappy she was, I couldn't get around that. I knew I'd be unhappy.'

Making mother unhappy is, of course, a technique used by domineering mothers to get their own way since time began. Tillie's next step was to remove Mae from immediate temp-

tation. She urged Mae to form a double act with the
unthreatening Frank, which was a good professional move anyway, as he was more successful than Mae. A partnership with
him could only increase her box-office value. Frank, who was
besotted by Mae, readily agreed. With this success under her
belt, Tillie urged them to accept a tour that had been offered,
which would neatly remove Mae from the object of her
affections.

Mae quickly recovered from her love affair and to hasten the
process went out with almost any attractive man who asked,
while still continuing her relationship with Frank. Social stric-
tures at the time were intense and, even by theatrical standards,
Mae seemed to be overdoing things. She became the scandal of
the company.

One of the cast, a middle-aged singer called Etta Woods, was
a distant relative and Tillie had urged her to keep an eye on
Mae on tour. Viewing Mae's reckless behaviour, Miss Woods
feared she might become pregnant, and urged her to acquire a
husband as soon as possible, so that if an accident did occur, at
least Mae would have the veneer of respectability.

Mae later claimed Frank and Miss Woods had connived to
get her to the altar. Mae often told the story of how she came to
marry, never varying it much. The *Premier* account is as good as
any:

> This woman on the bill kept talking to me about all the
> kissing with all the men in the show. She went on and on
> about how this would get me into trouble – if I didn't get
> married and become respectable. I think Frank must have
> put her up to it you know, buying her a dress and things
> and getting her to influence me. I didn't want to get mar-
> ried, I was having such a good time. But Frank kept beg-
> ging me and this woman kept on at me. So I married him
> – at seventeen – so long as he never told my mother. He
> never did.

Wallace also gave his account of the courtship, but not until
years later, when Mae was famous. According to him it was not

so one-sided. He and Mae went on moonlight jaunts together, took boat trips and country walks. She wrote him letters, which he kept, addressing him as 'My dear Frank', and gave him a diary as a present.

For all Tillie's plotting, unknown to her, Mae and Frank were secretly married in Milwaukee on 11 April 1911. On the marriage certificate, Mae lied about her age, saying she was eighteen, the legal age of consent in Milwaukee. Frank was twenty-one.

chapter four

THE VAUDEVILLIAN

In the cold light of morning Mae was terrified by what she had done. But Miss Woods emotionally embraced them, told them she envied them, and showered a cold-faced Mae with maternal kisses. Wallace jubilantly spread the news to the company, but Mae wiped the smile off his face by telling him he had broken Battling Jack's trust and Battling Jack had friends to be reckoned with.

Mae felt she had betrayed Tillie by becoming Mrs Szatkus – Wallace was Frank's stage name, his parents were Russian immigrants. She did not even have the consolation of having married a good-looking man for, with the flush of romance over, Frank's sinewy body seemed merely scrawny. She noticed his hair was thinning and Mae detested bald men.

Unaware of Mae's forebodings, the company manager gave the couple the evening off to celebrate, but it was not much of a celebration. Wallace later said he had nurtured the normal hopes of any young married man, and had wanted a family and a home. But Mae made it plain she was not interested in these things and that marriage was not going to alter her life style. She made him repeat his promise never to tell her mother they were married.

She continued to go to clubs every night to pick up men, sometimes not returning until three or four in the morning. She treated Wallace so cruelly the company turned against her and the manager told her he thought she was behaving disgracefully. After that she was more discreet.

She was trying to eradicate the marriage by behaving as though it had never happened. She made Frank suffer because, according to her twisted logic, she believed he had trapped her.

As the tour ground to its wretched close, she became increasingly fearful of Tillie discovering she was married. Frank, not surprisingly, agreed they should live apart. She had made his life so utterly miserable he was only too pleased to turn his back on her. Shortly after this he left town for a forty-week tour which Mae claimed to have arranged. He kept his bargain and never mentioned the marriage to either Tillie or Battling Jack. The fear of Battling Jack's displeasure was inducement enough to keep quiet.

The company, of course, knew she was married and the rumours spread. There was an occasion when Tillie asked her point blank if they were true, but Mae denied it. Astonishingly, Tillie never found out.

1911 was a year of great change for Mae. Not only was it the year in which she drove a wedge into the perfect trust she had shared with her mother, it was also the year in which she received her professional break. For the first time she attracted the attention of the Broadway producers and became a 'name' of sorts.

She was booked to do a Sunday concert at the Columbia Theater on Broadway. Although not the most prestigious of theatres, the Columbia presented the best in burlesque, and the Sunday concerts were known throughout the business as showcases, attended by the profession, where agents and producers had the opportunity to see little-known acts, without having to leave the precincts of Broadway.

Mae sang and danced, appearing for the first time since a child as a single. She looked good and moved with confidence, having learnt a great deal from Frank. Her singing was outstanding and Bert Waller, who was later to accompany her many times, felt her sense of rhythm and phrasing were reminiscent of black performers. She had had the opportunity to learn from the best black singers on the circuit.

Aware of her influential audience, Mae put everything she had into her performance. She wrote that she succeeded in impressing Florenz Ziegfeld, who sent word he would like her to call on him. Mae said that Ziegfeld made her an offer to appear at his theatre-club, 'The Roof', situated at the top of the New Amsterdam Theater, but she turned him down on the grounds that the room was too impersonal. She needed an intimate setting, she explained, where the audience could see her facial expressions.

The whole story seems unlikely. Ziegfeld would never have entrusted the responsibility of filling such an important room to an unknown, and had he done so such an offer would have been the stuff of dreams. Mae was later to play the largest rooms in Las Vegas and no one could describe them as intimate. Her style was broad, not cosy.

Ziegfeld certainly would not have been interested in her as a showgirl. Upon meeting her, people frequently remarked upon her daintiness. Daintiness is not a prerequisite for a showgirl, they need to be tall and willowy. Girls were meatier in 1911 but Mae would still never have made the grade.

What seems most likely is that Ziegfeld sent for her, as he frequently sent for promising young artists, in order to introduce himself and keep her in mind should anything suitable turn up. No firm offer was made. Ziegfeld died in 1932 and Mae did not start publicizing her version of this story until after his death.

She did, however, work on Broadway that year. Ned Wayburn, who still represented her, introduced her to Jesse L. Lasky. Thirteen years older than Mae, Lasky was a dashing figure who had risen meteorically from poverty. He had been a prospector during the Alaskan gold rush and had had a career as a cornet-player with the Royal Hawaiian Band. He then formed a double act with his sister Blanche, who also played the cornet, and who later married one Sam Goldfish, who changed his name to Goldwyn and became the Goldwyn of Metro-Goldwyn-Mayer. A showman to his finger tips it was inevitable that Lasky should have gravitated towards vaudeville, where he made a reputation for himself as a producer.

Lasky's latest venture was the Folies-Bergère, a plush theatre-restaurant on West 46th Street. The Folies was due to

open with a two-part cabaret, the first half of which was entitled
À La Broadway and the second *Hello Paris*.

Lasky, who had seen Battling Jack fight and betted on him,
needed ingénues for *À La Broadway* and was willing to give
Mae a chance. He placed her with the comedy duo 'Cook and
Lorenz' who were looking for a girl to play a maid in their
sketch as ham-fisted plumbers. She would also have a couple of
songs, one of which was called 'The Philadelphia Drag', for
which she wore harem trousers and a bare midriff.

Much of the music for the Folies was written by Harold
Orlob, but the lyrics for Mae's songs were written by a keen
young man called William Le Baron. Mae did not like the
songs, feeling they were not risqué enough. She was particularly unhappy about one entitled 'They Are Irish'.

This was a pattern that would be repeated throughout her
career. She was always unhappy about using material she had
not written herself, believing only she knew what she did best.
Such a philosophy stood her in good stead.

But she could hardly say so to Le Baron. She decided on a
less obvious course of action: 'At rehearsals I just sang the songs
they gave me, as they had written them. But I wrote them over
at home and put in the – oh, you know,' she told Ruth Biery.
But she did not yet have total confidence in her ability as a
writer and, to be on the safe side, she paid a professional gag
man to help her out, rehearsing with him in private. 'Cook
and Lorenz' were too busy with their own rehearsals to bother
about her – as far as they were concerned she was simply their
foil.

She did not have a great deal to do at rehearsals; while sitting around, she struck up a friendship with two athletic
dancers, Bobby O'Neill and Harry Laughlin. To while away the
time, they devised an act which featured Mae as the centre-
piece.

When the Folies' opening night arrived Mae was on her met-
tle. This was the classiest production with which she had been
associated to date. Tillie and Battling Jack were out in front, as
were Ziegfeld and the Shuberts. Despite this, or perhaps
because of this, she all but stole the show:

There were some shining lights in the cast, notably Miss
Mae West.   *New York Herald*

It was on Miss Mae West's appearance that the first real
hit was made. She seems to be a sort of female George M.
Cohan with an amusing, impudent manner . . .
                                             Evening World

A girl named Mae West, hitherto unknown, pleased by her
grotesquerie and a snappy way of singing and dancing.
                                             New York Times

However snappy her performance it still did not save Lasky
from closing the Folies in debt. In his autobiography Adolph
Zukor writes, 'The failure of his Folies-Bergère cabaret had not
been a small one – he dropped more than \$100,000.'* The
reason for Lasky's failure was that the club was too small to
sustain his lavish productions. Not enough revenue came in.

Once again Mae was out of work.

To fill in the time until something turned up, Mae practised
singing with a boyfriend of the time, Joe Schenck,** who was a
ragtime pianist. Schenck had formed a small band, which used
to rehearse in the Wests' rambling house, and Mae would sing
such numbers as 'Maple Leaf Rag' and 'Beautiful Ohio'.

By now, Battling Jack's eclectic career embraced theatrical
management, and he decided to handle the Schenck band. He
claimed to have put Joe in touch with another of his clients,
Gus Van, and they worked the clubs together and ultimately
became a top act. But by the time that happened Battling Jack
had ceased to look after them.

Boxing was Battling Jack's real vocation and he always had
his eye on up and coming fighters. As did Mae. One of her
father's clients, to whom she took a shine, was a villain called
Otto North, who hung out with the Eagle's Nest mob, a

---

* *The Public is Never Wrong*. Cassell, 1954.
** Not to be confused with Joseph M. Schenck, who founded Twentieth Century Productions and became head of Twentieth Century-Fox.

Brooklyn gang. One night the Eagle's Nest fought the Red
Hooks which, according to Mae, occurred because one of the
Red Hooks had made a pass at her. More likely it was a ter-
ritorial battle. Gang fights were not uncommon in Brooklyn
and all the Wests surged out into the street to watch.

Battling Jack could not resist the temptation offered by a
fight on his doorstep and, after a while, left neutral territory and
waded in to help out the Eagle's Nest boys. Whatever reservations Mae may have felt towards her father, she was very much
his daughter and whereas she did not actually wade in, she tells
us that Battling Jack cleared a space, nearer the action, for her
to stand so she could better view him knocking hell out of the
opposition. It is clear from her autobiography that this was one
of the few occasions in her youth when she felt unreservedly
close to her father.

North did not get killed – as he might well have done – and,
after the fight, presented himself to Mae battered and bleeding.
Tillie dressed his wounds. Mae found battered warriors sexually stimulating. Throughout her life she loved to have sex
with boxers on the night they had fought, and frequently did so.

By 1911 the movies had made an impact on the public, but to
vaudevillians they were not regarded as an attractive source of
income. Movie people were looked down upon, considered
even less meritorious than burlesque performers. But whatever
her own sentiments Mae, in any event, was not right for the
movies at that time. The leading ladies were petite adolescents,
girls trembling on the brink of womanhood. Mae was too
knowing, even at eighteen.

The movies themselves had suffered their ups and down. The
novelty had paled and cinemas now had to book variety acts, in
addition to the film, to draw in the crowds. Mae performed live
many times in movie houses between the screening of the
movies.

She had also developed another skill in picking up some
knowledge of drumming from the Schenck band. At first out of
curiosity she merely patted away at the drums, but discovered

she had a feel for them which she tried to develop into a routine. She became proficient, throwing the sticks in the air and catching them, and in general putting on a good show.

Around 1910 'talking' pictures revitalized audience interest in the movies for a while. However, they had nothing in common with the talkies of the late 1920s, which employed a soundtrack, but instead were silent films in which the screen actors mouthed their words while other actors sat behind the screen, out of sight, and spoke the lines aloud.

Most films were then made in the New York area but California, with its continuous sunshine and wide variety of scenery, was beginning to be seen as an ideal territory for film making. The movie companies started moving west. The pretty suburb of Holly Wood (the original spelling) became their preferred base. Screenwriter DeWitt Bodeen paints a portrait of the Hollywood of 1911:

Hollywood was then a pastoral village nestling at the foot of the Santa Monica hills. The clean air was redolent of orange and lemon blossoms, and in the spring wild poppies and Indian paintbrush coloured the sloping fields orange and purple. The fences and low roofs of the farmhouses and bungalows were covered with geraniums, morning glories, and Cecile Brunner roses. Hollywood wasn't a state of mind *then* – it was a little farming suburb of the thriving but still sleepy Southern California city known as Los Angeles, not too many years removed from its original status as a Spanish-mission trading centre called El Pueblo de Nuestra Senora la Reina de Los Angeles a Porciuncula.*

This Hollywood would not have attracted Mae. What did she care about Cecile Brunner roses, unless they were sent backstage with a diamond clip attached? Hollywood was provincial, the big money was to be made on Broadway and thus Broadway remained Mae's target. And in the autumn of 1911 it seemed

* *From Hollywood*, DeWitt Bodeen, Tantivy Press, 1976.

she was back on course. Lee Shubert, who had seen her in *À La Broadway*, invited her to appear in *Vera Violetta*, which was to open at the Winter Garden on 20 November. The Winter Garden was one of the most impressive theatres in New York, a far cry from most of the venues where Mae had already lifted her dumbbells.

Vera Violetta, described as an 'extravaganza', was based on a German production by Leo Stein, and contained songs by Edmund Eysler with a book by Harold Atteridge and Leonard Liebling. It is a series of musical vignettes bound together by a love theme. It was very Ziegfeld, which was Shubert's intention as the Winter Garden productions were set up in competition.

Vera Violetta followed the successful run of *La Belle Paree* starring Mitzi Hajos. But for all Miss Hajos's charm, the unexpected hit of the show had been an energetic twenty-five-year-old 'blackface', fresh from vaudeville, who sang Dixie songs in the new, syncopated jazz style. Al Jolson electrified the audience. As a result the Shuberts increased his salary from $250 a week to $400, and gave him two major spots in *Vera Violetta*.

Jolson signed the contract but was unhappy with the terms, believing he should receive better billing. His unswerving belief that he was being taken advantage of made him a difficult colleague. The star of his new show was Gaby Deslys and the highlight of the evening should have been her unique 'Gaby Slide' dance. The bill also contained operetta star José Collins, and comedy was to be provided by Barney Bernard, who had a big following.

Mae probably knew she was outclassed. In comparison with the rest of the cast her presentation had to seem rough and untutored, and if this was not enough to depress her, Jolson's jazz singing was so good it was certain he would gain a standing ovation. Among such high-powered company there was more than a chance she would get lost.

As rehearsals progressed Mae developed a cold which reached its climax as opening night approached. At the last moment she decided she was too ill to go on; the prospect of competing with real professionals may well have affected her decision. For whatever reason, Mae joined the cast later in the run.

In his biography of Gaby Deslys,* James Gardiner dispels the fiction that Mae was already a celebrity at this time when he describes her as a chorus girl.

As Mae suspected, Jolson was an enormous hit; he eclipsed Mlle Deslys in popularity and stole this show too. It was not to be a good year for Gaby Deslys. Following *Vera Violetta* she went to New Haven, Connecticut, where she appeared before students from Yale. Far from drawing applause, her performance unleashed a hail of eggs and vegetables, many of which found their mark. She could not bear it and fled the stage in tears. As was the custom in an emergency, the chorus girls were put on. They fared little better and, in addition to throwing food, the students ripped out their seats and also flung them.

Mae's situation was not as gloomy as Gaby Deslys'. Ziegfeld had obviously been keeping his eye on her, as promised, and now an opening became available, which he thought might be right for her. He offered her a part in *A Winsome Widow*, which was to open in April 1912 at the Moulin Rouge. This was to be another lavish production, with seats at a pricy $2 each. The producers were Klaw and Erlanger of the old 'Syndicate' – competitors of the Shuberts along with Ziegfeld. Variety was a cut-throat business.

The press received *A Winsome Widow* well: the *New York World* deemed it 'tip-top'. Mae, as a character called 'La Petite Daffs', sang a song called 'Piccolo' into which she poured her all, hoping to impress Mr Ziegfeld a second time round. Unfortunately, her all was rather too much for *Variety*, whose reviewer sniffed in distaste, 'A pretty melody, spoiled in the singing by Mae West, a rough soubrette . . . just a bit too coarse'. Part of the coarseness resulted from competing too hard with comic Frank Tinney.

Mae did not know which way to turn. To be described as too coarse for Ziegfeld was a terrible indictment. She reluctantly

* *Gaby Deslys*, Sidgwick & Jackson, 1989.

had to admit, once again, that she was not really Ziegfeld's type – a humiliation in itself.

After *A Winsome Widow* she 'rested' until she ran into Harry Laughlin and Bobby O'Neill, the two dancers from *À La Broadway*. They, too, were out of work. Recalling the act they had devised, they brushed up the routine and with Mae acting as producer secured a tour from Philadelphia through New England. The billing was 'Mae West and the Girard Brothers'. Mae dreamed up the name, probably after the little boy called Girard back in Brooklyn, for whom she had bought a cowboy suit.

The 'new act', as *Variety* termed it, angered its reviewer for the same reason as had her performance in *A Winsome Widow*. Once more she was rebuked for being coarse.

The act took $350 a week and out of this she paid her new agent, Frank Bohm, a 10 per cent commission. From the residue she was responsible for both travel and accommodation expenses and for the cost of the costumes. She paid the lads $50 a week each, which was not bad money for dancers, and kept the balance herself.

She began to look the part of the leading lady. Early photographs reveal her in the costume of an Edwardian lady, complete with beaver collar and wide-brimmed hat. Her hair is a soft brown framing her strikingly pretty face.

However, she did not confine herself to working solely with the Girard Brothers and sometimes, when appearing as a single, worked as a 'Muscle Dancer'. An item in *Variety* from 1912 reads, 'Mae West ... sings while making interesting movements in a seated position.'

In 1913 she billed herself 'The Original Brinkley Girl', which was not strictly true – her latest glamour girl image was created, as the name suggests, by the artist Nell Brinkley. Mae included among her numbers such titles as 'Isn't She A Brazen Thing' and 'It's An Awful Easy Way to Make a Living'. Another of her specialties was 'Good Night, Nurse'. There is sheet music still in existence, bearing on its cover a photograph of Mae, decked out in a nurse's uniform. Thanks to her unlamented husband, she had also mastered an eccentric dance in which she appeared with a life-sized rag doll whose feet were attached to her own. She was back in New York – in the autumn of 1913 appearing on a variety bill at the Fifth Avenue Theater.

Beverly, at Tillie's instigation, had also started a theatrical career, but Tillie could already see that her younger daughter did not have Mae's flair and consequently did not push her so hard. Tillie found total satisfaction in Mae. In Tillie's eyes, Beverly would always remain in her sister's shadow. Mae tells us that there were times when Tillie 'took the strap' to Beverly, but this never happened to her. Perhaps, if Mae had not been around, Beverly might have fared better but it seems likely that Tillie saw the impossibility of ever making her into a star. All of which built up a deep frustration within Beverly.

Nonetheless she teamed up with Mae for a while in a 'sisters' act, as that sort of act was then popular. 'Mae West and Beverly' played many halls together. In later years, at Mae's prompting, Beverly changed her name to Beverly Arden, the surname having occurred to Mae on leaving an Elizabeth Arden beauty salon.

During their travels Beverly heard whispers that Mae was married to Frank and Mae confessed but swore her to silence. Beverly never let her down; even so their act did not last, mainly because of their off-stage skirmishes. The girls, although bound by their blood tie, did not actually get on with each other. Their temperaments differed. Mae took her work seriously, but Beverly already had an air of hopelessness about her career which she disguised by giving the impression that she did not care much about anything except having a good time.

This was her defence against her elder sister. For while Mae had not achieved much in terms of public recognition she was, at least, earning her living playing vaudeville. Without Mae's help Beverly could not achieve even that. Throughout her life Beverly tried to assert herself, and she quickly found a way to get back at Mae and her mother. At an early age she took to drink.

Mae was appalled. She had seen how drink had altered her father's personality, and there were many examples among other vaudevillians of the destructive effects of alcohol. As soon as Mae had finished work, unless she was meeting a man, she went home to bed. Night life bored her; she fulfilled herself on stage. Not so Beverly, who even at a tender age would crash in at all hours, much the worse for drink. Noisy fights erupted in the dawn as the enraged Mae was rudely woken from her beauty sleep.

Mae blamed her failure to work with Beverly on her own preference for performing as a single. This was partly true, but was partly said out of loyalty. She never wrote nor made an adverse public statement about her sister. True, she mentioned her as little as possible but this was to keep Beverly out of the limelight for her own good. When exposed to publicity, Beverly often let the side down. The West family dignity, which Mae maintained so determinedly, meant nothing to her. By destroying it Beverly had a rare opportunity to get her own back.

Part of her act with 'Sister' (as the girls called each other) involved Mae leaving Beverly on stage to sing a song, while she changed into male attire to play Beverly's boyfriend. Male impersonation became a feature of her act to the extent that there was speculation, even at this early date, that she was in reality a man. She would end the act with a short speech, subsequently reported by *Variety*: 'It's the first time I have appeared with my sister, they all like her, especially the boys who always call for her, but that's where I come in – I always take them away from her.' Hardly a line designed to build up Beverly's confidence! She had to stand like a lemon, simpering, while Mae took the audience's applause.

The *Variety* writer, however, ended his review with the following less than flattering remark: '*Sister* isn't quite as rough as Mae West can't help being. Unless Miss West can tone down her stage presence in every way she might just as well hop out of vaudeville into burlesque.'

It seemed Mae would never get the measure of a true Broadway star and, indeed, she never really did.

In 1915 Mae was in a show called *Such Is Life*, and its tour took in the West Coast. While there she made her first professional contact with the world of movies. Universal Films, founded by Carl Laemmle and among the more go-ahead of the new studios, agreed to see her but whatever discussions may have taken place they led to nothing.

While on these long tours she got into the habit of whiling away the time by scribbling down ideas and material that she could try out in her act. She even wrote songs, one of which she made a standard part of her act. It was called 'The Cave Girl', and she performed it while draped in a leopard skin. The final couplet went:

> I learned to bill and coo from a turtle dove
> And a grizzly bear taught me how to hug.*

Once again the grizzly reared his head.

---

* *Goodness Had Nothing To Do With It*, W. H. Allen, 1960.

chapter five

MAE WEST TAKES OFF

Strangely it was Tillie, who had tried to see off all Mae's suitors, who introduced her to the man who was to become her lover for over thirty years. James A. Timony was a lawyer whom Tillie met when she consulted him over a legal matter. He was thirty-eight, Mae twenty-three, and at her most attractive.

Disapproving of younger, more handsome men who might dissuade Mae from becoming a star, Tillie considered the affluent Timony a suitable consort. A retired sportsman who still owned a baseball team, he retained traces of his former burliness. He was well-known in certain political and criminal circles and some people who met him thought he was a gangster himself. One actress, who knew him through working with Mae, simply called him 'a thug'. Although capable of charm, he did not often bother to exercise it.

He was a daring investor, however, and had made a fortune out of racing cars and aeroplanes. Tillie had a few plans of her own that required backing: the foremost was finding a vehicle which would star her darling daughter.

Like Battling Jack, Timony was of Catholic-Irish stock, and that was not all they had in common. He also looked uncannily like Mae's father.

Timony was smitten with Mae from the moment he saw her and his affections never wavered although there were times when he was to pay heavily for loving her. But, at the outset, he was the dominant partner. He telephoned her after their initial meeting and invited her to dinner where he convinced her to let him act as her personal manager.

They soon became lovers and when Timony proposed marriage Mae confessed her entanglement with Frank Wallace whom she still occasionally bumped into. Timony, or Jim as she called him, soon soothed any fears she may have harboured about Frank talking. With Mae at his side, he sought out the weaker man and, as Mae's protector, bullied him into remaining silent, drawing attention to the finery he had bought Mae and deriding Frank's obvious lack of professional success. Jim insisted Frank grant Mae a divorce.* After such a humiliation – to which, disgracefully, Mae lent her support – Frank's only desire was to continue to keep as much space as possible between himself and Mae.

At Jim's urging, Mae left Brooklyn and set up home in an apartment in Jersey City. Although Jim was a regular visitor he did not move in. Mae did not wish to be branded as flagrantly immoral.

Jim was a sharp dresser who carried a cane with a jewelled handle – an essential means of support given his limp. He was chauffeured about in a large, open car with Mae, lavishly attired in his gifts of furs and gems, lounging at his side. They made an exotic pair.

Mae, however, never loved Jim and made not even an attempt at fidelity although she kept her many indiscretions from him. Jim possessed a jealous streak and was not a man to be lightly crossed. She writes of the many other lovers she knew during this period and it is impossible to unravel the tangle of her various sexual relationships; in any event, such an effort would be pointless. Few meant much to her. Due to the amorality of her upbringing she was able to indulge her fancies without suffering pangs of remorse. The overriding morality Tillie had instilled in her was a desire to succeed at all costs. Like Dickens and Shaw she believed poverty and frustration were the real sins in life.

Jim sometimes joined her on tour and she was glad of his company. She no longer had to travel with the rest of the cast

---

* Account taken from *Mae West: The Lies, The Legends, The Truth*, George Eells and Stanley Musgrove. Robson Books, 1989.

but could arrive at her hotel accommodation in style. She never wore her heart on her sleeve, nor gave her confidence easily, but Jim was now in a position of supreme trust.

That same year (1915) she teamed up with pianist-singer Harry Richman. Richman was out of a job but received a telephone call from his agent telling him to ring Jim who was now handling Mae's business affairs. Jim told him that his client, Miss West, was forming a new act and needed a pianist. A meeting was arranged at the offices of the William K. Harris Publishing Company.

In 1934 Richman published his reminiscence of that meeting in *Movie Magazine*. He admitted he did not like Mae at first. She came over as hard and left him feeling uncomfortable. 'She did not speak,' he recalled, 'did not even smile. Instead her eyes swept me from head to foot, a long, appraising stare. Then she spoke. "Are you versatile?" she demanded . . . with a trace of what seemed to be scepticism in her intonation. "I need a piano player good enough to do speciality numbers while I change my clothes and keep the suckers on the jump . . . you've got to be able to put over a song."

'It struck me forcibly,' Richman continued, 'that Miss West might not be a particularly indulgent employer.'

Mae told Richman to play and sing for her. She listened without comment, then coldly announced, 'I'll have your script tomorrow and you can run through your lines.' She gave him 'a gesture of dismissal'.

'The next day I returned,' Richman resumes. 'Ran through the script and was hired. Two minutes later came our first difficulty. Miss West wanted the act to be called "Mae West & Co." while I held out for "Mae West and Harry Richman". I pointed out that, after all, I had been a featured act in vaudeville, and finally won Miss West over . . . We agreed on $500 for the act; $200 for me and the rest for Miss West.'

While on tour with Richman Mae performed a routine called 'The Gladiator' during which, according to Richman, 'the audience howled gleeful appreciation'. But not everyone was delighted. There were so many complaints of the indecency of Mae's performance that these filtered through to Edward F.

Albee, general manager of the Keith circuit, which had booked her act.

Albee telephoned Mae to demand an explanation. 'Miss West became highly indignant,' Richman remembers. 'She denied that there was the slightest basis for the complaints. The complainants were evil minded, she told Mr Albee, and to prove it she offered to do the act and let him be the judge himself.'

Albee accepted her offer and arrived at the theatre the next morning. In the empty building, with just a few cleaners shuffling about, Mae performed her act. 'She put on one of the most remarkable performances I have ever seen,' Richman swears. 'Using the same lines, but altering a gesture here, eliminating another there, she made the act seem lily white. No one could conceivably have objected to any part of it. When she . . . came to the line "If you don't like my peaches, why do you shake my tree?" instead of the sly wiggle, she raised her arms like an operatic prima donna and her face assumed a perfectly angelic expression. The listener might have supposed she was singing a paean to the beauties and joys of Mother Nature. Mr Albee was sold . . . and assured us that henceforth he would refuse to listen to such tommyrot.

'The next day we were engaged at Proctor's, Fifth Avenue, with an audience composed for the most part of travelling men. Miss West put in everything she had omitted for Mr Albee and added a few extra bits for good measure. The audience was in an uproar. We stopped the show. Then the manager stopped us. He insisted we tone the whole thing down. He said he just wouldn't have it.'

Mae said she would abide by Albee's decision and the next day a call was placed to his office. Richman recalls Albee's answer, 'I've seen the act and it's perfectly alright.' *Variety*, however, did not agree and continued to chide her: 'She loses much by occasionally overstepping the line between facetiousness and freshness. When she learns to draw the line she will have made a marked stride in the right direction.' Nevertheless her press *had* improved. Previously her act had been dismissed as 'turkey' or 'too rough', now criticism was tempered with constructive advice.

'The trouble was, we didn't play many places,' Richman says. 'Miss West insisted on $500 and she wouldn't take $499 either. It was $500 or nothing with the result that most of the time it was nothing. . . . Often we would walk out of a booking agent's office after she had haughtily turned down $400 for a week. . . . One time the telephone in her apartment in Jersey City was disconnected because the bill hadn't been paid.'

Elsewhere in the same article Richman claims, 'I was considering leaving her when she wrote a play. She felt sure that if we put it on it would mean fame and fortune for all of us. So Timony and I "angeled" the show ... We begged and borrowed scenery and costumes. We cajoled electricians and stage hands. We talked actors and actresses into working on "spec" ... When we opened in Greenwich Village the show laid an egg that any ostrich would be proud to crow about. I surveyed the wreckage ...'

This blows apart the foundation of the Mae West 'instant playwright' myth. Mae always insisted that the first play she authored was *SEX*, written in 1926 – and that it brought her immediate fame as a writer. But she had clearly been scribbling away a decade earlier.

Mae's autobiography is factually unreliable in that it presents a chronicle of uninterrupted success. She states that her appearance in *Vera Violetta* was a triumph (omitting the fact she never even played the opening night) and that by the time she was appearing with Richman she was already a Broadway star. At the height of her fame she maintained, 'I never had a failure in my life,' as if Mae West was unreservedly applauded from the age of five onward. It was a curious flaw in the make-up of this extraordinary woman that she could never concede failure, a flaw which would widen into a chasm with age.

Christmas 1916, however, was a truly happy period for Mae. She was having an affair with an accordionist, Guido Diero, who rates a mention because he had a profound effect on her life. Nearly an entire chapter is devoted to him in *Goodness Had Nothing To Do With It* while most of her lovers, if they stuck in her mind at all, merely merited a line or two.

Guido and Mae met when they appeared on the same bill in

Detroit. There they formed a duo which enabled them to travel together with impunity since it provided an effective smoke screen to hide their affair from the ever-vigilant Jim. Fortunately for Mae, Jim was unable to travel with her all the time.

Their affair lasted several weeks until Mae came down with influenza in Hamilton, Ontario. Diero never left her side, lavishing every care upon her, but his gentleness lessened his appeal and she did not feel the same way about him afterwards. Men should be men in Mae's book; they were sex objects and their ability to transport her sexually was all that mattered. If she had wanted a nurse she would have hired one.

When she was on her feet again she fell straight into the arms of heavyweight boxing champion James J. Corbett, whom she had seen fight in the ring. He was much more satisfactory and their relationship was sustained, on a casual basis, over several years. Diero, however, refused to be brushed off and his jealousy caused her concern.

Diero was further inflamed when he suspected Mae of having yet another affair, this time with Joseph M. Schenck, then in charge of the Loew circuit. He smashed Schenck's desk in a rage and Mae was frightened he might tell Jim. He did the next best thing and went to see Tillie, begging her to intercede on his behalf. He got a frosty response but Tillie was very frightened, believing him with some cause to be insane.

Schenck, who had reason to feel uncomfortable about both Diero and Jim, cautioned Mae about her behaviour, and hastily arranged a booking for her in Chicago which she felt it expedient to accept.

Meanwhile the country itself was in a state of unrest. In April 1917 President Wilson decided America could no longer stand aloof while Europe engaged in the bloodiest war in its history. Reluctantly he plunged his country into the war with Germany, a conflict in which Britain and its allies had already been engaged for three years.

At first the war made little difference to Mae and she continued with her endless round of tours. But it had a prodigious effect on the newspaper baron, William Randolph Hearst, who one day would turn his attentions on her. He had already discovered, years before, that accounts of bloodbaths sold papers. Fanatically anti-British, Hearst filled his 'yellow press' with biased, pro-German war coverage.

For all Hearst's sniping a new spirit emerged, an awareness that America had a vital part to play in the conflict. Overnight the country became patriotic. Conscientious objectors were victimised and frequently beaten up and a whole generation of American men joined the battered, but unbowed, British in the fields of Flanders. American women, along with their British counterparts, undertook jobs that had previously been done by men, volunteering for any work that would help the Allied war effort. There was a spirit of adventure in the land; as yet the war was thrilling since few American casualties had been shipped back home.

Theatres produced patriotic shows, with casts rigged out in service costumes and baton-twirling chorus girls dancing to march tunes. The theme was the conquering hero. But as the reality of the war began to bite, the mood of the American people became more sombre. The public turned to escapism and the movies came into their own. Theatrical artists reappraised their situation as they began to realize that greater fame could be achieved from one movie than from an entire life spent on the boards. Mary Pickford, 'America's Sweetheart', was now the highest paid woman in the world. Both Charlie Chaplin and Douglas Fairbanks had already become millionaires. The Talmadge sisters were national figures, as were Gloria Swanson, Harold Lloyd and Tom Mix.

In search of further diversion America went dance crazy. The 'Turkey Trot' became the rage and jazz the thing. Originating among black musicians in New Orleans, jazz had its roots in ragtime. This feverish music ignored formal rules and gave its practitioners the freedom to improvise. Mae was swept up by the excitement.

And she found plenty of opportunity in Chicago to listen to the new sounds. Chicago, with its large black population, was nearly as full of jazz clubs as New Orleans. It was definitely the place to be for hot music.

Mae was playing the Majestic Theater and one evening after the show went with some pals to an establishment she would primly describe in her autobiography as 'a low, coloured café'. This was the Elite No. 1 Club, situated on the south side of town. The music was wild and the clientele decidedly on the shady side (some of the men bore scars on their faces, Mae reported enthusiastically – she always liked men with scars).

Her olfactory organs must have been offended that evening as the atmosphere was heavy with cigarette smoke and alcohol fumes, not to mention the more pungent aroma of marijuana. While her party swigged gin and puffed on their cigarette holders, Mae sipped her beer and surveyed the scene. The dancing excited her. As she watched the sinewy black dancers, standing virtually on one spot, violently gyrate to the rhythm, she realized she could cause a sensation with this dance.

At the Majestic matinée next day she introduced the dance into her act, calling it the 'shimmy'. Unrehearsed, Mae started to impersonate the erotic dancing of the blacks. She shook her anatomy until it seemed her sequins must fly off. The more she shook, the more the catcalls and whistles erupted, inspiring her to even greater licence. She took ten bows.

So great was the pandemonium in the theatre that the management feared a police raid. The manager remonstrated that what she had done amounted to an obscene display and she must forthwith drop the shimmy from her act. He might as well have saved his breath, that wild applause was music to Mae's ears. Irrespective of managerial complaints she performed the dance at every appearance she made on tour.

She introduced it to Broadway in the autumn of 1918, when she took part in the Rudolf Friml musical *Sometime* at the Shubert Theater. Thus began a bitter feud between Mae and that other Broadway veteran, Sophie Tucker, for Miss Tucker would later claim to have introduced the shimmy to Broadway. She maintained that she had originally seen it danced by Gilda Gray, and had booked Miss Gray for her shows. What Mae found galling was that Miss Gray had an enormous success with the dance, far greater – and certainly longer lasting – than

she did. Miss Gray was a slim blonde with an ideally propor-
tioned dancer's body and, as far as posterity is concerned, the
invention of the shimmy, if it is remembered at all, is credited
to her. Mae never forgave this slight.

The insult was exacerbated ten years later in 1927 when Miss
Gray danced the shimmy in a film entitled *The Devil Dancer*.
When Miss Gray happened, off-handedly, to mention that it
was a 'native' dance, Mae demanded, 'Native to where? She's
Polish.' Miss Gray's real name was Marianna Michalska. Mae
eventually settled for disdain, quipping, 'Who wants to make a
career of the shakes?'

Mae was invited to take part in *Sometime* by producer
Arthur Hammerstein, uncle of Oscar Hammerstein II. The
show opened on 4 October and Mae played the small part of
Mame Dean, a wisecracking showgirl. Hammerstein allowed
her to perform the shimmy since Broadway audiences were
considered more sophisticated than their out-of-town counterparts.

Once again she encountered stiff competition from other
members of the cast. She was playing opposite Ed Wynn and
Frank Tinney, strong comics whom she respected. 'They put
me on the bill with two of the greatest comedians of the day,'
she complained in the Thirties to a reporter working for the
News of the World. She admitted she had badgered the lyricist,
Rida Johnson Young, to pep up her material, but Miss Young
viewed her request with displeasure. She had already written
her lyrics to the satisfaction of Friml, no easy taskmaster, and
was not prepared to alter them to suit a pushy, young vaudeville
turn. Miss Young fobbed off the persistent Mae, but as a sop
dashed off a few new lines for her. Mae was not impressed and
the lesson was brought home, once more, that if she was to
succeed in show business she must write her own material.

She found commiseration in the form of the stage manager,
who was none other than Oscar Hammerstein II. According to
Fred Nolan, biographer of Rodgers and Hammerstein,* Mae
was so low she took Oscar to one side and advised him, 'to quit

* *Sound of Their Music: Story of Rodgers and Hammerstein*, Dent, 1978.

the theatre while he still had the chance. "You've got too much class to hang around the stage, kid." ' He had caught her in a mood of despondency brought on by the smallness of her part.

Despite her tiny role she nevertheless managed to attract attention. 'I strutted on the stage,' she told the *News of the World* journalist, '... saying nothing, just walking. The audience forgot the comedians. I still walk like that.'

Her efforts secured a mention or two in the press. The New York *Herald Tribune* enjoyed her 'capital characterization' but considered the shimmy 'vulgarity'. *Variety* offered qualified praise: 'Miss West, with the assistance of what sounded like a well-placed claque, stopped the show with it.' The claque probably amounted to no more than Battling Jack, and his rough friends, giving the girl a warm hand. *Variety* further noted: 'Miss West has improved somewhat in looks but is still the rough, hand-on-hip character that she first conceived.'

She was getting heartily sick of *Variety*.

Journalist Leonard Hall was a member of the same audience. He later wrote an account of the first time he saw Mae for *Photoplay*: 'And there was Mae West – a beautiful ball of fire who performed as a speciality dancer in high kicks, cartwheels and fast taps. She was a tasty tornado and I fell madly in love with her.'

By now she had an idea of the stage personality she was trying to create but had not yet come to grips with it. Just as Glenn Miller was to spend years experimenting with different instrumental combinations before hitting on the right big band sound, so Mae had still to perfect her mix.

After a respectable run of 283 performances *Sometime* went on tour, but Mae turned the opportunity down. She went, instead, on another of her own lucrative tours, appearing in clubs as well as theatres.

The 18th Amendment, popularly known as 'Prohibition', was soon to become Federal law and under its terms alcohol was to be banned – and prohibited from being sold in clubs. Consequently, in 1919, clubs were full of partygoers indulging in a final boozy fling.

To quote Mae in *Goodness Had Nothing To Do With It*,* 'the repeal of drinking did not sit well on the American stomach'. Prohibition became a godsend for gangsters. The mobs invaded showbusiness, and set up illegal outlets for the sale and consumption of bootleg liquor. These 'speakeasies', which also served up jazz and girls, sprang up all over New York and Chicago, providing a rich source of income for the underworld.

Possibly the most famous speakeasy owner was Texas Guinan. Her age was a secret but she was born sometime in the 1880s. She was blonde and blowsy and could match any man in a fist fight. Her joint was frequently raided until she was finally imprisoned for her constant violation of the liquor laws. Texas provoked the line by the silent screen writer Grant Clarke, 'Reach down in your heart, Texas, and get me a piece of cracked ice.'** Texas was the star turn in her clubs and her gags – delivered defiantly with hand on hip – became synonymous with speakeasies. 'Give the little lady a big hand' was one of her best-known lines.

Texas was Mae's heroine and she visited her club whenever she could. She modelled her entire act on the 'Queen of the speakeasies' and owed Texas a vast artistic debt. Texas was her inspiration but, unfairly, Mae never acknowledged her contribution to building the Mae West legend.

Many stars, such as Sophie Tucker, regularly played the more upmarket speakeasies. Although not a star, it is likely Mae did the same, but not in the top venues. She knew most of the hoods who ran the joints and her act, now improved and refined by Texas Guinan's example, was perfect for the environment.

That September she was again appearing in New York. Confident after her successful tour, she bought herself new costumes, including a silver lamé sheath and a bejewelled gown in black and white which *Variety* deemed 'very tasteful'. It was the first and only time Mae was ever described as 'tasteful', much less in the superlative. She was now more disciplined on stage,

---

* W. H. Allen, 1960.
** *Louise Brooks*, Barry Paris, Hamish Hamilton, 1990.

her movements less unbridled. Her reviews continued to improve and even *Variety* puffed her: 'Mae West was an unqualified hit ... shows a marked improvement in method and delivery.'

At last Mae West was taking off.

chapter six

BIGAMY?

Movie houses were springing up overnight to accommodate the number of films now being made, and theatres vied with each other in the luxury they offered. The Capitol Theatre, New York, was one of the most sumptuous, and the stars themselves attended its premières, dressed to the nines, and arriving in Hispano-Suizas, Duesenbergs, or even an Isotta Fraschini – luxurious dream machines the like of which will never be seen again. Gloria Swanson was packing them in with her latest film, *Male and Female*, released in 1919.

William Randolph Hearst had diversified into films, and had just released, through his company, Cosmopolitan Pictures, a feature, *Cecilia of the Pink Roses*, starring Marion Davies. Hearst had arranged for thousands of pink roses to frame the screen at its première, and for enormous electric fans to waft their fragrance throughout the auditorium.

His Majesty, the American, starring Douglas Fairbanks, was the latest offering at the Capitol, and Mae's former agent, Ned Wayburn, who always had his finger in one pie or another, was producing the lavish stage show which accompanied the screening. With French themes still the fashion, this was entitled *Demi Tasse Revue*. Mae was booked to dance the shimmy, and sing a couple of songs.

In November 1919 she was back at the Winter Garden on a Variety bill, and she was still in New York, in August 1921, at the New Century Roof Theater in a revue, directed by J. J. Shubert, entitled *The Mimic World*. During its Boston and Philadelphia tryouts it had been called *The Whirl of the Town*. She played several characters: Cleopatra, Shifty Liz, and another called Jazzimova. The latter was a caricature of Russian stage and film star Alla Nazimova.

Nazimova was, perhaps, the screen's most glamorous star and presented a persona of studied eroticism. Billed as 'the Woman of 1000 Moods', not even Theda Bara could eclipse her. It was rumoured that no man was safe in her presence – which was true for she could not abide them. She was a rampant lesbian complete with her own personal harem. Gossip about her all-female orgies was wild. In 1923 Nazimova was to overreach herself financially with her production of *Salome*, for which, as a tribute to Oscar Wilde, she employed only homosexual actors. She lost a fortune but, being a feisty lady, she dusted herself down, survived the talkies, and continued to make films, although in largely subsidiary roles, until her death in 1945.

The Mimic World, alas for Mae, did not have as durable a fate as the glamorous Nazimova and closed within a month. *Billboard* contemptuously dismissed it as 'the very peak of worthlessness'. The show, however, gave Mae the opportunity to meet a man she revered above most others. On opening night, 15 August, the world heavyweight champion boxer Jack Dempsey was in the audience. In July 1921 he had won boxing's first million dollar fight by bettering Georges Carpentier.

The fight had attracted a stellar audience, including members of the newly elected President Harding's cabinet, the industrialists Henry Ford and John D. Rockefeller and Al Jolson, now a world celebrity. Jolson's smart appearance was marred that night by a bandaged jaw. His manager had devised a publicity stunt during which Jolson had sparred a few rounds with Dempsey. Not among his wisest decisions.

There was nothing courtly about Dempsey in the ring, he was out to kill; despite his ferocity, he was no lumbering halfwit. He stood at a graceful six feet two inches and weighed less than fourteen stones and for all the punishment he had taken his face was still handsome. He was suitable material to become a movie star and that was exactly what his manager, Jack 'Doc' Kearns, intended. He had plans for Dempsey and Mae to make a film together. Kearns brought Dempsey backstage after the show. Mae faced him appraisingly. He was twenty-six and she twenty-eight; the chemistry was electric.

Kearns asked Mae to take a screen test with Dempsey. Dempsey, monosyllabic in front of this glorious vision of womanhood, could only mutter 'sure, sure'. In order to persuade her Kearns proposed that Dempsey and Mae should first form a double act during which Dempsey would stage demonstration bouts with members in the audience. They would tour from New York to California. Dempsey's name would ensure a sell-out and, once in California, they would appear in a film which Kearns would produce. Mae was attracted by the idea. Dempsey was hard to resist. The deal, however, did not have the same impact on Jim, who could see that Mae would never be able to keep her hands off the boxer.

Later that week she and Jim met Kearns and Dempsey at the Pathé studios on 168th Street. Dempsey had already appeared in a couple of films but was still nervous about the test. In *Goodness Had Nothing To Do With It** Mae says she had to tell him to be more 'aggressive'. 'Look Champ, I won't break – hold me tighter,' she encouraged.

The test proved successful and Mae was offered a part in a projected film to be called *Daredevil Jack*. The title made it obvious who was to be the star. This may have been one of the reasons she refused the offer, going along with Jim when he put his foot down, giving his excuse that the scheduled three appearances a day when on tour would be too much for her.

She knew she had to accept his decision since she was now dependent upon him. He was an emotional and financial prop who could not be replaced. The loss of the film was probably a good thing. Films were not yet ripe for Mae West, nor she for them, and Dempsey never made a name for himself as a film actor and soon gave up the idea.

But the loss of Dempsey, the man, was a blow.

She could console herself by reading her now glowing press coverage: 'She rises to heights undreamed of for her,' quoted a *Variety* review on 23 June 1922, 'and reveals unsuspected

* W. H. Allen, 1960.

depths as a delineator of character songs, a dramatic reader of ability, and a girl with a flare for farce that will some day land her on the legitimate Olympus . . . Miss West has arrived and is a real wow.'

In 1924 Mae fell hopelessly in love and it caused her much heartache. Her feelings were so intense that she was prepared to break up with Jim and marry the man, if she could gain her freedom from Frank. Despite Jim's threats, Frank had still taken no steps to secure a divorce; Mae had no burning desire to marry Jim and, as long as Frank stayed out of her life, she had not pressed him for a divorce.

Although Mae never found it easy to confide her feelings about such things, she could not keep them from her mother. She still saw Tillie regularly and telephoned her every day when they were apart. Mae frequently forsook her own apartment to stay with Tillie, who could tell something was wrong. Mae blurted out her predicament.

Later, she spoke of the affair to Ruth Biery, but cautioned, 'I ain't never going to give his name. I've talked about him once or twice, a woman does, you know. But his name is sort of sacred.' She revealed, however, that he was a salesman, unconnected with showbusiness.

Night after night, while Mae mooned at home, Tillie brainwashed her. She persuaded Mae that Jim was the right man for her and that it would be foolhardy to jeopardize her career by becoming involved with a man who wasn't even in the business. She succeeded and Mae broke off the relationship, but not without pain. She resorted to her proven panacea by going out with other men.

'I wouldn't go out with a man who didn't remind me of him,' she continued to Ruth Biery. 'And then I'd rush home before the evening was over because he did remind me of him. I learned will power then. I learned determination. It took a lot of both. I had to talk to myself over and over and over. I can do it today. When I see a man I think I might like and I know he might interfere with my career, I can sell myself out of the idea of liking him. I finally took two months to figure it all out. I just argued and argued with myself . . . I knew I couldn't have both – marriage and a career.'

Yet facts which have now come to light indicate that Mae did seriously contemplate marriage at this time, career or no career. Thanks to the resources of the County Clerk of Harris County, Texas, two curious documents have surfaced.

The first is an application for a marriage licence made out to R. A. Bud Burmester, resident of the Rice Hotel, Harris County, and Mae West of New York City. It is dated 22 March 1924. Burmester gives his age as thirty-four and Mae lists hers as twenty-four. This is in keeping with Mae's practice at the time of lopping seven years off her age. Her driving licence stated her date of birth was 1900. She continued to subtract right up until she had a Hollywood career and would doubtless have carried on to the grave had evidence not come up to stop her.

The second document is the marriage licence itself, bearing the same date. It is signed by Burmester above a clause swearing 'that there are no legal objections to our marriage'. The licence, however, is unsigned by a licenced minister, and was not returned to the County Clerk for recording, so no record exists of a ceremony actually having taken place. But it seems likely that Burmester was the mystery lover.

Possibly Mae knew nothing about his application for a marriage certificate and Burmester intended to surprise her. And it would truly have been a surprise as she was already married to Frank. In the unlikely event she had confided her marital status to Burmester he would hardly have taken out a marriage certificate before the divorce was settled.

A more plausible explanation seems to be that, after having been knocked cold by Burmester, she seriously considered a bigamous marriage. Common sense – compounded by the knowledge that she would be losing Jim and alienating Tillie – prevailed and she called it off at the last moment and fled back to mother. Few people knew how deeply her feelings had run, and perhaps how very nearly she had committed bigamy.

A decade later, Mae was to tell Miss Biery, concerning her

break-up with her mystery lover, 'If I hadn't made such a big success, I'd regret it. If I hadn't got to the top, I'd be sorry. But as it is – you can't do two things in life. Mother was right. She saw it correctly.'

According to Mae she always did.

chapter seven

SEX

SEX was the play that put Mae on the map. Not because it possessed any particular production merit but because of the scandal with which it surrounded her, and her canniness in capitalizing on it. She was promoted overnight from vaudevillian performer to New York headliner.

Mae had become desperate. In 1925 she was thirty-two years old and her career was mediocre. She had reached a certain level but couldn't seem to lift off from there. She needed to star in her own show or she would never make the grade. 'I needed a full length play,' she stated in the *News of the World*. 'Nobody knew my style, what I could do best.' She remained confident that with the right vehicle she could fill a theatre. Jim started looking for plays which might be adapted to her talents.

Mae had been scribbling down bits of dialogue and ideas for years. As Harry Richman tells us, one of her plays had already been disastrously produced in Greenwich Village and after that she had written another entitled *The Hussy*, but couldn't get a backer.

Mae was bemoaning the lack of suitable plays to Tillie one day and, to illustrate her point, she took a script Jim had brought in and irritably pointed out its defects. According to Mae, Tillie replied, 'Dear, you can write your own play.' Conveniently forgetting her earlier disasters Mae recognized the wisdom of Tillie's remark. 'You know, this was a mother, watching, observing her own child . . .' she told Denis Hart. 'You know better what you want than anyone,' egged on Tillie.

In order to prepare herself for this undertaking, Mae tells us that she studied the great psychologists – Havelock Ellis,

Sigmund Freud and Carl Jung. She wanted to understand the reason for the strength of the sexual urge that dominated her life, and which would feature in any play she wrote. She may, indeed, have read a few paragraphs in the papers, or such like, about these men but she never studied their books. Mae never read so much as a novel in her life. If she needed to know what a book was about she would ask someone who had read it to tell her. When she became famous she made her secretary give her a spoken synopsis of any book with which she needed to be acquainted. But she was fascinated by pulp psychology and would intently apply its findings to her own life, and that of any stage character she considered portraying.

There are two versions as to how *SEX* came to be written. Mae's version is that her chauffeur (i.e. Jim's chauffeur), mistaking her directions one day, took her to the dock. There she saw sailors mingling with prostitutes. The sight of the sailors in their uniforms, and the whores in their flashy clothes, tantalized Mae. She told the chauffeur to stop for a while, while she soaked up the atmosphere of sex and commercial transaction. She realized that this was what she had been seeking. These were the characters about whom she would write.

The second version is supplied by George Eells and Stanley Musgrove, who postulate in their book about Mae* that Jim bought a play from a client and suggested that she adapt it with the help of her friend, the playwright Adeline Leitzbach, who had assisted her with the writing of *The Hussy*.

However the idea came into being, Mae became inspired and set about creating the play with a vengeance. Many minds shaped *SEX* including, to no small degree, Jim's and Tillie's.

The character Mae wrote for herself was the prostitute Margie LaMont. Margie discovers a drugged society woman and as she tries to help her, the woman recovers and reports Margie to the police for trying to rob her. In revenge Margie entraps the woman's son into marriage. But, at the brink of the altar, she is troubled by her conscience and relinquishes the boy, to return to her own true love, a sailor.

* *Mae West: The Lies, the Legends, the Truth*, Robson Books, 1989.

Amidst a pile of scribbled ideas the play slowly took shape. 'I don't bother with any approach,' Mae told reporter Ben Maddox. 'I just sit down ... and write the kind of show I'd like to see myself.' Having completed the play, and utilized Jim's office staff to type it neatly, she sent it to the Shuberts. She was too self-conscious to put her own name on the manuscript as she was, after all, a known variety artist, but her past record as a playwright was not exactly glowing, so she chose the pen name, Jane Mast. The name Mast evolved from the first and last two letters of her professional name, and Jane was not only her own middle name, but Tillie's as well. She thought this might bring them luck.

It did not.

A reader in the Shubert's office vetted it – 'some flunky in the Play department,'* was Mae's understandably sour description – and sent it back with a rejection slip.

Jim consoled her by telling her it was time for them to go into production as independents. Forget the big managements, no real money could be made working for them anyway. They must produce SEX themselves. He would, once again, underwrite the finance. Tillie would also act as partial backer. She had wealthy relatives and, as Mae knew well, considerable powers of persuasion. Another backer whom Jim persuaded to invest was the gangster Owney Madden.

Madden was one of New York's most colourful figures. He has been written of as 'small and soft spoken ... china blue eyes, and a gentle manner. He was nonetheless a very hard man who could be cruel and was believed by the police to have killed several men before he was out of his teens.'** Elsewhere he is described as 'the hard and sensible boss of the New York underworld'.† It was a title for which Madden had fought in many bloody clashes with rival bootleg outfits. His early career had been nipped in the bud as he had spent most of his youth in Sing Sing. He was a good friend to Mae.

* Article by William Scott Eyman, *Take One*, September/October 1972.
** *Duke Ellington*, James Lincoln Collier, Pan, 1989.
† *No Cover Charge*, Robert Sylvester, Dial Press, 1956.

Mae now had what she wanted. A play in which she could star and financial backing. There was even a part for Beverly – as understudy. What sister could ask for more?

But she still had trouble finding a decent director. Many of the desirable ones were committed elsewhere and the rest, when shown the script, turned it down. One director complained there were characters in the first act who did not return in the second. 'They're busy,' Mae told him.* Word spread that Mae was once again in business as a playwright and abruptly good directors became hard to pin down.

Eventually she and Jim went to see a play directed by Edward Elsner. Principally a drama director, but no longer quite the force he had been, he was nevertheless a man of flair. The best, by far, that they had seen and – he was available.

They met Elsner during the interval. According to Mae in her autobiography, *Goodness Had Nothing To Do With It*, he 'looked like something out of an Edgar Allan Poe story dusted off'. He agreed to meet them next day at his office for a reading.

The meeting did not start well as Elsner had broken his spectacles and Mae was obliged to read the script to him. She was pleased, however, when he laughed, unprompted, in the right places. When she had finished he leaped to his feet, yelling, 'My God, you've done it. This is just what Broadway has been screaming for.'** One way or another, Elsner was booked to direct the show.

The producer, who had also invested in the show, was C. William Morgenstern, a New York figure with contacts as varied as Jim's.

There was a month of rehearsals and after this there was to be a tryout at New London, Connecticut, followed by a New York première on 26 April 1926 at Daly's Theater on 63rd Street. Mae's rehearsals were a shambles. She was solely interested in her own role and kept changing the lines of the other players in order to accommodate her part better. The script,

* *Goodness Had Nothing To Do With It*, W. H. Allen, 1960.
** Article by William Scott Eyman, *Take One*, September/October 1972.

such as it was, changed drastically from day to day. Mae did not arrive until mid-morning but often stayed until late at night, which made the days very long for the rest of the cast, who came on time. If it ever occurred to her that she might be inconveniencing them, the thought did not disturb her.

Mae liked Elsner, mainly because he did not get under her feet and allowed her to run the show. She felt confident enough to improvise and he followed her line of thinking by encouraging her to ignore the plot and concentrate on selling her personality. He urged her to exaggerate her hip-swinging walk and to emphasize her Brookyln pronunciation.

Even so, when the company started to rehearse in the New London theatre her spirits dropped, and her depression pervaded the rest of the cast. The theatre was really a cinema and had been closed for some time. It was damp and the heavy drapes cloaking the interior of the building reeked of mildew. Complaints to the house manager were useless. He was a lacklustre individual who resented the company.

SEX started life under the working title *The Albatross*, but Mae knew it could not possibly open as this. It sounded like something by Chekhov. In a magazine article she revealed how the play came to be retitled *SEX*: 'One day, early in rehearsals, Elsner said that the play reeked with "Sex, sex, sex!" So that's what we called it. A lot of newspapers wouldn't print the word so the ad. would read, "Mae West in That Certain Play". Silly, eh?'*

Not so silly. Curiosity was aroused. But not because the newspapers refused to print the title; several, including *The New York Times*, did so. Rather it was Mae who invented and broadcast the fiction that the title was banned. She recognized the value of controversy and worded certain advertisements in a manner which implied a ban had been imposed. In addition she paid bill stickers to paste illegal bills publicizing the play on walls, windows, cars and anywhere else they could. Mae knew best how to generate publicity.

Jim worried that *SEX*, as a title, might repel audiences and

* *Take One.*

65

Morgenstern agreed. They tried to get Mae to change it. The house manager, who had developed a dread of Mae, sided with them. Mae told journalist Martin Sommers, 'They worked on me for hours.' But to no avail. Her mind was set.

It must be borne in mind that the Mae West of *SEX* was a different creature from the sophisticate of the feature films. Any comedy arose from the situation, not from hand-on-hip wisecracks: 'What many people don't realize about my plays,' she told William Scott Eyman, 'is that they weren't comedies; they were sex-dramas. I only rarely put any comedy in, and then just to break up the drama.'

On opening night, just before curtain up, the house manager smugly informed her that a mere eighty-five people had turned up. She could have strangled him. To try to create some atmosphere she invited all the patrons to sit in the stalls. Audience response was understandably polite after that, but there was no evidence that the play had shocked. It seemed unlikely there would be a stampede for tickets during the run.

She had not, however, reckoned on the navy. New London is a port and next day the fleet was in town. Word spread that some of the scenes contained what a newspaper described as 'strumpeting and trolloping'. Such being the traditional sports of the navy, the boys came to lend their support.

Mae explained to Martin Sommers what happened next: 'The second night, when I arrived at the theatre, a little discouraged, there were long lines of sailors . . . waiting to buy tickets.' The navy was Mae's sort of audience. She gave the boys a night to remember. She shook her physique, sashayed and wrung every ounce of innuendo from her lines. The men yelled their appreciation, stamping on the floor. 'Believe me,' she told Sommers, 'I'll never forget the navy.'

Mae had further reason to thank the boys. For Harry Cort, manager of Daly's, was also in the audience. Although he had given an undertaking to house *SEX*, it was not binding. Thanks to the navy, however, Cort was impressed.

Daly's was what could be described today as an off-Broadway theatre with no great passing trade, so Mae thought it best to keep the bill stickers busy. Her publicity now read: 'HEATED –

MAE WEST IN ''SEX'' ', but the reviews were anything but warm:

Poorly written, poorly acted, horribly staged, *SEX* does not even contain anything for the dirt seekers. The theme is trite and the lines are dull, while the action is simply disgusting. *Billboard*

We were shown not sex but lust – stark, naked lust . . . Miss Mae West, the featured member of the company, contributed a song and dance which . . . added but little to the art of the entertainment. *New York Herald Tribune*

After three hours of this play's nasty, infantile, amateurish, and vicious dialogue . . . one really has a feeling of gratefulness for any repression that may have toned down her [Mae's] vaudeville songs in the past. *Variety*

Variety, which had stopped knocking her of late, was back on form. Despite this press barrage *SEX* managed to stay in business and the *Herald Tribune* reviewer put his finger on the reason why. He wrote that the play presented 'stark, naked lust', but omitted to add that whatever else lust may be, it is never dull.

SEX was no box-office triumph initially, but some plays have a vitality of their own which has nothing to do with the acclaim they may or may not receive. It became a cult show.

Just as box-office receipts started to flag, *SEX* was given a further, much needed boost by the British Embassy. Comment about Mae's depiction of promiscuity in the navy provoked an enquiry. This amused the public and the play settled into a run of nearly a year.

In an unidentified magazine article, a Brooklyn neighbour of Mae's tells of going to see *SEX* and being not so much shocked as surprised. Not by the play, but by Mae's appearance. 'When I saw her in her stage costume, my eyes nearly popped out of my head,' she remarks. 'Mae showed me how she had padded her shoulders and hips . . . When I told her she was no more like her stage part in real life than I was, Mae laughed and agreed with me.' Clearly she did not walk about Brooklyn resembling an 'upholstered egg-cup', as her famous silhouette has been described.

Another of Mae's callers was George Rauft, an employee of Owney Madden's. He was outstandingly handsome in the Valentino manner and like Valentino had been a gigolo. He was regularly seen in Madden's Cotton Club where Madden encouraged him to fraternize with the female clients. But Rauft's main duty was to deliver Madden's bootleg booze to the clubs. Writer Lewis Yablonsky tells us that 'In addition to driving booze, George sometimes ran errands for Madden'.* One of those errands was collecting the receipts for *SEX* and delivering his cut to Madden. Yablonsky interviewed Mae towards the end of her life, and she said of George, 'I liked his style and dark good looks and wanted to use him in a new play I was writing, called *SEX*. But, somehow, he seemed nervous and felt he couldn't really do any serious acting.'

Rauft later managed to conquer his nerves. He went to Hollywood, changed the spelling of his name to George Raft, and starred in over one hundred films.

While Mae was appearing in *SEX*, a world-shattering event took place. In 1926 the great screen lover, Rudolph Valentino, died of peritonitis at the age of thirty-one. The hysteria that accompanied his funeral was unprecedented: suicides were committed and rioting broke out when his body was displayed at Campbell's Funeral Parlor as thousands fought to get near the bier. The parlor was wrecked and souvenirs were even torn from the coffin and the body.

Campbell's was situated near Daly's Theater and Mae never forgot the pandemonium caused by Valentino's extraordinary lying in state. Actor Scott Richards recalls her talking to him about it nearly half a century later. Richards, a believer in reincarnation, confided to Mae, 'in my previous life of forty-five years ago I was Rudolph Valentino and lived in Hollywood ... Miss West didn't appear to be surprised.' She herself was a believer in reincarnation by then.

* *George Raft*, W. H. Allen, 1975.

68

She was, however, surprised and indignant at the publicity accorded actress Pola Negri at Valentino's funeral, which upstaged any sensation *SEX* may have given rise to.

Miss Negri had been a mistress of Valentino's, an affair that had been professionally helpful to both parties. It shot Miss Negri into the limelight and helped Valentino ward off accusations of homosexuality. She arrived at Campbell's, after the first riot had been quelled, heralded by a ten-foot-square wreath of white roses, with POLA picked out in scarlet carnations, and fainted, as if on cue, beside the bier, thus starting another riot.

But Mae had something more worrisome than Pola Negri with which to contend. A legal suit was issued against *SEX* claiming it was plagiarized. Such charges are frequently directed against any successful theatrical venture and judgement can be difficult since no work of art is entirely original. The claim was eventually thrown out of court, but not for six fraught months. In the midst of the case another charge was brought against Jim and Mae alleging their financial accounts were less than scrupulously kept. To take her mind off her troubles, Mae decided to write another play.

She chose a subject, male homosexuality, which had always fascinated her. Homosexuals work in all ranks in the theatre and Mae knew many. She frequently wrote of them, never tired of discussing them, and did not object when female impersonators imitated her. 'I looked upon them as amusing and having a great sense of humour,' she writes in her autobiography. 'They were all crazy about me and my costumes. They were the first ones to imitate me in my presence.' Her quaint notion about homosexuals was that they were women trapped in men's bodies.

She was happiest in the company of effeminate homosexuals. Masculine types, particularly those whom she found attractive, left her uneasy; she did not want to believe that a handsome man could be sexually indifferent to her. With effeminate homosexuals she relaxed and felt she could talk freely. Most, in turn, enjoyed her company, feeling an affinity with a woman of such aggressive sexuality. It is not necessary to be male in order to be unadulteratedly sexual in outlook but, in Mae's day, it was the custom. In any event, few females are so upfront about it as Mae.

Another reason why Mae was drawn to homosexuals was that she owed them a debt for helping her to develop her persona. She paid tribute to two in particular: she had worked with both and both had left their mark on her.

Bert Savoy was an eccentric drag comedian who appeared in vaudeville and in Greenwich Village revues during the Twenties. Mae picked up many mannerisms from him, including some tips on how to roll her gait as she walked. An outrageous personality, he died as spectacularly as he had lived. During a storm he shook his fist, cursing 'Miss God', and lightning struck him dead on the spot.

Julian Eltinge, with whom Mae worked before coming into contact with Texas Guinan, was probably the most famous female impersonator of his day. The epitome of insolent elegance, he is credited as the inspiration behind her bold manner.

Mae's new play was *The Drag*, which she wrote as a plea for a greater tolerance of homosexuality. Police harassment of homosexuals was savage in New York and many times she had seen chorus boys bearing wounds after having been beaten up. She had witnessed such brutality herself and intervened against the police. More to the point she had recently suffered a bout of unrequited lust concerning a young actor to whom she had made advances. Even a lady as experienced as she was had her blind spots. The truth painfully dawned. Deep-voiced and manly as he was, he was also homosexual.

But her overriding reason for writing *The Drag* was the success of *SEX*. She realized that in order to keep the ball rolling, she would have to trump herself with something of even greater salaciousness.

Mae was not the first playwright to deal with homosexuality. Helen Menken and Basil Rathbone were already playing in *The Captive*, which concerned lesbianism. To the uninitiated the theme could pass unnoticed, but *The Captive* was closed down anyway by New York authorities at the same time as *SEX*. Mae had been determined that no one would miss her theme. She would hammer it home with a sledgehammer.

New York in the 1920s housed several transvestite clubs. Mae had always known of their existence, but with her newly inflamed interest she now wanted to visit a few. She and Jim accompanied some of the boys from the show on their late-night jaunts, and recruited several eye-catching transvestites into the show's cast. She also picked up useful dialogue from the boys' patter. Mae thrived on the atmosphere – in his dark business suit Jim stuck out like a sore thumb.

Once again she adopted the pen name of Jane Mast and Elsner and Morgenstern were again, respectively, director and producer. Timony took his usual role as financial director. She did not plan to appear herself in *The Drag*. It would have been impossible as the highlight of the play was a ball in which the transvestites vie with each other in the splendour of their costumes. If Mae West had come on and topped them, then her point would have been lost. She babbled excitedly of her plans to that distinguished actress, Constance Collier, who seemed slow to grasp the ethos of *The Drag*. 'You don't understand,' she told her, 'I've got seventeen real live fairies on stage!'*

But even seventeen real live fairies could not save *The Drag*, although, at first, things looked promising. It tried out at Poli's Park Theater, Bridgeport, Connecticut, in January 1927, after some difficulty in securing a venue – several managers had refused to house the play. As with *SEX* she plastered the hoardings with advertisements, this time proclaiming, THE DRAG BY THE AUTHOR OF *SEX*.

Opening night played to a full house. To ensure this she had made a special offer – tickets could be purchased two for the price of one. The steamy subject matter was well, if raucously, received and patrons travelled from as far away as New York, Boston and Philadelphia to see the play. There was, after all, nothing like it in New York.

The audience, when filing into the theatre, was treated to a bonus – a drunken Beverly was cavorting noisily outside. Mae

* *Mae West: The Lies, The Legends, The Truth*, Robson Books, 1989.

was genuinely horrified and tried to quiet her, but Beverly was determined to turn the evening into a celebration. Then she overheard a remark passed about Mae, which she construed to be insulting, and turned violent. She was arrested by the police and charged with disorderly conduct. Mae never forgave her.

Despite *Variety*'s condemnation – 'a revel on the garbage heap' – *The Drag* showed every promise of becoming another hit and transferred to Paterson, New Jersey, prior to its hoped-for opening in New York. But this never took place. Fate stepped in and gave her an unlikely but portentous break. Mae was arrested.

chapter eight

JAIL

Mae credits her mother with the creation of Mae West. The dedication in *Goodness Had Nothing To Do With It** reads: 'In loving memory of my MOTHER, without whom I might have been somebody else.' She might have given similar credit to Acting Mayor Joseph V. McKee for, unwittingly, he played as significant a role as Tillie in ensuring her daughter's fame.

James J. Walker, Mayor of New York, was a playboy who enjoyed both the company of good-looking actresses and rubbing shoulders with showbusiness personalities. In addition he numbered several hoodlums among his friends, including Owney Madden.

His deputy, Acting Mayor McKee, did not share his *laissez-faire* approach to life. He considered theatrical New York, in particular, to be a sink of turpitude and was revolted by the current spate of fashionable, sexually-orientated plays. He viewed *SEX*, and its star, as running sores on the back of Manhattan. Mayor McKee was a friend of John Sumner of the Society for the Suppression of Vice. When the time was right, both men wanted nothing better than to clean up the theatrical life of New York. This opportunity presented itself in February 1927 when Mayor Walker went on holiday, leaving McKee in charge.

By now *SEX* had been running for forty-one weeks but business was petering out. Mae and Jim had heard rumours of possible police raids, as had the rest of New York. While they would have preferred that this did not happen, if such a raid did

---

* W. H. Allen, 1960.

73

take place, it would bring publicity and a big boost to business.

On the night of 9 February, urged on by Sumner, McKee ordered the police to raid, on corruption charges, three theatres, Daly's among them. The other plays affected were *The Captive* and *The Virgin Man*. The casts, producers and directors of all three shows were taken into custody. It transpired, during the trial, that plain-clothes policemen had been planted among the audiences.

While being charged Mae came face to face with Helen Menken, star of *The Captive*. Miss Menken was a legitimate actress and outraged by her arrest. She further objected to being bracketed with Mae West. She did not disguise her distaste and the two leading ladies exchanged sharp words. After Mae had been charged she could not resist having the last word: 'Well, anyhow we're normal!' she spat out at Miss Menken. This from the playwright who boasted of having seventeen real live fairies on stage. The remark, uttered when she was aroused, throws Mae's apparent support of homosexuals into a different light: her principles were always sacrificed for a good exit line.

The artists were given the option of leaving their plays – which meant closure – and the charges would be dropped, or face court proceedings. Miss Menken opted for withdrawal but Mae chose to fight her case. Although publicity was her motivation she did make a stand. She felt she should be free to explore sexual themes, on stage, without bureaucratic interference.

Mae faced the General Sessions on 19 April 1927. She arrived at court in the company of Jim and Morgenstern (both of whom had been charged with her); the nineteen cast members of *SEX* who had also been charged; and Tillie and Beverly.

The court was packed for what promised to be some entertaining real live theatre. The prosecution stated its case: the character Mae played in *SEX* glorified prostitution. Selected dialogue was read out as proof. A dance Mae performed in the show was also cited as obscene. Mae offered to perform it for the judge but was advised against doing so. The arresting officer testified that 'Miss West moved her navel up and down and from right to left'. The defence asked if the officer had actually seen Miss West's navel. 'No,' he responded, 'but I saw something in her middle and it moved from east to west.' The gallery exploded with laughter but Judge George E. Donnellan did not join in. Neither was he amused when she responded to a question with: 'The audience wants dirt and I give them dirt.'

Writer Elizabeth Yeaman was present at the trial and wrote, 'The judge finally had to clear the courtroom when Mae started to make monkeys of the state witnesses.' However tempting, it is not wise when facing charges to make monkeys of state witnesses. Had Mae's bearing been more temperate, the decision might have gone the other way. As it was, she played to the gallery and alienated the jury.

The jury deliberated for more than four hours, but finally found Mae, Jim and Morgenstern guilty of corrupting the morals of youth. Judge Donnellan sentenced them to prison for ten days each, and fined them $500 apiece. Mae's sentence was to be served at Welfare Island.

The sentence came as a shock, because she had not anticipated failure, but she brazened it out, and told the press that she was viewing her sojourn in jail as a holiday and intended to spend the time writing scripts. Mae later wrote about her experiences, and the article was published in the *Observer*.

She quipped that 'the iron cot did not agree with her,' but in fact she bore her sentence with dignity and gained two days' remission for good behaviour. During her week inside she met thieves, shoplifters, prostitutes (one of whom, at the age of twenty, had already been imprisoned five times), and drug addicts, who jolted her equilibrium considerably: 'They all sat before me,' she wrote. 'All glaring at me; all filthy, dirty, tattered and torn; human derelicts.'

Upon arrival she had been asked to strip and remove her civilian attire: 'What?' she claims to have said, 'I thought this was a respectable place.' She was presented with a prison uniform which elicited the following comment: 'I didn't like it at all; no lines to it.' She was then handed burlap underwear, thick stockings and flat shoes. She complained to the warden, Henry O. Schleth, who permitted her to wear her own silk underwear.

75

She was assigned to dusting the library and ate her meals with the warden in his office. He also took her out for drives. She knocked along well enough with the other inmates, who viewed her with awe, and whereas she did not pal up with other prisoners, she exchanged guarded conversation with a girl called Lulu, a 'stick-up woman'. 'I liked Lulu very much,' Mae admitted, 'for it requires a lot of nerve to 'stick-up' a man. Of course, there are a lot nicer ways to take everything a man's got – although I must admit Lulu's was a lot quicker way to get results.'

She visited the sick ward and the narcotic ward, and in the latter met an eighteen-year-old, half-Chinese, opium addict who left an indelible impression. Another addict committed suicide during Mae's stay. As she wrote: 'If I had ever wanted to get local colour, I sure got it there.'

For all her bravado the experience left its mark: 'When the big sheet-iron doors swung open,' she confessed, 'and God's big blue sky smiled down and I was free! Well, just use your imagination.' Warden Schleth was sad to see her go. 'A fine woman,' he pronounced. 'A great character.'

Journalist Ben Maddox later wrote that Mae had told him the police had given her a million dollar publicity campaign free. She capitalized, fully, on her jail sentence but harboured resentment. In 1934 she told the *News of the World*, 'I went through a conviction based on evidence which today seems exceedingly slight.' A quarter century later, in *Goodness Had Nothing To Do With It*,* she wrote, concerning the evidence of the policeman who described the movements of her navel, 'it was on this moron stutter alone that a conviction was secured.'

She left jail an unsavoury figure, 'gaudy and publicity seeking', as the press put it. In pious circles there was public indignation that she had expressed no remorse for her crime and exaggerated stories circulated about her decadence.

Once out of prison she moved again, this time to a rambling, old-style apartment on 72nd Street and West End Avenue which Beverly shared with her. Although the sisters fought

* W. H. Allen, 1960.

Beverly was still Mae's closest confidante, Jim notwithstanding, and there were certain things, such as her marriage, that she couldn't tell Tillie. Beverly was unable to afford her own apartment since she had no job and had too strong a will to contemplate living with her mother. She had been Mae's understudy in *SEX*, largely a device to put money through the books, for the likelihood of Mae missing a performance was rare, as Beverly well knew. It is doubtful she could have carried the show in any case.

Despite Mae standing trial *SEX* closed. Mae claimed the strain had made her too ill to continue but, in truth, illness was also a face-saver. Although her arrest had brought a surge to the box office, official pressure became too hot for her to bear.

She was also forced to abandon any immediate plans for mounting *The Drag* in New York. Her public excuse for cancelling the run was that audiences were 'too childlike to face like grown-ups the problem of homosexuality'. But Jim had been warned by officials that there would be trouble if the show came to town. This time, if a charge was pressed, the sentence would be stiffer.

Mae was beside herself, she could have made a killing with both shows. She viewed the cancellation of *The Drag* as a postponement, and vowed she would revive it some day. Eventually the shock value of the piece became negated by more extreme productions, and, without the shock of transvestism, *The Drag* has little to offer. It was never revived.

Mae chose the tamer world of bathing beauty contests as the background for her next play, *The Wicked Age*. Contests were sweeping America in the 1920s and most were rigged. She planned to expose them. Once again, Mae was the campaigner. The idea had come to her while she was in jail. Those eight days of incarceration seem to have been responsible for much of her early creative output.

She assembled the same team about her, including Elsner as director and Jim, and his hoods, as backers. This time, however, there was a designated change of producer, and Morgenstern's place was taken by Anton F. Scibilia. One source* suggests this was a pseudonym for Mae, and that he was also billed as the author. He seems to have no other traceable Broadway credits.

As with *The Drag*, she began without a script. All Mae needed was an idea and the rest was made up as rehearsals shambled along. As *Screenplay* later noted, 'After making a few rough notes she calls a rehearsal. A script is not essential. She writes the dialogue and works out the situations during rehearsals to fit the cast she has hired. This is her method.' To describe Mae's rehearsals as possessing method is to dignify the process. What *Screenplay* failed to point out was the utter chaos which accompanied a Mae West production. No one seemed to know what they were doing. Mae disregarded most advice Elsner offered, and he was wise enough not to offer much. Often she could not be bothered to turn up for auditions, and had little idea as to the identity of some of her fellow actors, most of whom she ignored anyway.

But this did not include her former boss, Handsome Hal Clarendon. Hal was not so handsome nowadays and his fortunes had declined with his looks. He sought work as an actor and was grateful for anything he could get. When she learned of his plight she at once gave him a part, warmly welcoming him to the company.

The male lead went to movie actor Raymond Jarno. Jarno had a swashbuckling appeal and melodious voice, but his voice posed a problem. Being a silent actor he had never used it in a theatre. Mae had not bothered to discover this before she hired him; she had liked his looks and given him the job without an audition. But as soon as he started to rehearse she realized she was in trouble. Beyond the first few rows he was inaudible. He had been given a contract for the run of the show and quickly made it clear he had no intention of leaving.

Jim tried to cheer her up by saying Jarno would improve. He suggested that if he didn't, a few friends could be found to run Jarno out of town. Before this could happen, however, Mae

* *The Encyclopaedia of the American Theater 1900–1975*, Edwin Bronner, A. S. Barnes & Co., 1980.

took action of her own. She reduced Jarno's part and gave most of his lines to another actor. When he objected she told him she would free him from his contract if he preferred.

Jarno brought in his union. Actors had suffered such a history of ill-treatment at the hands of producers that they had, by now, formed themselves into various unions. Mae had to answer to Actors' Equity, something she resented. The dispute rumbled on through a tryout in New Haven, Connecticut, right until opening night at Daly's, New York, the former home of *SEX*. The cast had divided loyalties, which made an unpleasant atmosphere backstage.

Once in New York, Equity representatives insisted upon viewing both versions of the play before they would permit the curtain to rise. The cast, already scheduled to give an evening performance, had to give two earlier performances for the union representatives.

Four hours before curtain up the verdict went against Mae. Equity decreed that Jarno's part must be restored, or he had to be replaced. Mae would be liable for his salary for the duration of the run. She told Jarno that if he would play the truncated part, for just one week, until she could get a replacement, she would then pay his salary for the duration of the run. But he would not back down. There was no recourse for her other than to accept the union ruling.

The actors had read from scripts for the union and the original version of the script had to be re-learnt, by everyone, in four hours. Under these distressing circumstances *The Wicked Age* started its New York run. Mae describes the play as 'a hit and a headache'. There was certainly a deal of the latter but the former was wishful thinking. The show ran for a mere nineteen performances and received the usual appalling reviews to which Mae, the playwright, was accustomed. 'Disgusting,' stated the *Daily Record*, summing them up. She was criticized too for her matronly appearance and for looking 'podgy'.

Of the plays Mae had authored, two had not survived runs of more than three weeks and the third had landed her in jail. A lesser person might have given up. Then she heard of a Broadway success called *Rain*, staged in 1923, which gave her her second wind. Based on a story by Somerset Maugham, *Rain* told of an affair between a missionary and a prostitute. It was the hottest show on Broadway and no small measure of its success lay with its star, Jeanne Eagels, whose personal life was as sensational as the subject matter. Mae coveted Miss Eagels' success, believing that she might have more effectively played the role herself. Who better to act a prostitute leading a priest to damnation? Mae set about preparing a new play.

She was not sure about the story line at first, but wanted the period to be the 1890s – the Gay Nineties, a roistering decade exemplified by the figure of Lillian Russell. The fashions of the period suited Mae. The long skirts hid the eight-inch high heels she wore to give her height, and the corseted waists made her seem less dumpy, as did the big hats and elaborate hairstyles. Mae remembered Tillie wearing such fashions and by adopting the styles her mother had worn, she felt she could give her the stage career which had been denied her.

Mae claimed the inspiration for the period and character of her new play, *Diamond Lil*, came as a result of a conversation she had with a hotel receptionist. She was wearing one of her evening dresses and an armoury of diamonds at the time. The receptionist told her she reminded him of a young lady he had known in his youth in the Bowery. The Bowery was a colourful area, and not every lady would have been flattered by such a comparison. Mae, however, took it the right way, and the man went on to describe Bowery life as he remembered it. He sketched a picture of brothels, white-slave traders and gang warfare. Mae's eyes widened with excitement; it would be the ideal backdrop for her new play. 'Suddenly I visualized the character who was to become a part of American folklore – Diamond Lil,' she modestly wrote in her autobiography.

At first she thought she might call her character 'Diamond Til', in tribute to her mother, but 'Diamond Lil' seemed to roll off the tongue better.

The receptionist may have been confusing his memories with folklore, for there is a Bowery legend of a real-life Diamond Lil, a prostitute who wore a diamond in one of her front teeth. But if Mae had heard about her she never mentioned it.

Jim, again assisted by Tillie, organized the finances. Owney Madden owned over 50 per cent of *Diamond Lil*. Mae's productions were not the only theatrical ventures in which Madden invested, of course, but he was one of her stalwart 'angels'. She chose a friend, Ira Hards, to direct. He had just completed a successful run of *Dracula*.

Diamond Lil is a saloon singer who falls for an undercover detective who is posing as a Salvation Army officer. Their love story takes place within a white-slavery theme. The atmosphere of the Bowery permeates the play and Mae depicts it as a lovable, entertaining place where good triumphs in the end; the villains are victims of society and the tarts have hearts of gold.

After a promise of good behaviour was extracted from Beverly, she was given the part of Sally, a girl who becomes pregnant by a man who then abandons her. She attempts suicide only to recover and fall victim to white-slavers. Lil saves her.

Although *Diamond Lil* is Mae's creation, various sources shaped the play. Two of these were the brothers Jim and Mark Linder. They had heard Mae was preparing a play and brought her a script they had written, set in the Bowery, called *Chatham Square*. Mae turned it down, explaining she was already well into her own play. She did however give Mark, an actor, a part. Despite her rejection of the Linders' script, *Diamond Lil* carries the credit 'Locale suggested by Mark Linder'. Linder was of the opinion that he had suggested rather more and Mae later had to face a court case to prove otherwise.

Diamond Lil previewed at Teller's Shubert Theater, Brooklyn, and after little more than a week, transferred to Broadway's Royale Theater, where it opened on 11 April 1928 and played to packed houses until 12 January 1929.

In the vulgar, wisecracking Diamond Lil, Mae had at last found her true stage personality. All the ingredients had finally fused together, producing a rounded and convincing performer:

From now on, she's my favourite actress . . . From now on,
I intend to applaud her from the top lines of my column
and the front rows of theatres in which she happens, by the

grace of God and the laxity of the Police Department, to be playing ... she's simply superb.   *Evening Telegram*

Miss Mae West has become an institution in the Broadway drama ... now more admired by her public than is Jane Cowl, Lynn Fontanne, Helen Hayes or Eva LeGallienne.
Herald Tribune

Glamour Miss West undoubtedly has ... She is alive on the stage as nobody is in life. In *Diamond Lil* all roads lead indeed to Rome. This Rome of all roads is Miss West
The New Republic

The British photographer, Cecil Beaton, was on holiday in New York while Mae was playing *Diamond Lil* and like most tourists he went to see it:

Mae West is terrific, a huge, blowsy, lustful blonde with a very painted face, high gold wig and curved figure of peachy pink. It made one feel that this thinness really was unsatisfactory sexually. This fat, pink, creamy, fleshy creature looked so lewd and naturally, healthily, amorously, lustful that in one scene where a Spanish lover mauled her, felt her breasts and buttocks, one had to cross one's legs and scream hysterically with laughter.*

Lewis Yablonsky, George Raft's biographer, tells us that Raft was once again the runner for Madden. He would present himself at the theatre each night to collect Madden's takings from Mae or Jim. Mae was brisk in her dealings and one of her duties before leaving the theatre each evening was to check the box-office receipts. She would change from her Lil costume, sit at her dressing table and divide the money proportionately.

Pleasure Man was the title of Mae's next play and, although it was not yet written, producer Carl Reed was already interested in putting it on. *Pleasure Man* is the story of a promiscuous

---

* *Cecil Beaton*, Hugo Vickers, Weidenfeld & Nicolson, 1985.

actor who has an affair with a married woman. One day when the woman arrives to keep an appointment with him she discovers that he has been murdered by castration. Suspicion falls on her husband, but eventually a young man confesses to the murder. He is the brother of a girl with whom the actor had dallied and dropped. He had castrated the actor to ensure he would undo no further women. Many of the subsidiary characters are transvestites who provide bitchy commentary throughout. It is quite a moral tale and once again Mae was banging her drum.

The theme of adultery didn't happen by chance. During the run of *Diamond Lil* Mae had had an affair, and had not discovered until several weeks later that the man was married. She dropped him because she abhorred adultery. The idea of death by castration for an unfaithful married man therefore seemed attractive.

Pleasure Man owes more than a nod to *The Drag*. She borrowed much of its material, notably the transvestite party scene. Mae was determined to get her real live fairies on stage somehow since she did not consider castration, by itself, a sufficient crowd-puller. As with *The Drag* she did not act in the play because she did not wish to upstage the transvestites. In any case she was not free: she was still pulling them in at the Royale.

Mae was unusually diligent in attending rehearsals for *Pleasure Man*. This had nothing to do with a sudden attack of conscientiousness; the rehearsals enabled her to spend time with her new lover. Rehearsals were held at night, after the curtain had come down on *Lil*. Jim held the fort at the rehearsal hall until her arrival in the fond belief she was travelling straight from the Royale to him. In fact, she took time off before leaving the theatre to entertain her lover.

Pleasure Man's 'tryout' was on 17 September 1928 at the Bronx Opera House. It transferred for a further 'tryout' to the Boulevard Theater, Jackson Heights. As far as the reviews went she was once again in the doghouse. 'Such filth turns my stomach,' wrote critic Robert Littell. 'Muck by the jeerful,' mocked Gilbert W. Gabriel.

Critics can be jaundiced; they see too many productions and lose touch with the fact that an evening at the theatre is meant to be enjoyed. Anyone reading reviews for *Pleasure Man* could be excused for believing the evening to have been a disaster. But apparently not. Robert Littell added in his review: 'Pretty nearly the most nauseating part of the evening was the laughter of the audience, or at least that part of it which howled and snickered and let out degenerate shrieks from the balcony.' If that was the case then the 'filth' to which Littell alluded clearly did not turn the entire audience's stomach as it turned his. Many members of the audience seemed to have a whale of a time. Only *Variety* managed to capture the spirit of the evening: 'Go early,' its reviewer urged. 'Some of the lines can't last.'

The official opening was on 1 October at the Biltmore Theater. The advance box-office receipts totalled $200,000. And, as the play was written by Mae, a sizeable crowd gathered outside the theatre hoping to see some police action. They went away disappointed. Her name now blazed from two Broadway marquees. Hundreds had to be turned away and the crowd blocked the streets. Everything seemed set for another runaway success ... but it was not to be. During the third act, when the drag party was at its height, truncheon-bearing police entered the theatre and stopped the show. The cast was arrested and carted off to the night court, some men still in their frocks. The charge, again, was one of indecency.

This time, however, Jim had prepared for trouble. A court injunction was obtained, preventing further police intervention, and *Pleasure Man* was put on again the next night. The newspapers were full of the story. 'Mae West in Paddy Wagon Again', ran one misleading headline.

Mae later confessed that she had herself stage-managed much of the publicity. 'The way to be a theatrical success,' she told Ben Maddox, 'is to get the public talking about you. If they're whispering and gossiping about you before the curtain rises, your audience has a big build-up. I always used to put things in the first night that I knew would have to be cut out later. It sure aroused enthusiasm about me.'

The second night audience, of course, hoped for another

raid. The actors revelled in the sensation they had caused but were, nevertheless, worried in case they might be imprisoned. This was, after all, Mae's second 'morality' offence. The performance continued uninterrupted but furious activity had been taking place that day in the offices of the public prosecutor, with the result that the District Attorney invalidated the injunction. The police again raided the show upon its third performance. Once again the cast ended up at the police station charged with giving an 'indecent' performance.

Mae hurried to the police station to try to sort things out. Had she written the play? she was asked by the police captain. Her response was observed and written up by former policeman Jeffrey Amherst: 'Calmly she gazed at him, took her time and replied, "Don't ya read ya noospapers?" Are you going to provide bail for all these people? he asked. "Somepin' of the sort," she answered with the maximum of insolence . . .'* Just the attitude she had displayed in court during the *SEX* trial and which had won her a stint in the slammer. Mae again elected to stand trial, together with fifty-six other interested parties whose defence costs she personally underwrote. Nathan Burkan, the Marvin Mitchelson of his day, was hired to defend her. The trial was set for March 1930.

But again she lost her nerve. *Pleasure Man* stopped production after she was charged, and was never restaged. The box-office advances had to be returned. *Pleasure Man* had seen just two complete performances before being consigned to limbo.

---

* *Wandering Abroad*, Jeffrey Amhurst, quoted by Eells & Musgrove, in *Mae West: The Lies, The Legends, The Truth*, Robson Books, 1989.

chapter nine

THE CONSTANT SINNER

Diamond Lil finally closed its Broadway run, free from prosecution, on 12 January 1929, re-opening in Chicago on 20 January at the newly refurbished Apollo Theater. Beverly came with Mae to Chicago and, as the part of Sally was undemanding, she was also there in her official capacity as Mae's understudy.

Beverly was no fool and knew Mae would have closed the show rather than give the part to another actress, even her own sister. Broadway correspondent Edward R. Sammis highlighted Beverly's predicament: 'As Mae's double, she could never hope for a break for herself, unless misfortune befell her beloved sister, and that was the last thing in the world she wanted to happen. It never did happen. Beverly was on hand, waiting in Mae's dressing room with her make-up on, night after night, ready for the emergency that never came. Mae, in all those months, never missed a single performance ... The patter of applause coming to her out through the wings night after night was music to her ears.' If Sammis believed what he wrote he'd believe anything. Downtrodden all her life, Beverly was dying to have a go and she would not have been human had she not felt jealous.

Jim was unable to accompany Mae to Chicago and remained in New York on business. She tells us in her autobiography that she took advantage of his absence to indulge a legion of new lovers and describes several. She writes yearningly of a jet-haired mobster with insane green eyes, who sadly got shot before their relationship could be consummated. Another was an unnamed boxer with whom she purported to share a sex session that lasted fifteen hours. But one man tops them all in her outrageous account. She maintains he enjoyed twenty-three separate orgasms in a single night. She was certain of her figures because she swore she counted the number of used condoms the following morning.

Cary Grant summed her up after having made two movies with her: 'She never told the truth in her life . . . She dealt in a fantasy world; the heavy make-up she wore was one sign of her insecurity. We were all very careful of her.'* The construction of her stage personality had blurred her ability to separate fact from fantasy. She began to believe the tales she told about herself.

The reviews in Chicago were as glowing as they had been in New York, and after a successful season the company toured through Illinois to California. It was a happy time for Mae, who was fêted wherever she went. She enjoyed being on the move, living out of a suitcase. It was second nature to her. But the tour was not altogether trouble free. The police tried to close the show, on obscenity grounds, in Michigan, but an injunction was obtained preventing them.

While she was on the West Coast, Columbia Pictures expressed interest in filming *Diamond Lil* with Mae in the lead. She performed a screen test, which was disappointing, and when executives finally got round to reading the play it was pronounced indecent. The project was abandoned.

About this time she began to experience a serious health problem. The symptoms manifested themselves in bouts of abdominal pain. She had had the same symptoms, intermittently, for over two years but now they intensified. Sometimes, several attacks in a day would leave her exhausted. Doctors could find nothing wrong, but the attacks persisted. So great was the pain that, if it occurred while she was on stage, it would sear through her performance and mar it.

Jim found the cure. One evening he brought to the theatre an Indian whom he introduced as Yogi Sri Deva Ram Sukul, president of the Yoga Institute of America. The Yogi was a spiritual healer. Taking her hands, he sat before her and prayed

* *Cary Grant: A Touch of Elegance*, Warren G. Harris, Sphere, 1988.

in Hindi. After an intense silence he pressed his hands on her abdomen. He left after refusing a fee.

The pains never returned.

Mae experienced more than physical relief. As swiftly as Paul had been converted on the road to Damascus, she was converted to mysticism. A good thing, too, for Mae was shortly to need all the support she could get. Tillie had been seriously ill for some time with cancer of the liver. Mae had refused to accept that she was ill and blamed Tillie's weight loss on dieting. Like Mae, Tillie had battled with her weight all her life. Mae allowed no one to speak of cancer and bombarded Tillie with expensive gifts, as though they might in some wondrous way ward off the disease. Tillie's condition deteriorated while Mae was in California. She anxiously kept in touch.

From San Francisco, the company moved to Los Angeles, where Mae was informed that Tillie's condition had worsened. She had now contracted pneumonia and was not expected to live. Cancelling all engagements, Mae returned to New York as quickly as possible. But the journey took two worry-fraught days. To her relief, when she arrived in Brooklyn, Tillie had rallied and Mae was, once more, convinced her mother would recover.

Diamond Lil re-opened in New York. After the show each evening, Mae would rush back to Tillie, who seemed to be constantly improving. This was a fool's paradise. Mae was told one evening at the theatre that Tillie had relapsed. As soon as the show was finished she rushed back – just in time to hold Tillie in her arms before she died. Tillie was fifty-eight.

Mae screamed and dropped to the floor in a faint. A feeling of panic followed. Every time Mae had been in trouble she had run home to mother, now there was no mother to whom to run. She was terrified.

The suffering of the rest of the family was nothing as compared to Mae's. Mae and Tillie had been linked by a bond unshared by the others. As long as they had each other they needed no one else.

Mae had lost her innocence years ago, and whatever small

part of Mary Jane West remained unscathed was now securely locked inside her. She made no conscious decision, but from then on it became her sacred duty to consolidate the legend of Mae West. It was her trust to her mother.

Mae suffered remorse. She was guilty of deceiving her mother over her marriage, and there had been times when she had put Tillie off from touring with her, for fear her mother might cramp her style. Mae convinced herself that if she had only allowed Tillie to travel with her, she might still be alive. She could have been introduced to the Yogi, and his spiritual healing might have cured her too. Mae still could not bring herself to admit her mother had died of cancer. In those days a stigma was attached to the illness so she told people that pneumonia had been the sole cause of her mother's death. Eventually she almost convinced herself that this was the case.

In reality, she had nothing with which to reproach herself. No mother could have wished for a more devoted and affectionate daughter. Tillie was the only person to whom Mae was not afraid to show affection, the only person she totally trusted and, certainly, the only person to whom she was unswervingly loyal.

Battling Jack was as supportive as possible. In his bluff way he loved Mae and realized the depth of her grief. Who knows what private remorse he may have suffered over his cavalier treatment of his wife? Their marriage had stood up – mostly because they had not seen too much of each other – and Tillie had been absorbed in Mae, gaining vicarious fulfilment through her daughter's now blossoming career. She had viewed Battling Jack as an accessory.

His main worry now was who would continue to look after him, but he had to look no further than Mae. That younger version of his wife who also had his knock-about fighting spirit would see him through. Although Mae could not yet think coherently, the others instinctively knew that she would take over as head of the family.

John Jr, the spoilt darling of the family, was not abnormally upset. He still had his father and two elder sisters on whom to lean.

Beverly could get on well enough without Tillie too. Tillie

had been no inspiration to Beverly, given her little encouragement, and made it clear that her younger daughter was, if not exactly a disappointment, then clearly not up to expectations. In any event Beverly now lived with Mae, travelled with Mae and was supported by Mae. Circumstances had hardly changed.

Jim was the greatest prop for Mae during this terrible period, and it was to him she turned, rather than to her siblings.

Mae became unbalanced. She reacted hysterically, flailing her limbs and screaming until she had to be restrained. She moaned that she, too, wanted to die. She then lost the power of speech for a few days. She could not bear to look at her mother's belongings and these had to be removed. Even photographs of Tillie had to be put away.

She retreated into a private world. Battling Jack was so alarmed by her behaviour that he made her promise she would never look at his corpse. But it was not the spectre of death in general that had unstabilized Mae, it was Tillie's death in particular.

Tillie was laid to rest in a mausoleum which Mae had purchased, at the Abbey of Cypress Hills Cemetery, Brooklyn. She ensured there was room in it for the rest of her family, and for herself.

Tillie's life had been one of courage but unfulfilled promise. She had arrived in America as an immigrant full of hope for her new life, and her exceptional beauty had quickly attracted a dashing husband. The marriage, however, had been soured by his obvious preference for the company of his friends, his love of booze and his indifference to family life. She had found escapism in the theatre, and longed to be a part of it herself, but the needs of her three children prevented the realization of her dreams. Investing her hopes in her elder daughter, she had lived her life through Mae. Her finest hour had been when Mae's name shone from the Broadway marquees. But, immediately after her death, it seemed that the bright future Mae had before her was about to wane, and Tillie's love for Mae had backfired. Her overpowering devotion to her daughter had produced a dependence in Mae that could not be replaced. Tillie had produced a daughter who believed herself to be the centre of the universe, yet was an emotional cripple. Unable to give enough of herself to love someone, and yet in desperate need of security, the very brashness of her façade was an indication of her inner terror. Without constant reassurance Mae West spiritually collapsed.

After the funeral Mae returned to *Diamond Lil*. There was, after all, nothing else to do. But it took months for her to regain her feet and during that time she suffered fits of hysteria and lost two stones in weight. She eventually learnt to live with her grief, but she never completely recovered from it.

While Mae was in emotional turmoil, America itself was in crisis. Wall Street crashed, leaving the financial affairs of the nation in chaos. Stock became valueless and millionaires paupers. Those in rural areas found they could neither sell their produce nor earn money to replenish stocks. Thriving farms became dust bowls. The poor of the cities were reduced to a life of begging, but those from whom they begged were often nearly as badly off. Queues at soup kitchens stretched for blocks.

Mae was not hit by the Wall Street crash. Her main assets were gems. She believed in tangible possessions and her instincts served her well. Jim had always invested in the stock market and consequently suffered losses. But Jim was a gambler. He was used to winning and losing.

When *Diamond Lil* closed, Mae toured for a while, with a new act based on her Diamond Lil character. But, as with most other performers, business was poor, added to which her raunchiness, so well received in the cities, did not go down well in the boondocks.

She hastily pasted together a new project entitled *The Racket* – a rewrite of *SEX* – and toured with this for a few months for the Shuberts, opening at Chicago's Garrick Theater. She barely broke even.

Tillie had died in January 1930. By March of that year, Mae was still in low spirits and did not feel like coming to terms with the world. But she had no option. On 14 March the *Pleasure Man* case came to court and Mae testified, dressed from head to foot in black. No wisecracks this time; she seemed so uninterested in the outcome her inattentiveness was remarked upon. Judge Bertini was inclined to be severe and lectured Mae upon her lack of morals, but Nathan Burkan won her acquittal. The show was adjudged 'not basically an immoral performance'.

After the case Mae shelved all immediate plans for a further tour. She decided, instead, to write a novel, hoping this would distract her from her grief.

The book was to be called *Babe Gordon*, after its heroine. Mae describes Babe as one who 'uses her beauty and sexual allure as a soldier uses his weapons – without mercy or scruples. Her basic appeal attracts all types of men, from the bruisers of the prize ring to the more refined sons of the city's aristocracy. From her experiences with men, she is canny, worldly wise, quick thinking.'* In short . . . Mae West.

She persevered with the book and, as with all her artistic ventures, asked for ideas from nearly everyone she knew. If she thought them worth using, she incorporated them into her story and used Jim's staff to type out the document.

Even with this assistance the book was presented to its publishers, the Macaulay Company, not as a finished manuscript but as a collection of ill-ordered notes. It was left to someone else in the publishing house to render it literate.

Babe Gordon was successful, and in order to promote subsequent editions, Macaulay inaugurated a competition for readers to retitle the novel. Out of the entries, *The Constant Sinner* was chosen, and the book is now better known under this title.

The novel traces Babe's history from her days as a Harlem prostitute to her success as the mistress of a wealthy playboy, taking in a murder trial and various suicides along the way. The atmosphere is provided by drug pushers, addicts, hit men and nymphomaniacs – the sort of people whom Mae always enjoyed writing about. Babe embodies much of Mae's own philosophy and she remarked several times that the book contains more autobiographical material than *Goodness Had Nothing To Do*

---

* The Macaulay Co., 1930. Also known as *The Constant Sinner*, Sheridan House, 1949.

With It. Since it was written before she became a film star, it is not so tailored to suit her image.

Mae had an acquisitive mind and an aptitude for recalling snatches of dialogue and colourful descriptions, many of which she used in her book. No great conversationalist herself, she would encourage those who interested her to talk in her presence. She egged on the chorus boys with whom she worked and remembered their stories and their phraseology. She listened to the gossip in the boxing gyms.

Her style is lurid. In the following passage Mae introduces Babe's best friend, Cokey Jenny, who peddles cocaine – an occupation as fashionable then as now:

A soiled green dress, a flaming red felt hat and dusty satin slippers were the total wardrobe her rambling body carried. She struck a sporty note with a flashy black oilcloth purse. Jenny's gin voice was a scraping rasp. Her eyes resembled steel-headed prison bolts as the cruel purple mouth opened into a witch-laughing salute to Babe. Babe nailed her with a cross-examining eye, and stabbed her with slow words of pain that touched Jenny's pride. 'You walkin' gin house. What the hell's the meanin' of bein' late like this? I had three tumbles the time I've been waitin' for you.'

As if anyone could be in doubt about Babe's tastes after that, Mae continues:

Babe was the type that thrived on men. She needed them. She enjoyed them and had to have them. Without them she was cold and alone . . . There are women so formed in body and mind that they are predestined to be daughters of joy. These women whom the French call 'femmes amoureuses' are found not alone among women of the streets, but in every stratum of society. History's pages reveal the power of these women that thrive on love, whose lives are centred on men. Babe was a born 'femme amoureuse'. Her idea was that if a man can have as many women as he wants, there is no reason why a woman should not do the same thing. She was one of those women who were put on this earth for men – not one man but many men.

Babe Gordon was published in 1930. By then, Hollywood had done much to liberate sexual attitudes in America, but purity leagues still thrived. Middle America's basic attitude to sex was that it was for procreational purposes only, and acceptable within the confines of marriage and nowhere else. Sex was not to be discussed, except with a gynaecologist, and then in the strictest privacy.

There were, naturally, double standards. It was permissible for the upper classes to practise birth-control but the working class was expected to exercise abstention. The rich had physicians willing to prescribe for them, but birth-control pioneer Margaret Sanger was imprisoned in 1916 for running a clinic in Brooklyn.* She had outraged public opinion by openly displaying contraceptives. What was good for the gander definitely was not good for the goose.

Which raises the question, did Mae ever get pregnant? The sponge method she advocated was far from foolproof. Condoms were more reliable, but not infallible.** If she had abortions, were they the cause of the mysterious abdominal pains cured by the Yogi? Possibly she was barren.

Barren or fertile, she was as resolute in her struggle for sexual liberation as was Margaret Sanger.

In her novel she unconsciously reveals many of her sexual idiosyncracies and preferences. She relates, for example, the excitement she felt when having sex with boxers who had just finished a fight: 'The touch of her soft body against his own raw, irritated flesh which had been scraped on the ring ropes was soothing . . .' Her attraction to blacks is evident: 'Money Johnson was a huge, lordly lion with plenty of self-assurance.

* In Britain Marie Stopes was fighting the same battle. In 1921 she opened the first birth-control clinic in the British Empire.
** About the time *Babe Gordon* was published a pharmaceutical process was discovered which is highly likely to have enhanced Mae's enjoyment of life. The 1930s saw the appearance of the first latex condoms.

His sunny features and hot burning eyes held a magnetism that irresistibly drew the attention of women to him. His magnificent body, lynx-eyes, and pearly white grin had brought the women of Harlem crawling to him, hungering for even an affectionate glance.' And elsewhere: 'In that great mirrored room ... Money Johnson appeared like an army by reflection and she was like a shimmering white quicksand ready to consume these black battalions.'

Auto-eroticism appears in the book, too, for Mae loved to admire herself. Her apartment was full of mirrors and she would frequently comment, even to casual acquaintances, upon her own beauty: 'She looked at her glowing body with self-appreciation. The well-turned arms and legs, the smooth contour of curving hips, her pink curling toes, all combined to give her a thrill of sensuous pleasure and to remind her how she might captivate any man. "How nice I am," she thought.'

Her other great delight, food, is celebrated: 'Babe's appetites were always lusty and it was not till she had finished two large helpings of soup that she felt any desire to talk.'

And in any world created by Mae West there are homosexuals, one of whom answers to the name of Madame Jolly.

Babe was an extension of Diamond Lil. As she put it, she's 'the kind of woman every man wants to meet – at least once.'

The pre-movie star Mae West was a darker creature than her films depicted. There was a coarser side to her that cinemagoers never saw. This cruder aspect comes out in *The Constant Sinner*. Babe is not so fun-loving but more clinically obsessed with sex, more callous in her attitude. Babe compares the sexual prowess of her partners with her cronies, and they pass the men on, one to another. Men are just so much meat to be devoured, then abandoned. Love does not come into it. As Babe says, 'So, this is love! A goddam belly ache, that's what it is.'

A cynic is a disillusioned idealist. The sensitive become cynical, the obtuse merely numb. By expressing sentiments sceptical of human goodness, Mae reveals she still cares, but is armouring herself.

Her description of Babe's attitude to truth in *The Constant Sinner* could equally apply to her own understanding of life: 'It never occurred to her that she was lying. That is, it had no moral significance to her. To Babe, a lie was simply something one told to gain an advantage, to get what one wanted by the shortest route.' Mae's travels in vaudeville, since a child, had been long and hard and she had been taken advantage of in every way. The press had reviled her, her mother had died, her sister was a drunk, her father and brother ineffectual and, apart from Tillie, the only people to have helped and shown her affection were gangsters. Respectable people had done nothing for her. The only respect she had gained was through notoriety. Money was her sole security, the means of keeping the world at bay. At this stage in her life, only one person was going to take advantage, and that was Mae West.

Theatre critic Elizabeth Yeaman, by no means hostile to Mae, recalls the prevailing attitude held by 'legitimate' theatre-goers towards Mae during the 1920s: 'When I was living in New York, I never went to see Mae West on stage ... Discriminating theatregoers simply did not put Mae West on their list. Occasionally, some of the highbrows would venture to her theatre in something of the spirit that they would go on a slumming tour. New York ... regarded Mae West as *déclassé*.' She adds, 'Time was, in New York, when first class leading men never sought a job with Mae West. Although her plays always had long runs [sic], which guaranteed a steady salary for her cast, particular actors did not seek jobs with her, even though they might need the money badly.'

As good a novel as *The Constant Sinner* is, Mae did not see her future as a novelist. The stage was in her blood. She dramatized the book and the Shuberts agreed to stage the show; Jim set up a company, Constant Productions, to handle the financial transactions. Each production with which Mae was involved had its own company, but these rarely survived the duration of the play. She once whimsically had called one of her companies Moral Productions. As with *Diamond Lil* there was a big cast of supporting players, making the show expensive to mount, and there were many scene changes requiring a large backstage crew.

The Constant Sinner opened at New York's Royale Theater

on 14 September 1931. *The Times* thought it 'dull' and *Billboard* commended it to 'morons'. Audiences were equally unimpressed and the show closed after a run of just eight weeks. Mae blamed the Depression, which was certainly a contributory factor. The theatre, in general, was in grave difficulties.

Mae entered another period of personal depression. Her success in *Diamond Lil* seemed to have been forgotten and she was on the skids again. As always when depressed (and, it must be said, also when not depressed) her weight crept up. She regained the two stones she had lost at Tillie's death, and more to spare.

Jim's appearance was no incentive to slim. He, too, had put on weight and in addition he had lost the flashy smartness which had so impressed her in their early days together. It was not uncommon, nowadays, for people to mistake him for her father. Hardly the squire with whom a girl-about-town would wish to be seen.

In low spirits she announced to the press that *The Constant Sinner* was closing, and would re-open later in the year. This was a face saver. The eight weeks' run had taken its toll on Mae. The Royale was not air-conditioned and, like many plump people, she suffered in heat. There had been nineteen costume changes for every performance and she felt exhausted as well as depressed. There were no plans to re-open.

No offers of tours came in, and she had no ideas for a new play. She did not feel like writing one anyway. She reviewed her circumstances; she was a low-brow comedienne, good for a belly laugh maybe but never to be taken seriously. Out of work, she was also overweight, and her boyfriend an embarrassment. She had just passed her thirty-ninth birthday. Not a happy predicament.

chapter ten

NIGHT AFTER NIGHT

Mae could not help but be painfully aware that while she had been flogging herself to death in the heat of New York, largely to unappreciative audiences, several of her associates were making a financial killing in Hollywood.

Two such were Jesse Lasky and William Le Baron, both of whom she had worked with back in 1911 in the Folies-Bergère. Lasky now wielded hefty power in Hollywood as second in command of Paramount Pictures, answering only to its boss Adolph Zukor.

Le Baron had, more or less, stuck by Lasky, and was now a prominent producer in his own right at Paramount. In 1927 he had produced *The Popular Sin*, Paramount's most commercially successful film of the year, and his documentary-style *New York* had also won acclaim in that the stark, innovative sequences had involved location filming, a practice commonplace today but which broke new ground at the time.

For all his success, Le Baron's relationship with Paramount had not been trouble-free. He was a man with a stubborn streak and had crossed swords several times with both Lasky and Zukor. First in 1927. That had been the year in which Warner Brothers had shaken the industry to its roots with their release of *The Jazz Singer*, starring Al Jolson.

It was the first 'talkie'. It seems inconceivable today that most of the studios prior to 1927 could have had so little faith in the viability of sound, and were content to continue to plough money into silents. But Warners had persevered with experiments and invested courageously in *The Jazz Singer*. By no means a full-scale talkie, its full orchestral soundtrack included several songs by Jolson, augmented by a few snatches of dialogue. The novelty thrilled the public. An overwhelming demand arose for more. Overnight, silents were as dead as the dodo and heads rolled in the studios as executives were punished for not foreseeing the future. Plans for sound were hastily made, budgets mapped out, and schedules rearranged.

Le Baron had been one of Paramount's sacrificial victims. It was made plain to him that, whatever his past triumphs, there was now no place for him at Paramount. He went to the less prestigious RKO studios where his first project, released in 1929, was a sound version of *Rio Rita*, a former Ziegfeld success. Its star was Bebe Daniels, also previously under contract to Paramount.

Rio Rita was a huge success. Like Le Baron, Miss Daniels had double reason to feel gratified. She had a beautiful singing voice, but until *Rio Rita* no one had bothered to listen to it. An experienced actress, who had made her debut at seven, she had been widely used at Paramount during the Twenties but had never been given a proper break. Zukor had refused to allow her even to test for sound.

Rio Rita was an embarrassment to Paramount. Not only had the studio let Bebe Daniels slip through its fingers, it had also lost Le Baron. Far from being on the scrap heap, he had scaled the heights once again. He was hastily enticed back, readily responding to that irresistible persuader, the cheque book.

Not all members of the industry withstood the onslaught of sound so successfully. The careers of many were over the moment *The Jazz Singer* appeared. Some artists had voices which could not be satisfactorily recorded, others had foreign accents so thick as to render them indecipherable. A case in point was Vilma Banky, the gorgeous Austro-Hungarian star discovered by Sam Goldwyn. Sound killed her off as surely as a bullet through the heart.

The casualties were numerous, embracing names which shone in lights in their day, but which now mean nothing – a parade of cadavers like the members of the bridge party gathered in Norma Desmond's crumbling mansion in *Sunset Boulevard*.

Altogether, there was much weeping, a few suicides and a

deal of panic. But the slaughter continued. It brought unprecedented problems. Hollywood had always had a surfeit of stars and would-be stars – but so many artists had been dispensed with that there was now a dearth of competent actors. New stars were needed who could handle sound dialogue.

Paramount was quick to replenish its stable and several of their new artists were recruited from the stage, artists who had proven they could speak. The stars themselves were quick to accept the contracts waved under their noses by panicking executives since they'd never earned such sums before.

Among the more exciting of Paramount's signings was Marlene Dietrich. In 1930 Dietrich's German movie, *The Blue Angel*, had focused world attention on her, and much credit for this should go to her director Josef von Sternberg. A master of sensual camerawork, von Sternberg found his ideal subject in the skeletal beauty of Dietrich. He spent hours setting up each shot, finely balancing the light and shade, before allowing her in front of the camera. His erotic obsession with his actress is evident in every frame.

In her early days Dietrich accepted his judgement unquestioningly and the resulting movies are tributes to her allure. Von Sternberg's techniques stunned Hollywood but his perfectionism was too time-consuming and, consequently, too expensive to suit the colony. He fell out of favour and Dietrich moved on to other directors.

The Depression didn't initially make an impact on the profits of the motion picture industry. The novelty of the talkies provided just the escapism needed in such harrowing times. By 1930, profits of the Paramount Publix Corporation (later Paramount Pictures) had soared to $18 million, the highest recorded since it had started trading.

Paramount spent much of this profit on the acquisition of additional theatres, investment in radio, and the development of its music division (it was one of the biggest producers of musicals). Its moguls considered themselves immune to the Depression, but were to pay heavily for their arrogance. By 1931 the tide drastically turned. Audiences, now accustomed to the new sound movies, declined alarmingly. The following year

Paramount was in trouble as the company plunged into a disastrous twenty-one million dollar deficit.

Hollywood itself was in danger in 1932 of becoming obsolete as the world's movie capital. Some of its older stars who had, seemingly, made the transition into sound could no longer pull in the audiences. Despite the 1930 Academy Award success of *Coquette*, Mary Pickford, for example, was on the skids. Born in 1893, the same year as Mae, her adolescent pertness now came across as a bit jaded but her audiences would not accept her as an adult, preferring her in her *Rebecca of Sunnybrook Farm* ringlets. Whereas Mary was ready to oblige, her thirty-nine-year-old face could no longer accommodate the deception.

The ringlets, in any event, were tiresome for her. In its natural state her hair was as straight as a yardstick and bound in rags at all times when she was not in front of the camera. The lights soon made the curls wilt and filming then had to stop while the crew (for whom America's Sweetheart was paying since she owned the company) expensively sat around doing nothing until the 'Pickford Curls', as they were dubbed, were retied and set again. In 1928 Mary shocked the world when she bobbed her hair.

She knew it would be more dignified to retire gracefully but, like many others, once having tasted fame she was hooked. She made a couple of films during the early 1930s, but by 1933 America really had jilted its sweetheart.

Pola Negri fared only slightly better. Her Polish accent, distorted by the primitive sound system of the day, far from enhancing her appeal as she had believed it would, baffled the public. Her exotic image itself became unfashionable in America and she went abroad to star in German films in the 1930s.

Even Swanson, that giant of the industry, was on rocky ground. She had been around since the Teens and the studios and audiences were looking for new faces. Hopeless at choosing suitable vehicles she carried on for just two more years but, after *Music in the Air* in 1934, found it safer to bow out discreetly.

It was Garbo who prospered the most with the coming of sound. Her accent was a problem, but one which her studio, MGM, was keen to solve (unlike Pola Negri's). Garbo was MGM's biggest attraction and they chose *Anna Christie*, her first talkie, carefully. Her husky voice suited the new medium, the very constriction of its range a bonus, particularly if she was cast (as she always was) as a foreigner.

By 1932 gangster films were popular and among the most successful was *Scarface*, which told the story of a gangster based on the real-life Al Capone. It even flung in a whiff of incest for shock value. *Scarface* started a trend, and starred Paul Muni and Ann Dvorak. George Raft was in the cast.

Raft's path to Hollywood, it is alleged, had been smoothed by East Coast mobsters, who had invested in films and needed a trusted representative on the West Coast. But however he started, Raft's talent quickly assured his career. His first film had been *Queen of the Night Clubs* in 1929, but *Scarface* made him famous, as a gangster with a habit of flipping a coin. His latest film, *Night After Night*, was in production at Paramount in 1932, with William Le Baron as producer. Le Baron was dramatically about to re-enter Mae's life.

Mae liked people to believe that the Hollywood studios deluged her with offers for years, and finally enticed her to the land of imported palms with a contract she could not refuse. Others, however, tell a different story.

Adolph Zukor writes that, in her pre-Hollywood days, far from being a sought-after commodity, most producers dismissed Mae as a coarse joke. He added, 'Picturemakers had shied away, not knowing exactly how to use her. Certainly no one believed that the Mae West of the stage could be transferred almost intact to the screen.'* She was over-the-top, too blue and just too overblown. Even allowing for the depressed social conditions of the time, the short, unsuccessful run of *The Constant Sinner* speaks for itself. Mae was no great draw at the box office.

While Mae bleaky contemplated her future in New York, work was progressing on *Night After Night*. The leads were

---

* *The Public Is Never Wrong*, Adolph Zukor, Cassell, 1954.

already cast. Raft was backed by Louis Calhern, Constance Cummings and the British comedy actress Alison Skipworth, who had formerly worked as a stooge for W. C. Fields.

Le Baron felt that, despite Miss Skipworth's considerable talent, the film hung a little heavy. A lighter touch was needed, someone who could add a few belly laughs. Possibly a wisecracking actor or actress with a broad appeal? There was no broader comedienne about than Mae West.

Raft mentioned her name to Le Baron who, of course, remembered her. She had had a brief fling with Raft in her *Diamond Lil* days and, as was the case with most of her lovers, had remained friends with him. Both Raft and Le Baron regarded her, affectionately, as a character.

'George got me my first break in the movies,' Mae told Raft's biographer Lewis Yablonsky, 'but I had mixed feelings. He played the lead ... and I was in a supporting role. It was very hard on me since I had been a big star in *Diamond Lil, SEX* and other plays. I found it tough playing under him.'* Her 'mixed feelings' were expressed with hindsight. By then she had told the world for so long that she had been a big star before entering the movies that she almost believed it herself.

Neither Raft nor Le Baron thought she would have a career in Hollywood and neither, when informed of the decision to hire her, did Zukor. The general feeling at Paramount was that she would not last, but the public might be amused by her for a short while. She was worth gambling on for a supporting role. Mae's agents, William Morris, were formally propositioned and Paramount offered a two-month contract, at $5,000 a week. A handsome deal.

On 16 June 1932 Mae, with Jim and Beverly in tow, left New York by train for California. The last time she had travelled that line she had been journeying in the reverse direction, after receiving the news of her mother's impending death. On that trip Mae had been full of foreboding, dreading existence without her mother. Once again the future was imponderable.

No one could have predicted that Mae would become a star.

* *George Raft*, W. H. Allen, 1975.

She was not the Hollywood type, being too old, too short and too fat. After accepting the contract she had managed to shed a few pounds, but dieting always made her miserable and she was still overweight. The only physical assets she possessed were her pretty face and her hair, which she had now dyed a mildly indecent platinum blonde. But as Mae hurtled towards the film capital, she could have taken comfort from the thought that Hollywood was, as it still is, a madhouse in which anything can happen.

In those days, people of standing in the movies did not travel the full journey to Los Angeles, but got off at Pasadena, a suburb about half an hour's drive from Hollywood. Artists were met by studio executives in limousines and sometimes, for a real star, a brass band was on hand.

Mae dismounted at Pasadena and was met by Murray Feil, her representative from the William Morris Agency, but no one else turned up. There was no Paramount official and no limousine. Two years later, when she was Paramount's biggest star, and an estimated 5000 men a year wrote her marriage proposals, she wrote of her arrival in Pasadena for the *Sunday Dispatch*: 'That village (Hollywood) when I slouched off the train for the first time, handed me the coldest shoulder which ever came out of the ice-box ... The nearest cameraman was twenty miles away up at Paramount. Just for a minute, as I hiked to the taxi rank, I reckoned the old Mae West stock had taken a Wall Street highball ...'

Mae told Tom Baily, Paramount's publicity director, that she originally viewed her sojourn in Hollywood as 'a sort of vacation', a place where she could write a sequel to *Diamond Lil*, based on the low life she found there. She was hedging her bets against failure.

Paramount had arranged accommodation for her in apartment 611, at the Ravenswood, a handsome art deco block on Rossmore Avenue, a leafy boulevard in the smartest part of Hollywood. With the Wilshire Country Club just a few yards away and a picturesque Spanish-style church at the beginning of the road, Rossmore was the Hollywood equivalent of Beverly Hills. And it has housed almost as many celebrities, including

Vilma Banky, Dolores Del Rio, gossip columnist Hedda Hopper and, later, Nat King Cole. The Ravenswood had an arrangement with the studios and accommodated many of their stars. At different times Mickey Rooney, Judy Garland and Ava Gardner stayed there.

Beverly shared with Mae, and Jim moved into an adjacent apartment. The Ravenswood became Mae's home for the rest of her life. She seldom left it, unless work took her away, and she never took a holiday.

But her first days in Hollywood were glum. She did not think she would like it there. It was the height of summer and she looked askance at the brilliant California sunshine, which was bad for her skin. She lowered the blinds in her apartment on that first day and no one ever saw them raised thereafter. The Ravenswood had a pool, but no one ever saw Mae visit it or even take a walk in the garden.

As a matter of course Tom Baily set up a press interview for Mae. The journalist was Madge Tennant of *Movie Classic*. Miss Tennant noted how dispirited Mae seemed: 'She didn't look especially happy when we saw her at the Legion boxing matches the other night, with her manager [Jim]. She looked about her frowning and few people noticed her. "Oh, it's divine not to be recognized," Mae insists. "I'm so happy to be able to go about not followed by crowds." Her manager adds, "I have refused $1000 a night just to have Miss West visit a nightclub so that they can advertise that she has been there." '

A likely story.

Mae told Miss Tennant she was a Broadway legend and thirty-one years old. The unimpressed Miss Tennant observed,

If, as is claimed for her, Mae West is only thirty-one years old, she must have worked hard and fast to produce the enormous volume of Broadway successes, books, vaudeville acts, skits and popular songs that have appeared under her name ... Mae thinks that several of her plays would make good motion pictures, particularly *Diamond Lil* ... 'And I haven't dieted, either!' she avers. 'I never was fat. I never weighed an ounce over 119. That was padding.' Hollywood wonders if she will be a sensation in Hollywood, where sex is a trade mark and not a novelty. Time – and Mae, herself – will tell.

Time did tell, and in less than a year Miss Tennant would be less slighting and intensely grateful for any time at all that Mae could spare her for an interview.

Predictably, Mae fared better with a man. *Screenplay* journalist Clark Warren got more out of her: 'Mae, in a few husky words, left me gasping, all my previous idols shattered, my illusions trailing in the dust. Mae ... speaks as frankly about the more obvious emotions as most people do about onions. And when Mae discourses on the various aspects of that all important subject, you realize that you are dealing with an Authority.' To ensure Warren had some solid copy she insulted Clark Gable, the reigning King of Hollywood: 'He has as much sex appeal as a dish of leftover potato salad.' 'I glanced up,' Warren continued, 'to see Mae calmly exhaling a cloud of per-fumed cigarette smoke, entirely unconscious of the fact that she had just tossed a bomb into a million boudoirs.'

Mae continued with her assessment of Hollywood women:

I can't say that I think much of your screen stars for sex appeal ... the flat figure does not attract men and in spite of styles, the figure of Venus will always be the world's love ideal. Garbo is wonderful as an actress but she is cold – terribly cold. I can't imagine a man going crazy over her. Jean Harlow gives a very physical performance and so, in a manner, did Clara Bow, but Pola Negri comes nearest to having any real sex appeal among present screen stars ... I think that Dietrich's is in her voice more than in her famous legs.

Pola Negri only came in for a back-handed bouquet because it was common knowledge that her career was virtually over.

Mae went on to inform Warren that she had just completed another book, entitled *Frisco Kate*, which was being turned into a play.

Mae was trouble to Paramount from the start. She was not given her script until a month after her arrival in Hollywood and complained bitterly about this. Her keen business sense could not accept that the studio was happy to pay her $5000 a week to sit idly at home. When the script finally arrived she detested it. The part had 'nothing going for it,' she grumbled to journalist William Scott Eyman. 'It was unimportant to the story and flatly written.' Studio head Al Kaufman was sent to placate her, but was unsuccessful. Anyone could play her part, she fumed. 'Al was very disappointed,' noted Zukor.

Not as disappointed as Mae. 'They gave me my first dialogue sheet and I hit the overhead lamps,' Mae told the *Sunday Dispatch*. 'I didn't like it. I told them so in several different languages.'

She refused to start filming until she was given permission to write her own material. Kaufman threatened legal action but had to report to Zukor that she would not relent. Zukor was worried. 'The wardrobe and screen tests had been fine,' he continued in *The Public Is Never Wrong*. 'Everybody wrangled with Mae . . . but she wouldn't start the picture.'

Neither side had budged by 17 August, Mae's birthday. To diffuse the situation, Kaufman took Mae and Jim to dinner. It turned out to be a surprise party for Kaufman. Zukor takes up the tale: 'Towards the end of it, Mae opened her handbag, took out a cheque and handed it to Al. It was for twenty thousand dollars – her salary to date. "I'm leaving for New York tomorrow," she said.'

The little *bombe surprise* considerably concentrated the minds of both Kaufman and Zukor. And it seems extraordinarily idealistic of Mae. By returning the $20,000 she was rejecting the chance of a movie career. But she was convinced she would not be a success with the script as it now stood.

Rather than idealistic, perhaps the gesture was strategic and she gambled that her cheque would not be accepted. She later confessed to the *Sunday Dispatch*: 'I realized that whether I liked it or not the film people had got me.' Having signed a contract she could be sued for breach, and she could not hope to win a battle against such formidable legal and financial resources as Paramount possessed. And Paramount would have been well within its rights to sue. She had neither asked for nor been given script approval. She was also aware that no other studio would be keen to employ her once it become known that she had broken a contract. Troublemakers were not worth bothering about; there were plenty of aspiring and talented artists who could take their places.

Happily it did not come to that. Zukor instructed Kaufman to compromise. Mae could write her own lines but these would be compared to Paramount's script. It would be decided at a conference which version was most suitable. If Mae's material was preferred then it would be used in the film. If not, she would be released from her contract. It was a fair settlement.

Mae presented her script the next day. Le Baron boosted her morale by telling her that, rather than make a judgement at a conference, he was prepared to shoot both versions of the script. A more objective decision could then be reached. Mae thought him 'a fine man'.

She did not take so kindly to Archie L. Mayo, her director. Mayo was a fat little New Yorker and her principal objection to him was that he was a product of the movie industry, having started his career as a film editor. That he knew a great deal about films cut no ice with Mae: she thought he had had no theatrical experience. In reality he had not come to the Coast and entered films until 1915, after stage experience in the East.

Their first encounter did not bode well for the future. He told her that he preferred the original script, and did not find her lines funny. She accepted the insult coolly, determined to prove him wrong. Mayo had directed some of the biggest Hollywood stars, such as Al Jolson and John Barrymore, and knew his worth. He was experienced in comedy but his style owed much to the slapstick of the silent era, a school to which the wise-cracking Mae owed nothing.

She spent the days before she was scheduled to start filming sitting quietly on the set, absorbing techniques which were new to her. Jim and Beverly flanked her like lieutenants. She realized her delivery would have to be subdued. Many theatrical actresses had made themselves ridiculous by playing to the camera as broadly as they played in theatres. The result was a grotesque pantomime. Her timing would have to be swifter. The camera was intimate and jokes came across quickly; there was no opportunity to wait for a laugh, a practice that was second nature to Mae.

She did not take to the movie people. To Mae they were a fey, talentless and unreliable bunch. But she was a quick learner, as she demonstrated on her first day of shooting. Zukor writes: 'The director put her through the paces in the manner he had expected to and, a good sport and honest to the core, she did her best. Then she directed herself according to her own script and ideas. Plainly her own characterization was far the better.'

Mayo did not accept Zukor's judgement and tried to impose his own ideas upon Mae (he was, after all, the director), but she would have none of it. She insisted, impertinently, that all scenes with which she was involved had to be shot her way. Not surprisingly they soon had a row. The scene that sparked this off concerned her entrance into a nightclub. Bedecked in diamonds, Mae parks her fur:

'Goodness, what lovely diamonds,' gasps the hatcheck girl.

'Goodness had nothing to do with it, dearie,' Mae responds as, hand on hip, she saunters out of frame and, as one critic put it, 'into motion picture history'.

She wanted the camera to follow her up a staircase before she left the frame, a pause which would accommodate the laugh she knew would follow. Mayo insisted this was a waste of time and wanted to cut immediately after the line.

'I knew it was a great line,' Mae later told William Scott Eyman. 'That it would break up the audience; it had to be protected with footage. There was a big row about that. Mayo wanted to cut away . . .'

Mayo stood his ground. The scene, he insisted, would be shot his way or not at all. Mae refused to continue and the shoot ground to a halt. Hangers-about gathered interestedly as the atmosphere became overcharged.

Le Baron had to be sent for. He arrived with studio head Emanuel Cohen, a man who in his career seems to have made more enemies than he did pictures. At five feet, two inches, Cohen was no taller than Mae, but Budd Schulberg, whose father B. P. Schulberg was general manager of Paramount until 1932, described him as 'a calculating little giant'. He also wrote: 'Cohen brought to mind all the small, darting, predatory animals – ferrets, weasels, rats. Rats thrive and fatten on disaster, which is exactly what made Manny Cohen.'*

This was one disaster Cohen was determined to avert. Realizing Mae was the stronger force, he gave into her, and once again Mayo was overruled. The scene was to be shot as Mae intended. Privately, Cohen confided to Mayo, it could be cut afterwards if it did not work.

Filming resumed.

After Mae had made her exit upstairs, following her 'Goodness' line, she could consider herself lucky not to have walked up still more stairs into a court of law, answering a charge of plagiarism. The 'Goodness had nothing to do with it' routine was an old standby frequently used by Mae's Chicago heroine, the speakeasy owner Texas Guinan.

Their styles were so similar that Miss Guinan had been paid by a newspaper to pontificate upon the lawsuit when Mae was having legal problems with *Pleasure Man*. Texas Guinan had been Le Baron's first choice for Maudie Triplett, Mae's role, but she was older than Mae and not so well preserved. She had lived and it showed.

Miss Guinan could hardly have been pleased at the appropriation of her material, particularly in a role intended for her, but her death the following year brought Mae the consolation of knowing that the threat of litigation was ended forever.

Screenwriter William Fitts states that Mae was 'a notorious thief of material', so much so that when he came to the Ravenswood to show her some songs he had written, he was reluctant to leave them overnight in case he never saw them again. 'Most of her one-liners,' he says, 'were stolen from other people. She heard them, liked them, and made them her own.'

The one-liners of which she became undisputed mistress

* *Moving Pictures*, Penguin, 1984.

were an innovation dreamed up to suit the movies. She had rarely used them on stage and admitted as much to *Premier* magazine: 'For the pictures I had to write wisecracks ... I figured the only way to get material over, was to punch it across with funny lines. I mean, in the films, they wouldn't let me sit on a man's lap. And I've been on more laps than a napkin ...'

Mae was wary of Alison Skipworth. It was clear from the first scene they shared that Miss Skipworth could hold her own in any company of comedians. She had, after all, worked with W. C. Fields. Whereas she was no beauty – resembling nothing so much as a pantomime dame – her feel for comedy was strong.

During their scenes together Mae consciously altered her timing, quickening her delivery, something not usually a part of the laid-back West approach. There is a particularly funny scene which takes place while the ladies are in a club, drinking champagne. Alison Skipworth asks:

'Maudie, do you believe in love at first sight?'

'I don't know,' she responds, 'but it sure saves an awful lot of time.'

The advantage lay with Mae, as she had the punch line but, even so, she gave Miss Skipworth a rough ride, insisting on certain shots and tutoring the indignant Miss Skipworth on how to feed the line to her.

Hedda Hopper was present during the shoot and recalls their confrontation in her autobiography: 'Mae West and Alison Skipworth were ready to play a scene and Alison Skipworth was frightened Mae would steal it. During a break she told Mayo Mae's timing was ruining her performance. "You forget, I've been an actress for forty years," she told Mae. "Don't worry, dear," was Mae's reply. "I'll keep your secret." '*

The film was previewed before receiving its première at New York's Paramount on 4 October 1932. 'The preview audience went wild,' Mae told William Scott Eyman. 'The film went over. See, I was right. I've always known what's best for me.' As may be, but she was too nervous to attend the première. She sent Murray Feil and met him afterwards for his verdict.

* *From Under My Hat*, Hedda Hopper, Frederick Muller, 1953.

Reviews varied and opinions still differ. Leslie Halliwell dismisses it as 'a dim little drama'*, whereas John Douglas Eames enthuses, 'the film caught the bold, pleasure loving Prohibition era's atmosphere with style.'** When it came to Mae, reviewers were of one mind. *Photoplay's* Leonard Hall summed up all their reactions:

> There was a terrific explosion. A bomb had gone off in a cream-puff factory ... Blonde, buxom, rowdy Mae – slithering across the screen in a spangled, sausage-skin gown! Yanking our eyes from Georgie Raft and Connie Cummings! Battling for the scene with that magnificent, veteran trouper, Alison Skipworth! I dare say that the theatre has never sent Hollywood a more fascinating, spectacular and useful figure than Bounding Mae West, queen of the big-hearted, bad girls of show business ... she was like a blast of fresh air in the smokey atmosphere of Raft's swell speakeasy.

Despite the hysteria of the above, written shortly after the première, Mae does not actually do a great deal in the film. It was, after all, a George Raft vehicle and she was merely a backup character actress. But what she does is done exemplarily. Her scenes are iridescent. Her impact is immediate and elevates what is, in essence, a flatly directed piece of ephemera. Without Mae *Night After Night* would be undistinguished – it is only remembered today as the film which introduced Mae West to the screen. She made a tremendous impact in what amounted to little more than two scenes. Afterwards George Raft good-naturedly acknowledged, 'Mae West stole everything but the cameras.' Zukor was more succinct. 'She stole the show,' he said.

The success of her scenes depended on more than just the full flowering of her talent; in Maudie Triplett Mae created a new type. She brought humour into the deadly serious matter of sex

---

* *Halliwell's Film Guide*, 7th Edition, Grafton, 1989.
** *The Paramount Story*, Octopus, 1981.

and banished forever the concept of the sinister vamp. Sex was not only fun but it went unpunished. In Mae's hands sin made the world go round. Her philosophy – 'I'm a girl who lost her reputation and never missed it' – was underlined with every undulation of her hips.

In a way Mayo's directorial lack of imagination works in Mae's favour. In the 'Goodness' scene the camera does little more than frame the picture, creating a proscenium arch, and this enables Mae to use the set as a stage. The whole sketch, including her sashay out of frame, is essentially vaudeville, and allowed time for her to make the transition into the more subtle techniques of filming.

By fighting Paramount and bullying her director into submission Mae ensured her place in cinema history. Had she accepted Paramount's script and acknowledged as a newcomer that her director knew best, both she and the film would now, in all probability, be forgotten.

The techniques of filming, from the artist's standpoint, quickly filtered through to Mae, and she appreciated the value of effective lighting. Shadows could do terrible or wonderful things to a face. She liked the way Ernest Haller had lit her in *Night After Night* and requested his services whenever possible in the future. He was to work on several more of her successes.

Her plans to return to New York were forgotten. The script for *The Constant Sinner* could rest in a drawer to be taken out when, and if, required. Mae had other fish to fry. The first of which was to ensconce herself in Hollywood in style. If she was to be a star, then she would be the most starlike at the job. She had, after all, a natural aptitude.

Yet she kept her feet on the ground. Although showered with offers to star in more films, she had been too long in the business to get carried away. She liked the Ravenswood apartment and had no plans to abandon it for a Bel Air mansion. She did, however, refurbish it. It was carpeted throughout in white and furnished with French-style gilt and ormolu. A few pieces were genuine, others reproductions; who cared so long as it all looked right? She installed a grand piano, and had it repainted white and gold, with pastoral scenes brightening its panels. She commissioned a nude portrait of herself – her body so streamlined by the artist that the only link with reality was a certain resemblance to her face. This was hung in the living room.

The portrait was in Spanish style and a monkey is included in the composition, squatting near Mae and erotically contemplating her. She had heard that some of the grand Spanish ladies of the past had kept monkeys as pets, the theory being that the ugliness of the monkey would enhance their own beauty.

The bedroom was the *pièce de résistance*, housing a large bed with a brocaded canopy above which a mirrored ceiling was suspended: 'I like to see how I'm doing,' Mae cracked to the press, adding, 'I do my best work in bed.'

The general décor included several large, pink-tinted mirrors, pastel shades and blinds, and a large, white satin couch.

The apartment was photographed many times during her career, and looks enormous. In fact, it is quite small. There is a single, fair-sized living room – of which the grand piano took up a third of the floor space and the couch another quarter. Off this is a dining alcove, through which a small kitchen is reached and there are two smallish bedrooms (the larger of which was Mae's). Two shower rooms, a hall and a walk-in wardrobe complete the accommodation.

One reason she liked the apartment was that it afforded some protection against possible intruders. There were security officials both in the front lobby and in the basement garage. Mae had mixed with some dubious people and did not want to make herself too accessible. When the current occupant of the apartment, Donald S. Brady, took possession he was astonished to discover that the front door was reinforced by steel sheeting and that the window glass was bullet proof. Although Mae hated the sunshine, fear of violence was another reason for keeping the blinds drawn. Even though she was on the sixth floor she was frightened someone might take a shot at her through the glass.

If she had an extravagance, it was for luxury cars. She had the finest Rolls-Royces, Cadillacs and Duesenbergs. All were part of her image – Mae West could hardly travel in a Ford.

The way things were going it seemed she would never have

to. Throughout the country the reaction to her appearance in
Night After Night was phenomenal. Cinema managers re-ran
the film several times and clamoured for a Mae West starring
vehicle. Paramount, in grave financial trouble, saw, if not a
light at the end of the tunnel, then at least a glimmer. Zukor
wanted to strike while the iron was hot and was ready to allow
any reasonable request she might make. Diamond Lil was
Mae's alter ego, and she insisted that if she was to star in a film
for Paramount – and there was no contract to do so – then it
would be in a version of her play.

There was some demurring because Paramount's research
department asserted that any film set in the Gay Nineties would
be unpopular. Cinema audiences, the department assessed,
were comprised mainly of youngsters for whom the 1890s
would have no appeal. She was asked to consider other properties but refused.

Emanuel Cohen came up with a compromise. Why not
update *Diamond Lil* to modern times? He could not have misjudged his leading lady more. Mae was affronted. As she saw it,
by rejecting the Gay Nineties Cohen was rejecting Tillie who, to
Mae, epitomized the era. *Diamond Lil* was to be a tribute to her
mother. Cohen hastily retracted when she threatened to walk
out, and no further requests were made for her to change her
mind. *Diamond Lil* went into production and this time Mae
ensured she had script approval.

chapter eleven

WHEN A WOMAN GOES WRONG ...

Mae also made it clear she was not working with Archie Mayo. Lowell Sherman was to be her new director, a well-spoken man versed in the theatre and an actor himself. He had worked under Archie Mayo's direction himself in 1930 when he had appeared in *Oh! Sailor, Behave!*, so he could commiserate with Mae; he had also worked with some of the screen's most distinguished names, including Garbo and Barbara Stanwyck. He had even made an appearance in *Monsieur Beaucaire*, arguably the worst film Valentino ever made. Sherman was still acting in 1932* when he agreed to direct Mae in *Diamond Lil*. He endeared himself to her by telling her he had seen and admired her performance on Broadway. This, she decided, was her man.

Lowell Sherman is one of the many interesting Hollywood characters. His career had nearly been shot down in flames in 1921 due to his involvement in the Fatty Arbuckle scandal. He had been present at the party during which Fatty, one of the world's most popular comics, had been charged with the rape and murder of actress Virginia Rappe. Fatty had been acquitted of the charges, but the Hearst press had run a campaign of vilification which had hammered the coffin nails into his career.

The reverberations of the case were still echoing around Hollywood in 1932. A line Sherman uttered in *What Price Hollywood?* could equally have applied to his own private life. 'Let me tell you about Hollywood,' he states. 'Keep your sense of

* *What Price Hollywood* is perhaps the most memorable of Sherman's films. It was released in 1932, the same year he directed Mae. It is a fable about the mores of Hollywood life.

humour and you can't miss.' Despite the vicissitudes of his career, he had kept his sense of humour.

As an actor he specialized in playing lecherous villians and as a director his films had earned respect for his open treatment of bold sexual themes. For all his charm he had the reputation of being a cad in private life. Talented and attractive, with a touch of the maverick, he was just the man to look after Mae West in her real début as a film star.

Mayo's improvisatory work method had grated on Mae. She had watched him shoot take after take, wasting footage and time. She was disgusted when actors arrived on the set not knowing their lines, and when Mayo was unsure of how to shoot a scene, having not thought about it beforehand. Neither did she approve of the time-honoured practice of shooting scenes out of sequence. As a stage actress that unnerved her and made it difficult for her to find the nuances she sought in each scene. Therefore she introduced an innovation into the shooting of *Diamond Lil*. The film would be shot in sequence as though it were a stage performance. She also persuaded Sherman to rehearse the four leading actors for a week before the shoot, until they were word perfect.

It was unheard of in Hollywood to shoot a film in such a way and Emanuel Cohen advised against it, with as much success as he had had when he suggested the story be updated. Mae countered that to shoot the film in the normal way would take three months. She would have a wrap within three weeks. Paramount wondered exactly what it had taken on. In less than six months after her arrival in Hollywood she was taking over responsibility for an entire film.

But Zukor did not care how the picture was shot, just as long as Mae got a move on. The exhibitors were baying like wolves for a picture with her in it. Studio 8 was allocated for the shoot which, she felt, augured well. Mae believed in the science of numerology, and 8 was her lucky number. Her birthday was 17 August; 1 and 7 make eight, and August is the eighth month of the year. Her apartment was 611 which, added up, made 8.

The numerical combinations, however, were clearly not favourable when the time came to select the screenwriter. Mae had little time for wordsmiths; she believed implicitly that she was the best provider of her own material. John Bright was given the task of adapting her play for the screen. Eloquent as he was on the printed page, Bright could be salty in everyday conversation. He accepted Mae as a seasoned vaudevillian so did not bother to moderate his language in her presence. Mae could swear with the best of them when so inclined, but did not choose to do so in public. She resented Bright's coarseness and vented her frustration by objecting to his script, which made Bright swear even more. Mae demanded to be treated like a lady and Bright was replaced by another, more silver-tongued writer, Harvey Thew.

Leading men were always more important to Mae than writers. Part of Hollywood folklore is that Mae West discovered Cary Grant. This story was started by Mae and never denied, at least not too vehemently, by Grant. According to Mae, she first saw him as he was getting out of his car as she was walking across the lot with Cohen. She had to pause to catch her breath. At twenty-eight, suntanned, slim and six foot three, Grant stood out even in Hollywood, a town full of handsome men.

'Who's that?' she gasped when she was in command of herself. Cohen told her it was merely some bit-part actor, no one to bother about, but she insisted on being introduced. Her wish was Cohen's command and he nearly tripped over himself to summon Grant to meet the great lady the whole town was talking about. When the affable Grant left she told Cohen, 'If he can talk, I'll take him.' He was to be her new leading man. She required no screen test; he was perfect.

It's a good story but the truth is different. Far from being a bit-part actor Grant had already been a hit on Broadway and made seven movies before meeting Mae. He was currently under contract playing Pinkerton, the male lead in a non-singing version of *Madame Butterfly*,* a role rejected by Gary Cooper on the grounds that Pinkerton's dastardly character might alienate his female fans.

---

* As Lt Pinkerton, Grant had to wear a white naval uniform which enhanced his looks. He was wearing this when he stopped Mae in her tracks.

When she told Cohen that Grant was to be her leading man, he had protested that Grant was not free: he was assigned to *Madame Butterfly*.

'I don't care if he's making *Little Nell*,' Mae had snapped.* Rescheduling took place to allow Grant to film with Mae immediately after completing *Madame Butterfly*.

He proved the perfect foil for Mae West.

In his biography of Grant, Lionel Godfrey notes: 'She [Mae] had a good idea of the male foils she needed to appear at her most effective . . . Without sacrificing the virility, Cary Grant represented another "class", good manners, the aura of a gentleman . . . his implied morality existed merely to be slyly circumvented by her uninhibited lewdness, and his courtesy and breeding were not so much a rebuff as props to the expression of her outrageously healthy sexuality.'**

If Mae did not actually 'discover' Grant, as she claimed, she certainly gave him a leg up the ladder. He had yet to find his footing in the motion picture hierarchy.

As indeed had Mae. *Diamond Lil* was to be her first starring role and the character met with immediate opposition from the censors. The Arbuckle scandal, and others involving movie stars, had unleashed a moral backlash which led to the creation of a voluntary code of conduct implemented by the Hays Office, named after its president, Will H. Hays, who from 1922 to 1945 was also president of the Motion Picture Producers and Distributors of America. Hays had earned the nickname 'Tsar of All the Rushes' due to his reputation as a disciplinarian. Under the supervision of the Hays Office, a Production Code was issued in 1930. It was the job of the Hays Office to oversee the moral content of films and ensure they did not breach the Code. Many producers and artists regarded the Hays Office as simply an additional burden they now had to bear. To get past the Hays Office became an integral part of film making. Mae was firmly in their camp.

The Hays Office insisted the character of *Diamond Lil* be

* *Cary Grant: A Touch of Elegance*, Warren G. Harris, Sphere, 1988.
** *Cary Grant: The Light Touch*, Robert Hale, 1981.

toned down and much of her bawdiness removed. It also insisted the title be changed – *Diamond Lil* sounded morally reprehensible. Mae had no option other than to agree. *She Done Him Wrong* was finally devised as an alternative title and 'Lady Lou' became the character's name.

The plot, too, had to be watered down. In keeping with other changes, Mae reluctantly altered the status of Cummings, the Cary Grant character. In the original he had been a Salvation Army captain, but fearing public outrage, he was made non-denominational. The white-slave ingredient, which had been a powerful sub-plot, was also diluted. What remained was still pretty liberal for its time.

For all Sherman and Mae's compatibility, the shoot, as in every venture involving Mae, was not without friction. In 1934, just before his premature death, Sherman spoke of his working relationship with her. Although she had instigated the three-week schedule, and had complained of the time-wasting methods of directors, she herself was consistently late on the set. Sherman was responsible for maintaining the schedule, and he spoke to her strongly about her tardiness. She perfunctorily apologized, but continued to arrive late.

Mae was not a morning person. Typical of theatre folk, she was willing to work late, all night if necessary, but hated to get up early. The film industry was built around early morning starts; most stars were collected by studio car at around 5 a.m.

At whatever hour Mae arrived she went straight to make-up, then wardrobe. By the time she was kitted out in costume and ready for work at least three hours had passed. For Mae a nine o'clock start meant that she arrived at the studio at that time.

One morning when she was late yet again Sherman instructed the props department to block the studio door with a stack of furniture. He threatened to fire anyone who so much as lifted a hand to help Mae when she arrived. When she duly made her appearance, three hours late, she peered confusedly through the barricade in her short-sighted way, and angrily called for assistance. There was an unnatural silence and no one stirred. Sherman was seated in his director's chair, idly chatting to someone. She got the measure of the situation. Gingerly, for she was in costume, she moved enough of the props to squeeze through to the set. Sherman bid her a curt good morning, to which she responded, and work commenced.

The lesson hit home and she was never late again during the shoot. On occasion Sherman was heard to refer to her, behind her back, as 'the blonde bitch'.

Despite Mae's impact, Zukor was wily enough to impose a modest budget of $200,000 on *She Done Him Wrong*. To his surprise there was only an overspend of $60,000 – he had expected much more – and the film came in before time. Sherman completed the project within eighteen days, three days earlier than scheduled.

The film opened at the Paramount, New York, in February 1933, and Mae made a trip to the cinema to promote it. She sang 'Frankie and Johnny' and the public adored her.

Within a week of its release it was clear that *She Done Him Wrong* was going to be a hit:

> Miss West in picture hats, straight-jacket gowns and with so much jewellery she looks like a Knickerbocker ice plant ... as full of laughs as an agent is of alibis, the entire production depends on the personality of the *SEX* star who gets across each jibe and point with a delivery that will soon be imitated ... Her handling of lovers, past and present and prospective, comprises the whole picture.
>
> *Variety*

Fan mail arrived by the sackful.

Her success could not have come at a more welcome time for Paramount. The company had over-extended itself but instead of expanding, business was contracting. From a peak in the 1920s, when assets had totalled three hundred million dollars, the company now found itself in the grim position of being unable to meet its debts. Its chain of 1700 cinemas was about to be sold and the company had filed for bankruptcy.

It is no exaggeration to say that Mae saved the day. *She Done Him Wrong* was Paramount's most profitable picture for over a decade. It grossed profits of over three million dollars: not enough to bring Paramount out of the red, but enough to allow it to remain solvent and retain its cinemas. As Mae modestly announced: 'My picture saved the studio.' The film, it seemed, was just the tonic needed during the Depression. Money was scarce, but enough could be found to buy a ticket to laugh for an hour or so with the outrageous Mae West.

She Done Him Wrong is not a musical, yet it contains three songs, 'Frankie and Johnny'; 'A Guy What Takes His Time' and 'Easy Rider' – the latter a slang term for 'pimp' – a fact of which the Hays Office seemed blissfully ignorant. 'Frankie and Johnny' had been a part of her act for years although, for the film, she replaced some of the original lyrics with more sanitized ones.

The film contains some of her wittiest lines:

A man comments on a nude painting of her hanging in the bar. Mae agrees it is good, but opines, 'I do wish Gus hadn't hung it up over the free lunch.'

'When a woman goes wrong, men go right after them.'

'You know, it was a toss-up whether I went in for diamonds or sang in the choir. The choir lost.'

She introduced, in an exchange with Cary Grant, the much misquoted line, 'Why don't you come up sometime, see me?' For some reason the public repeated this as 'Come up and see me sometime.' The misquote became so popular Mae included it in her next film and used it for the rest of her life.

Inexplicably she did allow a wonderfully funny line to go to another actor. A singer sidles up to a pianist and remarks: 'You know, ever since I sang that song it's been haunting me?' The pianist replies: 'It should haunt you, you murdered it.'

Mae would not be taken advantage of, but was no bully. And she could be extremely kind to the defenceless. The large cast of bit-part players in *She Done Him Wrong* includes many washed-up vaudevillians whom she had known, and for whom she secured work. Quite a few former prizefighters and old lags – some had been lovers – also swelled the ranks. There was a regular trickle of callers at her dressing room, people who had known her and who were now down on their luck. All were seen, treated courteously and given handouts.

If actors were (by her standards) fair in their dealings with her, they could expect regular employment. Louise Beavers, who plays her maid, Pearl, frequently appeared with her. Rafaela Ottiano, who plays Russian Rita, had played the part on stage. Jack LaRue, although not in *She Done Him Wrong*, was to feature in other of her plays and films.

Several Mae West personality traits are evident in embryo in *She Done Him Wrong*. She had already become obsessed by her image; this is made plain during a scene she shares with Gilbert Roland. She shows him some photographs of herself, which he admires, but they are never seen on camera. Mae nonetheless insisted on using actual photographs of herself. The photographs were later purchased in the 1970s by a fan when they turned up at a curio shop in Hollywood. He showed them to her and she confirmed they were the same ones she had used in the film.

She hated her shortness and liked to create an illusion of height. In addition to her high heels, her hair was dressed elaborately and she wore large hats, topped by lofty feathers. The illusion worked: the public thought of Mae West as a tall, buxom woman.

She supervised all her personal publicity and paid scrupulous attention to the billboard, lobby and fan magazine stills. None were released until all signs of sturdiness had been eradicated. Her photographic figure was airbrushed until the rounded tummy had disappeared and a trimmer waist-line was substituted. The maternal bulge that was her bosom was enlarged and uplifted. No character lines were permitted to show in her face; her cheek bones were highlighted and whole areas shaded out to render her face more becomingly heart-shaped.

Paramount had cause to toast the success of *She Done Him Wrong*, but the celebration was not universal. The picture was banned in Australia after a single showing and much press comment resulted. All over America pockets of people were outraged by the film and Mae's attendant publicity, which focused on her blunt appraisal of sex with its underlying assumption that sex was to be enjoyed conscience-free by women as well as men. Many of the indignant were involved with religious bodies, and several of these formed themselves into morality groups who protested both to Paramount and to Congress. These groups numbered among their members some powerful people.

Mae shrugged it all off. She had always caused scandal, it was the essence of her success. Now that she was a star it was only to be expected that the comment would be wider spread and she enjoyed the sensation she was causing. She had clawed her way up from Brooklyn, earned her living in vaudeville, gained a reputation from a prison sentence, and the only big money she had made had come from business deals with gangsters. Her star status had been gained through her clever handling of sexual insinuation. What did she care about complaints from morality groups? Mae did not have the luxury of picking and choosing her morals; she had to go where her talent directed her and where the money lay.

Paramount's relief at still being in business temporarily overrode other concerns – it decided to deal with complaints in a corporate manner. Meanwhile the champagne glasses clinked.

But even Mae was not able to brush aside all press comment – and there were as many attacks as bouquets – particularly when it seemed the industry itself was turning against her. Journalist Malcolm D. Phillips published a typical fire and brimstone article in *Picturegoer*:

Hollywood must put its house in order if it is to survive: the moral outlook behind the great propaganda force of pictures is that of an immoral and dissolute community and nothing will more surely sweep Hollywood to extinction if that suspicion is not removed – not by a smokescreen of propaganda this time but by a thorough cleaning up of personal conduct . . .

The most high-powered publicity campaign I can remember has been devoted to the glorification of Mae West – whose loudly sexy screen personality has become the symbol of the moral irresponsibility, if not the decadence, of Hollywood today.

Let me admit at once that I liked Mae West as well as the next man in *She Done Him Wrong*. She represented a type that one might meet in any bar-room and almost any less reputable place. She was amusing in a flamboyant way and she was different.

But she should never have been invested with the glamour of a goddess or the importance of a prophet. She should never have been boosted to an eminence that sets a film character that is little more than a common courtesan up as an example and a model for the girlhood of the world.

The glorification of the type of woman Mae West portrays on the screen is, it is necessary to stress again, one of the most disturbing factors of the present Hollywood revolt against previous standards.

Previous standards? Where had Phillips been hibernating for the past thirty years? Hollywood during the Thirties was a paragon of restraint compared to the Teens and the Twenties. Phillips was apoplectic when he came across Mae's latest advertisement which read, 'When I'm good I'm very good, but when I'm bad I'm better.' He wrote about that in *Picturegoer* too.

Most stars might have thought it better to ignore Phillips's attacks, but not Mae. Her reply, under the banner headline 'Who Says I'm a Bad Woman?', was published in *Picturegoer* on 25 November 1933. She informed her readers that there was nothing so dull in the world as a good woman 'unless it be Malcolm D. Phillips', and continued:

Virtue may have its own reward, but it isn't at the box-office.

Men like women with a past – because they hope history will repeat itself. Women like to see them too, because almost every woman (although she won't admit it) would like to be a scarlet adventuress – without any of the penalties, of course ... The colourful, glamorous, great women of all time all had the courage of their convictions and I'll say they could have been convicted of breaking every convention in the book.

... Some girls are beautiful and dumb, but it's better to be beautiful and dumb than just dumb, and today you don't *have* to be dumb, anyway. And it's possible for a girl to be unconventional and exciting without being immoral. They've been admitted on equal terms with men in business, politics, science and the arts.

Why should I be attacked as a menace to movie morals because I present sex on the screen as it really is?

Is it not far less dangerous to do it that way than to give it a phonily romantic and mysterious label and a fancy foreign accent? Sex is not necessarily vulgar. I don't think it is any more so than eating. Sex is never vulgar except to vulgar people. Why is it necessary to weep over the processes of nature?

Love is a woman's stock-in-trade and she always ought to be overstocked. At any rate, you can't ignore or hide it away by a screen of hypocrisy.

The film public likes the characterizations I play because they recognize the fundamental honesty in them. I give them a character with all the works. No hooey. A real woman who is honest and fearless.

I deal with the fundamental things of life as it is being lived today and as it always has been and always will be lived.

But Phillips had his supporters, one of whom was Father Daniel Lord who, backed by his superior, Cardinal Mundelein, followed up Phillips's article with one of his own, denouncing the 'obnoxious pictures' of Mae West. Six months later, while *She Done Him Wrong* was playing to capacity audiences, the Catholic Bishop, Bernard Sheil, organized a protest group, the

National Legion of Decency, whose stated aim was to clean up the movie industry. Mae was its prime target.

Mae summed up her feelings about his crusade to journalist Ben Maddox, who noted: 'Mae West is an interesting and frank woman. She admits immediately that making folks talk about her is a business proposition . . . it keeps her on the go manufacturing new tricks to attract attention to her personal publicity.' He was not the first journalist to discover that for a women who dealt in fantasy she could be disarmingly honest.

The fashions of the Gay Nineties which Mae had championed became the rage. Her likeness was made for Madame Tussaud's wax museum in London. Twenty-five years later she preened in her autobiography: 'Mae West was a household word . . . I was better known than Einstein, Shaw or Picasso.'

chapter twelve

I AIN'T MARBLE

There was no doubt at Paramount as to who was the greatest star. Dressing rooms were allocated in pecking order and Mae was moved to the unassailable suite No. 1. No. 2 was occupied by Claudette Colbert and No. 3 by Marlene Dietrich. This triumvirate occupied the ground floor as did, in diminishing order of importance, Sylvia Sidney, Miriam Hopkins and Carole Lombard.

Lesser stars were relegated to the second floor and, if an actress was placed on the third floor, she was either on the way up or the way down. No one stayed on the third floor for long.

As for the men, Gary Cooper was God, followed by Fredric March, Bing Crosby, George Raft and Charles Laughton. Cary Grant was low on the Paramount priority list, but thanks to Mae, got dressing room No. 11 which, at least, was some form of recognition.

After finishing the picture, Grant paid her a generous tribute. 'I learnt everything from her,' he said. 'Well, no, not everything, but almost everything. She knows so much. Her instinct is so true, her timing so perfect, her grasp of the situation so right. It's the tempo of the acting that counts rather than the sincerity of the characterization. Her personality is so dominant that everyone with her becomes just a feeder.'*

Meanwhile, Zukor was anxious to feed her a script that would get her working again. He wanted to strike while the iron was hot. Mae felt the same way. It had already been announced that she would star in *Barnum's Million Dollar*

* *Cary Grant: A Touch of Elegance*, Warren G. Harris, Sphere, 1988.

Beauty, a biopic of American beauty Louise Montague. Before tying herself down, however, she ensured that she would receive control of script, casting and choice of director. Le Baron would be her producer, as before, and she insisted that Cary Grant, once again, was her leading man.

But while promoting *She Done Him Wrong* in the East, she had been visited by a friend, writer Lowell Brentano, and he had given her a treatment entitled *The Lady and the Lions* in the hope it would be her next movie. The story revolved around a lady lion tamer. It was no accident that Brentano came up with this idea, as she had previously confided to him that she was fascinated by lion tamers. He had, shrewdly, featured the very topic she favoured.

Big cats had intrigued Mae since childhood, when Battling Jack had taken her to the Coney Island circus. During her tours throughout America, she had visited literally dozens of zoos and circuses. Mae tells us, in numerous articles, that her fascination had become an obsession and, once *Diamond Lil* had been enshrined on film, her next ambition was to play a lion tamer.

Mae had few heroines. Texas Guinan was one, but another was Mabel Stark, the famous lion tamer, whom she eventually met.

Years later, when Zukor was preparing material for his autobiography, she wrote to him: 'I would stand before the lion's cage and see myself inside, in full command . . . There was no moment at the height of my success that I would not have gladly exchanged positions with any lady lion tamer – for a limited time, at least.'*

Her fixation never waned. Even as an old lady, she would visit circuses, escorted by her musclemen, and invariably pop backstage afterwards to pet the animals. Sometimes she was photographed nursing a chimp or a monkey.

She decided that Brentano's treatment would be her next vehicle, and she would write the screenplay. *Barnum's Beauty* could wait. She informed Zukor of her plans, and called a meeting at the Ravenswood, which both Le Baron and Emanuel

---

* *The Public Is Never Wrong*, Cassell, 1954.

Cohen attended. To keep her sweet, Cohen told her that the studio was prepared to make this movie big and expensive. 'They were anxious to make me happy,' she reminded Zukor, 'and I was willing to let them.'

But Cohen outmanoeuvered Mae on this one. According to *The Hollywood Story*,* Joel W. Finler's study of the major studios, the budget was set at $200,000, the same as for *She Done Him Wrong*. As production progressed, Mae became increasingly enthusiastic. A lion tamer was hired, and she spent hours with him, discussing how best to handle the animals. He assured her that the lions with which she would be working were elderly and tame. It was not assurance she had been seeking, however, but advice. Although the studio was against the idea, for obvious reasons, she was determined to enter the lions' cage herself, and master the great beasts.

As Lowell Sherman was unavailable, her new director was Wesley Ruggles, younger brother of actor Charles Ruggles. Wesley had appeared in films himself, as one of the Keystone Kops, a troupe of knockabout comics who made innumerable two-reelers, full of daredevil stunts, under the direction of Mack Sennett.

Filming for *I'm No Angel*, the new film, started on 11 July 1933. A reporter for *Screen Play* was there:

There is a director on the set, of course, but she generally directs herself and plays the scene as she believes it should be played. One of the most amazing things to me was the filming of a love scene between Mae West and Cary Grant. Mae delivered her love speech talking to the camera and the hanging mike. Her sweetheart Grant wasn't in the scene. Later that day, Grant arrived, sat on the chair opposite the one West had parked in, and delivered his love lines ... Yet when the scene is flashed on the screen Cary and Mae are talking feverishly to each other.

* Octopus, 1988.

This was a standard technique, devised for a mixture of reasons. Sometimes both artists were not available on the same day but, more often, it was a matter of diplomacy. It could be unwise to shoot a love scene with both parties present. Each would require the camera to favour them. Better they were both in ignorance of what the other had done.

Mae was expected to enter the lions' cage, but there was a hitch during the shoot. The trainer, under whose authority she was to work, did not turn up. She sat around for an hour and still he did not arrive. Unable to contain herself she suggested the scene be shot without him. Ruggles could not permit this as insurance was valid only providing the scene was shot under strict professional supervision.

Mae insisted, and Ruggles reluctantly imparted news he had hoped to keep from her. The trainer had not arrived, he said, because one of the lions had torn off his arm the night before. A deputy trainer was being sought but it was unlikely, now, he could come that day.

But Mae had steeled herself for the challenge and was determined to go through with it there and then. She informed Ruggles she was going to enter the cage anyway. As he could do nothing with her, he sent for Le Baron to arbitrate. Le Baron heard Mae out, even agreed that the shots would be a bonus for the picture, but the unalterable fact remained that she could not be permitted to enter the cage without a trainer being present.

She would not accept this so Albert Kaufman was then sent for. He reported the situation to Zukor, who wrote of it in his autobiography:

'This lion scene is the main reason I'm doing this picture,' she [Mae] blurted out. Kaufman, always the executive, tried to reason with her. We'll shoot around the scene, he told her, then shoot it last of all. She would not accept that, fearing that it was merely a delaying tactic. Finally Kaufman had no option other than to tell her the unvarnished truth, that she was too valuable a property to risk, and the film too expensive a project to be jeopardized. She understood the argument but, by now, nothing would stop her from getting into the lions' cage. Kaufman finally relented. It was either that or she walked off the film.*

Normally a scene is shot several times with a single camera. It was recognized, however, that there could be no retakes, and several cameras were set up around the cage to capture the scene from different angles. Riflemen were posted at the ready, should there be trouble.

Mae told Zukor of her feelings at the time:

At last here were lions surrendering to my will. They looked at me with great big beautiful but dangerous eyes. They were fascinating to me and seemingly fascinated by this stranger in dazzling white and gold. They snarled, they pawed at me ... curiously, I was not nervous or concerned for my safety. I do not call it bravery. It was something I can give no real name. Let's just say that this, and only this, was a fitting climax to the obsession which had driven me. I had to do it, and I did.

After the scene, she actually patted one of the lions, through bravado, and bowed to the crew.

Zukor wryly comments: 'It is pleasant to know that Mae was not shaking in her boots. I can testify that others were shaking in theirs — as far away as New York City. The long-distance telephones were humming that day. Mae will grant, I think, that film producers have their bad moments.'

As she stepped out of the cage, the crew burst into a round of spontaneous applause. She remarks in *Goodness Had Nothing To Do With It*, 'someone had to get the director a drink of water'.

The only stunt in the film Mae did not actually perform herself was a scene in which she is seen placing her head in a lion's mouth. This was a special effect added later.

Ruggles found that Mae constantly queried his decisions. She was never without her personal mafia of Jim and Beverly and,

* *The Public Is Never Wrong*, Cassell, 1954.

from time to time, they were augmented by other favourites. Whatever suggestions Ruggles made were instantly taken up by her lieutenants, who would whisperingly conspire with Mae, shooting glances at him that were frequently hostile.

One of her current favourites was a former vaudevillian called Boris Petroff. The way to Mae's heart was by praising her looks and Petroff did this lavishly, advising her on all aspects of beauty care. At Mae's instigation he was put on the payroll as Style Advisor to Miss West. While Mae was working he would wait on the sidelines, a beaker of iced spring water ready for her to sip. As soon as a scene was shot, Mae turned to Petroff and asked him what he thought. Excluding the director, she would mutter darkly with Petroff and they would leave together for her dressing room, followed by the silent Jim and Beverly, Petroff carrying Mae's handbag which he had nursed during the shoot. Ruggles loathed him. Gossip of Mae's brushes with Ruggles spread round the studio, enhancing her reputation for being difficult.

One morning, after keeping Ruggles waiting an hour, she airily announced she had been having her hair restyled. What did he think? Ruggles thought he would like to get on with the film so he smiled and said it was fine. Mae shot four scenes in quick succession. She returned to her dressing room while the cameras were being reset, only to return with yet another hairstyle. She told Ruggles that Petroff had not liked the earlier style and that she would be wearing her hair like this for the rest of the film. Ruggles pointed out that this could not be, since her new style would not match the rest of the shots.

Mae sat in her chair and started to hum, something she did when annoyed. She would neither speak nor look at Ruggles. After a few moments of silence, and still looking straight ahead, she repeated in a hideously calm voice that she was keeping her hair as it was. The entire morning's work had to be reshot.

In true theatrical tradition, Mae was superstitious. If she had a costume change she insisted on changing her underwear as well. Before each take she spat, and whistling was forbidden in her dressing room. She had bought a pet monkey, Boogie, and he was worked into the film as a talisman.

Boogie was responsible for the line 'Beulah, peel me a grape.' Mae had entertained the crew by getting him to perform his party trick, which was peeling a grape before eating it. When the time came for the shoot to start she called the line to her maid, Beulah, as a gag, hoping to make the crew laugh. It came out so well it remained in the film and became a Mae West trademark.

Boogie died when the film was completed. Mae was so grief-stricken she could not attend the première. He was an engaging little creature and the crew were genuinely sad, but a sigh of thankful relief went round that he had not died while the film was in progress. The effect on Mae would have been cata-strophic.

When the film was completed Ruggles was asked how he had enjoyed working with Mae. 'She's an interesting person,' he replied with some understatement.

She managed to keep her weight down for *I'm No Angel* but, although set in the 1930s, most of her gowns would have been more appropriate to the Gay Nineties, and the wasp waists and tight hips strained at the seams. Mae looks the picture of health, however, her skin and eyes are clear and – as with her bulging dresses – every movement overflows with vitality.

Mae went into training before filming which, in her case, meant cutting down on cakes and chocolates and abstaining from sex for a week beforehand. This ensured she was sexually ravenous and, so she thought, this beneficially translated itself on to the screen.

I'm No Angel is the story of Tira, the lion tamer, who does a little hustling on the side and becomes implicated in a murder case when a shakedown goes wrong. She is discharged and goes on to become a society success (shades of Mae's vaudeville days when convicted murderesses became theatrical attractions) and sues a swell (Cary Grant) for breach of promise. The ensuing court case is vintage Mae West exchanging witticisms with a judge who is clearly besotted by her. She wins her action but tears up Cary Grant's cheque for damages, and they end up together.

The film starts in a small-time carnival. There are seedy sideshows and the camera rests on groups of men clinching deals – it could have been Gus's Bar from the Bowery. The camera moves on to a kiosk which bears the legend '*Tira – Incomparable*'. Buglers blow a fanfare, and the barker announces 'Tira, the girl who discovered you don't have to have feet to be a dancer.' A mass of men crowd round the catwalk.

Mae makes her sequined entrance, a yashmak held seductively up to her face. 'The marvel of the age!' the barker yells. She undulates before the men. 'Get my meaning, boys?' she asks, before launching into her song 'They Call Me Sister Honky-Tonk', ending the number with the contemptuous aside, 'Suckers!' The whole item was stolen from Texas Guinan, whose catchphrase was 'Hello suckers'.

As in all Mae West films there is a blending of Mae the person with her screen character. Tira's birthday is 17 August, the day of Mae's birthday. When Tira is having her fortune told the gypsy says, 'I see a man.' 'What,' exclaims Tira, 'Only one?' When her horoscope is given her in manuscript form she is told, 'Put this where you can consult it frequently.' 'I'll take it to bed with me,' she says.

The film contains some of her best lines: 'I've been places and seen things,' a character tells her. 'I've been things and seen places,' she responds. Or, 'Do you mind if I get personal?' a man asks. 'Go right ahead,' she says. 'I don't mind if you get familiar.'

She briskly states her philosophy: 'Men are all alike,' she says. 'Married or single, it's their game. I just happen to be smart enough to play it their way.' She later declares, 'It's not the men in my life, it's the life in my men that counts.'

Ruggles contradicts accusations, current in Hollywood circles at the time, that she stole all her material. 'I can tell you this,' he said in an interview with *Picture Play* in 1934. 'Several occasions arose on the set when I asked Mae to give me new lines for such and such a situation. She thought it over and came back with the lines.'

When it became known at Paramount that Mae was about to film a song, the studio became crowded with onlookers. Everyone wanted to hear her sing. Both Maurice Chevalier and Marlene Dietrich came to watch her perform 'I Want You, I

Need You', one of her best songs in the film. As always, Ruggles was up against the clock and Mae felt she had been rushed. Everyone applauded wildly at the end but Mae was dissatisfied with her performance. Ben Maddox was present as, ignoring the cheers, she emphatically told Le Baron, 'I'm going to do that song again . . . I had to sing without a rehearsal . . . I must have time to rehearse so I can sing with feeling.'

The official opening of the film was 4 October 1933, but there was a preview at Grauman's Chinese Theater in Hollywood. Even in that town of premières Mae's preview caused the traffic, literally, to stop. There is newsreel footage in existence of Mae's arrival at Grauman's, depicting the bedlam.

Prior to her arrival the crowd is spilling from the pavement into the highway of Hollywood Boulevard, bringing the traffic to a halt. Searchlights stab the sky, and radio interviewees fight to get near the microphone stand. It is like a scene from Nathanael West's *The Day of the Locust*. Among the arriving stars are Loretta Young, Charlie Chaplin and Paulette Goddard. There is a roar as Mae's Cadillac arrives, and the police form a chain to keep the crowds from her. Ablaze with diamonds and draped in arctic fox furs, she makes her way to the theatre. A podgy Jim Timony inconspicuously limps at her side.

The announcer's voice-over commentary treats her arrival in the foyer as if he were a pilgrim at Lourdes given a glimpse of the Virgin. 'Here's the lady herself,' he breathes. 'The star of stars makes her appearance. Every feminine eye follows her dazzling gown, every masculine eye – oh, well. Mae West has come to town.'

Not just to town, but to the world. In its first week at the New York Paramount, *I'm No Angel* played to an unprecedented 180,000 people. Attendance records were also broken in America's other major centres: Dallas, Chicago, Detroit and Los Angeles. The success of the film was enormous, eclipsing even *She Done Him Wrong*. By the end of the year the two films combined had earned over a million dollars net profit for Paramount – a vast figure in those days. She was a phenomenon, the most sought-after star in the industry. As far as Paramount were concerned she could do no wrong. She had not only saved the company from bankruptcy but had restored optimism. She received full credit for the film's success and deserved it.

She had swayed fashion with *She Done Him Wrong*, and her influence now altered the very shape of women. Hips and breasts were again emphasized and, among the more daring society women, there was even an occasional glimpse of platinum blonde hair.

I'm No Angel is, arguably, Mae's finest film. There is a laugh in nearly every line; it contains some of her fruitiest sayings. In vaudevillian fashion the film's impact is immediate, hitting the audience between the eyes and leaving it clamouring for more. It is not so much a dramatic exercise as an extended and unfettered Mae West turn. There is a gusty freshness about the film. She has something new to offer and she knows it's good. Retrospectively, Eric Braun wrote, 'She had struck a blow for honesty in sexual expression that is still echoing around the world today, and she had done it all with supreme good humour.' That was the crux. Mae was thirty years ahead of her time and the subsequent feminist revolution of the 1960s. Yet her message was not shrill; some things, she realized, were better delivered tongue-in-cheek.

But the clouds that had dimmed the horizon of her success in *She Done Him Wrong* grew ominously more threatening with the release of *I'm No Angel*. Audiences were convulsed, but their laughter sounded sinful to the ears of the protest groups. As the press vied with each other to convey the film's outrageousness, Mae had the talent to exploit the situation fully, to her greater glory. But patience began to snap among religious leaders. Mae West, they decided, had to be stopped.

The famous could not wait to lay plaudits at her feet. Will Rogers considered Mae 'had to come out here to teach the other girls how to speak their lines.' Praise indeed, coming from such a master. D. W. Griffith ranked Mae, in terms of prestige, with President Roosevelt, and listed her among the ten most interesting people in America. Hugh Walpole wrote, 'Only Charlie Chaplin and Mae West in Hollywood dare to directly attack with their mockery the fraying morals and manners of a dreary world.' F. Scott Fitzgerald added, 'In a world of Garbos,

Barrymores, Harlows, Valentinos and Clara Bows, Mae West is the only type with an ironic edge, a comic spark, that takes on a more cosmopolitan case of life's enjoyments.'*

It was said that Garbo herself, in Sweden on a sabbatical, hastened back to America to regain her laurels, fearing Mae had snatched the crown from her classic, and enigmatic, head. It must be added that this was said, principally, by Tom Baily, Mae's publicist at Paramount – Garbo was contracted to MGM.

To capitalize on her success she issued, in cooperation with the Macaulay Company, who had published *The Constant Sinner*, *Diamond Lil* as a novel. The character was never far from her thoughts, inseparably linked, as it was, with Tillie. The book was written in her usual jackdaw manner, with help from many sources, not the least that of a professional writer from Macaulay who prepared the manuscript. Mae, as usual, gave it the once-over and added her inimitable touch. The book contains the same mixture of philosophy, rumbustious sex and knock-about humour as *The Constant Sinner*. It is slightly better bred, however, in that Mae was now a public figure and looking to her reputation.

Diamond Lil sold well, and she announced she was preparing another novel, to be entitled *How to Misbehave*. It, however, never saw the light of day.

The job of publicizing *I'm No Angel* fell to Arthur Mayer. As part of his campaign he had designed a poster of a swelling female bosom under which were the words, 'Hitting the High Spots of Lusty Entertainment'. Zukor, always the family man, was horrified when he saw it and summoned Mayer to his office: 'Mr Mayer, I'm shocked and surprised,' said Zukor sternly, reprimanding him for using such a 'dirty word as lusty'. Mayer explained lusty was from the German word 'lustig' [energy and vigour]. 'Look, Mr Mayer,' said the exasperated Zukor. 'I don't need your Harvard education. When I look at that dame's tits, I know what lusty means.'**

* Quoted in Mae's autobiography, *Goodness Had Nothing To Do With It*, W. H. Allen, 1960.
** *The Real Tinsel*, Bernard Rosenberg and Harry Silverstein, Macmillan, New York, 1970.

It was just as well Mayer's campaign did not travel to Britain, where pompous journalist Hannen Swaffer anguished in print about the effect of Mae upon a provincial audience. While appropriating some of her best lines to dress up his article, he claimed she would not be understood by the naive Brits. After making this point he did an about-face and proclaimed that she might be understood only too well, and that her influence would have a damaging effect on the very fabric of British life. He even brought in a negro lynching to heighten the effect. The article below appeared in a fuller form in the *Sunday People* in December 1933:

Her phrase, 'Come up and see me some time,' went right across the United States. Even chapel deacons used it, without knowing whence it came, or even what it meant . . .

I first heard of Mae West when *Diamond Lil* was a sensation. This was a play written by herself, produced by herself, and with Mae West herself as the one and only star.

She appeared covered with diamonds as one of those wicked women . . .

Diamond Lil cost nothing, and it ran for months and months. Sophisticated playgoers sneered – but they went, just as did the lowbrows . . . Hard-boiled playgoers, going 'for fun' would laugh at the pathos and jeer at the serious bits. But Mae West made a fortune. And if the police arrested her – well, it made people go all the more . . .

At the start, Mae West dealt with a Life of Pleasure. But her later plays were much more daring. They staged, frankly and crudely, a side of life still barred from the London stage . . .

The West End is now crowding to see her second talkie, *I'm No Angel*. As a consequence, everybody is asking why the Film Censor passed it. It is by far the frankest and most daring picturisation of Sex Appeal that London has ever seen. Told in a few words, *I'm No Angel* is the story of a woman who, in her own words, climbs to the top of the ladder 'wrong by wrong' . . .

The story is told with such a vein of satire and insolence that English audiences can only sit back and gasp; ... when Mae West says to a man, 'You put your body and soul into your dancing,' she says it in such a way that there is conjured up in your mind an infamy of meaning that is embarrassing.

Yes, the women sit there envious, not only of the diamonds, but of a woman who can sheathe herself with clothes that seem to grow on her. And, more than that, they feel themselves mere babies beside a woman who seems to Know It All.

As for the men in the audience, they are affronted that their sex can be regarded as a gang of suckers. They are intrigued by the insolence of it all. They know she could get *them* if she tried. This they resent. But they like it, in spite of that ...

A nation that can regard Tex Guinan a sport, and a people who can tolerate for years the existence of an Al Capone, are not nearly as shocked by the characters Mae West depicts as English audiences would be ...

A few weeks after *This Day and Age* was shown right across America, they have had an outbreak of lynching ... Negroes accused of assaulting white women are being threatened with death at the hands of a mob. Often, in such cases, the negroes are innocent ...

I often dread the effect of all these films, written for America, upon the English people. Then, on second thoughts I reflect that perhaps we are too sane to be influenced by them. We simply do not believe it ...

Well, Mae West is making hay while the sun shines ... Mae West has behaved, in real life, in the same downright manner that her stage characters do. She has dominated everybody. And, so far, she has more than justified it ...

'My goodness, what lovely diamonds!' says a cloakroom attendant to one of the Mae West characters.

'Don't kid yourself,' is the Mae West reply. 'Goodness had nothing to do with it.'

And with that, I am afraid, I must leave it.

While Swaffer worried about faraway Hollywood, the subject of his article was wondering how best to deal with a specific problem of her own. It had escaped no one's attention that she had a fuller figure than any other sex goddess. Now, with her success, and the accompanying dining out, her figure had ballooned. It was gently suggested at Paramount that the loss of a pound or two might be a good thing.

Part of the fault was genetic. Tillie came from German stock and Mae had inherited her Teutonic figure. Given the least encouragement her shape, freed from the restrictions of the Spirella corset company, assumed the form of a typical German *hausfrau*. Her rotundity was exaggerated by her shortness. Giving vent to her frustration to Ruth Biery, she complained that Hollywood had tried to alter her shape when she had first arrived, and viewed the slim Hollywood beauties around her with disaffection:

> I never saw so many poles in my life! I wondered how Hollywood men could stand them. But everyone said I had to get thin. I figured they knew this racket and I didn't, so I went on one of them Hollywood diets . . . It was pretty bad, but I'd been through a lot for art's sake so taking off twenty pounds or more was just one more piece of routine. I got down to 103 pounds. I stood in front of the mirror to study the results. I didn't like it. I didn't look – well, you know, voluptuous. And that isn't all, I didn't even look healthy. And man or woman, you got to look healthy to look right. Half-starved women can't have no life in them any more than a half-starved dog.*

The diet was not a success, and she complained about the ill-effects it was having upon her health, and that her energy was being sapped. She could never be slim, but sometimes she was podgier than others. She hit upon a ploy, aimed at studio heads, to prove that her shape was perfect for a movie star. She quoted the dimensions of the Venus de Milo:

* *Movie Classic*, April 1934.

That dame was supposed to be perfect. She was 5 ft 4½ tall
and weighed 130 pounds. I am 5 ft 5 in. I decided I'd stop
at 122 pounds because I knew, by that time, that the
camera added 10 pounds extra. A woman wasn't intended
to look like a man – and women never used to walk
around looking like beanstalks with the beans picked from
them. They got thin during the war, going without food for
their men. And they lost what their men wanted in them.
Curves!

Those French dressmakers saw the situation and hurried to take advantage. It took less material to cover a thin
woman and you could charge the same price. They
decided to make women stay thin. Women will do anything for fashion. Even to getting anaemia.

Mae was no more anaemic than she was five feet, five inches
tall.

She played on her fictitious verisimilitude to the Venus de
Milo throughout her life. 'I'm the identitical counterpart of the
Venus de Milo,' she stated elsewhere. 'But I've got it on her.
I've got two arms and I know how to use them. Besides, I ain't
marble.'

She was not marble but, nevertheless, could present a cold
façade. She refused to attend parties and never gave them.
Most stars enjoyed entertaining and flaunting their new-found
wealth, but not Mae. Such was her demand for hermit-like
seclusion that she gained a reputation for eccentricity. Few had
seen inside her apartment, and gossip flared as to its grandeur,
and what went on behind its steel-reinforced door.

'I don't like hot, stuffy rooms,' she told the *Sunday Dispatch*.
'I don't like high voice chatter. I don't like having to talk to my
hostess when 14 other guests are either treading on my toes or
resting their cocktail glasses in my eyes . . . And that's all there
is to it . . . I honestly prefer to talk about something with a little
more meat to it than the latest gossip. My idea of a good time
will always be just a bit different.' Like lion taming.

The truth was that, much as Mae disliked parties, she was
not invited to the best homes, and it stung. Her films had

earned her enmity, not just from morality groups, but from powerful Hollywood women – the wives of the studio bosses. These wives, while happy to swan from soirée to soirée in finery financed by the films their husbands had commissioned, could not actually bear to associate with the stars that made their husbands' money from earthy movies. Mae was *persona non grata* in Hollywood's upper bracket, and excluded from top-drawer social gatherings.

Joyce Haber, who took over from Hedda Hopper as the *Los Angeles Times* gossip columnist, remembers her mother dismissively referring to Mae as 'that filthy woman'. William Fitts recalls, idiomatically, that the *crème de la crème* did not court her company, 'She was a disreputable old broad,' he stated. 'People did not want to get mixed up with her.'

The hypersensitive Mae, easily hurt by criticism, was not prepared to expose herself unnecessarily to further barbs. The hostesses who did invite her might also invite guests who disapproved of her. It was more comfortable to indulge her natural reserve and stay at home with Jim and Beverly. Beverly was enjoying Hollywood and the status granted her as sister of the star of stars. She went with Mae each day to the studio and never left her side. She hoped that, with Mae's influence, she would soon be starting a movie career of her own.

Although Mae did not enjoy social gatherings this did not prevent her from enjoying certain public functions. She sometimes attended as many as three boxing tournaments a week. In his long-out-of-print book *An Innocent in Hollywood*, Clarence Winchester writes of a visit he made to the Hollywood Stadium, in the company of a group of luminaries, including Mae. The party also consisted of Johnny Weissmuller (the Olympic swimming champion who had become famous as Tarzan), Weissmuller's mistress and future wife, actress Lupe Velez, whose fiery temperament had earned her the soubriquet 'The Mexican Spitfire',* and Jesse Lasky, who was escorting Mae.

'Lupe Velez is already over-excited,' writes Winchester. 'Mae West takes her seat and stares implacably at nothing. Groucho

---

* She made a series of films of that title.

and Harpo Marx are here, Fredric March . . . A Mexican versus an American. That's enough to make Lupe Velez sit up and do her stuff. She soon does. "Keel eem, keel eem," she cries, jumping to her feet and swinging her right arm in an attitude of encouragement. "Heet eem 'arder – ah! That's right!" Lupe goes quite wild – oh, quite! While Johnny Weissmuller, who looks as though he ought to be in the ring instead of out of it, shows but little animation. Mae West continues to stare unmoved.'

Not for Mae any vulgar display. Whenever she was in public her behaviour was decorous and discreet.

Sometimes Ruth Biery accompanied her to fights – always in the company of male escorts, of course (Mae never went out in all-female company): 'I have watched her often,' she wrote in *Movie Classic*. 'She uses just two expressions. A steady stare at the fighters (if she is enjoying the punches the world never knows it). And a mechanical smile for the claps of her followers – when she enters and leaves.' Mae did have the most mechanical smile in the business. It had nothing to do with pleasure and was purely a physiological device. She told her friend Robert Duran, 'I never bother with a proper smile if I'm out. I just raise my top lip a bit, it does.'

Some have remarked on her surliness when in company. She was certainly no great mixer, and one of her escorts for an evening complained she did nothing but stare ahead with a bored expression, and hum to herself the whole time. As Wesley Ruggles had discovered, Mae hummed when she was annoyed, so clearly her escort had not been to her taste.

Even in the company of friends she was no conversationalist. Robert Duran, who spent many evenings with her, recalls, 'We would often sit quietly, not talking but there was a nice atmosphere. If we were in a restaurant then she would observe people. She'd sit there, tapping her fingernails against the back of a chair, or the table, and not talk much at all.'

She was equally tight-lipped when discussing her boyfriends. 'Men?' she responded to press enquiries. 'Sure, I've known lots of them. But I never found one I liked well enough to marry. Besides I've always been busy with my work. Marriage is a career in itself, and to make a success of it you've got to keep working at it. So, until I can give the proper amount of time to marriage I'll stay single.'*

The reason she stayed single was because she was married to Frank Wallace, although, at times, she had to remind herself of the fact. She had not seen him nor heard from him for years.

Mae did have her camp followers – such as Petroff – but these were non-sexual affairs. The Petroffs in her life acted like unpaid secretaries; after the novelty wore off, they seldom stayed the course for more than a few months. She was too demanding.

In her way she remained loyal to Jim. Many stars might have shrugged off a former lover when hitting the big time, but it never occurred to Mae to abandon him. Their affair stretched two ways. Her well-being was his sole concern, and Mae received emotional security from him. But he was rarely her lover nowadays, and that was the blight in Jim's life. Whereas she had never seriously pretended to be sexually monogamous, Jim had been included on her rota, but her nocturnal visits to him were becoming infrequent. Jim's great regret in life was that he could not completely satisfy her sexually. But no man could have done that. Her looks were her emotional security, upon which everything else was built. The parade of lovers was essential for her to maintain her confidence. Promiscuity is one cover for insecurity. Another reason explaining the hordes of men was that she loved sex compulsively and had become hooked. Sex can become a habit, as addictive as nicotine or alcohol, and Mae was a sex junkie.

Jim could not come to terms with this and was fiercely jealous of Mae's lovers. She took pains to be discreet and not flaunt them, partly so as not to hurt him and partly not to outrage public opinion, but her men were plentiful, if not varied. She went for a specific type.

Her active sex-life was another reason she did not encourage callers at the Ravenswood. She did not want prying eyes in her

* Tom Baily.

145

sanctum. She fostered the smoke screen that she led a life of moral rectitude and that the Mae West persona was just an image, a jape that was the reverse of the truth.

She very nearly got away with it.

chapter thirteen

RE-ENTER BATTLING JACK

The power of Mae West is not confined to the United States. In Paris she is a sensation. All summer long the social élite of Paris have entertained with Lady Lou parties, at which the feminine guests came attired in costumes made popular by Mae in *She Done Him Wrong*. This country's most exclusive women's magazine has devoted much space to pictures and comments on those Lady Lou parties of Paris which were inspired by Mae West.

So wrote Elizabeth Yeaman in 1933. And it was not just the glossies of Paris that were running features on Mae. It was a similar story all over Europe. In America *Vanity Fair* had featured her on its cover posing as the Statue of Liberty, 'freeing the sexually shy from their binding emotional blocks and repressions,' explained Mae magnanimously in *Goodness Had Nothing To Do With It*. George Jean Nathan saw the photograph and responded, 'She looks more like the Statue of Libido.'

She became the darling of the intellectual élite, and Miss Yeaman went on to note that Mae's approach had always been more wholesome than that of several other esteemed contemporary artists:

Today the highbrows of Park Avenue are her fans ... However, those same highbrows assiduously patronised the Theater Guild, which produced Eugene O'Neill erotica such as *Mourning Becomes Electra* or *Strange Inter-*

147

lude. But then the Theater Guild was not criticised because it operated under the aegis of ART. Mae West was frowned upon because she sponsored plain, wholesome sin without the trimmings of art. Personally, I regard Mae West's popularity today as a healthy and wholesome trend of public mind.

Mae Tinee of the *Chicago Tribune* observed how Mae's challenge to conventionality was gathering momentum:

Mae West has chosen to wear disregard for the moral code like a sunflower in her buttonhole and has the world admiring her boutonnière. This dame with the swinging hips, the bedroom air and the throaty growl of an amorous cat again frankly displays her wares in *I'm No Angel*. As I see it, Mae West's pull lies in the fact that she really and truly doesn't give a damn. The world is full of people who would like not to and she provides vicarious easy shoes and relaxed stays for their inhibitions.

The police reserves were called out to keep Mae West fans in order the day the picture opened at the Paramount, and continuous performances of the entire show, screen and stage, were scheduled from 9 o'clock yesterday morning until 5 o'clock this morning to accommodate the crowds.

Mae was freewheeling so fast there was a danger that if she hit the least obstacle she might overbalance.

Further financial blandishments came her way in the form of a deal with the Paris perfume house Gabilla. She sponsored 'Parfum Mae West'. The advertisement read: 'You can enjoy that strange fascination which is Mae West's. Parfum Mae West is loaded with lure ... dripping with sex appeal. A few drops behind your ears – and it's all over but the wedding march!'

But wedding marches were the last thing on Mae's mind. Her celebrity had brought her to the unwelcome attention of criminals, something she had dreaded since her success began. The newly rich of Hollywood were prime targets for a breed of scoundrels who hoped to feed off them. Extortion was practised under threat of disfigurement, kidnapping or bodily harm, and there was a spate of armed robberies of celebrities in Hollywood, the most recent victim being Jeanette MacDonald.

On an evening in the autumn of 1932, Mae's nightmare came true when she was confronted by a thief and robbed of cash and jewels to the value of $15,000. The incident occurred as she was waiting in her chauffeur-driven car for Jim to join her. A masked man wrenched open the door, aimed a revolver at her face, and demanded her handbag and the jewellery she was wearing. Her chauffeur was armed, but he dared not intervene, he later explained, for fear of provoking the assailant into a panic attack.

A few days later Mae received a telephone call from an unidentified man offering to sell back her diamonds for $5,000. He named a nearby site, where he promised to leave her empty handbag as proof of his credentials. Despite a warning not to tell the police, Mae informed a detective about the call. Disguising himself as Mae, in wig and female clothes, the detective went to the appointed spot and retrieved the handbag, finding no sign of the depositor. But there was a hitch to the thieves' plan: Mae had refused to pay for the return of her jewellery.

The police had a lead, and it pointed to the complicity of Mae's chauffeur, Harry Voiler, in the robbery. Although Voiler had not worked for Mae for long, she had known him for years, as he had been an associate of Texas Guinan's. He had, however, fallen on hard times and, sucker for a sob story that Mae was, she had given him the job of driver until he could get back on his feet.

By questioning associates of Voiler's, the police uncovered the identity of the thief and arrested a known criminal called Edward Friedman who, after a grilling, eventually confessed to the crime, naming Voiler as the brains behind the project – hence Voiler's reluctance to shoot when Mae was threatened. Mae was not surprised. It was not the first time a friend had betrayed her. She had been taken for a ride so often that she used to say, 'People think of me as a bank.'

Mae had to testify in court and this was the beginning of an even more frightening episode. She was bombarded by telephone and letter with threats of both death and disfigurement. She was told that acid would be thrown in her face if she did not drop the charges. She placed herself under police protection and countered the intimidation with a plucky official statement: 'I'll fight this thing single-handed if no one will come forward to help me. The police are helpless if those on whom the gangsters prey will not go to court on the side of the law. The gangsters threaten us in the film colony under penalty of having acid thrown in our faces. And they don't stop at acid threats. They threaten to kill. It is time someone called their bluff – and it looks as if it will have to be me.'

Instantly, in the public eye, brazen hussy Mae was transformed into public heroine number one, upholder of the law. What, it may be wondered, did her moral opposition make of this?

The police guarded the Ravenswood twenty-four hours a day and Mae was protected by two bodyguards, an ex-marine and a former boxer. Director Leo McCarey felt the full force of her security when he called on the off-chance to try to interest her in a deal. He was taken to the police station and detained for an hour until Mae identified him.

Eventually Friedman was brought to trial and, despite the threats, Mae gave evidence. She told the jury that at the time of the robbery he had seemed so nervous that she was frightened he might hit her in the face with his gun: 'I could make back the money anytime,' she said, 'but I couldn't get myself a new face.' Friedman was sentenced to imprisonment for a period of between thirty years and life.

Mae was a heroine to the public and her bravery had stolen the thunder of her detractors for a while, but this latest wave of Mae West publicity was resented by certain members of her profession. Perhaps her high-handed attitude to some of her colleagues had left them disenchanted, or perhaps straightforward jealousy was the motive but, whatever the cause, her

Battling Jack.

Tillie.

Mae at six months, 1894.

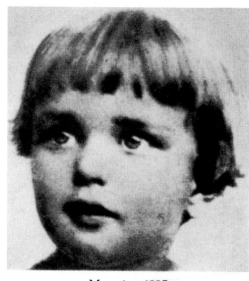

Mae, circa 1897.

Mae, matronly at thirty-four, five years before stardom in Hollywood

The salacious variety performer, circa 1917. Her stage performances had already provoked the wrath of the moral purity brigades.

Belle of the Nineties.

Karl Struss brought a new, more becoming softness to Mae's looks in *Go West Young Man* (1936) in which she starred with Randolph Scott.

Her psychic advisor, T. Jack Kelly

Mae loved musclemen, but married the unbrawny Frank Wallace in 1911. Their marriage barely survived the secret ceremony.

own industry now seemed to turn against her. The following item which appeared in *Picture Play* was merely one of several of the same tenor:

> Mae is clever – very clever . . . But is Mae clever enough to know where cleverness ends and discretion begins? . . . A Mae West director cannot be held entirely responsible for a Mae West picture. Not so long as she writes her own stories . . . A splendid scene is wrecked when the camera cuts from one player to a close-up of the star before that player has actually finished his scene. We may want to see the star, but we don't want to see her to the detriment of the story. If this occurs too often in a film, it becomes a monotony and a bore to the most lenient of audiences. Mae is a genius at making wisecracks, but it takes more than wisecracks to justify six reels of celluloid. It takes an interesting, fairly plausible story that is different from previous stories in which the star has appeared . . .

But Mae's eventual Hollywood demise would have nothing to do with the number of close-ups in her movies. It was the constant pressure of the purity leagues that rang her professional death knell in Tinsel Town. Directly spurred on by the runaway success of Mae's two starring films, the guardians of public morals intensified their attack in 1934 against what they believed to be the Hollywood erosion of decency standards, and to the moralists she seemed to epitomize all they considered malign in the movies. Episcopalians had already formed a Committee of Motion Pictures to oppose immorality in films, and the Catholic Church, soon after, encouraged its members to form picket lines around cinemas showing movies it considered offensive.

There was definite support for these pressure groups among certain sections of the nation, and this plunged Zukor and the other studio bosses into a dilemma. On the one hand they were determined to continue to utilize Mae's lucrative services, but they were embarrassed by the unhealthy attention she was bringing to the studio. There were millions of Catholics in

America. Some of them were already boycotting cinemas. Their activities could not be allowed to gather momentum. For studio moguls it was a case of having to reconcile their nerves with their interest in the money she made.

Mae, however, was not nervous. She enjoyed her position as the world's most famous sex exponent. It was excellent food for her voracious ego to feed upon. She knew how greatly she had transgressed and the extent of the outrage she had caused, but her movie star persona was forever gathering power over Mae the woman. She could not draw back or temporize her professional or public behaviour. An element of getting her own back underlay her stubbornness. By cocking a snook at so-called public decency she was evening the score for the many humiliations she had suffered at the hands of the respectable. She now called the tune. Mentally she was putting her thumb to her nose and extending her fingers.

She was also making a fortune.

When work started on her new movie, which had the provisional title *That St Louis Woman*, she was determined it would be just as spicy as the previous two, more so if possible. She discovered, however, that making films in 1934 was not so much fun as it had been in 1933. The era of non-censorship had ground to a halt.

In addition to the Committee of Motion Pictures, Bishop Sheil's National Legion of Decency seemed to be getting stronger daily. Its executive, comprised largely of Roman Catholic bishops but including a number of Anglican and Jewish bigwigs, set out to view new releases and grade them as to their moral acceptability. Millions of Catholics signed the Legion's pledge: 'I condemn indecent and immoral pictures . . . and promise to stay away altogether from places of amusement which show them as a matter of policy.'

The *I'm No Angel* furore had come at a particularly bad time for Paramount as it was already in hot water with an earlier film, *The Story of Temple Drake*, released five months before *I'm No Angel*. Based on William Faulkner's novel, *Sanctuary*, it told of a society girl who is kidnapped, raped and kept captive by a sexual pervert.

Despite its sensational theme it was a serious film, but what chiefly infuriated the morality campaigners was that far from being repelled by her life of debauchery, the girl took to it and was reluctant to abandon it. To enjoy any form of sex was reprehensible in the eyes of the Legion, but to be seen to enjoy perversion was beyond the pale. The outcry was enormous. The Legion urged Catholics to boycott *Temple Drake*.

Terrified by the thought of a loss of revenue in the new puritanical climate, the studio bosses had looked for a remedy and came up with the idea of pledging their whole-hearted support to the Hays Office, thereby reinforcing what had been a rather lacklustre organization to date.

Tsar Hays rose to the occasion and had the Production Code of 1930 strengthened and expanded, taking ostentatious care to consult prominent religious leaders for advice. He appointed Catholic journalist Joseph Breen to be in charge of the new Production Code Administration. And in this capacity Breen was currently holding discussions with Paramount as Mae's new film moved into production.

The Hays Office, under Breen, became Hollywood's watchdog. Breen became involved in all phases of film production, from vetting the script to viewing the finished commodity. A film had to receive the Seal of Approval or Purity Seal, as it was called, before release. Any violation of the Code meant a $25,000 fine and, although that could be absorbed, the ensuing Legion condemnation could result in a public boycott and a crippling loss of funds.

Under Breen's administration Hollywood entered a new era, which was to last until the 1960s: 'The Production Code Administration diligently policed the industry – saw to it that sexual passion was kept within bounds on the screen, virtue rewarded and vice punished. Mae West's new film ... was toned down so much that she was reported to have burst into tears over the carnage wrought on her script.'*

Bursting into tears, at least publicly, was not in Mae's repertoire but she was anxious about the attempt to dilute her

* *Hollywood Anecdotes*, Paul F. Boller Jr. and Ronald L. Davis, Macmillan, 1988.

art and upset at any effort to bridle her. She was not going to give up without a fight. For her new film, now retitled *It Ain't No Sin*, she decided to return to the Gay Nineties. Once again, she would play a saloon singer but the setting would be New Orleans rather than the Bowery and, as in *She Done Him Wrong*, two men would love her, one crooked and the other straight.

In accordance with the new regime the script was sent to the Hays Office for approval. This had been the form with previous films, but only minimal attention had been paid to the Office's verdict. Now its judgement was awaited with baited breath. Its reader progressed no further than the title before raising two objections. *It Ain't No Sin*, given its religious connotations, was an unacceptable title. Aside from any moral objection, the title in itself was also a corruption of grammar and shouldn't be used – such was the weight the Hays Office could now wield.

Paramount suggested *It Isn't A Sin*, as a replacement, but this was vetoed as it still carried religious overtones. Someone came up with *St Louis Belle*, but the film finally appeared as *Belle of the Nineties*.

This threw the Paramount press office into chaos. No one had bothered to inform the press office of the title changes and, as promotion for the film, it had been decided to make a gift of a talking parrot to all key distributors. The birds had been taught to repeat the phrase, 'It Ain't No Sin'. With the change of title the birds were useless as publicity gimmicks. Paramount's offices rang to their screeches for weeks as they were distributed to various departments.

A number of posters advertising the forthcoming film as *It Ain't No Sin* had already been displayed on Broadway, and a group of priests had assembled beneath one of them, holding aloft banners proclaiming the words 'It Is'. Another inducement for Paramount to change the title.

Le Baron was again the producer and Leo McCarey the director. Although McCarey was not a product of the theatre, he was experienced in comedy direction, having just completed the Marx Brothers hit *Duck Soup* for Paramount – a film that had impressed Mae. He had also directed Laurel and Hardy in their early days. Mae was satisfied that she was working with someone who knew comedy; in fact, she referred to him as 'one of Hollywood's best directors'. Rare praise from Mae who, in truth, was convinced all directors were merely living off her back.

After having seen some of the 'dailies', she was also pleased with the work of cameraman Karl Struss. She believed he had captured her beauty on celluloid better than any cameraman to date.

Breen was determined that Mae would not transgress the Production Code. He vetted each day's lines before filming began and insisted on numerous amendments. As if this were not intimidation enough he personally came to the shoot, and stood on the sidelines while she performed her scenes.

Another formidable opponent took an interest in Mae at this time: the press baron William Randolph Hearst. He was dubbed 'the Father of Yellow Journalism', a well-earned soubriquet for the mud-slinging dished out in his newspapers across America. Yellow Journalism destroyed the careers of innocent people, yet bolstered his circulation figures. His biographer William A. Swanberg wrote of the Hearst press: 'They [Hearst's news-papers] were deficient in the newspaper's first requisite – news ... Truth, the touchstone of news value, was unimportant to Hearst because circulation, money and power were his goals – he specialized in attack, and in attack he was pitiless.'*

Hearst was seventy in 1933 and lived in a magnificent moun-tain-top castle in San Simeon, California. Long before the roads to the castle were built, Hearst had had his labourers sweat their way along the trails heaving some of the world's greatest art treasures up to his lair. He, and his castle, were the inspiration behind Orson Welles's classic film *Citizen Kane*.

Such was the social cachet accorded an invitation to the San Simeon castle, it was said that there were just two categories of people in Hollywood: those who had received an invitation to visit and those who had not.

Hearst claimed to support family values – despite the fact he had ditched his wife to live with movie star Marion Davies –

---

* *Citizen Hearst, A Biography of William Randolph Hearst*, Longman, 1962.

and backed the Legion of Decency. His writers denounced anything which Hearst considered undermined family life. Mae became their chief target.

Hearst employed some persuasive writers. Louella Parsons, equal to Hedda Hopper in her vituperative gossip, was on his payroll. Many actors were so terrified of 'Lolly' [known behind her back as Mrs Velvet Finger, as her husband was a specialist in the treatment of piles] that they sometimes telephoned her with family news even before discussing it at home. One husband discovered his wife was pregnant only when he heard the news on Lolly's radio show. If Lolly did not get her 'exclusive' she could cut up rough: those who did not play the game were crucified in print.

It was ironic that Mae alienated Hearst as she was precisely the sort of person he most admired. Fred Lawrence Guiles writes of him: 'If Hearst recognized any society as such, it was that of the amusing and successful, those who had wit and had made it – statesmen, film people, fellow publishers.'* Hearst was infatuated by the movies, and had been in the business himself since 1913, when he had produced serials and newsreels. He went on to own Cosmopolitan Productions, a company which, many said, was created as an instrument to further the career of Marion Davies.

His antipathy to Mae arose because she was alleged to have made slighting remarks about Miss Davies, although the content of these remarks has never been made public. Mae denied the allegation, which indicates the rumour was groundless, since she seldom held her tongue when it came to knocking other actresses.

Aside from his newspapers, Hearst had another weapon he aimed at Mae. He held a substantial financial interest in *Motion Picture Herald*, the trade magazine of the film industry and, by writing in its columns of her feuds – some true, most faked – with directors, as well as the escalating costs of production owing to her unpunctuality, he tainted her professional reputation.

* *Marion Davies*, W. H. Allen, 1973.

By and large she did not tackle Hearst. How could she defend herself against a man who owned most of the country's newspapers? Who would print her reply? What reply was there against insinuation? She, of all people, knew the power of innuendo. Now, in a more sinister guise, it was being directed at her.

While Hearst squandered literally millions at his castle, Emanuel Cohen, back at Paramount, was coping with Mae's budgetary demands. He had been hoping to get her to accept a paltry $200,000 salary, but Mae, conscious she had been ripped off last time, was not having it. Cohen realized his days of securing a cheap West film were over, but her current demands were astronomical.

Mae's salary soared. She signed a four-year contract which called for two films a year, with an escalator clause specifying each would be paid at an increasing rate; for 1934 she was to receive $300,000 per film, plus a script fee of an additional $100,000.

She was determined that the studio splash out on production values. She had long admired the bandleader, Duke Ellington, who had fronted the orchestra at Owney Madden's Cotton Club and told Cohen she wanted him and his orchestra for her next film. Black, handsome and permanently randy, Ellington was just her sort of man. He was also an outstanding musician and composer. Just as Joseph Haydn had woven folk songs into symphonic form, Ellington had fused popular material into the newly designed swing idiom. But Cohen did not care about his creativity, it was his cost that mattered. Ellington was a star and would be expensive to hire. Cohen protested, reasonably, that the studio already had an orchestra under contract, why bother to hire another? But Mae would not waver and Ellington appeared in the film.

She insisted on an even larger cast of extras than before and, once again, many of them were vaudevillians or pals of her father, and small-time hoodlums she had known in New York or on tour. Libby Taylor was, once again, her maid.

Her bodyguards still travelled with her and accompanied her each morning to the studio. They were carried away by the glamour of their surroundings so, as a reward, she put them both into the film as extras. They were thrilled. By now she was in the midst of an affair with one of them, the boxer Mike Mazurki.

Mae managed to prevent press scrutiny into her amatory affairs by a mixture of dextrous footwork and her choice of lovers. Nearly all her boyfriends were boxers, wrestlers and musclemen; unlike ego-heavy actors – the traditional squires of Hollywood beauties – these men managed to deal with their day-to-day aggression by letting it out through physical combat. They did not frequent the gossipy milieu of the movie crowd and were therefore unlikely to meet the columnists who could damage Mae. Of her ex-lovers who did break their silence, most seemed to remain fond of her. She was considered a good sport who never caused trouble.

Mike Mazurki discovered this. After he had decided he had had enough and wanted to return to the square ring, he came clean with Mae and told her his decision. There were no scenes, no recriminations. She accepted the circumstances, metaphorically shook his hand and gave him some money as a gift. It was a present, not payment for services rendered. Mae never paid her men and she was too vain to hire prostitutes, but she had no objection to passing on a lavish gift if the occasion called for it or the man had been particularly memorable.

Boxer Max Baer was a one-off lover. After she had bedded him, she noticed him standing at her bedroom window waving to someone in the street. She asked what he was doing, and he confessed he had had a bet with a friend that he would be able to get her to bed and the wave was the signal this had been achieved. Mae burst into laughter.*

The Chicago *Sunday Tribune* on 8 July 1934 ran an article claiming that *Belle of the Nineties* had had to be withdrawn from circulation at the insistence of the Hays Office, and would

---

* Both Max Baer and Mike Muzurki accounts taken from *Mae West, The Lies, The Legends, The Truth*, George Eells and Stanley Musgrove, Robson Books, 1989.

not be released until substantial alterations had been made to it. It made a good Mae West story, and the piece was lavishly illustrated with shots of Mae in her Ruby Carter (her character's name in *Belle*) costumes. But the article was misleading in that *Belle* had not yet been completed, and the Hays Office had not insisted on any alterations.

Paramount had hoped to première the film in New York at its huge Paramount Theater and, with this in mind, a rough cut had been sent to the New York Board of Censors, who had to determine if the film would be acceptable for display in New York. The Board promptly banned it, sternly recommending: 'The said film be rejected in toto upon the grounds that it is indecent, immoral, would tend to corrupt morals and would intend to incite to crime.' But this was part of Mae's master-plan. Suspecting that the Board would ban her film on principle she had deliberately included, when Breen was not about, scenes which she knew would be unacceptable. When the film had been rejected, she removed the offensive material, and substituted her intended scenes. In the presence of the representative from the Hays Office, she then meekly shot the new material within a few days. The revamped film was then returned to the Board, who passed it, satisfied in the knowledge Mae West had been put in her place.

Unyielding as the initial New York pronouncement seems, the Board had the reputation of being among the more liberal of censors, and other states tended to take their lead from New York. 'If New York rejects Mae West films, it is certain that several other states will do so,' announced the BUP special correspondent from Hollywood.

That conclusion had struck Paramount's executives too. That's why they had dispatched the film so speedily to New York, with alternate endings up their sleeves. Once the hurdles were crossed, and the finished product passed censorship in New York, then in all likelihood it would not run into too grievous trouble elsewhere.

The special correspondent continued patronizingly: 'Mae West is a very distinct character on the screen, and she depends largely on her "wisecracks" and her manner of speech to make her effects. Take those away from her and there is not a great deal left.' Remove the gags and style from any comedienne and there is not a 'great deal left'.

Despite the interference of the Hays Office, the film in its completed form is still a lusty, bawdy celebration. Mae's version of the 1890s comes strongly across and, although the action opens in St Louis, as far as the ambience is concerned it might just as well be the Bowery, with Gus's Bar only a step away. And Ruby Carter might as well be called Diamond Lil. The whole film smacks of vaudeville, with several artists performing numbers between the action, and there is a chorus of some of the heftiest dancing girls ever filmed. None of Mae's despised 'beanpoles' here.

Belle of the Nineties is Mae's most glamorously packaged film, and credit for this must lie, to a large extent, with art directors Hans Dreier and Bernard Herzbrun for the stunning backcloths against which Mae poses for her opening shots. They set the whole tone. A tenor warbles 'My American Beauty' while Mae, in shimmering gown, regulation hand on hip, is featured in turn as a butterfly, a glittering bat, a rose, a predatory spider and finally the Statue of Liberty.

She is gorgeously dressed by Travis Banton, who makes even Edith Head – that doyenne of costume design who dressed Mae in *She Done Him Wrong* – look to her laurels. Mae may have had to wheedle the money out of Cohen but at least he could see where it was spent. Mae wears several shoulderless gowns which show off her peachy skin, but the *décolleté* is modest. She never believed in revealing cleavage. It was unusual for her to show as much of her bare arms as she does here.

Hollywood did not seriously eroticize the bosom until the early 1940s, when Howard Hughes introduced to the world that magnificent Amazon Jane Russell, in *The Outlaw*. Until that time, the bust had principally been the symbol of maternity. Hughes had become besotted by Miss Russell's breasts and had spent weeks developing a special brassiere which would display them to maximum advantage as far as the law would then permit. After Jane Russell established the tradition of the erotic bosom, it was subsequently upheld by various standard bearers, including Marilyn Monroe, Jayne Mansfield, Anita Ekberg and Sophia Loren.

Mae never emphasized her bust. Her hips were the 'flagship of her sexuality', as the London critic Alexander Walker has put it. Her bosom, which she padded to keep balance with her hips, was never actually defined.

Belle has the distinction of being the first of Mae's films in which she wore a wig throughout. She had worn wigs earlier for various scenes, but had now developed a serious hair problem which was to be the bane of her life. The peroxide which had been used to bleach her fine hair had permanently damaged it; much had fallen out and what was left was decidedly wispy. She was never seen in public from then on without a wig or head covering of some sort.

McCarey spent a long time lighting Mae. The shading he achieved is magnificent and in certain shots, aided by Banton's frocks and her altitudinous shoes which the frocks hide, she seems almost slim.

Mae borrowed from *The Constant Sinner* for the plot, and it is a good enough vehicle to enable her to strut through the action spouting her wisecracks. There is no shortage of ready wit:

'All she thinks about is having a good time,' a character says of Ruby. 'I don't only think about it,' she replies.

Walking through her hotel with the manager, he points to an oil painting of a lady. 'This one, in particular, is an old master,' he boasts. Ruby quips, 'Looks more like an old mistress to me.'

'A man in the house is worth two in the street.'

A man embraces her and moans, 'I must have you. Your golden hair, your fascinating eyes, your alluring smile, your lovely arms, your form divine . . .' 'Is this a proposal or are you taking an inventory?' she asks.

'May we ask what kind of men you prefer?' a swain enquires. 'Just two. Domestic and foreign.'

'It's better to be looked over than overlooked.'

'If he was the last man on earth, I wouldn't . . .' she says. 'The last man?' interrupts her maid. 'Well,' she says, 'Maybe I am taking in a little too much territory.'

'Weren't you nervous when he gave you all those presents?' 'No, I was calm and collected.'

'His mother should have thrown him away and kept the stork.'

There are lots more.

Mae had been right to insist that Duke Ellington appear in *Belle* since he clearly inspired her. She sings the best she ever did on film. There are several blues arrangements, performed by her with a sureness of touch that sometimes compares with no lesser singers than Bessie Smith or Dinah Washington.

She also sang the haunting torch song 'My Old Flame'. For some reason this song, and Mae's interpretation of it, irked Beverly. Mae's friend Robert Duran recalls Beverly, as an old lady, watching the movie on television with Mae. When the number came up Beverly mocked, 'How could you sing it, Sissie? He's your old flame, but you can't even remember his name, it doesn't make sense.' This seems like a scene straight from *Whatever Happened to Baby Jane*: although Mae did, at times, snap back and even yell at Beverly, she tolerated many insults from her.

For all the restrictions Breen had placed on Mae's script there was not much he could do to suppress her 'libidinous personality or the walk that launched a thousand female impersonators' hips across the length and breadth of the country.'*
The only obvious evidence of the Hays Office is the sub-theme of gospel music and religiosity which runs throughout. At one point the maid asks for time off to attend a prayer meeting. Ruby not only grants this, and gives her money for the collec-

* *The Hollywood Musical*, Clive Hirschhorn, Octopus, 1981.

tion, but asks her to say a prayer for her. Diamond Lil would have given her the time off and money but not bothered about the prayer. Censorship, however, didn't lessen the film's appeal:

25 DEEP TO SEE NEW MAE WEST FILM

Twelve shows daily and the patrons standing twenty-five rows deep throughout the day is the custom in Atlantic City at the première of Mae West's new Paramount production *Belle of the Nineties*. Unhurt by the censor's scissors, the famous West wisecracks are still abundant. It is predicted that the film will probably be the most successful picture of the Mae West collection. It has already made an even better box office showing at Atlantic City than the tremendously successful *I'm No Angel*.*

In a syndicated interview, published by the *Sunday Dispatch*, Mae gave her opinion as to why her films were so successful: 'People don't go to the pictures to be instructed. They don't want uplift. They don't want education. They want entertainment. And that, let me say, is my aim in every picture I make – 46 million people have seen those pictures of mine so far. That's bigger than the entire population of some of the biggest countries in the world.'

Throughout her success, Mae had kept in touch with her family. Beverly was already with her at the Ravenswood, and she now sent for her brother John, who was not having much luck in holding down a job in the East. She got him a job at the studios as a carpenter. Charming though he was, John was no respecter of hard work and had inherited the West weakness for alcohol. He was found drunk and asleep on several occasions and was finally dismissed. Not even Mae could save him.

But she did not give up. Battling Jack, among his various

* Unidentified press cutting.

careers, had dabbled in real estate and she had inherited an interest in property from him. She now started to invest her earnings. During the 1930s, property was cheap in southern California and, among other properties, Mae bought a rambling hacienda in the San Fernando Valley. There was a paddock attached where horses could be exercised.

Apart from drink, the only real interest John seems to have had was horse racing, to which he had lost a fortune. Mae moved him into the hacienda, or ranch as she called it, with a stable of horses which, she hoped, he would train and race, thus building up a business for himself.

This move was doomed from the start, however, as the necessary licence to train the horses was not granted to Jack. And although Mae kept horses as pets at the ranch, Jack spent the money with which she had entrusted him to train them on an expensive sports car, which he gleefully drove around Hollywood.

Battling Jack had remained in New York, where he had various business interests, and occupied a house on Long Island which Mae had bought him. But his concerns were widespread, and a real estate investment had taken him to Florida. It was now plain that he was, again, in financial trouble, so Mae decided to bring him to California as well, where she could keep an eye on him.

She disposed of the Long Island home, thus severing her connections with New York forever, and put her father up at the ranch along with his son. Battling Jack had, after all, worked with horses, so he could lend a hand with the prospective business venture John was supposed to be building up (the training licence had not yet been refused).

Battling Jack arrived at Los Angeles station and was met by his son. Mae was on the set at Paramount. Before proceeding to the ranch, John had instructions to drive his father to the Ravenswood, where Beverly would be waiting for him, and where Mae would join them later when she had finished her day's shooting.

The press, tipped off by Paramount, covered the story, but Mae refused to pose with her father. This was the sort of intrusion into her personal life she abhorred. She would assist the press to write any stories they liked about her as long as they steered away from her near and dear.

This disappointed Battling Jack, who would have liked to have seen his picture in the paper. As it was, and to Mae's annoyance, he garnered quite a good press for himself; column upon column in the newspapers were devoted to the 'former top-notch ring gladiator' and 'father of the world's most famous blonde'. He was described as 'a stocky, well-built man, bearing none of the usual physiological mementoes of the ring', which presumably meant that he had neither a broken nose nor a cauliflower ear.

When cornered into making a comment, Mae dramatically stated, 'He fought for me with his hands when I was a child, now I want to do something for him.' This was so far removed from the truth that it could in no way qualify as an intrusion into her personal life. Battling Jack would have fought for anyone, on any pretext.

Her father sometimes accompanied Mae and Jim to the studio. He got on well with Jim, and the two superannuated ex-sportsmen had much in common. Battling Jack became a familiar and somewhat popular sight in certain quarters at Paramount. He held no official position other than being Mae West's father, but this afforded him kudos and opened many doors, particularly those attached to liquor cabinets. Good old Jack was always game for a chat and a laugh, even if these did tend to become protracted, causing his hosts to regret their largesse. There were times, it was whispered around Paramount, when busy people actually hid when they saw bluff Jack swaggering down the corridors.

When he was not at the studios Mae later confessed, 'He spends his time reading the sporting editions, one foot on the mantelpiece and the other tucked under him . . . As sound as a bell himself, I guess he brought me up that way, too.'*

It might also have been better for Beverly had she put up her feet on the mantelpiece and enjoyed herself, but she could not.

* *Sunday Dispatch*, c.1936.

Beverly now rarely went with Mae to the studio, as it was clear Mae was not going to promote any ideas Beverly had of becoming a film actress. Beverly had been left much to her own devices at the studios while Mae busily pursued her own career. This was not indifference on Mae's part but a genuine fear that if Beverly was put in the limelight her alcoholic tendencies were bound to surface, exposing both Beverly and Mae to humiliation. The resulting ridicule would have been disastrous for Beverly's mental well-being. In this instance Mae was more concerned for her sister than for herself, but Beverly, naturally, did not see it this way. She had become increasingly embittered by Mae's success.

Beverly's reunion with her father did nothing to bolster her morale. He was so stupefied by Mae's lifestyle that, in keeping with the rest of the world, he expressed little interest in his second daughter. With the arrival of all her family, Beverly could not stand still being a nobody, and decided she would make an effort to pick up the threads of her career and have another stab at making a name for herself. There was nothing Mae could do to stop her, and she realized that if she tried she would only fuel Beverly's resentment further.

Mae was willing to let Beverly trade on the fact that she was her sister, which would have a novelty attraction for audiences. Perhaps producers would see her as a gateway to the elusive superstar, and be inclined to give her a hearing.

Bearing in mind her physical disadvantage, Beverly chose to go in for a career as a radio singer and impressionist. An impression of Mae was to be the pivot of her act. She told Broadway correspondent Edward R. Sammis, 'It got so you couldn't step into a vaudeville or motion picture house anywhere without finding someone who was doing an imitation of Mae. I thought to myself, "After all, who knows Mae better than I do? Who is more familiar with her every little inflection and mannerism than I, after all those years of understudying her parts? So why shouldn't I be doing imitations of Mae on the radio?"'

Sammis commented, 'Mae would have you think that she knows nothing about Beverly's activities. She won't talk about her sister.' But she decided to break her silence regarding Beverly to help launch her new career. Beverly had made another of her periodic attempts to stay off the booze, but there was a dread in Mae's heart. Alcohol is a hard taskmaster. Mae doubted Beverly's abstention would last. However, for the moment, Beverly was happy, inspired by her new ambition and full of good intentions.

Mae arranged for Beverly to be put into contact with executives of the New York Station WHN. As long as Beverly was working, she did not mind where she was sent and the sisters welcomed a break from each other's company.

For a few months Beverly appeared on WHN, but she soon ran out of material. Whenever the sisters were apart they rang each other every day: Mae advised Beverly that sketches were the answer and recommended her to Ned Joyce Heaney, who had written material for Mae during her touring days. Heaney knew Mae well and could therefore write satire of her which Beverly could perform in her impressions.

Mae told Beverly to cast the sketches with actors who had formerly appeared with her in her various shows and who might now need a job. Among those who accepted was actor Robert Baikoff, a Russian emigré who claimed to be a prince, and who later married Beverly.

Billed as 'Beverly West and Company', and constantly guided by Mae, Beverly made some headway with her show, but before the year was out returned to the Ravenswood with no further offers. Unfortunately Mae never heard Beverly's show as the transmitting station was unobtainable on the West Coast.

chapter fourteen

EXPOSÉ

Throughout her forty-eight years' residence in Hollywood, Mae published her telephone number and address in the directory. She had her ex-directory numbers as well, but she never wanted to be in a position where a producer could not personally contact her if he wanted to. The listed number was the switchboard of the Ravenswood, and the operators had instructions to announce every call before it was put through. All buttons on the Ravenswood switchboard were red except for two white ones – the manager's and Mae's. Yet, she was not difficult to get hold of and callers were often startled when making an enquiry to find themselves suddenly confronting her on the end of the phone.

She was a newsman's delight; quotes from her were sought on nearly every topic, but she would not tolerate fools. Frank London, writing for *Collier's* magazine in June 1934, recalled a female cub reporter who rang Mae for a story:

> Reporter: 'Miss West, do you think you would like to be a mother, and would you be a good mother if you were a mother?'
> Mae West: 'Are you a mother yourself?'
> Reporter: 'I am not, nor am I even married.'
> Mae West: 'Neither am I. This ought to be a real helpful conversation.'

In her memoirs Hedda Hopper recalled she once asked Mae, 'How do you know so much about men?' 'Baby, I went to the right school,' Mae told her.*

* *From Under My Hat*, Frederick Muller, 1953.

168

In August 1934 she gained a new fan in the person of Benito Mussolini, the dictator of Italy. Il Duce was campaigning for larger families, and pronounced Mae a prime example of 'virile, healthy, womanhood'. Mae doubtless agreed.

Belle of the Nineties was released on 21 September 1934 and the moral crusade against Mae flared up again: 'Churchmen of every creed are conducting a crusade for wholesome movies – or none,' announced one newspaper. In New York, the State Board of Regents, the censoring body, was seriously reconsidering its decision and debating whether the film should not after all be withdrawn, but the debate took so long that by the time a decision had been reached it was too late.

Happily not all churchmen were against her. She had a champion in Canon John S. Mitchell, assistant rector of New York's Little Church Around the Corner, the 'actors' church'. According to the rector, when Mae had lived in New York she had been a frequent member of his congregation. He told the press: 'She is a good soul. A charming and generous woman. She attends church frequently ... She is a good, hard-working human being.'

She was certainly generous to the church and regularly donated considerable sums to Catholic charities. This was not general knowledge, as she did not want the image of a charitable woman to dim her sparkle as a sex goddess, believing the two to be incompatible. Mae gave genuinely and generously, yet insisted the recipients keep quiet about it. One such was the priest of the church at the foot of Rossmore Avenue; he had only to ask and Mae readily sent a donation.

Nuns of a nearby order also benefited from her charity. Whenever she bought a new limousine – and that was often – she donated the old model to the nuns. She had once seen a nun getting on a bus and it had dismayed her. She believed nuns 'deserved the best'.

Perhaps an element of guilt underpinned her generosity – by donating to the church she was really storing up favours in heaven. But Mae gave to diverse charities – the church (of all denominations) was merely one. If guilt was a contributory reason it was not the overriding cause. She had a genuine respect for goodness and believed herself to be a good woman; her only disagreement with the church was that she could not subscribe to the view that a delight in sexual promiscuity was sinful.

This did not inhibit her from sometimes visiting the nuns and discussing different problems with them, problems which most people might have considered outside a nun's province. On one occasion Robert Duran was staggered when she casually remarked to him, 'You know, blow jobs ain't wrong. I asked the nuns about it today.' Either Mae and the nuns misunderstood each other, or the area of responsibility assumed by the sisters was wider than that for which they are usually given credit.

Religion came over Mae in phases. When the mood was upon her she would enter any religious edifice to gain solace, be it Anglican, Catholic or Jewish, for all three faiths were within her birthright. Although no great walker, she did sometimes saunter down Rossmore Avenue dressed in slacks, scarf and dark glasses to call at the church where she would sit alone and contemplate.

Not that there was much time for contemplation. Paramount drove their willing workhorse as hard as they could. Shooting for a new film started just before Christmas 1934. The title eventually settled upon was *Goin' To Town*; it had had working titles of *How Am I Doin'?* and *Now I'm a Lady*. The script was set in modern times and Mae played Cleo Borden, a brash, Western oil heiress who decides to move up in society. The original story was by Marion Morgan and George B. Dowell, but Mae wrote the screenplay. Karl Struss, whose work she so admired, was again her senior cameraman.

Le Baron produced under Cohen's supervision and her director was Alexander Hall. He had been directing only since 1932, but he had spent many hours in consultation with Mae, having been film editor on *She Done Him Wrong*. In the short time he had been directing he had notched up a goodly number of successes, notably the Shirley Temple hit *Little Miss Marker*. Hall had been assigned the property before casting his junior star, and he had invited Miss Temple to test for him. Still a child, she was nevertheless aware of her prestige and for her test read just three words, 'aw', 'nuts' and 'scram'. She was hired on the spot.

Hall's main difficulty in working with Shirley Temple was that her baby teeth kept falling out and had to be replaced by false ones. The dislocation could take place overnight, so a dentist was constantly on the set. Mae, on the other hand, had had her teeth capped well before coming to Hollywood; with her Hall had another problem with which to contend: her weight had crept up again. She attempted to control her figure with the help of her Merry Widow, a corset with laces at the back which could produce a waistline on even the most resistant of torsos.

Her weight did not stop her from mastering several new skills for the film. She took lessons in judo, shooting, card shuffling and dealing, and she played the drums and the piano. She had learnt to drum whilst in vaudeville, but now that she was about to commit her efforts to celluloid she had a kit installed at the Ravenswood – happily for the neighbours the block had thick walls – and she practised for hours.

Mae in modern dress merely meant Mae in evening dress, and Travis Banton again produced some outstanding, swirling, ankle-length confections. One gown alone was so encrusted with ornamentation that it weighed forty-five pounds. Moving around the set under the scalding arc lights and supporting that weight on precarious heels might have caused a stormtrooper to stagger. Mae never complained.

While filming was underway she had to turn down an invitation to address the 70,000 members of the Associated Sportsmen of California, who had invited her to be guest of honour at their Christmas dinner on 10 December. 'It's tough to say "no" to one good man,' she lamented. 'But saying it to 70,000 is even worse.'

She had adopted the habit of rewarding her directors with statues of herself, two-foot-high effigies which she scrutinized as carefully as her publicity stills before they left her hands. Alexander Hall was to be the recipient of one of them. The sculptor brought his work-in-progress to Mae in her dressing room for approval. He did not get it. A reporter, who merely signs himself DWC, was interviewing Mae at the time, and noted her reaction: 'It's too big there, and not big enough there,' she told him indicating her hips and bust.

DWC went on to note Mae's comments on the film:

> This is going to be the best picture I've done. I know now what they want and what they don't want. I've found out that things that the censors think are bad I think are all right, and I've learned that there are a number of things that I shy at that they see nothing wrong in ... When I wrote this one I got all the difficulties straightened out before I began and the censors approved it. So now all I have to do is follow my scenario ... The kiddies like me. That's because I always think of things to put in my pictures that they'll like ... In this one I lasso a man and shoot through his hat, and the kids are going to get a great kick out of that.

Mae pointed out that the film was four days ahead in its shooting schedule to allay rumours that she had been arriving late in the mornings.

As before, a Hays Office representative was present on the set while she filmed and, despite her hopes to the contrary, there were problems. If anything, Breen was even more vigilant than before, since the release of *Belle of the Nineties* had renewed controversy. She fought the restrictions but the film was inevitably weakened. The good lines, however, still emerged:

'Delilah? That's one female barber that made good.'

As always, there are several songs in the film, and the songwriters included Sammy Fain, Irving Kahal, Sam Coslow and, surprisingly, the French composer Saint-Saëns. He had composed thirteen operas, the most successful of which was *Samson and Delilah*. Delilah's music is written for contralto and her three major arias are show pieces which offer an opulent range for the voice. 'Softly Awakes My Heart' is the best known of the three, and Mae chose it to sing in *Goin' to Town*.

Burlesquing prima donnas was an old vaudeville tradition which she had seen and done herself in her days on the boards.

Now she brought it to the screen. In the film the aria is sung at the operatic evening Cleo holds to impress society and prove she is cultured. Wearing an outrageous parody of the costume of a Philistine, she prepares for her performance. In time-honoured prima donna fashion she is hysterical with nerves, crashing about, bumping into people and shrieking from time to time as she tries out the high notes of her voice.

Aside from its comedy value, the skit is interesting in that it provides the only example, on film or record, of Mae's top register. Technically, she was a natural contralto with an extended upper range capable of producing notes as high as top A and B; she may even have had a C but does not attempt it. As soon as her voice scales above the stave, its vibrato quickens into machine-gun rapidity, and its timbre becomes hideously pinched. What emerges is strangulated and harsh. This serves her burlesque perfectly, making her performance even more brittle. Had she so chosen the harsh tone of her singing might have been refined. She possessed a voice that, with training, could have sung comfortably the contralto/mezzo repertoire.

Her aria is performed as a duet which she sings with Tandie McKenzie, one of the leading tenors of his day. He is done up in a costume as absurd as her own and looks a complete buffoon. His powerful voice nurses Mae through and disguises her vocal deficiencies.

She kept a gramophone record of the accompaniment at the Ravenswood and would sometimes play it to sing the aria to her business acquaintances. One of the privileged was William Fitts. He recalled: 'She was really proud that she had sung the aria and wanted me to know how scholarly she was. She had the range for it but I remember thinking how nasal it was in the upper register – that nasality was not apparent when she sang ordinarily. In America we have a certain sound associated with a deprived socio-economic group and she had that sound.'

Fitts had called on her in the hope of interesting her in performing two songs he had written. In typical West idiom, they were entitled 'I Want a Cool Guy With a Hot Rod' and 'A Lady's a Lady No Matter What Cooks'. After some discussion she gave him $35 each in exchange for a straight sale and a waiver of royalties. She never used either song but this was not unusual: she frequently purchased material for which she might, possibly, have a future use. Rather than risk being sued she bought properties outright.

Because the censors weakened the innuendo Mae appears sometimes to be digging for laughs in *Goin' To Town*, and Mae West without innuendo is Mae West without bite. The Samson and Delilah sketch is possibly the funniest thing Mae ever did on screen. Her pleasure in doing what she did best – her vaudeville routines – communicates itself to the audience.

The film is smoothly directed and very pacy. There is a florid aspect about the sets which enhance the Mae West atmosphere, suggesting rococo at its most extreme. The gambling casino is magnificent, glittering with filigree work and crystal. This provides the perfect setting for her and, happy in these surroundings, she dominates the film throughout.

Like most of Mae's work the film carries its own message: Mae's revenge on Society. She had been wounded by the ruling class and she would now show them up for the double dealing frauds they are, but the satirical message gets swamped by the Mae West character. Any film in which Mae struts about, hand on hip, constantly adjusting her golden hair and playing with her diamonds as she makes mincemeat of the men, is artificial. Instead of attack her message becomes comedy. Her sarcasm gets swamped by the fun.

The film opened on 17 May 1935. The Hearst critic, as might have been expected, damned it by calling it 'trite'. By contrast the *Herald Tribune* found it 'amusing stuff'. Critic John Douglas Eames remarked 'Of course, Mae could no more be separated from sexual insinuation than Donald Duck from his quack, but her shafts of wit were now toned down from the outrageous to the merely naughty, and the audience reaction to the film was similarly subdued.'*

Maybe, but people still turned out in droves. Once again West had come home triumphant. Her personal fortune was also robust. In 1935 her income topped $480,000, which made

---

* *The Paramount Story*, John Douglas Eames, Octopus, 1985.

her America's most highly paid woman. She was such big business that Cohen formed a separate unit, detached from Paramount, which traded under the name Major Pictures, purely to handle Mae's films.

Goin' To Town did equally well in Britain, opening at London's Plaza. The *Daily Express* critic was censorious but amused. 'It is a film emphatically not for children,' he wrote (so much for Mae's claim that she always worked with children in mind), 'but its raucousness has a polish which seems to excuse much of its moral tone. No "purity drives" or censors can quench Miss West's unique personality.'

Ideas of morality change. In 1989, Britain's Channel 4 ran a season of Mae West films on television. The transmission time was 5.40 p.m., the time traditionally allotted to children. No complaints were received from viewers.

Although Mae never revealed her age she was nearly found out when the following item appeared in a Los Angeles newspaper on 27 October 1934:

YOU WORK IT OUT

Some time ago, Mae West was quoted as having lived in a certain house in Brooklyn, New York, until she was twelve years old. It is known that her childhood home was demolished and a church was built there – in 1905, twenty-nine years ago. You have an interesting problem in simple mathematics. How old is Mae West?

To her embarrassment, such simple mathematics made her forty-one years of age – bang on target. And the age she had recently declared when filling in an application for an endowment policy.

Mae tended to invest in insurance, diamonds and property – such as the ranch – and she had been adding to her real estate. When driving with Jim one Sunday afternoon, she had come across a large plot of land for sale in the Van Nuys area. She wanted to buy it as an investment but Jim told her it was a white elephant – property in such a sparsely populated area would be difficult to resell. Nevertheless, she bought the plot for $16,000. Taxes were high and, indeed, for a few years it did seem a poor investment. She considered reselling it at a loss, but Jim so gloated over her lack of business acumen that she became stubborn and decided not to. She later confessed that she had simply kept the property to spite Jim. In the 1970s, she sold just a portion of the land and it fetched over a million dollars. She used to boast that she was an ace property speculator ('I only made the first million or so out of movies, the rest came from real estate') but, in this case at least the property remained in her possession by default rather than judgement. She had no more foreseen the property boom than had Jim.

A widely circulated rumour had it that she owned the Ravenswood building. But, according to Robert Duran, she never even owned her own apartment there; it was leased for the entire duration of her tenancy. She did, however, enter into a financial arrangement with the owners at one time and held the deeds as security for a period, which possibly started the story.

Mae was aware of the tales of her reputed business acumen, which spread around Hollywood with the speed of a bush fire, and positively encouraged them. They were good for her image and sound professional insurance against the Hearst papers' slurs.

To keep herself fit she engaged a physiotherapist. James Davies was a well-known Hollywood figure who gave her a daily massage and put her through a series of physical workouts: 'She has the finest physique of any woman I have ever seen,' he said stoutly, bearing in mind who paid the fees. 'She is so strong that with one arm she can lift me off the floor. When she first came out here from the stage, she suggested reducing, but I warned her against it. There is not an ounce of fat on her.' It was probably true that she could lift him off the ground. She had kept up her barbell training and was proud of her biceps. Towards the end of her life, when her mind was inclined to wander, she would invite journalists to feel the still sinewy strength of her upper arms.

Although she was now the highest paid woman in the USA, 1935 was not a good year for Mae. Three calamities disrupted her life: first, 1935 marked her decline in popularity; secondly her husband, Frank Wallace, emerged from the mists of the past; and thirdly her father died.

Battling Jack lost his final battle on 6 July. He did not put up much of a fight and died in his sleep from a heart attack. He was seventy-one, and had been ailing for weeks. Mae had moved him from the ranch into an apartment at the Ravenswood in order to ensure he was near her and properly looked after. Mae had often apprehensively reflected that heart conditions ran in the West family.

The funeral was held in Hollywood, but the body was returned to Brooklyn for burial, where he was laid to rest next to his wife in the family mausoleum which Mae had purchased.

Whatever may have transpired between Mae and her father in the past, she was saddened by his death. They had become close in his final months. In Hollywood she had even referred to him as 'my best friend'. She had grown to realize that the things to which she objected in his character, such as his temper, his buccaneering spirit and his refusal to conform, were the very qualities which he had passed on to her and which had helped make her a star.

Battling Jack's death affected her, but by no means as severely as had Tillie's. Unlike Tillie, her father had lived to see her become famous, and that was a consolation. She had the twin battlements of fame and fortune to buffer her against the harshness of the world. The feeling of panic which had accompanied her mother's death did not overwhelm her again.

All things considered, Battling Jack had had a good life. He had spent his youth as a prototype lager lout, good-naturedly punching his way to local fame; he had married a beautiful and spirited woman who gave him three surviving children, the eldest of whom had kept him in luxury in his declining years. His middle years had been spent coasting about America, and he had roistered around Hollywood in his twilight. Not a bad innings. There had not been a single moment when he had been burdened by life's responsibilities. Mae viewed life far more seriously.

And it had been a particularly serious time for her that spring, when news of Frank Wallace percolated into the newspapers.

The press had been trying to dig up scandal about Mae ever since she emerged into the limelight, but without success. She behaved impeccably in public. Her private life seemed a closed book and apart from a few provocative jibes at her co-stars she never indulged in gossip. Jim lived next door and was ostensibly her manager. Aside from him, her closest companions were her family. She did not have a boyfriend and had announced publicly, many times, that she abhorred women who carried on with married men. Pretty poor pickings for the press from the world's greatest sex bomb, and too good to be true.

There were, of course, her lovers and gossip thrived, but no one could prove a thing. Most of the couplings took place in her apartment and the toing and froing was conducted with discretion. When scandal erupted, it did so quite unexpectedly, from a forgotten corner of her life. Her marriage was uncovered by accident.

She had married Frank Wallace in 1911 in Milwaukee. They had never divorced but given Jim's threats, Frank had disappeared 'permanently' from her life. What Mae could never have foreseen was that the marriage certificate itself would come to light. This happened when municipal workers in Milwaukee decided to index marriage records. Mae's certificate suddenly surfaced. Within hours the press were in Milwaukee in droves. A married Mae was big news.

On this occasion she regretted her listed telephone number. Ignoring the physical evidence of the document's existence, Mae continued to deny her marriage. Many times. An annoying side issue was that the certificate recorded her age as eighteen at the time of her marriage. The press seized upon the point. It did not need an Einstein to work out that she was not thirty-five as she claimed.

'Mae West, the woman who captivated the cinema fans of five continents with the phrase "Come Up and See Me

Sometime", was engaged today in a desperate attempt to discredit reports that, far from being a spinster, she was married ... twenty-four years ago,' reported the *New York Times*. 'She has issued denial after denial from her headquarters in Hollywood. Miss West says she has had to rebuff no fewer than eight gentlemen convinced that they have matrimonial claims on her.'

At first she tried to treat the discovery as a joke, but the press were not going to allow her to get away with that. Two Frank Wallaces were traced to whom the details on the marriage certificate could apply – coincidentally, an actor called Frank Wallace had appeared in *Diamond Lil*. He had played Jimmy Biff, but he had died two years previously so now he was not much use to the journalists.

The other Frank Wallace was Mae's husband. He was living in New York, scratching a living by appearing in what was left of vaudeville. He admitted he had married Mae but claimed they were divorced in 1916. 'I never heard of the guy,'* Mae responded tersely.

As a result of the publicity Frank gained several bookings which might otherwise not have been offered. People wanted to see what he looked like. Having broken his silence he now refused to keep quiet, and cheerfully repeated his claim. What he did was understandable. He had never had a break. Now that the spotlight was shining on him for the first and only time in his life he could not help but milk the situation. Those who saw him perform say he was a fine dancer in the Astaire mould. But while his wife had been luxuriating in California, he had been working the flea pits of New York. If the boot had been on the other foot, and it had been the husband who had achieved success and abandoned the wife, public outrage would have known no bounds. Those were not days of sexual equality, however, and Wallace was regarded as a clown. He was held up to ridicule and Mae refused to have anything to do with him.

Frank, however, also had something to hide from the press. He had stated he was divorced from Mae – not out of regard for

* *New York Times.*

her – but because he was a bigamist. Frank had taken a second wife. Had Mae married Burmester in 1924, as she had surely intended to, that would have made both her and Wallace bigamists. What a beanfeast the press could have extracted from that situation.

Since Wallace could not say he was divorced from his second wife, by sticking to her guns, Mae was able to deflect most of the flak on to him. She continued to maintain she was a spinster. To compound the fiction, she gave an interview to Ruth Biery, expressing hopes that perhaps one day she might find Mr Right. The two ladies had exchanged their much publicized confidences as they glided through town in Mae's Rolls-Royce: ' "I haven't met him yet, but I will, I will," gushed Mae, clearly in a panic and determined to douse the flames engulfing her image. "And I'll know him the moment I see him. And I'll grab him. And we'll have plenty of years, yet."

"And Timony isn't that man, Mae?" asked Miss Biery.

"Timony!" Her voice was startled. The habitual mask crept slowly over the softness that had been so sweetly revealed for that one, brief interlude. "Timony is part of all this!" She waved her hand at the back of the chauffeur, including the rich upholstery of the town car.'

'Timony belongs to Mae West, the public institution,' Miss Biery explained. 'But there is going to be another . . . and she will know him the moment she sees him. When love, real love, comes again, she isn't going to let the Public Institution or anyone who is a part of it, hold her back.'*

Good old Ruth Biery, who had probably guessed the truth or some of it anyhow, was proving her value as a friend. The real Mae, however, shines through at the end of the interview. Miss Biery was too astute a reporter to let romance completely blur the picture. She continues: ' "Of course," she [Mae] was lying back now, her furs snuggled imperiously around her, "a woman can marry, anytime. But you got to hold on to fame as long as you've got it. You can't let anything interfere. You've got to live for your public . . . I don't regret it." '

* _Movie Classic_, c. 1935.

Miss Biery ends her piece, 'I found myself shaking my head.' More likely, Mae shook her hand. Very warmly.

The furore by no means put her off men. In the autumn of that year she met another lover. The identity of the featherweight champion boxer, Chalky Wright, came to light years later under exceptional circumstances. The following account of conversations between Chalky and the male dancer Maxie Bailey, plus Bailey's observations of Mae, was given by Bailey to Public Notary Fred Otash in a sworn statement.*

Bailey had come to Los Angeles in search of work. One night he found himself standing outside the Club Alabam, with just four cents in his pocket, hoping to tap some of the entertainers for a handout when they came out. He was approached by a wiry black man who told him he was a boxer. He said his name was Chalky Wright, and when he discovered Bailey was destitute gave him $10.

The following night Wright and Bailey met again and Wright passed over another $10 and told Bailey that he worked for Mae West as her chauffeur. Bailey asked why he did not wear a uniform and Wright replied the job was 'a front'. 'I am not the chauffeur,' he said. 'I am the man.'

The two men continued to meet and Wright always tipped Bailey $10. When Bailey asked where Wright lived he told him he lived with Mae West. Wright added that he had to keep coming into town as he needed other women, one woman was not enough for him. He then divulged to Bailey certain specific details about Mae's sexual anatomy and performance, but added that if Bailey ever saw him with 'the boss' he was to stay away.

Bailey did see the two of them one evening when a limousine pulled up in front of the Hotel Dunbar at 3 a.m. and Mae and Wright got out. They did not enter the hotel but crossed the road to an after-hour spot which they went into, arm in arm, and sat down at a table.

Bailey followed them into the club and propped himself up at

* It is through Otash's good offices, a distinguished private detective formerly with the Los Angeles Police Department, that the following information can be recounted.

the bar where he could get a good view of the pair. Chalky was sprawled on his chair and Mae had her arms draped around him. Bailey thought they looked as though they were in love.

A week later Bailey saw them again, in the same joint. 'I almost died at what I saw,' he said, 'and wished that woman's bosom was against me, like it was against Chalky Wright. While I was observing them, Miss West yelled "Just a minute!" and Chalky hit the table real hard. Up to that point Mae West was all smiles, but now it looked like there was going to be an argument.' Bailey left.

Bailey and Wright met the next day and Wright confessed he was in love with Mae. Wright then reached in his pocket and took out a wad of dollar bills. Peeling off $100 he gave them to Bailey and repeated that chauffeuring was 'only a front. I am the man of the house'. He then told Bailey that if he [Bailey] was as generously endowed sexually as was Wright then he, too, could be in good financial shape. Wright further told Bailey that Mae loved 'men like him, but a lot of movie stars do also'. So, it appears, Mae sometimes did go out at night.

As with most of her lovers Mae was good to Chalky. She not only gave him cash, but took over his management, backed him as a boxer and, at his admission, helped him gain a world championship. She continued to help him financially throughout her life. And, in his way, Chalky was a chip off the old block: when in funds he was always a soft touch, particularly to down-and-out blacks – viz. his handouts to Bailey.

chapter fifteen

CENSORSHIP

Klondike Annie is different from any other Mae West film. In it she allows us to see the morose side of her character for the first time. In the first half of the picture she comes over as bitter, even chilling – hard-boiled enough to commit murder and not regret it. Her performance shows that she was capable of portraying a wider range of emotions than she'd previously demonstrated. She is an accomplished dramatic actress. But Mae was not interested in acting; she was interested in remaining a star, and, in keeping with the mentality of most stars, she required her films to serve as vehicles for her personality.

The script for *Klondike Annie*, by Marion Morgan and George B. Dowell (who had worked on *Goin' to Town*), had been sent to Mae by William Le Baron. He had been plying her with stories long before she finished *Goin' To Town*, but none of them appealed to her and she had refused them all. Six months went by in such shilly-shallying and it was now time for her to get back into harness.

Klondike Annie bore a similarity to her own play, *Frisco Kate*, upon which she had been haphazardly working since her pre-Hollywood days. She now saw an opportunity to bring *Frisco Kate* to the screen by combining her story with the Morgan/Dowell script. She wrote a screenplay which she sent Le Baron and told him she was prepared to start work. The credits for the film include an acknowledgement for 'additional material' to one Frank Mitchell Dazey, of whom Mae writes, 'I can't remember this boy or how he got into the act.'*

* *Goodness Had Nothing To Do With It*, W. H. Allen, 1960.

183

Set once again in the Nineties, the story concerns Rose Carl-
ton who sings in San Francisco's Chinatown in a club owned by
her Chinese lover. She plans to escape his jealousy by bolting
on a ship bound for Alaska. He discovers her plans and tries to
kill her, but during the struggle she accidentally stabs him to
death – just as she had stabbed Russian Rita to death in *She
Done Him Wrong*. She flees to the boat and, once on board, has
an affair with the captain who learns she is on the run.

En route a nun boards too, but she soon dies of a fever.
When the law subsequently appears looking for Rose, she
switches clothes with the corpse, makes up its face, and it is
assumed by the police that the dead nun is Rose. She maintains
the deception at the Klondike mission for which the nun had
been bound. Through her efforts the mission is revitalized and
begins to bulge with converts.

Meanwhile she has another affair, this time with a mounted
policeman. The captain learns of it and confronts the mountie.
Realizing she is ruining the mountie's career, Rose decides to
leave the mission. She does so in a spectacular fashion, donning
her tart's clothes and making up her face to resemble a prostitute's. In the captain's company she returns to San Francisco to
prove her innocence.

Shooting started in the autumn of 1935 and, as usual, the
film underwent several title changes, including *The Frisco Doll*
and *Klondike Lou*. Raoul Walsh,* her director, was a former
actor who had been in films since the days of D. W. Griffith. Of
mixed Irish and Spanish descent, he wore a patch over one eye
which gave him a raffish look.

There was little about the motion picture industry with which
Walsh was not acquainted. Gloria Swanson, with whom he had
appeared in *Sadie Thompson*, adored him and described him as

---

* Walsh had directed Theda Bara's silent hit *Carmen*. 'Destiny's Dark Angel'
had retired and was now Mrs Charles Brabin, a wealthy Beverly Hills matron.
But was security a fair exchange for stardom? Now and then the calm of her
mansion was rent as Mrs Brabin's fist crashed against a hard surface and her
voice was heard to scream, 'I started out as a star and remained one!' (*From
Hollywood*, DeWitt Bodeen, Tantivy Press, 1976).

'tall and robustly good-looking, with a huge, boyish grin and a shock of curly fair hair, and so shy that he blushed . . .'

Fortunately he did not blush over Mae's problems with the censor, who was already vehemently objecting to her script. Not just the customary *double entendres* but the religious theme were found distasteful. It was considered objectionable to portray a love affair between mixed races. Rose and her China-man were not on.

Mae did much for racial equality (providing this did not damage her appeal at the box office, in which case she would always back down). Enjoying black lovers herself, it was as though she was trying to redress the balance for the injustices perpetrated by white racist America against black people.

In Walsh she found a strong ally. He had experienced censor-ship trouble himself while *Sadie Thompson* was being made. He and Swanson had faced insuperable difficulties. Swanson writes of these in her memoirs: 'In any discussion of frankness and censorship in Hollywood, the play *Rain* [*Sadie Thompson* is based on Maugham's *Rain*] inevitably came up . . . Such things might be all right for theatre audiences, Hollywood censors felt, but movie audiences must be spared . . . Raoul and I sat around a table under the trees and conspired about how best to break the Hays code.'* Nine years later, Walsh was again sitting with his star, conspiring how best to break the Hays Code.

Mae wanted her new film to shock. Her novelty value was beginning to pall. *Goin' To Town* had been a big success but its receipts were not as huge as they had been for *She Done Him Wrong* and *I'm No Angel*. The effects of the Hays Office had been felt: it was no longer so easy to shock an audience. Previously she had been described as 'a monster of lubricity, menacing the sacred institution of the American family' – that would now take some living up to.

John Douglas Eames writes of this period in her career, 'Mae West didn't give a damn, just as long as they kept talking about her and the dollars kept rolling in.' This was not quite the case. She certainly had to ensure that the dollars kept rolling in, but

* *Swanson on Swanson*, Michael Joseph, 1981.

she also had to give a damn or the morality groups would have finished her career and she knew it.

She was sensitive about her position with Paramount. Although still Queen of the Lot, Marlene Dietrich was at that very moment making *Desire* with Gary Cooper, Paramount's greatest male star. The papers were full of Dietrich stories.

Dietrich had, at first, conducted her own press interviews but was no longer allowed to do so, as she had disgusted Zukor by chatting to reporters about her baby. This was not the sort of weak stuff a *femme fatale* was supposed to dish up. Zukor insisted a publicity man accompany her at interviews to ensure the right air of enchantment was woven about her.

Many people expected there to be animosity between Mae and Dietrich but there was not. The two stars got on well. Dietrich was impressed with Mae's down-to-earth attitude to the business and, in her autobiography *My Life*,* she pays tribute to her:

> She ... gave me good advice. She gave me the strength I lacked with a sensitivity that astonished me ... She was never a 'mother' to me, since she wasn't the motherly sort. For me she was a teacher, no, a rock to which I clung, an intelligent woman who understood me and who divined all my problems. At that time, I don't think she was aware of what a great influence she had on me ... When I read Ernst Lubitsch's screenplay for *Desire*, I was horrified: the film was to begin with a close-up of my legs ... Yet, for me they had only one purpose; they make it possible for me to walk ... But Mae West advised me to ... let the producers have their own way. She always had a thousand good reasons for her opinion and I listened to her ... Mae West was wonderful, intelligent, shrewd and understood her metier.

Mae mentions in her book, *On Sex, Health and ESP*,** that while at Paramount she was attending her hair one day when a

* Weidenfeld & Nicolson, 1989.
** W. H. Allen, 1975.

female star walked in and offered to wash it for her. Mae declined. 'I was afraid it wasn't all on my head.' Various writers have identified the star as Dietrich and the story is in keeping with Dietrich's persona. She seemed to encourage speculation about her sexual ambivalence. During the 1930s she took to wearing men's suits around Hollywood, which she sometimes exchanged for a tuxedo and monocle. Kenneth Anger describes her as 'a joyous bisexual'.*

Mae's leading man was Victor McLaglen, whose burly appeal owed much to his truck-driver image, unlike the more subtle drawling sexuality of Cooper. McLaglen's physicality contrasted well with that of the stage actor Philip Reed, who played the Mountie Jack Forrest. British-born McLaglen was a fine actor, but Mae had chosen him for a more fundamental reason. Even she admitted that she was now 'slightly over-weight'. That was an understatement. She was as plump as a pouter pigeon, the fattest she had ever been on screen.

Such embarrassing plumpness would have been emphasized had Mae co-starred with a lean actor like Cooper. McLaglen's very heftiness made her seem slimmer. She also liked him and, apparently, the feeling was mutual. Some years later he was asked about Mae in an interview and burst into spontaneous laughter, shook his head as though at the misdemeanours of some naughty child and said affectionately, 'Oh, dear!'

Midway through filming, while the project still bore the title *Klondike Lou*, Mae had an appointment with Idwal Jones, a features writer for the *St Paul Daily News*. He never got to meet her, being cut out at the last moment by the arrival of million-aire Gordon Selfridge, from the London store that still bears his name. Mae never slighted a millionaire; she never knew when she might need backing. But Jones still wrote his piece:

> The other morning I came to see her stage on the Paramount lot, a vast concrete hangar with a door a foot thick. Before it was posted the grimmest of armed sen-tinels. I proferred him the documents; letters of marque

* *Hollywood Babylon*, Arrow Books, 1986.

and *carte blanche*, a gate pass and a special set pass, all graced with high-priced signatures. He thumbed them with distrust. Then he spoke inward, from the threshold, to the assistant director, and a slow wink from that gentleman delivered me from the secular arm, who withdrew with reluctance, as if he didn't know what the world was coming to.

There isn't much to do on any set, once you are into it, except look around.

The off room, where the cameras were grinding on Miss West, was full of smoke, bright lights and furnishings even more lurid, for it was a bed chamber. You can either look on or else sit among the palms and smoke. Nobody cares how much you smoke in the studio. But you can't make any noise when the cameras are turning. They make a faint buzz, everybody hushes at once and stands frozen as in a *tableau vivant*.

The silence is mesmeric. In all progress there is some loss. The mad, careless ease of the silent days when players could yield to song, snores, rows over black-jack and the adorable clamour of the melodeon and cornet, pumping out mood music, we have bartered for the tyranny of the microphone.

Goethe said one may not walk under palms with impunity. Something is bound to happen to you. Quite as insidious is the effect of sitting among Miss West's abundant and synthetic palms.

Miss West came out of her off room, hemmed about with maids, secretaries and cinema adepts. She was in platinum and black, moved with larger dash than usual. There was some argument. She was strong for a crushing 'Oh yeah?' remark in the dialogue. Nobody ever said that in the Nineties, the dialogue writer was pleading. 'Nobody ever!'

They were still arguing when a group of distinguished visitors bore up. Only eminent persons visit a Mae West set. They look in awe at the players, and the players look in awe at them. One of the visitors, the central one, was notable in the extreme, with *pince-nez*, moustache and a hearty clubman geniality. He looked remarkably like Gordon Selfridge. For a wonder it was Gordon Selfridge, fresh from London. The meeting of the modern Aphra Behn and the merchant prince was brief but exuberant. This was the colloquy: 'How Do you do, Mr Selfridge?'

'How Do you do, Miss West? I liked your last picture.'

'You mean my latest, I hope? Thanks. I hope you'll like this one. And I hope to be in London in a few weeks.'

'By all means, come up and see me—'

Mr Selfridge said it first and merriment prevailed as it invariably does on these bright occasions. Miss West smiled amiably, she always allows her visitors the prerogative of this *bon mot*. Some say she is tired of hearing it; some insist she isn't and that she is gratified at the viability of this trademark, which hasn't yet showed signs of fading, any more than if it were cut in immemorial bronze.

'*C'est très ennuyeux, cette phrase,*' sighed Madame Wong Wing, offering me some watermelon seeds. 'Even in Peking and Canton one hears it much.'

Mae was always saying she was going to visit London or Paris. These cities held a fascination for her.

By 1935 the movie business was finding its feet again. Under President Roosevelt's 'New Deal' the worst of the Depression was over and, although it wasn't all roses the American economy had in part stabilized. Change was in the air at Paramount. The studio was solvent. In order to cash in on its renewed prosperity the company employed a new breed of executive, men who neither cared about, nor understood, artistic integrity and whose only master was the budget sheet. Personnel disappeared overnight and new faces arrived. Such was the turmoil that Zukor, based in New York, had to travel to Hollywood to sort out the upheaval.

There were many new faces around the front office, too. Hard-boiled faces whom Mae did not know. Among them was Ernst Lubitsch.

German-born producer/director Lubitsch was the new production chief at Paramount. He had gained a reputation for
excellence by directing a series of elegant comedies. The
'Lubitsch Touch' became synonymous with sophisticated
humour. He went on to direct Garbo in *Ninotchka*, for which
the sultry Swede traded in her escutcheon of tragedy for comedy at which, surprisingly, she excelled. 'Garbo Laughs!' proclaimed the publicity. So she did, and so did the audiences.

But Mae was not laughing. She could not abide Lubitsch.
Although he was production chief, which was a desk job, he
was an artist to his fingertips and had strong views about how
comedy should be presented. He had, indeed, been a comedian
himself in the silent era. Mae had her own strong ideas too and
they did not coincide with those of Lubitsch.

His habit of puffing a cigar did nothing to endear him to her.
She did not see their joint futures blossoming, and they got off
to a bad start: shortly after assuming his new position Lubitsch,
with monumental insensitivity, issued a press release which
Mae considered insulted her:

> Mae West has proved beyond a doubt that she is one of the
> greatest international stars in Hollywood. But she is not a
> director's star. Her personality is quite powerful enough to
> fill out any picture, and there is no room left for directorial
> technique. Her films are vehicles built around her, and I,
> personally, cannot make a good picture unless I am deal-
> ing with someone more pliable.

Although this was not necessarily derogatory, it was certainly a
criticism. It inferred that Mae West was difficult. It was a dis-
loyal statement for any company executive to voice publicly
about one of his senior artists.

In an interview with journalist William Scott Eyman, Mae
told of a skirmish she had had with Lubitsch:

> He had a habit of picking out the best scenes in all the
> films shooting on the lot, going on the set the day that
> scene was to be shot and doing it himself. What could the

other directors say? He was the head of the studio! So one day he shows up at my dressing room with a script.

'I want to direct you in a scene.'

'Oh yeah? How about doing a whole picture?'

'I'm head of the studio now, and I don't have much time – just this one little scene.'

'Which scene?'

'How about this one?'

'That scene is the best in the picture. It doesn't need you. Why don't you take a weak scene, one that could use the famous Lubitsch touch?'

He got this funny expression on his face, jammed that big cigar (which he was never without) in his mouth and walked away. But what else could I do? Stuff like that just wasn't fair to the other directors. I think I hurt his feelings.*

It was not just his feelings she hurt, she once slapped him across the face in front of the crew. No studio head would accept such humiliation.

Lubitsch's dour personality seemed to permeate *Klondike Annie*, making it the least convivial of her projects to date. He was an unhappy man who should never have accepted his position at Paramount in the first place; he did not have the right disposition for a desk job. He lasted just a year before relinquishing the job to William Le Baron, who had been hankering after it ever since it had been given to Lubitsch. Le Baron stuck at it until 1938, by which time he, too, had had enough.

Mae then began to argue with Raoul Walsh. Karl Struss – her favourite cameraman – was not with her on this film and she felt she needed him. Because of her weight she was feeling vulnerable about her looks. Struss was working elsewhere and could not break his contract. She blasted Walsh for being inefficient because he hadn't secured his services beforehand. She distrusted the work of every cameraman assigned to her, com-

* *Take One*, 1972.

plaining she was being badly shot and insisting on retakes. Her figure made her unduly sensitive about her clothes and she rejected numerous specially designed gowns. Because she was unhappy at work, she did not rush to get there and was consistently late. When Lubitsch ticked her off she arrived even later to spite him.

She did not completely lose her good humour, however. Among the ex-boxers who (as usual) padded out the cast was Italian Kid Moreno. He was rather slow-witted but had been given a single line to say, 'There's a boatload of guns in the harbour.' Not a quick learner, the taut atmosphere of the studio made the line difficult for him to remember. Kindly stagehands taught him the line as 'There's a boatload of cunts in the harbour.' This he duly delivered to Mae during the shoot. 'Bring them ashore,'* she answered without missing a beat.

The Hays Office was also giving her headaches; she still employed the technique of inserting provocative lines, which she knew would be expunged, then replacing them with her original ideas. The ploy no longer worked. The completed film was released on 21 February 1936 (having come in behind schedule and over-budget) to withering reviews. According to the *Boston Transcript*, 'There was a singular lack of variety in her acting. Not only is she the same in one part after another, but there is an unvarying sameness to her expression within a given characterization.'

The East Coast Preview Committee damned the film as 'Replete with insinuations, a typical Mae West picture with the usual amount of risqué wisecracks and obvious sex appeal.' From 1950 onwards, to be described as possessing sex appeal was to receive a compliment, but in 1936 it amounted to an accusation of wantonness.

The Hearst press, whose proud boast was that its thirty different newspaper titles were on fifteen million American breakfast tables every day, was predictably outraged. Hearst's

* *Mae West: The Lies, The Legends, The Truth*, George Eells and Stanley Musgrove, Robson Books, 1989.

indignation hit boiling point when he learned of her 'blasphemy' in impersonating a nun. Editorially, he fumed, 'Is it not time Congress did something about Mae West?' Much later Mae laconically retorted in *Goodness Had Nothing To Do With It* that 'The nearest Congress came to that was almost naming twin lakes, round ones, after me.'

Hearst was a vicious enemy and his papers refused to carry advertisements for the film. This policy reached the heights of ridiculousness when the New York *Daily Mirror* published an advertisement for the orchestra scheduled to play on the same bill as *Klondike Annie* without mentioning the main attraction, the film itself. Likewise the Seattle *Post-Intelligencer*, belying its name, printed details of a film entitled *Every Saturday Night*, which was the B picture playing with *Klondike Annie*.

In Chicago, a Hearst editorial cited *Klondike Annie* as evidence that 'the Hays organization cannot be depended upon to suppress the kind of film of which *Klondike Annie* is an odiferous example'.

The scene which caused most offence was the one in which Rose made up the dead nun's face to resemble that of a prostitute. Such was the outcry that the whole scene had to be deleted. Inveighing against this scene, the *Hollywood Reporter* noted, 'Situations rather than lines offend.'

Somehow, cinema managers, who after all were out for a profit, managed to dupe Hearst. His own papers carried small ads which read, 'Important Feature. For information call VA-2041' (the number varied from town to town). This was the number of the local cinema. Every citizen who rang a number was given details of the local showing of *Klondike Annie*.

The Paramount publicity department, out of touch as usual with the main office, hardly defused the situation by saturating the country with posters proclaiming 'She Made the Frozen North . . . Red Hot!'

Mae was hoisted by her own petard. She had hoped that the religious content of the film might gain her support from the moralists, and had even included very un-Westian lines, such as 'Any time you take religion for a joke, the laugh's on you.' But her intentions backfired horribly, and the purity leagues

were up in arms – how could Mae West have the temerity to
even pretend to portray a missionary?

Klondike Annie was banned from exhibition in Lincoln,
Nebraska, after the intervention of county attorney Max Towell.
The attorney was joined in his denunciation of the film by
Bishop Hugh Ryan of the Omaha Catholic diocese, who urged
his parishioners to boycott it.

The Legion of Decency backed these gentlemen and issued a
press release stressing the need for continued vigilance 'on the
part of all persons interested in the maintenance of a wholesome screen':

> The subject in question, being of low moral character,
> widely advertised and presenting a performer who both
> upon the screen and the stage has in several instances
> been associated with plays which have elicited widespread
> disapproval, creates an apprehension that unless there is
> renewed vigilance, together with a determination on the
> part of the public to discourage the production of such
> films the excellent progress in the improvement of the
> moral character of the films in the past several months
> may be lost.
>
> This film and all such films are held to be in some
> measure an invasion of public and private morality, cre-
> ating as they do an unwholesome impression upon theatre
> patrons and particularly the youth. This film has been
> classified by the Legion of Decency as being 'objectionable
> in part' because while under the Legion's classification it
> is not held to be vicious in its entirety, yet it is regarded
> as a subject which contains numerous objectionable inci-
> dents and consequently should be avoided by the Catholic
> public.
>
> The National Legion of Decency urges the producers of
> motion pictures to avoid the production of subjects of this
> character and to direct their attention exclusively to those
> wholesome types of picture for which the American public
> has repeatedly demonstrated overwhelming preference.

The American public, currently, was demonstrating an over-whelming preference for *Klondike Annie*. Business was boom-ing. In New York the film had opened at the vast Paramount Theater and crowds literally fought with each other to get in and see what all the fuss was about. Normally, the theatre opened its doors at 10.30 a.m. and started its last show of the day at midnight. But such was the demand for seats that the opening time was put forward to 8.30 a.m., with the final screening taking place at 2 a.m.

In San Francisco the story was the same. The movie opened at the Warfield Cinema and the Hearst press carried a series of statements by prominent citizens denouncing it. There was a stampede for tickets.

Mae did not take any of the accusations of immorality lying down. 'The trouble is,' she explained in a newspaper item cap-tioned 'Mae West's Cross' (which must have delighted her Catholic persecutors), 'that when any other actress says an ordi-nary line it's all right with everybody. When I say the same line, everybody reads a double meaning into it . . . Sex, or glamour, whatever you like to call it, is how I earn my living. It's my particular style, and it's getting harder to put across. Any other actress has a whole troupe of bright, young writers thinking up things for her to say. I think up my own things to say, but I have a troupe of experts to tell me I can't say them. It simply isn't fair.'

The Legion of Decency continued to gain support from public figures, including Mrs James F. Looram, Chairperson of the motion picture faction of the International Federation of Catholic Alumnae.

An extraordinary anomaly occurred when the Massachusetts Department of Public Safety, the body which administered the state censorship law, passed *Klondike Annie* as suitable for exhibition. This was the very department which had rejected *Rose Marie* as being unsuitable a short time previously. *Rose Marie*, the film version of Rudolf Friml's musical, tells the story of a mountie's chase after a criminal and his romance with a sophisticated opera singer. Starring Jeanette MacDonald and Nelson Eddy (with Gilda Gray, Mae's rival 'shimmy' dancer, in

a cameo role), it is the epitome of innocuous charm. It is difficult to imagine what Massachusetts could possibly have objected to. The department realized it had made a blunder by
banning *Rose Marie*, and to the Legion of Decency's consterna-
tion opted not to make any more waves and passed *Klondike
Annie*.

Amidst the chorus of disapproval, support was offered Mae
from an unlikely source. The National Society of New England
Women expressed the opinion that, 'This film is not without
value to a certain class of adult audiences.' It did not specify
which class.

As the dispute raged, Mae did as she customarily did and
made a coast-to-coast promotional tour. Her appearances drew
vast, noisy crowds and sometimes violence broke out outside
the cinemas where she appeared. Her act was as undiluted and
full of brazen innuendo as ever. It seemed little else filled the
columns of the newspapers.

On 6 June 1936, still promoting the film, she made the first
air flight of her life. The journey was from San Francisco to Los
Angeles. Mae told the press she enjoyed the experience but, in
truth, she had loathed it. Aeroplanes terrified her and in the
future she would only fly in an emergency. But Mae West could
not admit to personal vulnerability so, as far as the press was
concerned, it had been a great experience.

In Kansas City the *Journal Post* devoted a whole page to a
largely hostile article about her. It included the paragraph,
'Mae West has been fired by one movie producer and hired by
another. Though her pictures draw big crowds, there are many
cinema patrons who would not have felt bereaved if Mae had
not got that second contract.'

She had not been fired, but the article was true in substance.
A change in her fortunes was being brought about by the
machinations of the machiavellian Emanuel Cohen, whom
Budd Schulberg had likened to a 'watchful toad'.

chapter sixteen

THE FREELANCE

Budd Schulberg's father, B. P. Schulberg, did not mince words either. He went further and called Cohen a 'master of the double-cross'. This description is justified given what Cohen did when he was production chief at Paramount, the position occupied in 1935 by Ernst Lubitsch.

As the contracts of various artists expired, instead of offering them new Paramount contracts, Cohen signed them up to his own personal management. In effect the stars were his to use as he thought fit. Among the artists he had stolen, via this system, were such high earners as Gary Cooper, Bing Crosby and Mae.

Both *Goin' To Town* and *Klondike Annie* were made under the aegis of Major Pictures, the company Cohen had created. His next step was to place Mae under his personal contract. Mae's advisors, among them Jim (who, be it remembered, was an attorney) and Murray Feil of the William Morris Agency, participated in Mae's transfer of allegiance. Paramount, it seems, was not on the ball. By the time the company attorney Henry Herzbrun discovered the sleight-of-hand, Cooper, Crosby and Mae were no longer technically Paramount artists, but under contract to Cohen.

Cohen was not on the lot at the time of the discovery, but on the luxury Santa Fe Chief train on his way to a Paramount business meeting in Chicago. Sam Katz, financial director of Paramount, reacted swiftly. A telegram, firing him out of hand, reached Cohen while he was still in transit.

When Herzbrun discovered that Mae had signed a contract with Cohen to start production on a new picture as from April 1936, he declared her in contempt of her Paramount contract.

Murray Feil rose to Mae's defence by announcing, 'Miss West notified Paramount six weeks ago her contract had been abrogated by the studio when it failed to have a picture ready for her last July.'

Mae's contract with Paramount specified she had to make two movies a year. She argued that she had made only one complete picture for the company in 1935 – *Klondike Annie* – the shooting of which had begun in September and concluded just before Christmas. Her previous film, *Goin' To Town*, had been started on 18 December 1934 and wasn't completed until February 1935. She had Paramount over a barrel, as she obviously had not completed two pictures in 1935.

But, although the company had been negligent, it had fulfilled the spirit of her contract. Whichever way the dispute is viewed, Mae had been less than straightforward. Paramount had given her her start and she had used a legal anomaly to free herself. In her defence the company was not made up in 1936 of the same people with whom she had begun to work. She detested most of the new executives and believed, accurately, they were prepared to use her until the public tired of her and then they would discard her. She moved in a cesspit of dishonourable people. Katz has been described as a 'monster' and Cohen a 'rat'; Mae proved that even if she was not like them she could certainly handle them.

Although Cohen's behaviour was indefensible – he had been a Paramount employee while appropriating the company's artists – he, too, was justified in what he had done. Lubitsch was squeezing him out and he had his back to the wall.

Legal action loomed. On 14 March 1936 the *Motion Picture Herald* reported:

The end of Mae West's career at Paramount is not news, but the technicalities of the abrogation are ... Mae West and the Paramount studio in Hollywood are jointly accusing each other of voiding her contract ... Out of a welter of conflicting statements and whatnot only one fact seemed clear – that Mae West would make her next picture, and the one after that, for another company, presumably Emanuel Cohen's Major Pictures. A Paramount statement . . . charged Mae West with being guilty of 'an anticipatory breach of contract', adding, 'an executive who would not be quoted said, "The studio does not waive any of its rights to her services." '

The crux of the matter was expressed by Murray Feil who explained, 'The new Mae West deal with Manny Cohen called for Mr Cohen to pay the star some $300,000 each for two pictures.' As always, Mae had responded to a cash offer, but this was not the main reason for her transfer of allegiance. She was convinced Paramount held no plans to promote her career; under the new administration, she knew her demands to control her pictures would not be sympathetically treated. As far as the new executives were concerned Mae represented the old days (four years is a long time in the movie industry). It was also predicted that she was burning out and her drawing power would fade. Despite the revenue she generated she was too much trouble. The new élite wanted to bring in artists of its own choice.

After much wrangling both sides reached a compromise. They had to, otherwise the matter would have been tied up in the courts for years, running up thousands of dollars in expenses to both parties. 'The score here is even,' announced *Motion Picture Herald*. 'Paramount apparently not wanting to continue producing Mae West pictures and Mae evidently desiring a change to Manny Cohen.' 'Paramount didn't seem like home to me anymore,' wrote Mae of that time.*

On the brink of letting her go, Paramount learnt of an offer Mae had received from a rival studio, RKO Radio Pictures. Unaware that Mae had actually signed with Cohen, RKO had offered her a contract for $300,000 per film, with $100,000 for each story line filmed, plus a share of the profits – a similar deal to the one she had already accepted from Cohen. Columbia had also expressed interest in her.

These offers caused Paramount to rethink. If Mae was con-

* *Goodness Had Nothing To Do With It*, W. H. Allen, 1960.

sidered such a valuable property elsewhere, it would be profligate to discard her. An amended deal was finally agreed upon by all parties, whereby Mae would make films for Cohen, and these would be released by Paramount, for screening at the Paramount cinema chain.

Hoping to start their partnership on the right footing, Cohen presented Mae with a diamond and ruby brooch. As in the old days, everyone gathered to celebrate in the front office. Champagne flowed and toasts were made.

It was like starting all over again for Mae. Her past successes counted for nothing. Understandably, she viewed the celebration a little sceptically. She was, however, off to a good start. A Maine newspaper announced, 'Mr Hearst's ban has given Mae more publicity than a million dollars could have bought. *Klondike Annie* has smashed all records in hundreds of American cinemas.'

No champagne was served at the Ravenswood. Poor Beverly. Mae was heavily into health foods by now and carrot juice and bottled water were the order of the day. She believed tap water was bad for her skin, and washed and bathed in natural spring water which was delivered to her apartment in carboys.

Despite Mae's reluctance to invite guests to the Ravenswood, she did not object, when the occasion demanded, to using the apartment for promotional purposes. Journalist Luis Alonzo arrived to interview her one morning and wrote of the domestic confusion in which she seemed to thrive.

She received Alonzo in bed. She was eating her breakfast, which had been served by her maid, Daisy, who came in each day. While answering his questions she made, and took, several telephone calls from the three phones on her bedside table. She rang Murray Feil each morning, and then Jim, although he was only next door. Beverly and her brother Jack were next (if they were not actually in the apartment with her as they often were).

Feil was trying to persuade her to accept some of the lucrative radio offers he had received but she would not agree. 'Hold out for a better offer,' she told him.*

---

* *Picturegoer*, 17 August 1935.

While Alonzo was there Feil arrived in person, followed by two interior decorators. Mae planned to revamp the apartment. They had brought along a photographer to take pictures from which they could work.

Then, Alonzo writes, in came 'a seedy individual', an ex-boxer and former colleague of Battling Jack's. Down on his luck, he had rung Mae the previous day and been told to come round. Shouting for Daisy to bring her handbag, Mae then gave him some money. Alonzo recalled her words: 'Glad to see you,' said Mae. 'Yeah, times are tough. I'm trying to find a spot for you somewhere in the studio . . . Poor devil,' she added when he had left.

Another journalist arrived to interview her but was interrupted by Daisy, who announced that Marianne, Mae's pet chihuahua, was unwell. Marianne was an addition to the household and Mae doted on her, taking her everywhere either tucked under her arm or with the dog trotting along beside her on a jewelled lead. The vet was phoned; he promised to come round immediately.

Beverly then dropped in followed by Mae's hairdresser. Meanwhile Le Baron rang, urging her to read a script which he was sending round by courier. His call was followed by one from Cohen, who suggested Mae should have some new studio portraits taken and could an appointment be made? After this an unknown Englishman rang. He was a friend of a friend. Would she possibly see him for a moment? 'Yeah, why not?' said Mae.

The mail brought hundreds of letters, which were sorted by a secretary who came in five days a week. Mae dictated her replies. No request for a photograph was turned down and no fan letter ignored. There were many letters from hopefuls requesting advice on how to start a film career. Whole forests must have been cut down to provide paper for the numerous charities who besieged her with requests to attend functions and to donate personal items for auction.

Jewellers sometimes called when they had something special to offer her and she became an expert on gems. Her favourites were star sapphires and rubies. She never touched a stone with an off-centre star. A New York correspondent who interviewed her noted, 'On her left hand she sported a giant sapphire ring, widely circled with diamonds. On the same arm were three dazzling bracelets. The one nearest the wrist, about two inches wide, was of diamonds, surmounted by a star sapphire of 125 carats. The other two were wide bands of diamonds. Her right hand flaunted a ring in which an enormous diamond was held by invisible prongs.' That would be what Mae termed her 'small dinner set'.

If she had a couple of days off, Mae would sometimes stay at the ranch with the family. She had a pair of overalls she would don before she tottered off on her stiletto heels to pet the horses. Marianne nervously trotted at her feet, shivering, because of the refinement of her breeding.

After Boogie's death Mae had purchased another couple of monkeys, but they were generally kept at the ranch; it is impossible to housetrain monkeys and, love them as she did, there was no way they could be allowed to defecate over her French décor. The monkeys were put in diapers for her visits as she liked to nurse them, but did not want to risk spoiling her clothes. If one had an accident she would squeal and hand it quickly to John.

Her trips to the ranch never lasted long, but even so it was a relief to John and Beverly (who sometimes stayed over with John) when she had gone. They could not enjoy a drink with bossy Mae there. They had to get sloshed behind her back.

Mae had spent too long in cities to be happy away from the masses. 'I like to know that there are crowds passing in front of my place,' she told an unnamed paper. 'I guess that's left over from New York . . . those great open spaces get on my nerves.' Now and then she toyed with the idea of buying a town house but could not be bothered. The Ravenswood suited her needs.

Mae never met Salvador Dali, but he was fascinated by her. About this time he was working for the Paris-based couturière Elsa Schiaparelli, celebrated for her collaborations with such avant-garde figures as Cocteau, Picasso and Tchelitchev. Schiaparelli gave Dali a free hand and his designs became positively hallucinatory. His compositions included hats shaped

like an upturned shoe, a female ensemble built around the
theme of a lamb chop, and a handbag shaped like a telephone.
Dali paid his tribute to Mae by designing for Schiaparelli a sofa
in the image of Mae's lips. Schiaparelli deemed it frivolous –
clearly not on a par with the exalted lamb chop.

Dali further celebrated Mae with a *trompe l'oeil* in the form
of an entire room reinventing Mae's features. Her hair provides
the curtains, the lip-couch her mouth, and the three steps leading into the room are designed as treble chins. Her eyes are two
framed paintings.

Dali's creation enjoyed a vogue and did much to enhance
Mae's standing with intellectuals, a standing which the French
writer Colette further endorsed: 'Can you honestly name
another artist, male or female, in the cinema,' she asked,
'whose comic acting equals that of this ample blonde who
undulates in little waves . . . whose throat swells with the coos of
a professional dove?'

Madame Schiaparelli recovered from her distaste at Mae
being a source of Dali's inspiration. So much so, that when
Hollywood later beckoned with an offer to design Mae's wardrobe for a film, she accepted. Proving, yet again, the power of
the cheque book.

Mae claimed she found the sofa 'amusing', but she was the
reverse of amused when she was nearly robbed again in the
autumn of 1936.

The garage entrance of the Ravenswood is at the side of the
block. Residents can drive in, park their cars, and take an elevator up to the main building. Mae often left the building around
noon by car and every morning a group of fans would gather
near the garage entrance to watch her leave. She never disappointed them and was always dressed to the nines, with her
gems glittering about her. Sometimes she would get Jack to
bring one of the monkeys over and she would take it with her,
cuddling it as she waved to her fans. Since her first robbery,
however, there were always at least two men with her in the car.
One was Chalky Wright, her lover-cum-chauffeur, and the
other was a bodyguard. Both carried guns. Mae was nervous in
public and for good reason.

A gang of four men entered the Ravenswood garage one afternoon, after the crowd had dispersed, attacked the garage manager whom they tied up and gagged, and held up each car as it arrived, stripping the occupants of their valuables and leaving them gagged and bound. They were a band of cold-blooded professional criminals who systematically robbed the occupants of nine cars. Mae was their prime target. Fortunately for her something alarmed them and they left before she got back.

The news of the attempted robbery, which greeted her upon her return, merely added to her worries. The Legion of Decency was still attacking her; her dispute with Paramount had not yet been settled; and Frank Wallace was refusing to disappear a second time, and had started the first of a series of lawsuits against her.

Having stated the previous year that he was divorced from Mae, he now changed his tactics, admitted that they were still married and sought legal acknowledgement of the marriage. In June he had filed an affidavit in New York, and Mae had been served with a writ. But the action had been dismissed by Justice Cotillo on the technical grounds that the writ 'had been improperly served'. Wallace appealed and a second writ was served on her in September in Los Angeles. She was now forced to take action. On 12 November she filed an affidavit at the New York Supreme Court denying the marriage had taken place and requesting Wallace's suit again be thrown out.

Wallace counter-attacked by stating he could prove she was his lawful spouse and that she dare not appear in the New York courts and face him. Mae fielded his attack by saying that, as a California resident, the New York courts had no jurisdiction over her. She would not give the matter credence by making a court appearance.

Wallace, however, refused to go away. Mae tried to fob him off and among the many press comments attributed to her is the following from a Los Angeles paper: 'Hollywood even gave me a husband,' Miss West laughed. 'It wasn't until I'd been here some time that I ever heard of the gentleman who keeps suing me in New York. I don't know whether to thank Hollywood for that touch or not – after all, I haven't met the man yet.'

During this barrage of publicity, a misprint occurred in a major newspaper which caused her irritation. A New York paper mistakenly printed the year of her marriage as 1905 and this started a run of conjecture as to her real age. Some papers claimed she was forty-nine. Estimates varied, fuelled by the fact she looked neither young nor old. As directrix Marilyn Gaunt says, 'Mae West was born looking forty and stayed that way.'

Eventually the litigation again came to court and New York Supreme Court Justice Callahan took a month to examine the evidence. By now Frank had admitted that he was a bigamist but swore he had divorced his second 'wife'. This revelation, although legally worthy of censure, in no way affected the legality of his marriage to Mae.

Justice Callahan directed Wallace to submit the 'additional proof' he claimed to possess to support his claim on Mae. It duly arrived in the form of letters and a diary, which he claimed was given to him by Mae after they were married. The letters addressed him as 'My dear Frank' and were signed 'With love, Mae'. They offered little proof of marriage and on 16 December 1936 Wallace's suit was again dismissed.

Meanwhile Mae and Cohen were planning their first film together under their new partnership. The rights for Lawrence Riley's stage hit *Personal Appearance* were owned by Paramount, who intended to turn it into a vehicle for Gladys George, who had made it a hit on Broadway. But Mae wanted the story, so Paramount jettisoned Miss George and sold the property to Cohen.

When she received these joyous tidings, Miss George was working for RKO making *Valiant Is the Word for Carrie* with Wesley Ruggles, one of Mae's former directors. The film earned an Academy Award nomination for her, which eventually softened the harshness of the blow Paramount and Mae had jointly dealt her. She would also gain long-term satisfaction from the fact that Mae's version of *Personal Appearance* was her least successful film to date.

Mae insisted on writing the screenplay and changed the title to *Go West Young Man*, a gratifying play of words on her name.

Go West Young Man centres around film star Mavis Arden. During a personal appearance tour throughout America, her car breaks down in rural Pennsylvania. She puts up at a small hotel with her long-suffering press agent, only to fall for a husky young inventor, the boyfriend of the daughter of the house. Through a series of misunderstandings a kidnap alert is put out by the police who are looking for her. As this mess is sorted out, love triumphs in the shape of her press agent, and the inventor is returned to his girl. Mae West never stole a man from another woman.

Henry Hathaway was the director. He was a former child actor who first trod the boards at ten years of age. He had made his directorial début in two-reeler Westerns and had the reputation of being an 'action' director. The same year he worked with Mae he also directed *The Trail of the Lonesome Pine*, the first outdoor film to be shot in Technicolor. He went on to direct numerous hits, including *True Grit*, which provided an Oscar for John Wayne.

Critic Eric Braun wrote of *Go West Young Man* that 'Hathaway . . . failed to make the most of the comedy potential of the situation.' This was not his fault. Mae, as usual, directed her own scenes, which was most of the picture, and brushed aside Hathaway's advice. She did not require innovative directors; she was convinced she could handle that side of things herself. She required directors who made her look beautiful. Hathaway pleased her on that score, and some of his portraits of Mae are striking. Using sometimes unorthodox shots he brings a softness to her face that no other director had achieved.

Randolph Scott is excellent as her leading man. Gauche in manner, he possessed the stunning looks, if not quite the charm, of his live-in friend, and former Mae West leading man, Cary Grant.

The part of Mae's chauffeur in the film is played by boxer Johnny Indrisano. It was common knowledge around town that Indrisano, who sometimes chauffeured Mae in real life, was another of her lovers. He, too, spent much of his time at the Ravenswood where, among his other duties, he supervised her physical training programme.

Indrisano and Chalky Wright inevitably met but, being men of the world, no blood was shed. They joined forces, and sometimes Indrisano was the bodyguard while Wright drove. Neither man touched alcohol, above an occasional beer, when with Mae and both abstained from smoking. Occasionally one or the other would escort her on a short, and reluctantly undertaken, jog along the beach.

In *Go West Young Man* it is impossible to separate Mae West from Mavis Arden. Both are playing each other. Mae makes the moviegoers believe she is taking them into her confidence and permitting a behind-the-scenes peek at her real self. Such intermingling of persona and reality is epitomized by Mavis's curtain speech, a speech she makes at each of the venues across America where she stops to publicize her new film *The Drifting Lady*, much as Mae publicized her own films.

It is pure parody. Mavis undulates to the microphone, stands between two columns of flowers and, hit by a spotlight, addresses her public:

> That, my dear friends, was *The Drifting Lady*. But it was not, please believe me, the real Mavis Arden. I say please, oh please, let me play a part that expresses the real me. A simple, unaffected country girl who finds her happiness in a garden and a swimming pool, but Mr Greenfield [her Producer] always says 'No, no, Mavis, you are a great artist and it wouldn't be fair to deprive the world of your genius.' So, that is why I play these fascinating sirens you seem to like to see. But, oh, I'm such a different person really. Beneath all this glitter, Mavis Arden is a very human person, like yourselves. If you, my dear public, could only come up and see me in my little Italian villa in Hollywood, I'm sure you'd be disappointed in the dullness and simplicity of my life there. I know it's cruel to disillusion you in this way, but I have to be honest and you must take it in the right spirit.

Although Mae's language was less mocking, Mavis's speech bore a resemblance to the speeches Mae was later to make at the curtain calls of her plays. It was her smokescreen to fool her public into believing that the real Mae West in no way resembled the licentious characters she played.

In the 1930s women wore short skirts, but Mae is in full-length gowns throughout the film. This, of course, was to hide her block-like shoes, but such an eccentricity started rumours that her legs were poor, even deformed. There was nothing wrong with her legs apart from the fact they were not very long.

Her shortness had become a complex and she insisted Hathaway photograph Randolph Scott, who was six foot three, so he would not appear too tall in comparison with her. He had to stand in a trench for close-up two-shots. The conversations Scott had with Cary Grant, when they compared notes on working with Mae, can be imagined.

Critics have been unduly harsh to *Go West Young Man*. True, there is less shock value in the dialogue than previously, and the one-liners are poorly represented owing to censorship. Not only did she have the Hays Office with which to contend but Cohen's own nervousness. The film was his baby and he would be in a sticky position should it not pass censorship. Mae's pacing had also slowed down from her earlier films, making her statuesque rather than flamboyant, and inclined to strike poses. It is as though she is discarding her movie technique and reverting to her theatrical style – perhaps a physical manifestation of her psychological condition.

There are, nevertheless, amusing scenes, notably when Mavis is unexpectedly confronted by fans just as she plans to seduce Randolph Scott; and her dealings with a star-struck maid who performs impressions. Her dialogue with Scott is charming and in their scenes together she reveals a previously unknown warmth.

Quick to strike, the Hearst-owned *Motion Picture Herald* vindictively crowed, 'She sings rather pitifully ... and virtually throughout the picture undulates and weaves, giving visual as well as verbal point to the tiresome series of suggestive lines. Incidentally, the fight with obesity seems to be getting her down.'

This oversteps the bounds of criticism. Her singing, particularly in the romantic 'I Was Saying to the Moon' is, as always, delightful. She was a confident vocalist and it is stupid to pretend otherwise. Certainly she is plump, but since when has beauty been the sole prerogative of the thin?

As in all her films, Mae wore a great deal of her own jewellery. Because of this, and her brushes with robbers, the insurance company insisted a small security force should permanently accompany her. Each morning armed outriders waited outside the Ravenswood and travelled alongside her car on its journey to Paramount. Despite the stick-ups and threats, nothing would part Mae from her booty.

'My love of diamonds is just part of theatre tradition,' she said. 'I came up through the school of the road show, vaudeville and so forth, and I have the trouper's point of view. Anyway, it's nice to know the diamonds are there, just in case.'

She made an impressive sight driving about town. She had bought for $20,000 a magnificent *coupe de ville*, chocolate-coloured Rolls-Royce. It is the perfect movie star's car and can be seen in *Go West Young Man*. Mae rented it to Cohen for use in the film. The coachwork was built to her specifications: it is a streamlined art deco masterpiece. Mae would recline among the lace cushions in the back while Chalky drove, a black bodyguard sitting next to him, both men kitted out in matching uniforms to blend with the car. Mae habitually wore white and shone like a pearl midst the dark car and the dark drivers. She stood out even in a city of stars.

When she arrived at her destination both men leapt out. Chalky opened the door and saluted while the bodyguard stood to attention. Despite the fact she was sleeping with Chalky – and probably the bodyguard – she insisted on being addressed in public with scrupulous courtesy as Miss West. All her lovers, throughout her life, publicly addressed her as Miss West without exception.

She had the dignity of an empress, and this was no accident for Mae's heroine was an empress – Catherine the Great. She had researched the great lady's life and drafted a script which, she hoped, she could cajole Cohen into producing as her next movie. She was besotted by the revolutionary Technicolor process and keen to make the new film in Technicolor, envisioning the splendour of her costumes against the backdrop of the imperial court of St Petersburg.

Cohen, however, could not have cared less about Catherine the Great or St Petersburg. Paramount had already dealt with the subject in *The Scarlet Empress*, starring Marlene Dietrich. He suggested that Mae's next film should place her firmly back in the New York of the Nineties, a world she had made her own in terms of box-office appeal.

Although he did not yet have a property he wanted to start filming as soon as possible and had already commissioned certain sets to be made, including a replica of Rector's restaurant, former haunt of Lillian Russell and a place where Mae, as a child, had dined with Tillie and Battling Jack.

He guessed, shrewdly, that the combination of the Nineties and Rector's would be too much for the sentimental side of her nature to resist. To her, turning down both Rector's and the Nineties meant rejecting Tillie. She could not do it. Cohen promised her that a film of Catherine in Technicolor would be his next priority.

Even so, Mae was unhappy about the new project and her troubles pressed down on her, making her subject to fits of melancholy. Frank Wallace was still agitating and she was worried lest the truth would out, making her seem a disreputable joke. The thought of the now toothless and bald Wallace emerging as her husband was too much to bear.

She was uncertain of her future. The box-office returns for *Go West Young Man* had been disappointing and she thought she might have made a mistake by signing up with Cohen. She had worked continuously since her arrival in Hollywood. It occurred to no one that the indestructible Mae could be tired, but she was. Ironically, the title of the new film (although there was still no story line) seemed a mockery in itself – *Every Day's A Holiday*.

Once again her director changed. Having once experienced Mae, most directors flatly refused to work with her again. In turn, she was usually glad to see the back of them, blaming them for any deficiencies the films may have had and for discomposing her spirits by crossing her.

Her new director was Edward Sutherland, a hard-drinking rabble-rouser in the Errol Flynn tradition who had once been married to the silent screen actress Louise Brooks. He had been born in London but made his career in Hollywood where he had worked as assistant director to Charlie Chaplin and had himself directed W. C. Fields. His reputation had been enormous during the 1920s, but by 1937 when he came to direct Mae his career was on the skids – the reason he had accepted the job.

Of all her directors, Sutherland became her favourite. She was pleased when she learned that he had directed a film called *Diamond Jim*, taking the similarity to *Diamond Lil* as a propitious sign. In 1972 she told William Scott Eyman: 'As far as directors were concerned, they just didn't make that much difference to me. Leo McCarey was good, Lowell Sherman was good, but I guess my favourite was Eddie Sutherland. Eddie was always so tasteful, so enthusiastic. In fact, assuming his health was good, I'd hire Eddie to do a picture today. Eddie was always just great.'*

Sutherland suited her because his demeanour was gentlemanly. Many men had come to grief because they assumed, from her image, that she was 'one of the boys', but she would not be treated coarsely.

There are two versions as to how the story line of *Every Day's A Holiday* came into being. In her autobiography Mae implies the idea came to her like a bolt from the blue at a meeting involving Sutherland, Cohen and the songwriter Sam Coslow. Although there was no script for the film, there were songs, and Coslow was at the piano playing the group his new number entitled 'Mademoiselle Fifi'.

Mae liked the song, as she liked most things French, and in a flash of inspiration the plot for the film tumbled into her brain. She excitedly related the story to the group and a stenographer took it down before anything was forgotten. The rest was developed later by many hands.

Twenty years after the publication of *Goodness Had Nothing*

* *Take One.*

To Do With It, however, she elaborated on the account and explained that the revelation had been not so much an inspiration as a psychic experience. She had clairaudiently heard a voice dictating the story line and had merely related what it had said. The entire story had been given her in precisely fifty-six seconds; she knew it was that length of time because Coslow had been playing the chorus to 'Fifi' and that was the amount of time it took. She had kept silent at the time because the experience had been so precious to her – it was her first awareness of 'The Force', that discarnate power that was later to influence her life so greatly – and she did not wish to vulgarize this intimate moment by being accused of publicity seeking. Presumably, as an old lady, she no longer cared.

She does not relate whether or not the Force also warned her against continuously denying her marriage to Wallace, but she decided that she would have to come clean. The deception was getting out of hand, particularly in view of the tangible evidence of her marriage certificate.

The *Daily Mirror* for 8 July 1937 carried the following item: 'Miss Mae West admitted in the Superior Court at Los Angeles yesterday that she had been Mrs Frank Wallace for twenty-six years, but denied that she and her husband had ever lived together as man and wife.'

Most of the truth was now out in the open. It was tough to acknowledge that the puny Frank Wallace was her husband, but it was a relief. She vainly hoped she could now forget about the whole unpleasant episode but this was far from the end of the matter. There had to be more in it for Frank than a few paltry variety dates performed as Mr Mae West. In the desperation brought on by poverty, Frank was after bigger pickings and, as Mae was soon to discover, he had further nasty surprises in store for her.

In blissful ignorance Mae started preparations for her new film. Peaches O'Day was the name of Mae's character. She liked the name 'Peaches' because it harked back to her childhood – the kids in Brooklyn had called her that. Peaches is a confidence trickster who repeatedly sells the Brooklyn Bridge to tourists. As a result of one such transaction, she has to leave town hurriedly to dodge the police and assumes the identity of 'Mademoiselle Fifi', a fictitious French cabaret star. In this guise she wears a brunette wig.

She said she had always wanted to go brunette (which seems strange since she had merely to cease bleaching her hair to do so), but having once worn the wig she showed little inclination to do so again. She did, however, keep the wig, as she kept most of her props, and it eventually resurfaced in the 1970s when Robert Duran found it in a bedraggled state in a cardboard box in the garage of Mae's Santa Monica beach house. By that time the beach house, purchased in 1952, was stuffed with mouldering souvenirs of her career, most of which she had forgotten.

Duran ran into the house to show Mae the wig, hoping it might amuse her. 'Oh yeah,' she said without interest, 'I wore that in *Every Day's A Holiday*. You can have it if you want.' He has it to this day.

Mae assembled a strong cast of comedy players about her for the film, among them Chester Conklin, Lloyd Nolan and Herman Bing. She was equally well served musically for, apart from Coslow's songs, additional material was provided by Hoagy Carmichael. A star orchestra was now part of a Mae West production and this time Louis Armstrong did the honours. Her gowns were designed by Madame Schiaparelli. No one could accuse Cohen of stinting on production costs.

But for all these trappings, nothing could put a stop to the ceaseless intervention of the Hays Office. It was wearing Mae down. She stated in *Take One*: 'Movie censorship was so silly. They'd sit in a projection room watching my film, screaming with laughter the whole time. As soon as there was a lull and they stopped laughing, they'd lean over and say, "That can't possibly go in; we'll have to cut it out." That meant we had to go back and re-shoot, which is very expensive . . . All that movie censorship was so petty . . .'

'Petty' was an understatement. The censor cost her her audience. The returns for *Every Day's A Holiday* were worse than those for *Go West Young Man*. The weakness lies in the tame character of Peaches who, while undoubtedly a wicked girl, is not the maneating Mae West of yore. Worn down by the Hays Office Mae had presented it with a script to which there were hardly any objections.

She had succeeded so well, she was informed by the censorship board, that if she cut just two one-liners (two more from the many she had already expunged) then the film would be given an 'A' rating, equivalent to a 'U' certificate in Britain. Children could attend without the accompaniment of an adult.

The one-liners were two of her best: 'I wouldn't lift my veil for that guy' and 'I wouldn't let him touch me with a ten-foot pole.' She wearily agreed.

For all the laundering, there are plenty of Westisms left, none as salacious as her earlier films, but still very funny: 'My motto is keep a diary and one day it'll keep you,' which owes something to Wilde's *The Importance of Being Earnest*. And, when she is arrested, the officer remarks to a colleague, 'She's only been arrested twenty-five times in the last month.' 'What do you expect,' responds Peaches. 'No woman's perfect.' On another occasion she observes, 'That guy's so crooked, he uses a corkscrew for a ruler.'

As Mademoiselle Fifi, she speaks in a cod French accent and actually indulges herself in a few sentences in French. She sings in French, too, and her presentation differs from her customary style. In her earlier films she is almost stationary as she sings, focusing attention on her face. But, as Mademoiselle Fifi, her hand movements are more eloquent, a gesture to what she considered to be the French manner.

Most critics liked the film. Columnist Sheilah Graham declared, '*Every Day's A Holiday* is a better picture than *She Done Him Wrong* – and clean, which should make it a hit all round.'

But Miss Graham's praise and the generous words written about her by Miss Graham's lover, F. Scott Fitzgerald, did not endear the couple to her. She did not care for them, as a comment in her memoirs displays. She dismisses Miss Graham as being 'busy just then trying to sober up her fallen down drunken lover F. Scott Fitzgerald'.

Despite her declining popularity, as far as tourists were con-

Above: Whatever the role or the period in which it was set, Mae's costumes rarely varied.

Left: Fiction mirroring reality. Mavis Arden was the character played by Mae in *Go West Young Man*, a film closely based on her own theatrical experience.

Below: Sextet on tour, circa 1962, before it became the movie, *Sextette* (1977).

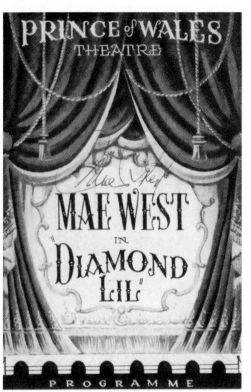

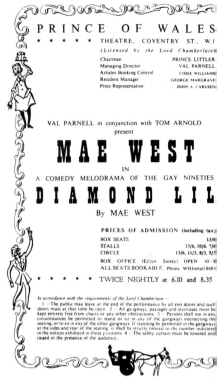

The London version of *Diamond Lil*.

Its London cast, 1948.

While touring Britain with *Diamond Lil*, Mae made a public appearance at the Dunlop factory in Birmingham, 1947.

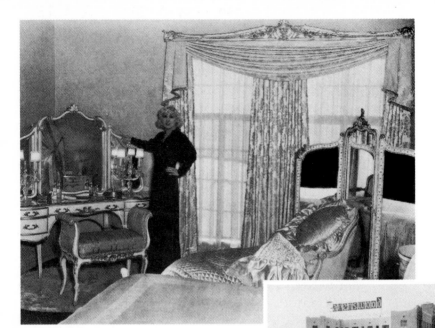

In her fabled, if tiny, bedroom at the Ravenswood (inset).

Mae with Beverly to her left, an unidentified man to her immediate right, Jim Timony and her brother John.

cerned she was still the most glittering attraction in Hollywood. Only the VIPs got in to see her, of course, but among those she received in her dressing room were mobster Benjamin 'Bugsy' Siegel ('How y'doin', Bugsy?'); the Sultan of Johore (the world's third richest man) and later Viscount and Lady Byng (who brought her an invitation to visit London and attend the jubilee of King George V, but she did not go). The press stated, tongue-in-cheek, that she called Lady Byng 'Dearie'.

Someone else who sought her attention was the novelist and playwright Anita Loos. Miss Loos was desperate to see the inside of Mae's apartment but, try as she might, she never gained admittance.

Miss Loos was working on a project in which she hoped to team up Clark Gable with Mae. Mae had never found Gable sexually attractive (and the feeling was mutual); he was, however, the number one male box-office star and there is no doubt that their screen combination would have been sizzling.

Miss Loos and her partner Robert Hopkins had written a scenario in which Mae was the owner of a male hockey team, of which Gable was the lead player. Miss Loos had already been in discussion with both MGM and Paramount about the matter, the latter still important in Mae's business life due to its distribution of her movies. MGM were prepared to put up the money providing Cohen and Paramount had no objection to loaning out Mae. These obstacles had been sorted out and now it was down to Mae.

In her memoirs Miss Loos writes of Mae: '[She] was difficult to pin down. The main tenets of a film star psychology are to be mysterious, difficult, irrational and suspicious, thus bringing about confusion and giving a star the whip hand. When ... asked ... for a conference at MGM she refused. "I never go off home base!" said Mae.'

Miss Loos persevered and finally Mae agreed she would meet her. She was informed that Mae's limousine would pick her up from the Beverly Wilshire Hotel. Miss Loos gushes:

No fan could have been more excited than I, as I waited on the pavement for that creature who was already a legend.

Hopefully, Mae would drive me off to her apartment where our conference would be held in her fabled white-and-gold drawing room . . .

Presently a chocolate-colored Rolls-Royce town car pulled up in front of the Beverly Wilshire with a handsome chocolate-colored chauffeur and footman, dressed in uniforms of the same color. The effect was a symphony of chocolate, except that Mae was decked in a cloud of white ostrich feathers . . . 'Get in, honey,' said Mae, 'and we'll hold our conference while we drive around Beverly Hills.' The reason for that ploy still baffles me. Perhaps Mae wanted to feel she could end our session at will by dumping me. So, I was cheated out of a look at the mysterious hideaway that all Hollywood longed to see.

Driving about the streets of Beverly Hills I told Mae our plot. She was not impressed. And at a time when every other star in Hollywood would have made any sacrifice to play with Clark Gable, Mae turned him down.

Then she explained her reason. 'Look, dear, I can't see myself horsing around with hockey players in a business way. It would make me feel unappealing. Any time I show my authority over the male sex it's got to be 100 per cent emotional. Your story line's okay, sweetheart, but take it from an old pro and cast that part with an MGM starlet named Roz Russell.'*

* *Kiss Hollywood Goodbye*, Anita Loos, Penguin, 1979.

chapter seventeen

PSYCHIC FORCES

In 1937 in order to promote *Every Day's A Holiday*, Mae accepted one of the many radio broadcasts offered her. This was *The Chase and Sanborn Hour*, an NBC peak time, network Sunday variety show hosted by ventriloquist Edgar Bergen and his dummy Charlie McCarthy. Bergen was the father of movie star Candice Bergen.

Mae's contribution was to be in two segments: she would trade jokes with the dummy in part one, and in part two, play Eve in a sketch based on the Adam and Eve fable with Don Ameche as Adam and the dummy as the serpent. The script was by science-fiction writer Arch Oboler, and had been broadcast before with a different cast.

The Chase and Sanborn Hour was transmitted 'live' and, although it was a coup to get her, the sponsors were nervous. The script was, understandably, vetted by executives before being submitted to her and she did not see it until the read-through at the NBC studio on 11 December, the day before transmission.

Mae arrived at the studio for the read-through in furs, sporting a large orchid boutonnière. She read her script with the aid of glasses perched on the end of her nose so they'd not collide with her false eyelashes. She gave a bland, professional reading which indicated nothing as to how she would interpret the part on the night.

Mae, as usual, was not chatty. She would enter a studio, always with her entourage, politely shake hands and sit silently, casting a chill over the premises until it was time for her to start work. She would then do her stuff, shake hands once more and leave.

Don Ameche recalls, 'She did little more than say hello and do the necessary work.' Ameche was the regular MC for the show. The vocalist was Dorothy Lamour, a star herself, famous as the 'sarong' girl who had featured with Ray Milland in *The Jungle Princess*. Miss Lamour was also a Paramount artist but had not had much to do with Mae. She speaks of the enormous respect Mae commanded on the lot. People did not trifle with her.

Miss Lamour, who appeared on the night to sing the title song from *Every Day's A Holiday*, recalls in her autobiography, *My Side of the Road*,* Mae's performance in *The Chase and Sanborn Hour*.

It was stipulated in Mae's contract that she could provide her own special material. She had, clearly, been attending to this matter during the day, for at her reading prior to transmission she provided a vastly different interpretation from the one she'd given the previous day.

Everyone pleaded for Mae to tone down her material. Miss Lamour remembers, 'As usual, she had inserted some bawdy Westisms. The minute the censors read the script, blue pencils appeared like magic. Mae innocently agreed to all the changes. Then she went on the air and read her script exactly as she had written it, word for word. Right in the middle of the skit we were cut off the air. The repercussions were incredible. Church groups were outraged and the mail came pouring in.'

As Mae proudly put it: 'I had caused a situation of national shock not to be matched till we dropped our first atomic bomb.'** NBC was furious and slapped a ban on her which stayed put for several years.

The Hearst press was swift to put the boot in; the *Motion Picture Herald* labelled her 'a symbolism of attainable sex, garnished with the ostrich plumes of the red plush parlour period,' which was tantamount to saying she was a whore. The *New York Sun* damned the show as 'the all-time low in radio'.

* Dorothy Lamour, Robson Books, 1981.
** *Goodness Had Nothing To Do With It*, W. H. Allen, 1960.

Such was the uproar that for a while NBC were in danger of losing their broadcasting licence. The Motion Picture Theater Owners officially protested to NBC, and Chase and Sanborn, the coffee manufacturers whose name endorsed the show, wrote a letter of apology to NBC, as did J. Walter Thompson, the advertising agency working for Chase and Sanborn.

For its part NBC broadcast an apology the following Sunday, and personally apologized to the Federal Communications Commission, whose task it was to ensure the airwaves remained unpolluted. The response did not placate the Commission, which stated in a letter that it 'rebukes NBC for the Mae West broadcast and refuses to accept the corporation's apology'. It added that the skit 'violated the ethics of decency'.

Paramount executives were incensed. They had spent years mollycoddling the Hays Office in order to secure the release of Mae West's films, and she had in one fell swoop undone all the studio's good work. A statement was issued by Paramount repudiating all responsibility for the broadcast.

Audience research, however, revealed that the ratings for *The Chase and Sanborn Hour* had leapt a substantial seven points from the beginning of the broadcast to the end. Word had clearly spread that Mae was broadcasting something worth listening to. The telephone lines had been in uproar as listeners urged their friends to tune in quickly so as not to miss an opportunity to be shocked. Most of the furore was caused because the broadcast had taken place on a Sunday and the subject matter was biblical. And for Mae West to portray Eve was asking for trouble.

It is easy to dismiss the outcry as typical of the prudishness of the times but, listening to the broadcast today, there is something shocking about it. Arch Oboler is a strong writer and there is a realism about the Paradise he created. Both Ameche and Mae were powerful actors (as she had demonstrated in *Klondike Annie*) and the sketch is not a bundle of belly laughs, but a dramatic sequence with one-liners added. Mae stressed that her early stage plays were not comedies but sex-dramas, and something of that ilk comes across in the Adam and Eve skit. Wantonness characterizes the way in which Eve is bored with Paradise and capriciously engages the services of the serpent to ruin the easy-going Adam. Those holding strong religious beliefs could still be offended.

Cohen and the Paramount executives probably had a worrisome Christmas as a result of the broadcast, but Mae remained unrepentant. The papers were full of her and, with the imminent release of her new film, the time was right for saturation exposure.

After Christmas, she embarked on a ten-week tour promoting *Every Day's A Holiday*, making up to eight appearances daily, and wherever she appeared the film played to packed houses. In New York alone, thousands turned up at the railway station to cheer her.

On her return to Hollywood, she told Cohen she was now going to make the Catherine the Great film whether he liked it or not and spent four months preparing material. During this time, however, she was to be given the coldest shoulder Hollywood had ever given her. In addition, for all its initial promise, the box-office returns for *Every Day's A Holiday* dropped when her public appearances ceased.

Paramount, its patience finally exhausted by the *Chase and Sanborn* outrage, severed its connection with Mae. Cohen, too, turned his back. The two films she had made under contract to him had not lived up to his financial expectations and he wasn't going to offer a new contract.

Mae was confident she needed neither Cohen nor Paramount. She believed that if Cohen had gone ahead with her plans for a Technicolor version of Catherine she would still be top box office. That she was no longer in this enviable position was rammed home with the publication in the *Motion Picture Herald* of a list of artists deemed 'Box Office Poison'. She could take comfort in the fact that she was in exclusive company; the other supposedly poisonous artists included Joan Crawford, Garbo, Fred Astaire, Katharine Hepburn and Dietrich.

All these had, in some way, caused trouble for their various studios, either by refusing to film certain stories, insisting on executive rights or, as in Mae's case, becoming the object of scandal. They had refused to toe the studio line and all had elicited the unwelcome attention of the Hays Office. It has been suggested that the studios cooperated with the *Herald* in the publication of its 'blacklist' and that by so doing a dual purpose was served. Hays Office approval was gained for the studio and the artists were duly disciplined.

However distorted its perspective, the list did indicate changing tastes. Just seven years after her first Hollywood film Mae was already yesterday's news. The mountain of press comment had produced overkill.

Undeterred, she prepared a preliminary script for *Catherine* which, her ego blinding her to the intensity of dislike for her at Paramount, she submitted to Ernst Lubitsch. It was swiftly returned.

She took Lubitsch's rejection as a personal slight, which it probably was, and moaned what a mistake it had been to have sent it to him in the first place. What, she demanded of Jim, made Lubitsch's opinion so important? By this time Le Baron was production chief at Paramount but, even had he wanted to, he could do nothing to help.

When it was pointed out to Mae that Dietrich had already made a biopic of Catherine the Great, Mae blamed its disappointing financial returns on Dietrich's performance, which she likened to that of a 'hollow cheeked doll'. Her Catherine would be less enigmatic and more basic (which would seem to fit in with what is known of the Tsarina). Mae believed Catherine to be a 'pre-incarnation' of herself, her alter ego, and likened her to Diamond Lil.

She never forgave Lubitsch and claimed in later years, as evidence of his spite towards her, that he stole her idea. He did, indeed, make a film about Catherine which starred Tallulah Bankhead, but not until 1945. To be fair to Lubitsch, *A Royal Scandal* was a remake of his own silent *Forbidden Paradise*.

Mae decided she would humiliate herself no longer by seeking outside backing and would finance the project herself. With Jim's help she formed the Mae West-Empire Pictures Corporation while he explored the viability of making the film as an independent. But war had broken out in Europe, the repercussions of which made finding financial backing impossible. The Mae West-Empire Pictures Corporation never traded.

The news that Mae had been unable to secure finance became common knowledge. It reinforced the stories already circulating that she was washed up. These rumours contained more than a grain of truth and inevitably came to her ears. Her personal predicament was galling in that Hollywood was booming again. The war began to have a stimulating effect on the box office – people again wanted escapism.

But no film offers were made to her which she could seriously consider accepting. She did what she had always done when in difficulty and took to the road, authorizing William Morris to organize a variety tour for her commencing at Loew's Theater, New York.

Meanwhile a new novelty had hit Hollywood. In 1939 David O. Selznick's *Gone With the Wind* had just been released. Shot in Technicolor and based on Margaret Mitchell's best-selling novel, this story of the Old South was the most lavish film Hollywood had ever seen. When Clark Gable had been named as the male lead, female stars had thrown themselves at Selznick to be considered for the role of Scarlett O'Hara, the part that eventually went to the then little-known British actress Vivien Leigh. Hedda Hopper had been so furious by Selznick's choice of a British girl, which she construed as an insult to American womanhood that, with spectacular failure, she urged the public to boycott the film.

Anyone who was anyone had fought for a part in the movie and there has been speculation that Selznick had considered Mae for the role of Belle Watling, madame of the local brothel. Many of Selznick's confidential memos have now come to light, however, and one of these dispels this rumour, yet shows how the speculation arose.

On 6 December 1938 Selznick dictated a memo concerning the casting of Belle, which, in part, reads as follows: 'Would Tallulah Bankhead play Belle Watling – she might go for it as a stunt, just as it has been suggested that Mae West (who is out of the question, of course) might be glad to do it as a stunt.'* Mae was never seriously in the running and the part was eventually played by Ona Munson. *Gone With the Wind* forms such a part of our movie heritage that it is now impossible to associate any actress, other than Miss Munson, with the role of Belle. Yet, the character was within Mae's range. Judging from her performance in *Klondike Annie* she could have come up with the necessary disillusioned bravery required. She was also capable of pathos, *viz* her balcony scene in *Belle of the Nineties* and her warm exchanges with Randolph Scott in *Go West Young Man.*

During her tour Mae had been badgered by enquiries from her fans about when her next film would be out. As there was no new film, their entreaties grew increasingly embarrassing. She parried them with a wisecrack, 'Give Venus a chance to take off her corsets.'

She had been offered certain film scripts, of course, but these had been from second division companies and she quite rightly refused to consider them. Thanks to her investments she could afford to be choosy. A standing joke about town was that the well-heeled suburb of Westwood was named after her because she now owned so much property there.

But as time rolled by she realized she would have to accept work or admit defeat. Then an interesting, even audacious, idea came from Universal Pictures. It was the first proposition she had seriously considered in months. Her interest was roused by an item in the trade press, written by Bosley Crowther, who noted that Dietrich was having a success at Universal with the comedies *Destry Rides Again* and *Seven Sinners.* Crowther wrote, 'If Miss Dietrich and her comedies were just both a little broader Mae West would be in the shade.'

Universal was a studio with a pedigree. Up to the 1930s it had built up an enviable reputation by producing some of the most successful films of Valentino, von Stroheim and Lon Chaney. But by the mid-1930s it had lost prestige and largely restricted its output to low-budget B films. Then Deanna Durbin had come along, whose zinging soprano revived the company's

* *Memo from David O. Selznick*, ed. Rudy Behlmer, Macmillan, 1973.

fortunes. This rise in status was augmented in 1939 when Dietrich and James Stewart co-starred in *Destry Rides Again*, about which Lord Beaverbrook is alleged to have enthused, 'Marlene Dietrich standing on a bar, in black net stockings, belting out "See What the Boys in the Back Room Will Have" is a greater work of art than the Venus de Milo.'

Universal were keen to cash in on the success of *Destry* by making a follow-up. Dietrich was unavailable so why not use the eminently available Mae West? And for a male lead, instead of a handsome leading man, why not go for parody and cast the great comic W. C. Fields? Together they might prove an unbeatable duo.

Fields was undeniably very funny. He was also a stingy, irascible alcoholic whom Mae had known since she had appeared with him in vaudeville when he was a juggler. He was not her cup of tea at all with his raucous behaviour and bouts of intoxication that rendered him incapable of work.

He and Mae had both worked for Paramount, but had maintained a respectful distance from each other. This was usual. Few of the stars socialized. They made their own films in their own studios with their own bands of workers. Apart from civilities, they seldom mixed.

Mae signed a deal with Universal which included options for two more films and which also contained certain stipulations. She must have top billing above Fields; she must have script approval and the right to provide her own dialogue; and she inserted a clause insisting that Fields abstain from liquor while working. Though still a big name, Fields was no longer the star he had been and had no option other than to agree to her conditions.

But, like Mae, Fields had it written into his contract that he would receive payment for script material and she could do nothing to stop him. His ability to write scripts was real; he had devised the stories and much of the material for many of his films. Consequently he received a credit as co-writer, something that was a constant source of chagrin to Mae. At the age of seventy-nine she was still fuming, as she made clear in an interview with *Take One* magazine in 1972: 'Bill Fields got co-script credit, which was a farce. He wrote one scene, between himself and another guy in a bar room. One scene! I liked Bill and all that, but he could be miserable when he wanted to be. I guess he hounded them and hounded them until they gave him screen credit just to get rid of him. I never saw the picture until after it had been released, and by then it was too late to do anything about it. That irritates me.'

It was predictable that they would not get along together. Years later, when asked how many films she had made with Fields, she replied, 'Once was enough', but in *Goodness Had Nothing To Do With It* she is fairer. As one vaudevillian to another she acknowledged his talent.

Their comedy styles were diametrically opposed. Mae polished her one-liners until they shone like diamonds. In this sense she was a disciplinarian. Fields, on the other hand, relied on improvisation and ad-libbed his way through a situation, using the script purely as a springboard.

She says she thought she was too strong for Fields. Sometimes, after she had performed a particularly good piece of business, he would burst into a fit of alcoholic tears. When this happened, she said, she would take the offending business out. This must be taken with a pinch of salt. There is no way Mae West would remove any material guaranteed to get a laugh unless, confronted with the Hays Office, there was absolutely no choice.

She remained civil about Fields during his lifetime but after his death gave vent to more genuine feelings. Their director was Edward Cline and sympathy must be extended to him. To be assigned two such egomaniacs, neither of whom was prepared to give way to the other, must have been a nightmare. Fortunately, he had had experience in dealing with difficult temperaments as he had previously worked as a Keystone Kop with Mack Sennett and his Bathing Beauties, and with Buster Keaton. He had also worked with Fields before, on the Paramount satire *Million Dollar Legs* – which had nothing to do with Betty Grable, but concerned a mythical country which decided to enter the Olympic Games.

Owing to Mae's personal prohibition law, Fields (who had no intention of abiding by it) had to devise ways of smuggling booze onto the set. He brought it in in various camouflaged containers, including paper parcels and Coca-Cola bottles. But Mae had her spies.

On one occasion (it is said) he was caught drunkenly persuading the child actors – for whom he had an aversion – to play in a busy main road, and she had him dismissed for the day. He exited in front of her, sarcastically tipping his hat with exaggerated courtesy. Her cheeks burned with rage. There were times when Cline's job owed more to his talent as a referee than to any directorial ability. It was agreed by all parties that Fields and Mae should share as few scenes as possible. Both concentrated on doing their own thing on days when the other was absent from the set.

Filming was difficult, not helped by a heat wave in Los Angeles pushing temperatures up to 107°F, followed by a period of torrential rain. Tempers were easily frayed. The friction was intensified by a union dispute which threatened production and was only resolved by a 10 per cent wage increase.

Mae was furious when Fields caused delays by forgetting his lines. He blamed his poor memory for this, but Robert Lewis Taylor, Fields' biographer, points out, 'This was an old and specialized lack, for his memory about other things was faultless.'

Fields was as churlish about direction as Mae. Sometimes Cline would make a suggestion about how a scene might be improved, but Fields would only grudgingly agree to a dry run. He spiked any attempt to film this by inspecting the cameras before rehearsing to ensure they were empty of film.

Fields took revenge on Mae for attempting to ban his booze by ruffling her fragile dignity. Robert Lewis Taylor records:

The part called for such extravagances of wooing on Fields' part that he couldn't shake it off between takes. His voice took on a permanent note of endearment, and he pranced around, holding his preposterous hat, like an adolescent. His style was enriched by frequent doses from the flask. The bouncy quality of his conduct began to get on Miss West's nerves. One afternoon on the set she said,

'Bill's a good guy, but it's a shame he has to be so God-damned cute!'*

Fields was even more lax in his time-keeping than Mae, arriving on the set at whatever hour best suited him. Remonstrations were frequent, after which he would retire to his dressing room and drink solidly, refusing to respond to the entreaties of the luckless Cline. On these occasions Mae would sit frostily in her dressing room, her unyielding face primped and powdered by make-up artists.

The film, finally titled *My Little Chickadee* after Fields' catchphrase, was based on an original idea by Mae, called *The Lady and the Bandit*. Universal had originally offered them a story called *The Jaywalker* but both Mae and Fields rejected this. During these script discussions Fields wrote Mae letters and she later quoted a portion of one. It begins, 'I take, my dear, a very dim view of the studio's mental equipment, to put it mildly.'

The story pre-dates Mae's beloved 1890s by a decade. It is the fable of Flower Belle Lee who undergoes a fake wedding with card sharp Cuthbert J. Twillie because she believes he has money. She leaves him on their wedding night to meet a mysterious masked bandit lover. During the daytime, Flower Belle takes over as teacher at the school and the local newspaper proprietor, a crusading knight-like figure, falls in love with her.

In the meantime Cuthbert, who is a pauper, is caught cheating at cards and is believed to be the masked bandit. He is taken away to be hanged but is saved at the last minute by a gun-toting Belle. She is left with a decision at the end of the film: both the bandit and the editor love her, whom should she choose? The real choice, of course, is between wickedness and goodness. Maybe she'll have neither.

Compared to the parades, bands, costumes and hundreds of extras in *Every Day's A Holiday*, *My Little Chickadee* seems sparse in production values, and it has become the norm in

* *W. C. Fields: His Follies and Fortunes*, Doubleday, 1949.

critical circles to dismiss it as inferior, a film which does no justice to either star. An accusation which, as a programme written for the National Film Theatre makes clear, 'has not prevented audiences from rolling up whenever the film is revived'. It is the most frequently shown of all Mae's (and Fields') films.

' . . . an inspired coupling of the suggestive art of America's leading mental strip-teaser with the comic talents of one of the funniest men on earth. Together they make a comedy which is more hilarious than its grab-bag plot.' *Time*.

The London *Times* was not so keen: 'Miss Mae West and Mr W. C. Fields are a weighty combination, but somehow or other they cannot persuade this film to run at all easily . . . Perhaps Miss West herself is partly to blame. She has one or two effective tricks of gesture and speech, but repetition of them becomes wearisome and she has little else to fall back on. Mr Fields is magnificently flamboyant and rhetorical . . . but hard as he works, *My Little Chickadee* obstinately refuses to gather momentum.'

They both turn in eccentric performances. Fields is splendid as the bottle-swigging cheat, integrating several of his well-tried bar room sketches into the plot. His anachronistic court-ship of Mae, which is never consummated, is a tragi-comic riot. 'What symmetrical digits,' he sighs as he kisses her hand. 'Soft as the fuzz on a baby's arm.' 'And quick on the trigger,' she responds, rolling her eyes to the ceiling.

They are backed by a strong cast, many of whom had worked with either Fields or Mae before. Worthy of mention is Margaret Hamilton, as the vinegary, hatchet-faced Mrs Gideon, who epitomizes all the narrow-minded prudes who ever spoke out against Mae. Miss Hamilton has been described by Christopher Finch* as possessing a profile 'as sharp as a sickle fresh from the whetstone', a description equally applicable to her approach to comedy.

In *Chickadee* Mae did manage to get some of her own back

---

* *Rainbow: The Stormy Life of Judy Garland*, Michael Joseph, 1975.

on the prudes; even the Legion of Decency is mocked – a protest against her is organized by the fictitious 'Ladies Vigilante Committee'.

Always, technically, a slow mover, Mae's pace in *Chickadee* is positively leisurely. She was so much mistress of the medium that some of her lines are muttered in a throwaway style well in advance of its time, and not to become popularly in use until the early Fifties.

Taken chronologically Mae's films show her development as a screen actress. In *Night After Night* she offers a filmic version of a stage performance, her voice shrill and 'projected', needing a wide canvas to get her points across. With *Chickadee* she uses the camera as a confidante. In all her films, particularly in *Klondike Annie*, there are moments when she transcends caricature and transforms herself into a fine actress, but she had to keep the latter quality suppressed in order to continue as Mae West.

Chickadee contains some classic lines: 'Are you trying to show contempt for this court?' Belle is asked by a magistrate. 'No,' she replies, 'I'm doing my best to hide it.' After being kidnapped by the masked bandit, she announces, 'I was in a tight spot but managed to wriggle out of it.' She is also asked, almost autobiographically, 'Aren't you forgetting you're married?' 'I'm doing my best,' she responds. Parodying her famous line in *She Done Him Wrong*, she drawls, 'Anytime you got nothing to do, and plenty of time to do it, come on up.'

Many of the scenes between Fields and Mae were shot separately. Mae preferred to work this way. She never acted 'with' a performer, she merely did her thing and her co-actor had to perform around her. Often she did not even look at the person to whom she was supposed to be talking. The camera was sufficient object at which to emote.

Mae possessed a repertoire of gimmicks. One of them was the way she used the telephone in her films. She would stare straight to camera front, start speaking barely as soon as the receiver had been lifted from its rest, bring it to her ear for a brief second, then replace it, still talking. Another was to insert malapropisms into the dialogue when she felt the scene could do with a lift. She describes Cleopatra as an 'hysterical' character. At the end of the film both she and Fields salute each other by each using the other's catchphrase. 'Come up and see me, sometime,' Fields invites, while she coos in reply, 'My little chickadee'.

Some of the best lines in the film were edited out, including one of Fields'. When Flower Belle substitutes a goat in the bed for herself, the unsuspecting Twillie murmurs, 'Darling, have you changed your perfume?'

At the time of its release in 1940 *My Little Chickadee* was deemed disappointing by all three protagonists – Mae, Fields and Universal. Universal did not pick up her option. It did not look good. Most major artists stayed with one company throughout their careers; that way both artist and studio could structure a career. When Anita Loos offered Mae a Gable film at the king of studios, MGM, she had turned it down by saying proudly, 'I never go off home base.' Now there was no home base to abandon.

She was still set on producing a film of Catherine the Great but each day, it seemed, brought depressing news. The very sets and costumes would cost a fortune and world circumstances had changed drastically since she had first thought of the idea. Not only was war raging in Europe but Russia, once Britain's ally, had now alienated itself by attacking Finland. A film eulogizing the Tsarina would hardly go down well in the all-important British market.

And the British had proved to be loyal fans of Mae. She was touched when she learnt in 1941 that an inflatable life-jacket, worn by RAF fighter pilots around their chests, was to be named after her. She considered it a 'tribute to my sex appeal in practical form'. The name of the eponymous garment is still in most dictionaries.

She wrote to the RAF to thank them for the honour and ended her letter, 'I've been in *Who's Who* and I know what's what, but it'll be the first time I ever made the dictionary.' She signed off, 'Sin-sationally, Mae West'. She frequently signed her photographs and publicity material 'sin-sationally', or 'sin-cerely', or sometimes 'sex-sationally', depending on her mood. Her signature contained two large loops, and towards the end of her life, she explained these had a special significance. She told Robert Duran that the loops were meant to represent her breasts. It amused her to think that under the all-embracing gaze of the censors she was getting away with a naughty private joke.

Universal eventually offered her a further film, but she did not like the script so declined. Columbia made an offer but she considered the production budget insufficient. The fees that accompanied these proposals were now less than a quarter of what she had received in her heyday.

She started work on another script, a story based on a Broadway play by Myron Fagan, in which she would play a private detective, and she wanted John Barrymore as her leading man. As a matinée idol, Barrymore had been as famous for his profile as his talent, but he was now an alcoholic who had drunk his way to ruin. If Fields had maddened Mae by his drinking, Barrymore would have driven her insane. It is odd that she ever considered him as a leading man, but Mae could never resist a villain and his attitude amused her – at a distance. It is doubtful that her admiration would have survived a working relationship. And Barrymore was certainly no box-office draw in 1940; at fifty-eight years of age he looked at least ten years older.

Barrymore seemed the only person unworried by his declining state. He enjoyed his rumbustious life and did not care what he looked like. When propositioned, he happily agreed to make a film with Mae. At that time – in fact, for most of his life – he would have done almost anything for money.

Mae had conferences with Barrymore and presented her synopsis to several studios. It was returned without interest. No one was prepared to risk money on an alcoholic debauchee coupled with a passé *femme fatale*. She was heartily sick of the movie business. There must, she felt certain, be something else in life. 'I began to feel that I would either live a very wicked life, or develop spiritually,' she later remarked on this phase of her life. The decision, of course, was not so clear cut. She could not at the age of forty-eight decide to be good or bad; either one quality or the other would already have dominated her personality.

Elsewhere she says she considered throwing in her lot with gangsters. That was never a serious consideration either. The cold heart of gangsterism would have terrified her; she could never have sustained a life of such potential violence. Her vision was blurred by the sex appeal radiating from those ultra-macho figures; Mae would always be fascinated by hoods, but she ensured she remained on the periphery of their world.

Jim no longer provided the emotional support she needed and their roles had gradually reversed. He now took his lead from her and she no longer sought his judgement. Jim's area of responsibility in her life had contracted. He represented her at the bank, looked after her itinerary and guarded her privacy. That was about it.

He was aware he had lost his grip over her and this made his jealousy even fiercer. He would go to pathetic lengths to discover what she was up to, spending hours sitting in the open doorway of his apartment, ostensibly reading the newspaper, but monitoring who came to see her. If she was out he would wait in this position to see if she returned alone.

She developed a technique to outmanoeuvre him. The Ravenswood's reception would ring when a lover arrived and, after this signal, she would saunter out to where Jim was sitting in the doorway with his paper and start to chat, perhaps pointing out something in the news. While doing so she carefully obstructed his line of vision, and the lover who had arrived at the sixth floor by now could sneak in through the open door of her apartment. It was all part of the fun of having an affair with Mae West. Her ploy was remarkably successful but only because Jim was becoming senile. When in full possession of his powers he would have seen through her at once.

Chalky Wright had left her employ and Mae, who was still subsidizing his expenses as a boxer, replaced him with his brother who took over his chauffeuring duties for a time. The brother had had a brush with the law and Mae gave him financial security until he found his feet.

Mae realized Jim was becoming morbid and needed something to occupy his mind. To give him something to do she bought an old church hall on New Hampshire Avenue and converted it into a theatre. The idea behind the project was that the Hollytown Theater, as it was called, would mount small-scale productions to try them out before a possible transfer to Broadway. It also provided an opportunity for Mae to meet promising young actors who might later prove useful. Jim took to the new project and under his supervision the theatre gained a reputation of sorts. Actress Yolande Donlan remembers Jim running the place and several productions that were put on there. One of Jim's plays, *Clean Beds*, did actually transfer to New York. If she had nothing better to do Mae would sometimes sit in during rehearsals.

On one occasion while she was there, the Mexican-born actor Anthony Quinn arrived for an audition; he was twenty-five, dangerous-looking and woundingly handsome. Mae's head spun. He was interviewed by Jim, a 'jolly, red-faced man', while Mae stood by 'looking like a queen'. Quinn describes the meeting in his autobiography: 'She stared at me for a minute and said, "Come over here, boy." I walked up to her. There was something tantalizing and almost coarsely sensuous about her. "What do you do?" she asked, on four different levels . . .'*

Quinn auditioned for the part of a sixty-four-year-old and the director turned him down, but Mae interceded. The director protested Quinn was too young, 'You can put make-up on the kid; he'll be sensational,' Mae told him. Quinn got the part.

John Barrymore turned up one day while Quinn was working at the Hollytown Theater. Mae had wanted him to play in *Clean Beds* and he had agreed in order to get the fee, but then lost interest. The author of the play, George S. George, admonished him and (according to Quinn) Barrymore 'told the writer to go and fuck himself'. Without doubt Mae would have received the same treatment had she and Barrymore teamed up and she would not have liked it.

It did not take Mae long to lure Quinn up to her apartment. He continues: 'Mae herself came to the door, a most dazzling

---

* *The Original Sin*, W. H. Allen, 1972.

creature, with beautiful translucent skin, like white silk with a light behind it, and soft, lively eyes, and the blonde hair worn loose. She was dressed all in white, a négligée that just barely covered her breasts; the cleavage was dizzying.'

She told him she had a black lover, one Tiger Jones, and that she had tried to bring him into the Ravenswood one day and had been stopped by the management because he was black. 'So I told them to go fuck themselves and I bought the joint,' Quinn recalls her telling him. She was always telling people she had bought the Ravenswood; it was an impressive chat-up line.

Quinn relates that she took him into the bedroom and told him, 'Turn down the lights, boy; they hurt my eyes.' Then she removed her négligée and started to writhe about on the bed, but he did not respond so she did not waste any more of her time and got rid of him.

Quinn's book was published in 1972 and Mae indignantly repudiated his account. It was unacceptable to her that any man could resist her, particularly a man as rugged as Quinn. 'I'd like to get him for that!' she raged.

But by 1941 the young Anthony Quinn was banished from her mind, together with a horde of other men. Mae was into spiritual matters. She had resumed contact with her Sri and was studying yoga. This calmed her down but did not provide the answers she sought about the meaning of life. She decided to devote the following six months to investigating the mystery. She particularly wanted to discover if there was life after death because she wanted to believe that she would see her mother again and, at her low ebb, sought proof.

Mae started her search by questioning ministers of religion. Could the Catholic Church, which had campaigned so virulently against her, contain the answer she sought? Apparently not. Mae spoke with priests but they could not supply her with what she was seeking. Neither could the Anglican Church nor the rabbi. It was something else she needed.

The breakthrough came in November 1941. She read in a Los Angeles newspaper that a Spiritualist convention would be held in town, which would include a public demonstration of clairvoyance by the famed medium T. Jack Kelly. Obviously

Mae could not attend a public gathering as she would create too much of a diversion, but Jim was dispatched along with one of Mae's bodyguards, a young boxer known as Mickey. Jim was to report whether Jack Kelly was genuine or, as she put it, 'just a lot of phoney showmanship'.*

Jim was not exactly thrilled at the prospect but Mae's wish was his command so he took his place among the congregation. Kelly was doing his demonstration blindfolded but nonetheless pointed to Mickey and told him he heard a name, spoken from Spirit, that sounded Russian or Polish. He then ran off a polysyllabic name beginning with S. Mickey whispered in astonishment to Jim that this was his family name. He had told no one this before and, as far as Jim was concerned, he was Irish.

Kelly went on to say that Mickey's deceased father was with him and wanted Mickey to know that he had been murdered and that his body had afterwards been thrown into water. This was astounding evidence of Kelly's capacity since Mickey had been told by his mother that his father had died by drowning. The excited men returned to the Ravenswood to break the news to Mae.

She invited Kelly to hold a seance at the Ravenswood. A dozen people attended, two of whom were Beverly and Jim. At his request Kelly was blindfolded and tied to a chair. He then slumped into a trance and while in this state various voices spoke through him. 'Some of the things he told us at that meeting were astounding,' Mae told *Psychic News*. 'Things about which he could not possibly know in advance, and some of which would be decidedly embarrassing to certain people if made public.'

Mae never revealed the precise nature of what transpired, but she did say that Kelly had predicted America would become involved in the war, and that there would be a surprise attack on Hawaii by Japan within months. He also predicted that the war would last between five to six years and that President Roosevelt would not finish his fourth term of office. The seance

* *That Ghost I Saw*, Danton Walker, Dodson.

took place in 1941, so these events had not yet happened, and it was only with hindsight that Mae recalled their accuracy.

There was still more to Kelly's demonstration of his astonishing powers. Written questions were placed in sealed envelopes and he proceeded to pick up the unopened envelopes and answer the questions written inside. The envelope was then opened and the question verified. Kelly appeared to be repeating answers given him by ethereal voices he heard, which remained inaudible to the other sitters. Mae thought she could hear whispering sounds and Kelly confirmed they were the voices of spirits. They would not harm her.

The question reading feat is, in a corrupt form, an established variety act, its effect achieved by the 'medium' planting an accomplice in the audience. The first question the 'medium' answers does not exist, and when the envelope is opened and the question supposedly verified, it is the accomplice who verifies it. In reality the 'medium' is reading the second question while purporting to read the non-existent first question. And so the act proceeds.

Mae believed Kelly to be a genuine psychic, and she was not only intelligent but possessed a developed sense of cynicism. She had been in vaudeville all her life and seen numerous mentalists at work. She was also accustomed to confidence tricksters with whom the theatre abounds.

Against this must be set the fact that at this spiritually barren time of her life she needed religion; a conviction that there was a deeper purpose to life than the cut-throat existence which had been the sum total of her experience so far. Spiritualism proved to her that there was such a purpose.

The proof became stronger when Mickey, the recipient of Kelly's original public message, reported to her that he had questioned his family about his father's death and they had confirmed what Kelly had said.

Mae's quest was fulfilled. She was now a Spiritualist. Not only did this satisfy her existential cravings but it was a route that could lead to reunion with Tillie. She told Kelly she wanted to develop any latent psychic powers she might possess.

Kelly introduced her to a woman who taught her the techniques of meditation; through meditation Mae would be able to hear her 'inner voice'. Within three weeks she was able to concentrate on any one subject for up to twenty-five minutes at a time. She realized that her 'inner voice' had been subconsciously guiding her for years, and remembered how, as a child, when Tillie had sent her to Sunday School she had developed headaches. With her new knowledge she attributed these to the unfolding of her psychic powers.

It was not until the 1960s that meditation, welded to aspects of Eastern philosophy, became fashionable. Mae's metamorphosis predated the hippy revolution by twenty years. Religion was an intensely personal thing to her and she did not make her beliefs common knowledge until the publication of *Goodness Had Nothing To Do With It* in 1959. Much ridicule was heaped on her head as a result. Her revelations, however, are in terms that to her were simple statements of fact. 'I got no loud ringing answers,' she says, 'but I have experienced enough psychic phenomena to be convinced that there is some kind of hereafter.' A reasoned statement. Another decade passed before she provided details of the psychic phenomena she had experienced.

After his successful seance, and his guidance of Mae, Kelly returned to his home in Buffalo. But Mae could not let him alone.

Beverly was in trouble. A few days earlier a man, introducing himself as a friend of her parents, had called and stayed the afternoon. While she was pouring the tea the police were searching for her guest who that morning had battered his wife to death. Beverly had been questioned by the police and, as always when in a crisis, she had called on Mae for help. Mae contacted the police and told them she might be able to assist them. She telephoned Kelly while the police waited, and he told her that the criminal had been arrested just twenty minutes earlier. This was news to the police who swiftly contacted headquarters. But it was true. Once again Kelly stunned her.

Although Mae's spiritual breakthrough came through her meeting with Kelly, she had been dabbling in seances prior to this time. She later divulged that some years before she had taken part in a table-tapping seance together with aviator Amelia Earhart. Miss Earhart disappeared in her plane in 1937 during an attempted flight round the world.

The first psychic voice Mae heard was that of a little girl who bid her good morning. The voice, she stated, was inside her ear. The next morning a deep, masculine voice spoke to her from the region of her solar plexus. Mae rang Kelly who reassured her the voices belonged to intelligences that had passed over.

Given encouragement, Mae loved to talk about these things. As columnist Danton Walker discovered, '[Miss West], far from being evasive in discussing such things, is eager to spread the word – to the right people – about something that has answered a spiritual need for her and given her a deep inner satisfaction.'

chapter eighteen

LONDON

In 1941, in San Bernardino, California, Frank Wallace surfaced again. He sued Mae for maintenance of $1,000 a month. The presiding Superior Judge, Charles L. Allison, dismissed the case. But the more Mae's name hit the headlines, the greater was Frank's incentive to cash in. He later admitted he had a new girlfriend and she was the real power behind the throne. In July 1942 he lodged a further claim for alimony, plus a $500,000 lump sum, which his lawyers estimated to be half the communal value of Mae's property. At this stage Frank had no choice other than to proceed; he could not afford to drop matters. His lawyers had already run up fees of $27,500; how could he pick up that sort of money playing second-rate vaudeville houses billed as *Mae West's Husband?*

Mae counter-sued for divorce and won her case. This did not come about, however, until she had made an out-of-court settlement to Frank. It was worth it for her piece of mind.

With the divorce behind her she spent most of 1942 pursuing her new-found, all-consuming interest in Spiritualism. There were no serious film offers, but Spirit told her something would be coming along soon. She was full of optimism for 1943 and a numerologist confirmed that the digits commuted to the occult number of 8 – her lucky number. It was bound to be a successful year. As if on cue an offer for another film came on the first day of the new year.

It arrived in the form of Gregory Ratoff, who had played the part of Benny Pinkowitz in *I'm No Angel*. He asked her to star in a new movie he planned to direct. She liked Ratoff and always preferred, if possible, to work with people she knew. She distrusted all strangers.

Ratoff was quite a character. He was born in St Petersburg and claimed to have trained as an actor in the imperial Russian theatre. He had fought with the Russian army in the First World War, and spoke English with a thick Russian accent.

He had worked with the best. As an actor he had been directed by both George Cukor and Howard Hawks and, in turn, had himself directed Peter Lorre and Erich von Stroheim. His direction had been acclaimed for *Intermezzo* which had starred Ingrid Bergman and Leslie Howard.

Throughout his career he continued to appear as an actor, giving memorable if bizarre performances, and he also directed film untils his death in 1960. The last film he directed, *Oscar Wilde*, which starred Robert Morley, is steeped in controversy. One critic, David Thomson, considers it 'a hopeless mess', whereas another, Leslie Halliwell, thought it a 'competent, well-acted version'. Both, however, agree that *The Heat's On*, in which he directed Mae, was a disaster.

Ratoff, who came to the Ravenswood with Murray Feil, told her he had a story based on a hit musical which would suit her down to the ground. There was no script but he acted it out for her. Mae, who was desperate to film, said she would do it providing she liked the script. Ratoff assured her she would love the script. It was a measure of her desperation that, for once, she did not insist on writing the screenplay. A contract was signed there and then and the new movie was to be called *Tropicana*.

Ratoff was finishing off a film so she heard no more for several weeks. When he reappeared he told her he was already supervising the construction of the sets for *Tropicana* and that filming of the chorus routines was completed. But there was now a hitch. He could not use the story line he had enacted for her but had another up his sleeve that was much better. She did not like it and demanded release from her contract.

Ratoff pleaded with her. He had managed to secure the finances only by using her name as collateral. If she backed out he would have to declare himself bankrupt. For her part, Mae was nervous rumours might circulate that she had walked out on the film and enhance her reputation for being difficult. Since Ratoff had assembled a solid line-up of supporting artists, such as pianist Hazel Scott and the Xavier Cugat orchestra, she decided her best course of action was to bite the bullet and go ahead.

The setting was contemporary; Mae grandiloquently informed the press that this was because she could refine her Diamond Lil character no further. She had played it in every possible permutation. Now it was time to shake off the bustle, but she still ensured the film would have one Nineties sequence in it.

The story concerns a musical star, Fay Lawrence, who becomes involved with a show she knows is going to flop. The action unfolds around her relationship with two bent producers who are trying to raise finances for another show. One of the producers has a sister who runs the Legion of Purity. The film was made under the banner of Columbia Pictures, who changed the title at Mae's prompting to *The Heat's On*, a title she felt better reflected the West persona.

She had put on a great deal of weight while not working, but now went on a diet and managed to shed over a stone. Unfortunately it was still not enough and she looks pretty hefty on screen. Mae was unhappy when dieting and particularly unhappy about Ratoff's film and it shows.

The film was a miserable ordeal for Mae and her leaden performance reflects her state of mind. She was humiliated by taking part in a film which was clearly cut-price. Ratoff's direction is clumsy; he obviously was working in a hurry to save money.

Mae had come full cycle, and *The Heat's On* is like a parody of *Night After Night*. In her first film she had not had a great deal to do but managed in doing it to illuminate the entire picture; her bold shafts of comedy elevated what in essence was a run-of-the-mill gangster film into a permanent tribute to her powers. She does not have much to do in *The Heat's On* either, but succeeds whenever she is on screen in actually slowing down the film to a funereal pace. What little that is good about *The Heat's On* comes from its supporting players.

Her appearances are separate cameos slotted into the film. She arrogantly lumbers through her paces indifferent to their lack of sparkle. Her musical items are appalling. The songs themselves are uninspired as are the arrangements. No effort is made to show off her voice and she grinds her way through a few chorus items in such a way that if it weren't for the fact that she is centre screen it would not be clear she is the star. She is plonked in the middle of a troupe of dancers whose very animation enhances her heaviness; she is so sewn into her costumes that she seems unable to move, even had the block shoes, tucked beneath her skirts, permitted her to do so.

The film loses its way from the start. Ratoff had tried to capitalize on the thriving South American market created by Carmen Miranda, who had arrived in the States with a bang. The Brazilian Bombshell, fantastically garbed, was pulling in audiences in a big way, much as Mae had done a decade ago with *She Done Him Wrong*. Mae, however, was pure Brooklyn; the nearest she came to South America was when she bought a bag of Brazil nuts.

Mae knew she had failed to deliver the goods and denounced the film herself as 'dismal'. As she was her own greatest fan, for her to take such a stand meant that she was sickened by it.

There is only one scene where the real Mae West shines through. This she shares with Victor Moore in the role of an elderly suitor who arrives for their meeting wearing a toupee. He dances excitedly around Mae; when about to embrace her, his hairpiece suddenly becomes dislodged. 'Don't look now, honey, your hair's skiddin',' Mae mutters.

The film retained its title of *Tropicana*, in England, where it arrived in 1944. Distributors did not consider it worthy enough to play as a feature and it was mangled into a B movie.

Just as Garbo had fled the industry in 1941 after the release of her flop, *Two-Faced Woman*, now Mae turned her back on films. Mae West appearing in a B movie was too great an insult to bear. She wanted no more of it. She did not even want to be in Hollywood where, she was convinced, she could see mockery on every face.

She was bitter and hurt. When Hollywood wanted her back, it would have to crawl on its knees to her. She did not doubt that Hollywood would want her back, but she could not have conceived how long it would be before the movie industry came knocking on her door again. In fact, twenty-six years elapsed before she returned, and then in the most extraordinary circumstances.

It was now or never for *Catherine* she decided. Not as a movie of course. That was all-too-painfully out of the question, but she was an actress and she could still command a theatrical audience. She converted her filmscript into a stage play, renaming it *Catherine Was Great*. She had remained friendly with Lee Shubert and that friendship paid off. He told her she could still draw audiences and, putting his money where his mouth was, said he would be honoured to stage *Catherine*.

The producer whom Shubert recommended – mainly for his enormous energy – was a foul-mouthed, cigar-smoking, thirty-seven-year-old tyrant named Mike Todd. Todd was later to achieve fame in 1956 from the only film which he personally produced, *Around the World in Eighty Days*, in which most of Hollywood played cameo roles. It was filmed in the wide-screen Todd-AO system which still bears his name. He married Elizabeth Taylor in 1957 and was killed in an air crash in 1958.

Todd had a flair for producing Broadway spectaculars and, although he had a personal investment in *Catherine Was Great*, he did not hold back on expenses. Mae's gowns were among the most lavish she had worn. One costume alone, heavily encrusted with rhinestones, and with a towering oriental headdress, weighed seventy-five pounds.

As with Mae's other theatrical sex-dramas, *Catherine* was not a revue, but a full-scale play containing elements of comedy. There was a single song entitled 'Strong, Solid and Sensational'. She took a personal interest in the casting of the male chorus, travelling to New York to audition applicants, and selecting the tallest, handsomest and most muscular actors she could find. There were, of course, rumours as to how Mae actually auditioned the boys. One of her attacks of sexual voracity, however, was no rumour, but was authenticated by Yolande Donlan.

Miss Donlan, whose father had acted with Mae in *Belle of the Nineties*, saw *Catherine* in performance and afterwards called with a young couple backstage to pay her respects to Mae. While mingling with the cast Miss Donlan's friend suddenly noticed that Mae and her boyfriend were missing. The girl went to Mae's dressing room and unceremoniously flung open the door. They had been missing only a few minutes, but the pair were locked together. 'I don't know if she was as sex-obsessed all the time, as she claimed,' says Miss Donlan, 'but she certainly had a spurt of it then.'

The director of *Catherine* was Roy Hargrave, and in her memoirs Mae acknowledges his difficulties in staging such a lavish play. Her film directors are barely mentioned in the book and, if they are, usually disparagingly, in relation to how she overcame their interference. Mae was contemptuous of the film industry, but she was sympathetic to the problems of a stage director.

The play opened for a pre-Broadway run at the Forrest Theater, Philadelphia, on 11 July 1944, during a heat wave. The temperature on stage under the lights hovered around 90–100°F, getting hotter as the evening progressed. Sweat poured from under Mae's heavy wig, and it took an effort for her merely to walk, particularly in the coronation scene – the weight of her train took four men and two pageboys to lift. She wore, as always, her platform shoes, the straps of which cut cruelly into her flesh. After each performance her feet had to be massaged painfully back into shape.

She played to a packed house and the Philadelphians loved her. She was a great, glamorous movie star: an exotic bloom in a fantasy setting. There was thunderous applause as the curtain fell and the hard-boiled broad from Brooklyn admitted that she had tears in her eyes. A very un-Mae Westian reaction.

The rehearsals, however, had been very Westian with Mae and Todd constantly snapping at each other. Despite the successful preview Todd was convinced there was a lot wrong with the show and that New Yorkers, accustomed to stars, would expect something more than Mae's mere presence to stir them. And there were too few laughs.

The fault, he believed, was that Mae had too much reverence for Catherine and was treating her subject too seriously. Something drastic must be done. A meeting was held between Todd, Izzy Rappaport (who was one of the play's 'angels') and Jim. Jim was designated the one to straighten Mae out but he did not have the nerve and flatly refused. Todd did have the nerve and, according to Art Cohn,* Mike Todd's biographer, this is what took place:

He told her she must play the show broader, for laughs. She replied that this changed the conception of the play and if she had to do this then she would not be ready for the Broadway opening. Todd bluntly informed her they were opening on Broadway in one week's time come what may.

'I got a new scene for you,' Todd told her.

'Another one?'

'Don't fight me, Miss West, we're only trying to improve the show.'

'But there's a limit,' she protested. The previous evening she had been handed a new song a quarter of an hour before the curtain rose. When she protested she could not learn it that quickly Todd had informed her someone would speak the words from behind the curtain. Although she had sung the song she had not been happy about it.

Todd now described the new scene to her. She was to receive the Turkish ambassador and say, 'The Turkish situation interests me mightily ... Come into my boudoir and we'll talk turkey.'

There was a pained expression on Mae's face. 'You're trying to make a caricature of Catherine the Great!' she complained.

* *The Nine Lives of Michael Todd*, Random House, 1959.

'Let's face it, Miss West, this isn't a Helen Hayes vehicle.'

Mae bristled. 'And who is Helen Hayes?' she demanded sternly.

A replacement scene which better pleased Mae was then suggested by Todd. She is inspecting the male courtiers and conspicuously keeps her eyes at crotch level. After passing several of the men she pauses and, peering down, says, 'You're new here?' She so liked the scene she used it not only in *Catherine Was Great* but for the rest of her life, having it written into *Myra Breckinridge* a quarter of a century later.

An original West line, according to Art Cohn, came about when a mishap occurred on stage between Mae and Gene Barry, who was playing Lieutenant Bunin. Barry's scabbard accidently stabbed her in the abdomen during an embrace. 'Oh,' she said, 'Is that your sword, or are you just pleased to see me?' That line, too, was used for the rest of her life and she later created her own story as to how it came about. Mae liked Gene Barry but objected to his habit of darkening his moustache with lamp-blacking as it transferred to her face during their kisses. Mae had no humour where her looks were concerned.

Mae grudgingly inserted a few of Todd's ideas into her script, but by and large, pursued her own course. As Cohn states, 'She had been one of Hollywood's foremost stars ... She knew what she was doing and she had no intention of backing down for a Michael-come-lately-Todd.'

There were disputes about the casting. Mae decided at this late stage that her leading man, Coburn Goodwin, was not right. She had met someone she preferred and wanted to substitute him in the show. This was Wee Willie Davis, a professional wrestler. Todd auditioned him but reported to Mae afterwards, 'He's a big, handsome brute all right, Miss West ... but he seems incapable of reading difficult lines like "Yes" and "No".'* He was not included in the cast.

*The Nine Lives of Michael Todd, Random House, 1959.

Despite the skirmishes the show opened on schedule at the Shubert Theater on Broadway on 2 August and played to a capacity audience. An element of patriotism surrounded the production as part of its takings was converted into bonds to help the war effort, but this by no means softened the hearts of the critics:

A dirty-minded little girl's essay on the Russian Empress, played like a chatelaine of an old-time *maison de joie* ... Even the staunchest West disciple felt faintly surfeited and would have settled, with loud cheers, for Cornelia Otis Skinner in Bible readings.   GEORGE JEAN NATHAN

... her script is monotonous and her acting is more limited than ever.   *Herald Tribune*

MAE SLIPS ON THE STEPPES! This morning the Siren of Sex lies self-slain by her own pen ... it should have been turned into a fifteen-minute blackout revue and somebody else might have better written the script.
                                    LOUIS KRONENBERGER

... the specific gravity of lead, and the results, when not merely sedative, were often crushing.   *Time*

But Ed Sullivan, later to host *The Ed Sullivan Show* on television, but at that time writing a column, noted, 'If you doubt the box-office oomph of Mae West, consider that she converted *Catherine Was Great* into a box-office hit. I don't know any other star strong enough with the public to have accomplished it!'

After each performance Mae would make one of her curtain speeches for which she had a fondness. She would announce that she was not a bit like the character she portrayed and would wind up, 'Catherine was a great empress. She also had three hundred lovers. I did the best I could in a couple of hours.'

The show notched up a seven-month run yet was not a

financial success. Todd had budgeted $150,000 for *Catherine* and it never recouped that amount at the box office. His judgement had proved accurate about how the show should have been played. Mae eventually came round to Todd's way of thinking and admitted to reporter Cecil Wilson: 'It's no good trying to be serious. I tried it . . . by playing Catherine of Russia, but when I held out my hand to be kissed the audience weren't happy until I raised my eyebrows in that way they like. So, gradually, the whole thing became a burlesque.'

After the Broadway run, *Catherine* went on tour in Baltimore, Boston and Washington DC. While in the capital she gave a special performance for wounded soldiers. Mae gave generously to the war effort. She entertained the troops both in live performances and on radio (despite the NBC ban), but never talked about her patriotism. She also took part in various training films made for the forces. In addition to this Mae found another practical way of helping her country. She sold many valuable pieces of jewellery and donated over one million dollars to bond funds. Her jewels were replaced by paste replicas. Some of the reproductions were auctioned at Christie's in London in 1989.

However she never took part in any of the famous Hollywood Canteen evenings where service personnel not only danced with the stars but were served food by them. She was no good on a one-to-one basis, having no small talk, and was inclined to come over as glum. Neither did she go on any bond-selling tours. She was probably not pressed to do so since Hollywood was as disaffected with her as she with it.

The publicity stills which accompanied the run of *Catherine* were magnificent. Her hair is pulled away from her head in a sophisticated style and she'd adopted a new, arched shape for her eyebrows. In reality she had little in the way of eyebrows, just a smattering of baby down, which gave her freedom to paint in whatever shape best suited her. Actuality shots, however, which she tried to suppress, reveal her more frayed appearance.

From Washington the show moved to Pittsburgh and ended its run in Chicago in May 1945. The New York run and tour had lasted almost a year.

When the war ended in September 1945 a spirit of euphoria filled the air. The film business had new heroines, and frothy musicals were in demand. Mae's brand of sexual pastiche was old fashioned. No film offers had come in while she was on tour. Shubert offered her another tour but this time there was no Broadway date scheduled. Although confident she could draw a provincial audience, Broadway was another matter and he wasn't prepared to take the risk.

Since she wanted to work she took the tour. Shubert had in mind a contemporary comedy by Miles Mander, Fred Schiller and Thomas Dunphy called *Ring Twice Tonight*. It was set in Washington DC and she was to play an FBI agent, Carliss Dale. Topicality was served in that Carliss was on the track of Nazi agents. At one point, and the reason why is unclear, a shower of balloons descended from the window of Carliss's apartment in Embassy Row, each bearing the legend 'Come On Up' and her address. What ensued, of course, was a parade up to the apartment of would-be lovers all determined to bed the lovely Carliss.

Mae adapted the play and converted it into a vehicle for herself, while Jim went to New York to discuss the details with the Shuberts. The title went through various incarnations and finally emerged as *Come On Up, Ring Twice*.

As the play was due to open in Long Beach, California, Mae remained at the Ravenswood. Like all professionals she did not believe in wasting money on accommodation. *Come On Up, Ring Twice* opened in May 1946 and was due to tour until February 1947.

Mae was now having serious hair problems. She had worn hairpieces for years and these had been provided by a particular establishment on Sunset Boulevard. But her special requirements were not easily met as she insisted that real hair, baby fine and as near natural blonde as possible, was used to make them.

Ann Rea, who now lives in Glendale, California, had looked after Mae's wigs for some time, but she had never met Mae personally since her chauffeur delivered and collected her hairpieces. One day, however, he arrived and asked for Miss Rea.

She recalls, 'He told me, "Miss West is in the limousine and would like to talk to you." So I went outside and, boy, there she sat in the limo, it was about half a block long. When I went up she said, "Hello, dear. Come in and sit down. I want to talk to you." Well, I got in and sat there beside her, she was all in white. "How would you like to travel with me?" she asked. "In one of my touring shows? Look after my hair?" I didn't know what to say, so I said it wouldn't be fair for me to walk out on my boss. "You can always come back," she said. So I travelled with her, on and off, for the next nine years. Miss West never discussed the money with me, that was always done through an agent.

'When she wasn't touring, I used to go to the Ravenswood about three or four times a month. There would be dresses and fur coats thrown about all over the place. I'm small, like she was, and she'd get me to put them on and model them for her while she decided which to buy. And hats, too, I was always modelling hats for her.'

Despite Mae's reputation for not getting on with other women Miss Rea liked her: 'She was a beautiful person, I thought she was marvellous and I wouldn't have stayed nine years with her if I didn't like her. When she travelled by train she had a compartment of her own. Sometimes she would get headaches if she was nervous and send for me and I'd massage her head. She was not temperamental, but if someone did something wrong she panicked. Mr Timony would travel with her, he was always nice to me but he was quite a bit older than her, and he looked like an old, old man. He was jealous of all the other men in the show, but he really behaved more like a father to her.'

Miss Rea was also required to dress Mae's hair prior to her making her stage entrances. She paints an interesting picture of Mae on tour. 'She always took pictures of her mother with her and had them up in her dressing room. She never mentioned movies and I think the stage was more important to her. Her complexion was very beautiful and it showed up better on stage. She always wanted to look beautiful, it was more important to her than the lines or the plot or anything. I had to do things her way but I figured she was paying for it so that was all right. We got along fine. Off stage, she didn't say much to anyone, she was very quiet. But she did love the men and they loved her.'

As always, the family had to visit and Miss Rea remembers both Beverly and John arriving at various times. 'I liked Beverly,' she says, 'she was lively and enjoyed going out. We went out together a couple of times after the show but Miss West objected. Beverly drank too much and she was annoyed at me for encouraging her. Beverly had one leg shorter than the other and Miss West was always frightened she would fall and hurt herself when she had had a few drinks as had happened in the past. Her brother John drank as well; he liked to enjoy himself. She would let them travel with her but she'd never allow them near her before she went on. She was the sole saviour of them, you know. She had a big heart.'

Come on Up ended its run back on the West Coast with performances in both San Francisco and Los Angeles. Mae still hoped for a Broadway run but it never materialized. What did materialize was far more exciting.

Mae had long nurtured an ambition to visit Europe. It was after all her ancestral home. Battling Jack had been of Irish stock and Tillie, German. She claimed to have discovered, somewhere along the line, that the Wests originated from the town of Long Crendon in Buckinghamshire and dated back to the time of Alfred the Great. The more celebrated Mae became, the more illustrious became her family tree. She eventually included knights and royalty in her genealogy and gave out that French blood flowed through her veins – and royal French blood at that.

She frequently told newsmen she was about to appear in both Paris and London and, whereas she never made Paris, in August 1947 she set sail on the *Queen Mary* for Southampton to tour Britain in *Diamond Lil*, culminating with a run at London's Prince of Wales Theatre. She left America in a blaze of publicity, photographed alongside Mr America.

Mae was no better sailor than she was air traveller and even aboard the well-stabilized *Queen Mary* found the ocean voyage unsettling. She stayed on board the boat for a night after it had docked to recuperate, but issued a press statement saying it was a wonderful ship with wonderful people and wonderful food. It was as well she had enjoyed the menu: Britain was in the throes of food rationing and the huge steaks she so loved were virtually unobtainable, even for ready money. She arranged to have food parcels sent to her.

When she made her appearance the crowds that had gathered were disappointed. She wore a plain black dress done up to the throat and hanging to her feet. She now wore evening or tea-gowns most of the time. The only touch of colour was a pink headscarf and her fabled jewellery consisted of a single bracelet and ring. Her bearing was modest. This was not at all what was expected. People had imagined that *Diamond Lil* herself was going to swagger down the gangplank.

'If a gal has her legs covered she can concentrate on hips and bust – and so can a feller,' she wisecracked, compensating a delighted throng for her quiet appearance. She had certainly come prepared, for she had brought six trunks of personal clothing plus two more containing *Lil* costumes. She had heard that clothes like food were rationed in Britain and that there was nothing to buy. She did not want to be caught out.

She also brought along half a dozen pieces of her best jewellery which she wore in her performances. Not everything had been sold for war bonds. The reason she wore so few jewels and plain clothes when leaving ship was that she had now reversed her policy about flamboyance in public. She believed that people should pay to see her in her finery. If they got the show gratis they might not come to the theatre.

She told the press the things they wanted to hear: 'I can't sew and I can't cook but, boy, I do everything else.' And 'I'm just crazy to meet Englishmen – one of my favourite leading men was an Englishman, Cary Grant—have they got something.' She created a favourable if low-key impression, and the *Daily Express* account of her arrival is typically warm:

Most schoolgirlish complexion, gentlest voice and demurest manner in London today belonged to Mae West.

But she also had the longest false eyelashes – fully a clear inch – the blondest, longest hair-do on the *Queen Mary* coming over.

Only dress in her ship's wardrobe which could be described as daring is a *décolleté* one of flame-coloured satin which shows those curves. But that is only for her play *Diamond Lil*. Her only make-up was a mere suspicion of pink lipstick, a little powder – and, of course, the eyelashes. Pink, too, was a chiffon scarf over her platinum hair. Her face is as unlined as that of a twenty-year-old girl.

Miss West still insists she has come to England 'because of your men – I love the way they talk.' She wants to see 'just everyone', but particularly John Bull, the King and Queen, and some of her ancestors in the north of England.

Mae was staying at one of London's loveliest hotels, the Savoy, where a riverside suite was awaiting her. She checked in on 17 September 1947 and immediately presented a problem for Scotland Yard. She had brought with her gems to the value of a quarter of a million pounds and when not in use they were kept in the hotel safe. Although Mae had personal bodyguards the police insisted on detailing an additional two of their own men to guard her.

Diamond Lil was to open in Manchester, then tour Blackpool, Birmingham and Glasgow before coming to London. Other than Richard Bailey and Hal Gould, her two leading men whom Mae had brought from America, she intended to cast the show with British actors.

To promote *Lil* she took part in the peak-time radio show *In Town Tonight* in which visiting celebrities were interviewed. Also on the show were Gilbert Harding and actress Googie Withers. Miss Withers's husband, John McCallum, recalled the event: 'The ... interview [was] ... very funny. We sat behind her [Mae] in the BBC studio while she was being interviewed. Googie said to me, "Look at her bottom." Every time she said anything, it wiggled. It soon became obvious that she couldn't say anything without wiggling it. Answers to the most mundane questions, nothing whatever to do with her famous sex image, got the full husky voice treatment and the bottom wiggle. It became quite hilarious, until everyone in the studio, including the sound engineers in the glassed-in control room, were in fits of laughter.'*

One of the actresses hired for *Diamond Lil* was Margaret Stallard. She remembers her audition and the 'utter confusion' that reigned:

'There were lots of ladies of the town and tarts among the girls. At that time Equity was not so strong on restricted membership. They picked up everyone who looked right. Among the men – and I'm sure Christopher Lee was there – was a Fiji boxing champ, and boxer "Kid" Lewis, who had one line, "Swing it, Lil", said in his cockney accent although he was supposed to be American. There was also a little man who sold newspapers nearby. I think Mae had seen him as she went into the theatre and thought he looked right so he was booked. He had ginger hair and a moustache and they took him just for that, as though wigs didn't exist. They put him in the bar scene to look colourful. The whole thing was totally disorganized. The producer just pushed people about on stage, there was no real direction. I went with lots of lipstick and my hair like Veronica Lake's.

'Mae West behaved very badly at rehearsals. Sometimes she wouldn't turn up for hours, then she would arrive in her long, black dress and blonde hair set immaculately.'

'There wasn't a particle of femininity about her, she was a pastiche of femininity. She was not truly sexual, she sent it all up like a female impersonator sends it all up. It was extraordinary. But she certainly had a sense of humour in a wry way. Little quips would come out, like, "Say, who is this guy Big Ben? I want to meet him." '

After days of auditions, Mae eventually selected Bruno Barnabe as her Latin Lover. He had already been rejected on the grounds that he was too old, but she found no one better, and with just a week to go before the pre-London run was due

* *Life With Googie*, Heinemann, 1979.

to start the role had yet to be filled. It was decided that Barnabe was the most suitable applicant after all.

He was working at the time at the Strand Theatre in *Separate Rooms* and during the interval he received a phone call from Jim who told him Miss West wanted to audition him again. Barnabe, though frail now, still recalls those events of over forty years ago: 'I was rather peeved,' he says. 'I replied to Mr Timony, "It was thought I was too old, well, I'm three weeks older now. I'm sorry, but I won't audition again."' But the temptation of working with the legendary Mae West was too much to resist and he agreed to meet her at the Savoy. 'I thought that I could dine out for years on the story,' he admits.

'I arrived next day at the appointed hour and Mr Timony let me in. Miss West was seated on a sofa, wearing a pink feathered négligée. Next to her were Noele Gordon and Francis de Wolff who were also in the cast. "Come right in, honey," she said and Mr Timony handed me a script.

' "We'll just run through the bedroom scene," she told me. "Now, I'm fixing my hair in front of the dressing room table and you come up behind me and put your hands on my bosom, OK?"

' "OK." I put my hand on her left breast.

' "I meant both breasts, honey," she said.

' "I put the script between my teeth and my right hand on her right breast, as directed, and gently rotated both hands. "You're in," she said briefly.'

The late Noele Gordon, beloved of the British as Meg in the TV soap opera *Crossroads*, did not get on with Mae. She loathed her. But not one to bandy gossip she would shut up like a clam when Mae was mentioned and refuse to discuss her publicly. She did, however, confide her feelings to her close friend, the comedian Larry Grayson (not to be confused with the American of that name who was later in Mae's employ). One of Mae's habits that infuriated Noele was that she would never address her by her name, always referring to her peremptorily as Rita, the character she was playing.

Miss Gordon played Russian Rita but got the part as an afterthought. It had originally been given to Malya Woolf, who provides more details as to why Noele hated Mae. *Diamond Lil* was being presented jointly by Tom Arnold and Val Parnell and Noele was the mistress of Parnell. Miss Woolf was informed at short notice that her part was to be given to Noele and that she would now understudy her. Being the girlfriend of the producer meant Noele could chose her own wardrobe and she selected some rich, period frocks.

That was before Mae came on the scene. '[Noele] had chosen all her wardrobe,' Malya remembers, 'but then Miss West arrived and wouldn't let her wear any of them. She was determined no one was going to outshine her. That didn't endear Miss West to Noele. I felt sorry for her because she had been publicly humbled and commiserated, but Noele was still in a temper. "Don't you touch me!" she screamed, before I had the chance to utter a word.'

Even Parnell's intercession could not get her frocks reinstated. Mae was adamant and Noele had to put up with the drab rags Mae thought suitable.

'Many years later I got a part in *Crossroads*,' Miss Woolf continues. 'Noele was, of course, the star. During a break I casually asked her, "Do you remember those days with Mae West?" "Don't you mention that horrible woman!" she snarled. But later she apologized. She was actually very nice but I had jarred terrible memories.' Terrible memories and physically painful, too. As Russian Rita Noele had to wear heavy make-up and developed a painful rash as a result. But Mae would not permit her to wear less.

As is the case in every company rumours started circulating about the star. Because she was never seen without a head-covering or a wig (and wigs were uncommon then even for actresses), one of these rumours was that Mae was bald. When the wig was not in use it travelled in a large box in the close possession of her hairdresser. One day it dropped and skidded along the floor. Mae screamed.

Another rumour, which persists today, was that Mae was a man. 'She had a make-up girl who used to talk to us,' Miss Woolf recalls, 'and she told us Mae had scars on her breasts as though she had had an operation. Word got around that she had had surgery to give her breasts. The poor woman didn't have a chance.'

As an understudy, Miss Woolf was no threat and Mae could be kind in such circumstances. Miss Woolf could sit back and watch the altercations without becoming involved and she saw a side of Mae that was denied Noele Gordon, 'She was a dear, an enchanting woman, so kind to me,' she says. 'Obviously her head was screwed on all right, but she was extremely nice. Her costumes were marvellous and the chorus all admired them. 'You can come in and try them on, sweethearts,' she said. But we were too in awe of her to ask, we never dared. I'm sure she wouldn't have minded if we had.'

The *Diamond Lil* company started the first leg of its tour in Manchester. Mae, always a nervous passenger, insisted on making the journey by train as she did not like the idea of travelling on England's narrow roads, fearing there might be a head-on collision. She arrived in the north-west in a fog: 'I'm sure they'll love me,' she cracked, 'if they ever see me.'

The cast consisted of thirty-eight speaking parts and fifteen walk-ons which made it expensive to mount. Economies had to be made. These started with the salaries of her fellow artists. Bruno Barnabe remembers, 'I was one of the lucky ones, I got £40 a week, that was all that was left after Mae took her cut of £2,000 per week. In order for the management to make any profit at all, it was essential we play to full houses. The dearest seat in a theatre in 1947 was around £3.'

Lil opened at the Palace Theatre, Manchester, and its publicity plus the drawing power of Mae's name ensured the house was full. But, as with *Catherine Was Great* the critics were not enthusiastic about her on stage:

Miss West did not entirely succeed in projecting for the stage the forceful character so well known on the films. Though always a colourful character she was sometimes inaudible.   *Manchester Evening News*

Mae stayed at the Midland Hotel – perhaps the finest hotel in the north. The rest of the cast had to fend for themselves and several stayed at the guest house of Alma McKay, one of the best known of theatrical landladies. Her home in Daisy Avenue has hosted generations of stage and film personalities. Miss McKay still recalls the *Diamond Lil* visit: 'She [Mae] found out that I was feeding my people better than she was getting at the Midland. She sent word she would like me to cook for her so I sent her round food every day. She liked my chicken and mushroom pie.

'I found out that she was a bit miserable because she couldn't go out; if ever she tried there were crowds all round her. Everywhere she went she had four big he-men with her, guarding her. So I sent word through one of the actors that if she wanted an outing in peace she should go to a village near here that was full of gravestones. There wasn't one person buried there who didn't have a title. Americans like anything like that, and there was a lovely pub that did lunches. "She'll be all right there," I told him. She got really excited about it, and nothing would stop her from going. She sent me an autographed picture afterwards.

'I never got paid for feeding her, of course. All the American stars are like that. Laurel and Hardy were just the same, inviting themselves and thinking they're doing you a great honour, then disappearing afterwards and you're out of pocket as a result. But I looked after her very well even though she didn't pay me for it.'

Next stop was Blackpool, where *Lil* was running for six weeks at the Opera House. She stayed in a suite at the Clifton Hotel and Joyce Wright, who was employed there, remembers the occasion: 'No one except her own staff was allowed to see her until she was fully made up. Then she allowed hotel staff in while she sat up in bed, very glamorous. We were all given tickets to see the show.'*

Mae intended to spend a quiet Christmas with Jim at the hotel, but accepted an impromptu invitation to spend Christmas Eve with a Mr and Mrs Olsberg at their home in Fairhaven Road, Lytham. Apparently Mae had made friends with the

---

* Which indicates business was less than capacity.

Olsbergs' son, who was serving in the armed forces in America. Mr and Mrs Ike Freedman were also present at the celebration. Mr Freedman recalls: 'Miss West arrived with her lawyer, Mr Timony, and an actor from the show, a big chap well over six foot tall [probably Kid Lewis, her bodyguard], and they all had dinner with the family. The Olsbergs' house was pleasant, but nothing extraordinary and there had been a great deal of razzmatazz about Miss West in the papers, but she was delightful. After dinner she sat on a pouffe by the fire and chatted with Mrs Olsberg's mother about what was put into the dinner and how it was made. Everyone was struck by how quiet and ordinary she was. It was a very homely little party. She didn't want to discuss her showbiz life at all, she simply wanted a quiet evening away from the theatre.'

There was a Christmas party for the cast in Blackpool, held on the stage of the Opera House. Someone got a huge gold chair from the props department and Mae sat on it like a queen.

'While the rest of us danced she sat on her throne,' recalls Bruno Barnabe. 'But after a while Mr Timony called for silence. "Miss West has some presents she wants to hand out," he said. "Will all the men line up on one side of the stage and pick out a piece of paper from this bin." We did this, and some of the papers had crosses on them. Seven of us got crosses, including me, which meant I was to go up to the throne and get a present. We each received a pair of socks. But all the women were passed over. I don't know how she could have done it.'

That party is also remembered by Margaret Stallard: 'She didn't contribute one penny towards it,' avers Miss Stallard. 'Mae West never entertained the company in any way whatsoever, she was stingy. We paid for the party and she put in an appearance.

'Afterwards, James Timony came to the girls' dressing room – he was a rough old thing who looked like a thug – and he was holding a brown paper bag, not a box, a brown paper bag of loose chocolates. He shoved this bag at us, stuffing the odd chocolate in his own mouth at the same time. "Miss West wants you to have some chocolates for Christmas," he said, and chucked the bag on the table without another word. He went out and slammed the door. You could have heard a pin drop in the room.'

That heart-warming scene was enacted, it must be remembered, in Mae's absence. What probably happened was that she had told Jim to buy the girls some chocolates for Christmas and he had brought the cheapest kind he could find, delivering them with the old-world charm Miss Stallard has described. It was undoubtedly a similar situation regarding the non-payment for Alma McKay's food and the lack of financial contribution to the cast party. Mae was like royalty. She never carried money. She left this to Jim, who clearly let her down. She was never mean and often generous.

There are several accounts of Jim being rude to people when Mae was absent, but he never dared to be in her presence, as Ike Freedman's account of the Christmas Eve party illustrates. When in her presence he had to watch his Ps and Qs, but behind her back he could, and did, throw his weight around.

As Malcolm Dodds discovered. Dodds, who describes himself as 'Mae West's greatest fan', sent her a Christmas present of a collection of over 1000 of her press cuttings mounted in a scrap book. Such devotion was rewarded and she invited him to meet her and to see *Diamond Lil* as her guest.

Beforehand he stood with the crowd and watched the 'dazzling' Mae arrive at the stage door, escorted by her bodyguard. After she had entered the theatre Dodds spoke to Jim, whom he recognized from photographs, and said he was there at Mae's invitation. Jim brushed him off and left him standing dumbstruck.

In distress Dodds sent word to Mae that he was there. A 'secretary' soon arrived, full of apologies, and took him to Mae in her dressing room. 'Miss West greeted me with a kiss,' he says, 'and said, "Malcolm, I am so delighted to meet you." Mr Timony shook hands and apologized and left the room. Miss West asked me why I admired her and asked me to read some cigarette cards to her, which I still have.' (Mae was featured on them.)

Dodds saw the show every night for a week and every evening

he went to Mae's dressing room. On the last night of his week he again shook hands with Jim and while doing so Mae said, 'Jim, give Malcolm what's in your hand.' He handed Dodds £50. She corresponded with him all her life and on learning of the death of his mother in 1958 sent him a long letter of condolence. When her autobiography was published she wrote and apologized because she had been unable to include a reference to him in it. She was considerate to her fans, often beyond the call of duty.

chapter nineteen

HOME AGAIN

Lil's next port of call was Glasgow. 'We took sandwiches and flasks for the journey,' Malya Woolf recalls, 'but no one had thought about her. I gather she had some sandwiches but had brought nothing to drink. Anyway, some old drunk* came stumbling down the corridor asking, "Has anyone a cup of coffee they can spare for Miss West?" So we poured her one in the cap of the thermos flask. As soon as we got to Glasgow she came over to us on the platform. "Who was the girl who gave me coffee? I want to thank you," she asked in that slow drawl she always used. We were overcome, she was such a big star. She was the sweetest woman.'

But Bruno Barnabe recalls she was disappointed by her lukewarm reception at Glasgow station: 'She stepped off the train expecting the usual vast crowds and was extremely displeased to find a thinner mob than usual.'

Mae was staying at the Central Hotel, just a couple of hundred yards from the now demolished Alhambra Theatre where *Lil* was playing. No matter where she was Mae would visit a Spiritualist place of worship and while in Glasgow she went to the St Vincent Street Church to see the famous medium Helen Hughes.

Barbara F. Baird, now of North Yorkshire, was among the congregation. 'She came in just before the service started, accompanied by two men,' remembers Miss Baird. 'One was the president of the church and the other was her bodyguard. She was dressed in a black fur coat and hat, very subdued. She

---

* This was the producer.

sat near the front, between the men, and left at the end of the service before the congregation. She did nothing to draw attention to herself and I got the impression she would rather have liked it if she could have gone there without anyone knowing who she was. I understand that she had specially requested that there was to be no fuss, she just wished to attend the service like anyone else.'

Mae had been invited by the president, Charles Hodgkinson, to sit on the platform with the VIPs but declined, making the excuse that her exclusivity contract prohibited such appearances. Such clauses prevent commercial ventures which might harm the box office, but no one would have sued her had she chosen to sit upon the platform during a religious service. She never exploited her religion.

Mr Hodgkinson noted, 'I regret to report that the audience ... appeared more interested in catching a glimpse of the curvaceous Mae than in the service.'

It was clear that Helen Hughes impressed Mae: while chatting to another Spiritualist, John Winning, she confided that she would sacrifice her screen career if she could become as good a medium as Mrs Hughes. She booked a private sitting with her to take place later in her hotel room.

The show moved to Birmingham from Glasgow. By now Bruno Barnabe was getting used to her and able to separate the woman from the star. 'I found Mae easy to work with and not one to throw tantrums,' he says. 'The nearest she came to having one was when she lost a laugh on one of her lines. The laugh should have come soon after her first entrance, which she made with me. When she came off she snapped, "I lost that laugh. You watch during the next performance and see who was moving during that line." I did, and realized it had nothing to do with anyone moving. The loss was Mae's fault. I didn't have the courage to tell her then but eventually when the laugh still failed to come, I came clean. "About that laugh," I said. "The line only makes sense if the audience hears the preceding question. You've been overlapping that line and losing the last word, so you've been losing the laugh yourself." She accepted that and regained the laugh, but later on she lost it again for the same reason. "Who was moving?" she demanded once more.'

London was the highlight of the tour and the entire reason Mae was in Britain. The show still wasn't making enough money but she was again ensconced in splendour at the Savoy. For reasons of economy Margaret Stallard found herself promoted to doing a scene with Mae. 'They started sacking people,' she remembers, 'and making people double up. There was lots of shifting about and economizing that would not have been allowed today. I found myself suddenly cast as the girl who was sent to Rio.

'To rehearse my scene with Mae I was summoned to her suite and subjected to the full Mae West experience. She was lounging on a couch in her négligée which had marabou feathers all over it. She said something and I answered in my normal English accent. It was the first time she had heard it as we played Americans in the show. "Say," she said in surprise, "you've got a real English accent. I thought you was authentic." She meant it as a compliment and seemed quite pleased with me in her distant way.

'But during rehearsals at the Prince of Wales she was underpowered. We assumed she would give a lot more on the night but she didn't, that was all we ever got.'

Several critics complained of Mae's inaudibility on opening night and after that microphones were strategically placed about the stage. Theatrical historian Joe Mitchenson recalls, 'It was the first obviously miked show in London. Every time she moved she went to a new microphone position. If she moved to the bed, for example, there was a microphone in the bedpost. If she moved to a table there was a convenient microphone in a vase of flowers. You knew she couldn't work without a mike.

'She used a spotlight, too. Whenever she came on she was hit by a spot. It followed her all over the stage and detracted from the rest of the performances. Everyone else seemed to be working in darkness. It shows the power of a spot – she would have known that from her days in Variety. All in all it was a very poor show.'

The critic for the *Sunday Express* of 25 January 1948 agreed: 'Mae West had a success last night on her first appearance in

London – not as the author of *Diamond Lil* – not even as its shimmering and bejewelled star, but as a woman at a microphone. *Diamond Lil* is a fifteen-minute vaudeville act, crudely and casually padded out to two hours.'

Critic Dick Richards was even more damning: 'The Mae West joke is over ... When Mae West glided on to the stage last night in a gaudy purple outfit she stopped the show – but soon we realized that a little of her technique goes a long way. Her stock-in-trade remains the same – but its effect has gone. Nowadays we want our sirens a little more subtle and streamlined ... If Mae West had visited us as a variety act – singing the three songs which were so well received in the second act – all would have been well. But, as it was, an over-enthusiastic, determinedly-kind, first night audience applauded Miss West and the play for all they were worth. In fact, for rather more than they were worth.'

Margaret Stallard remembers, 'She would just sway from one mike to another, hands on hips and deliver her lines. There was no attempt at acting. But she was magnificent in the songs and she had a stand mike for them so there was no trouble with sound. She just stood in front and let it all happen. I used to really look forward to that part. Her pianist, Bert Waller, was superb. She certainly cared about that bit of the show, and got the best musician available and stuck with him.'

Bert Waller has affectionate memories of Mae: 'She was a great character, but a stickler for no one upstaging her. If they tried they'd soon get a letter from the company manager. She had had a very good schooling in that direction. She loved singing but she was not at all a good musician. She did a seventeen-chorus version of 'Frankie and Johnny' but I had to play the melodic line throughout to support her. But she was good rhythmically. I'm sure she must have worked closely with black people as she had the same instinctive timing. She mostly sang point numbers. We had long sessions after the show, though, and she loved to sing all the old songs, things like 'Creole Love Call' and 'You Made Me Love You'.

'Timony was always with her and rumour had it he was a gangster. But we had no time for him, although she was lovely.

She had a perfect skin, lovely firm breasts and beautiful teeth and when she came out on stage you've never seen anything so clean, or beautiful, in your life.

'I'm sure she was every bit as interested in sex as she claimed. I remember a time at the Savoy when Timony was out. She had a young university student in there with her. Well, Timony came back unexpectedly and she literally had to shove the student out on to the window sill and make an excuse to get Timony out of the room to get the boy out again.'

Waller came from Hartlepool and at the time his father was still living there. Waller Snr had never been to London, but made the journey to see his son on stage with the famous movie star. When Bert told Mae about the visit she insisted he bring his father along to say hello. According to Bert: 'She came waltzing out in her négligée. She always believed in everyone getting an eyeful. Well, the eyes nearly popped out of my father's head, he had never seen anything like it in his life. I was embarrassed as he was a shy man.'

Mae often chatted to Bert about boxing. She told him she 'owned a part' of the famous 'Brown Bomber' – heavyweight champion Joe Louis.

The critics may not have been impressed with Mae but to the London audience she was the thrill of a lifetime. A Mrs Grace H. Marsh of Cambridgeshire saw one of the early performances of the London run and states with relish, 'She would have made mincemeat out of today's women. The thing that struck both my husband and myself was the standing ovation at the end. I've never seen anything like it. This was genuine applause, genuine appreciation of a wonderful performance.'

Margaret Stallard remembers how Mae had to battle against her short-sightedness: 'She was as blind as a bat. These were the days before contact lenses and she would never wear glasses, so she was led on to the stage. I don't think she could see the other actors, certainly not their facial expressions, but she never looked much at all at her fellow artists anyway, she just did her thing and ignored the rest of us. She wasn't nasty, merely indifferent.

'She had a style of her own and she was consumed with her

own image. Part of this meant that she had to have young men about her the whole time. Without doubt, she made sex a reality for the older woman long before Joan Collins . . .

'She always wore false eyelashes and in those days they were not fashionable, but I never saw her without them. They were very long and she extended them to about half an inch longer than her natural eye-line.'

Malya Woolf also remembers those extraordinary eyelashes: 'There was a moment in *Diamond Lil* when the police rush on stage, waving truncheons, like Keystone Kops. The truncheons were filled with sawdust and one burst one day. Mae was so short-sighted she didn't see this but she was suddenly aware of great blobs of dust stuck to her lashes. It looked bizarre. She had to play the scene like that and when the curtain came down she asked bemusedly, "What happened, what happened?" She had a heart of gold. A nice lady.'

Miss Woolf gained the impression that Mae was lonely: 'A call boy would lead her to the wings and she'd stand there, never anyone with her. I was not on stage at the time and she'd say to me, "Where do I go on, honey, where do I go on?" Off stage she was a mixture; it sounds strange but there was a quality of innocence about her. She was introspective, anything but a loud-mouthed American.'

Mae did not escape censorship problems in the cosmopolitan atmosphere of London. 'There had been cries of protest en route,' Bruno Barnabe recalls, 'and by the time we got to London the Lord Chamberlain's office stepped in and insisted that the bedroom scene, for which I had auditioned, be cut. There had been trouble about it in Blackpool and Mae had built it up even more for London. Now, as I came in, I would place my hands on her breasts, at which she would give a growl of pleasure and she then turned round so that I could kiss her left breast in front of the audience. It was very daring for the time and the manager of the Opera House, Blackpool, objected. "Ours is a family theatre where patrons bring their children. We don't want them corrupted," he told her.

'The Chamberlain's office had insisted Mae leave out this piece of business for London but, within a short space of time, we were playing to less than capacity houses. She told me to reinsert the bedroom high jinks to buck things up. "They would put us in jail if we did," I told her. It was a mistake. "Say," she said thoughtfully, "That would be great publicity." I told her that with her in jail for contempt there would be no play at all.'

Another actor in the London run was Roy Fewins. Like Malya Woolf, he gained the impression she was lonely. 'She always seemed to be on her own,' he says, 'which is unusual. Most big stars have someone with them all the time.

'Americans have this habit of spitting for good luck – we thought it was terrible – but she always used to spit into a tissue and then jam it in the scenery before she went on. But it was wonderful to watch her revving up. As her cue got nearer she'd start swaying from side to side, grunting, patting her hair, and by the time her entrance came she was Mae West.

'She was utterly different from her stage persona. Very quiet and very kind, I loved her. But when it came time for her to leave, the limousine would arrive, full of bodyguards, and off she would go as Mae West.'

Fewins recalls how Spiritualism was part of her life: 'In between my scenes I would nip out for a smoke by the stage door. Many times I saw a young lad arrive with his father, delivering a bunch of flowers for her which they left with the stage doorman. I knew her quite well by this time and would chat with her in her dressing room. She had just a slight Brooklyn accent, not nearly as pronounced as the heavy Brooklynese she used in films. I told her I'd seen the flowers arrive and she said she wanted to meet the donors. She did, too. She told me her father had come through to her at a seance and said she was to take care of the boy's education. His name was Michael Peters and he came from Luton. She invited the boy and his father to the Savoy and even travelled to Luton to spend a weekend with them.

'There was a sequel to this. When I was in Manchester, some years later, long after she'd gone back to America, I bumped into Peters in the Kardomah Coffee House and he told me Mae was still supporting him.'

While in London she had a sitting with the famous medium

Lilian Bailey. Miss Bailey, a redoubtable Welsh woman nearly six feet tall, numbered several celebrities among her clients, including the film star Merle Oberon. When Mae consulted her she announced that the prima donna Grace Moore, who had been killed in a plane crash the year before, wished to speak to her. This came as no surprise to Mae, who explained that Miss Moore had been a friend of hers and she had spoken to her before through other mediums.

What Miss Moore said at that sitting is unknown but from then on Mae was convinced the dead singer was communicating with her on a regular basis. Mae sought her advice to improve the second act of *Diamond Lil* which, she thought, might not be going down too well in London and be contributing to the disappointing box office. She picked the right person to ask for advice as, like Mae, Miss Moore had been as sharp as a needle when it came to cash.

The singer's namesake, Paddy Moore, was doorkeeper at the Prince of Wales. He recalled an occasion when he knocked at Mae's dressing room one afternoon, announcing, 'It's me, Paddy.' 'Come in,' said Mae.

When he entered she looked at him 'as though in a trance' and said, 'I thought it was Grace Moore. There's something I have to discuss with her. She usually calls around now.'* Tea was the usual time for Grace to call and word spread around the company that Mae was incommunicado at 5 p.m.

The luckless Noele Gordon had the misfortune to intrude while Mae was in conference with Grace, and Larry Grayson remembers Noele telling him of the incident. 'What do you want?' Mae demanded. 'Don't come in yet, I'm talking to Grace Moore.' Noele felt a chill pass through her body as she surveyed the room and saw to her unpsychic eyes that it was empty.

People journalist Hannen Swaffer, who had inveighed so sternly against the immoral effects of Mae's sexuality when reviewing *I'm No Angel*, was himself a Spiritualist. Upon learning that Mae shared his beliefs he abandoned his reservations

---

* *Empire News*, 4 March 1956.

and became a devoted follower. Presumably her sexuality was not detrimental in the incorporeal realm of the spirit world.

Mae had some jewellery stolen at the Prince of Wales. She told Swaffer of the theft and he suggested she telephone T. Jack Kelly. Mae did so in Swaffer's presence and he wrote that Kelly not only described the thief but gave his initials and told Mae he was a stagehand. She discovered the identity of the thief but did not prosecute as Kelly had advised against it.

Another of London's celebrated psychics whom Mae consulted was the Direct Voice medium, Leslie Flint.* Mae wrote to him, sending tickets for the show, and asked him to visit her afterwards at the Savoy.

The suite contained several hefty men ('not a woman in sight,' says Flint). He congratulated Mae on *Lil* but she quickly brought the subject round to psychic matters: 'It was well after midnight by now,' says Flint, 'and I was flabbergasted when she asked, "Mr Flint, would you be kind enough to hold a seance for us?"

'The conditions were far from ideal,' Flint recalls, 'but she put out the lights. The suite, however, overlooked the embankment and there was still far too much light coming from the street lamps. 'Mr Timony,' she requested, 'Would you be kind enough to draw the curtains?'**

Mr Timony was so kind but Flint was still uncertain anything would take place. 'I did not think much would happen but Mae's mother came through. But before accepting her identity Mae asked, "If you really are my mother, then what was the pet name we used to call you?" The reply came loud and clear, "Diamond Tillie".' As Mae became more successful she had bought her mother various pieces of jewellery. Battling Jack had dubbed her 'Diamond Tillie'.

'I could see Mae was deeply moved,' Flint continued. 'and after the seance, when the lights were back on, she told me, "Mr Flint, no one in the world except my sister and me knew that pet name for my mother." '

* Direct Voice mediumship is when spirit entities can be heard by all present not just the clairaudient.
** *Voices in the Dark*. Leslie Flint, Psychic Press, 1988.

From then on whenever Flint was in California he was a welcome guest. He continued to hold seances with her and still holds her in the greatest affection: 'Poor dear,' he says, 'she was so kind and generous. She helped a lot of people financially through the Catholic Church.'

Flint also remembers another example of her kindness, though this time the cause was closer still to her heart: 'There was a young man nearby, a schoolteacher, who had posed nude for a pin-up magazine. When the education authorities got to hear about it they sacked him. Mae saw the picture and thought him a fine specimen and she personally went to the school and pleaded on the boy's behalf, explaining that a beautiful body was something of which to be proud. Whether through her or not I don't know, but he got his job back.'

While Mae was in London she visited Asprey's, the Bond Street jewellers, to replace her stolen diamonds. She was given a private appointment and arrived early in the morning before the store opened, but most of the staff had hurried in anyway to catch a glimpse of her. They huddled behind a curtain at the back of the shop and peeped out from behind it.

Complete with two bodyguards, she made her usual spectacular entrance, wearing a long black dress and huge hat, fully made up despite the early hour. A Mrs Daisy, who used to work at Asprey's, still remembers Mae's visit and the 'gracious' way she conducted herself.

She wanted diamonds to wear at a special occasion to which she had been invited. The Sitwell family (among whom were the brilliant, eccentric Dame Edith and writers Sacheverell and Sir Osbert) thought it might be rather fun to hold a party and adorn it with theatrical folk, including Danny Kaye, who was in London, and Mae. Mae, who detested parties, could not resist the idea of hobnobbing with the British aristocracy and accepted. Her escort for the evening was Sir Henry 'Chips' Channon, who noted the event in his diary:

This evening, wearing my ruby and diamond buttons and very elegantly dressed, I went to pick up Miss Mae West, the famous comedienne. We were nearly mobbed – a crowd jumped at the car shouting for autographs, and I feared that the Rolls would be damaged. In the car she asked if she should 'make a knee' to the Duchess of Kent, and I said yes. We duly arrived at Georgia Sitwell's party, where we made a spectacular entrée, Miss West looking like little Lord Fauntleroy with her long blonde curls. I quickly presented the star to the amused Duchess of Kent, whom she shook warmly by the hand – no 'knee' – and I then led up Emerald, Mollie Buccleuch and others to her. Danny Kaye also arrived – a theatrical-cum-haute monde evening which lasted, alas, until nearly 5 a.m. Emerald suggested that Mae West should sing but she would not – I think because Danny Kaye was there.*

Mae's refusal to sing had nothing to do with Danny Kaye's presence at the party. If silly old Chips (not to mention the even sillier Emerald [Lady Cunard]) had been as well versed in theatrical protocol as they wished Mae to be in social etiquette, then they would have known it is never done to ask a professional artist to perform at a social gathering. An artist can only give of her best when conditions are as near perfect as possible. Mae never simply launched into a song – all were special arrangements requiring a knowledgeable accompanist and a microphone to amplify her voice.

If she would not sing to order there were times when Mae would lend a helping hand, particularly if she liked the look of a person. Micky Webber was starting out as a photographer at this time. She met Mae at a function held at the Grosvenor House Hotel. Miss Webber was about to take Mae's picture (with Mae's permission) when Mae interrupted: 'Honey, you get someone to take you with me.' Micky Webber reports, 'I was thrilled and as we went to have our picture taken a crowd of show business people gathered around. It's a lovely photo and I've treasured it all these years.' So much for Mae's alleged hatred of other women.

* '*Chips*', *The Diaries of Sir Henry Channon*, ed. Robert Rhodes James, Weidenfeld & Nicolson, 1967.

While Mae was gadding about town *Diamond Lil* ran into deeper financial trouble. 'We never picked up after the initial opening, for which Mae blamed the Lord Chamberlain and, after a London run of just three months, we closed,' Bruno Barnabe recalls.

'We played to poor houses,' Margaret Stallard adds. 'It all ended in a whimper. She just went at the end, there was no party, no celebration. There was nothing to celebrate.'

But Barnabe said goodbye to her. 'When we parted, I said jokingly, "I wonder if I'll ever come across such wonderfully firm breasts as yours again." She took me seriously and replied, "It's only because I exercise every day." Whereupon she interlocked her fingers and with her arms raised breast high brought the palms of her hands together with a jerk. "If any woman does that for a few months they will get firm breasts," she said. She told me she travelled with a six-foot plank of wood which she placed with one end on the seat of a chair and the other on the floor, then she lay along it with her head at the bottom; "The blood goes to your head and feeds the brain," she said. "I do it every day for a quarter of an hour." '

Among those who called to wish her luck was actor Barry O'Neill, who had played Gregg in *SEX*. Mae claims that he was astounded by her undiminished loveliness and told her she had not altered since they had worked together in 1926. It might be assumed that she had been around long enough to recognize gallantry when she heard it, but whenever such a remark was made she no longer accepted it as flattery but as a simple statement of fact. Her strange conviction she was ageless had begun.

chapter twenty

LAS VEGAS

A barrage of litigation awaited Mae in Hollywood, including a lawsuit for $100,000 damages from two men who speciously claimed she had plagiarized their material in *Catherine Was Great*. Mae underwent seven weeks of court appearances before Judge Samuel R. Blake of the Los Angeles Superior Court dismissed the case.

Next the United States Supreme Court ordered Mae to pay $21,000 to a Mr Golan Bogue, who sued for breach of an agreement under which he was to receive 5 per cent of the London takings of *Diamond Lil*. This had not been paid.

Her name then featured in unsavoury publicity concerning one Eli Pearson who, owing to his business interest in scrap metal, was known as the 'demolition king'. He had entertained Mae lavishly when she appeared in Birmingham (England), but had suffered a reversal of fortunes in the meantime and lost his mansion and four cars. He now lived in a modest bungalow in Budleigh Salterton. He was due to face the Official Receiver and explain how £250,000 had 'slipped away'.

During his palmy days he had had his photograph taken with Mae when he had given a reception for her and it was now splashed across the papers. But he denied stories that the bill for her party had exceeded $1300 and dismissed as rubbish 'fantastic talk of one hundred magnums of champagne'.

As if this weren't enough, an incident then occurred which many actresses would have considered a compliment but which Mae deemed an insult. Director Billy Wilder offered her the lead in his new film.

Wilder had already notched up a number of successes,

including *Double Indemnity*, which he co-wrote with Raymond Chandler and which starred Barbara Stanwyck, Fred MacMurray and Edward G. Robinson. The film gained Academy Award nominations for best picture, script, direction, photography, music and best actress for Miss Stanwyck. He had followed this up with *The Lost Weekend*, a stark drama about dipsomania. The film won Academy Awards for Wilder as director, its star Ray Milland, and for best picture and script.

His latest release had been *A Foreign Affair*, starring Marlene Dietrich and Jean Arthur, and this had also picked up a couple of Academy nominations. He had also co-written the 1939 Garbo hit *Ninotchka*.

Mae knew she was dealing with a man not only talented but commercially successful – someone with whom most leading ladies would have given their eyeteeth to work.

When Wilder first arrived in Hollywood as an emigrant from Austria in 1934 he had been keen to meet the movie stars. Top of his list was Mae West, then at the height of her career. He managed to meet her while he was working at Paramount. Wilder's biographer, Maurice Zolotow, writes: 'Billy had always found Mae West's image irresistible, ever since he had seen her early talking films ... She and Billy often got together in the commissary and over at Lucey's to swap licentious stories. Billy had a mysterious affinity with Mae West. She represented a plationic idea of The Whore, whose mystery Wilder was forever trying to unravel. There was about her a certain superb vulgarity and fleshiness which reminded him of Viennese and Berlin prostitutes.'*

Together with his partner, Charles Brackett, Wilder was now working on a new project for Paramount: a film that was designed, as the saying goes, to blow the lid off Hollywood and the movie industry. Appropriately, it was given the working title of *A Can of Beans*. When released, under the title of *Sunset Boulevard*, it proved to be one of the most explosive films ever made. It is one of the great Hollywood classics.

Undoubtedly, the stupidest mistake Mae ever made in her

* *Billy Wilder in Hollywood*, Pavilion Books, 1988.

life was to turn down the role of its tragic heroine, Norma Desmond, a part later brought eerily and unforgettably to life by Gloria Swanson. Her refusal was symptomatic of Mae's ever-increasing megalomania, a condition which was to undermine so much of her subsequent career and signalled her descent into a way of being that consistently, though not entirely, lost touch with reality.

Sunset Boulevard is a story that could only be set in Hollywood. Norma Desmond, a star of the silent era, has become deranged. She lives in a crumbling mansion on Sunset Boulevard, attended solely by a menacing butler who was once a former husband. Her only other companion is a chimpanzee whom she morbidly adores. The chimp dies and on the day of the funeral a young scriptwriter comes into her life with whom she falls in love. Her attempts to revive her career become intertwined with her fear of losing her lover. In the end she kills him and withdraws into insanity.

As Otto Friedrich writes in *City of Nets*, *Sunset Boulevard* is 'about Hollywood power and Hollywood imagery, about its worship of youth and its worship of its own past'. It is also about coping with ruined beauty, lost fame and the vileness of age; the torment of loving someone younger and, as Friedrich adds, about 'self-consciousness, infatuation, shame, anguish, incongruity, obsession, absurdity, and love's refusal to accept any of those things.'*

Norma Desmond was a magnificent role for any actress past her physical prime. Mae was fifty-five when Wilder offered her the part and he wanted her to play opposite one of the most gifted young actors of his day – Montgomery Clift. The part would have been a challenge for her, a change of direction. But Zolotow writes, 'She recoiled in disgust ... She did not consider herself a faded flower. She was in the prime of her life ... Mae West would not discuss the project. She would not look at an outline. She was insulted. She reacted exactly as Norma Desmond herself would have reacted.

Sunset Boulevard eventually collected seven Academy Award

---

* *City of Nets: A Portrait of Hollywood in the 1940s*, Headline, 1987.

nominations, plus an Award for best script and music. Mae might have been at the centre of this, as it was she chose an alternative – to revive *Diamond Lil* yet again and trail around America with it for the next four years. On the surface this seems pathetic, but it was not within Mae's power anymore to accept that her sex appeal could fade. All the potential Oscars in the world could not compensate for such a blow.

She was also not interested in developing as an actress. She saw herself as a creature whom no man could resist and that was all she ever wanted to be. Therefore, instead of committing herself to playing in a controversial new movie, the ageless sex symbol dragged out her suitcases, packed her sequins, wigs, eyelashes, corsets and stacked shoes to belt out 'Frankie and Johnny', twice nightly on the road.

Billy Wilder quickly discovered he had bitten off more than he could chew by asking former beauties to play Norma. After Mae spurned the part he turned to Mary Pickford. Miss Pickford had no such reservations and in her first meeting with Wilder made plans to build up the part. She told Wilder exactly how she envisaged the role. So much so that he realized that working with America's Sweetheart would be the shortest route he could take to a nervous breakdown. He withdrew his offer and considered he had had a lucky escape.

Pola Negri was next on his list. Still very striking-looking, her disposition had not softened with time. Wilder made another hasty exit.

Wilder's friend, George Cukor, finally suggested Gloria Swanson. She had forsaken Hollywood for New York a decade earlier, where she was mainly known as a television talk show hostess. Someone made the grave arror of asking her to come to Hollywood for a screen test. Zolotow records her reaction: 'I suddenly got a call from somebody at Paramount – my old studio, you know, the one you might say I built – and some nauseating little creep said they wanted me to fly out to the coast at once – at once, mind you – and take a screen test for the role in this movie. Test for a part in a picture? Me? Test? I was revolted.'

Swanson continued to refuse to be tested until George Cukor

asked her to do so as a personal favour. When that was settled Montgomery Clift, who had already accepted the part of the writer, decided he did not like the idea after all and broke his contract, claiming he could not convincingly make love to an older woman. Since Clift's closest companion was an older woman, the notorious murder suspect and torch singer Libby Holman, this seemed an odd excuse. He was homosexual anyway and every performance of love-making with a woman, whether old or young, was an acting job.

Clift later divulged his real reason for withdrawing from the contract. He was frightened his audience might not accept him making love to an older woman – a subtly different version of his original escape attempt. In the end William Holden played the part.

Sunset Boulevard is a masterpiece as it stands. With Mae as Norma it would have been a different film. It is tantalizing to imagine what she might have made of the part. She had already proven in *Klondike Annie* that she could handle a strong dramatic role and her Norma would have been a more bitter, darker creation. Swanson made Norma sinister but in Mae's hands she would have been evil. The sympathy engendered for Swanson's Norma at the end of the film would not have been present, and the film would have suffered as a result. It would have been more monochrome and the malicious observation might well have toppled into farce. For art's sake it's probably as well Mae chose to hit the road.

Mae opened in *Diamond Lil* in New Jersey on 28 November 1948 and transferred to New York's Coronet Theater later. By and large the reviews were good and the show did well. One critic noted that Mae was now considerably more famous than she had been in 1928 when the show had originally opened.

Richard Watts Jr. of the *New York Post* noted, 'Mae West is now a legend and an institution, rather than just an actress, and *Diamond Lil* is an American phenomenon, instead of merely a drama. She and it are, in a way, modern classics.'

But the run was overshadowed for Mae as Jim was not with her. There were many times throughout the years when she had wished Jim far away, but he had been a loyal friend and champion. Now he was feeling tired and listless and preferred to stay at home in California. Although her new-found freedom seemed desirable at first, she soon missed the security of having him around, even having to dodge him when she was entertaining. As always, when Mae had to fend for herself, she felt vulnerable.

On 26 February 1949 she was scheduled to take part in a television show hosted by John Chapman. It would have been her first appearance on television. This meant a tight schedule as she had a matinée that day and the television show would have to be squeezed between the afternoon and evening performances, at a time when Mae normally would be having a nap.

She was staying at the Chatham Hotel, New York, and rushed to get herself ready. In Jim's absence she had taken on a private secretary, Larry Lee, who helped her with her make-up. Just before leaving the hotel she went to the bathroom to check her appearance since she planned to go straight from the studio to the theatre and was wearing her Lil costume. In the rush her foot caught on a rug and she went sprawling head first on the floor. A sickening pain seared through her left ankle and when the doctor arrived it was diagnosed as a break.

Her television appearance was cancelled, as was *Lil*, and $200,000 was refunded in lost bookings. She remained in New York with her leg in plaster until June, but the humidity made her uncomfortable, and she returned to California. In the autumn she felt well enough to resume work.

She had stayed so long in New York because she was enjoying the company of David Lapin, her accompanist from the show who also went with her to California.

Mae lost no time in sueing the Chatham Hotel for loss of earnings and damages, which she estimated amounted to a quarter of a million dollars. She alleged a 'defective' floor mat had caused her fall and that she had become 'sick, sore, lame and disabled', and was thus unable to continue earning her weekly $3000 salary. The case dragged on until 1953, when she accepted a settlement of $20,000.

The *Diamond Lil* company was back on Broadway – this time at the Phoenix – by the autumn of 1949. Queues for tickets stretched down 45th Street and Broadway. After this she took the show on a coast-to-coast tour and while touring the West was made an honorary Indian Princess of the Lakota Tribe and given the name She-Who-Mountains-in-Front. She used it widely. Any crack about the voluptuousness of Mae's figure was taken in good part; she positively encouraged it.

Returning to New York, she played the Auditorium Theater, Rochester. But she was not feeling well and the strain of the tour was telling. Jim once again remained in California because of poor health and Mae herself had to travel with a doctor.

On the evening of 16 February 1950, almost a year after her accident at the Chatham Hotel, she collapsed on stage. She did not want the public to think that her health was less than perfect, so issued a statement maintaining she was suffering from food poisoning. A denial instantly came from her doctor, who announced she was suffering from 'sheer exhaustion'. She was back on stage the following evening.

It was not the tour that was exhausting Mae, but having to cope without a man in her life. It was not just a case of sexual deprivation, for she had not had sex with Jim for years, it was the lack of emotional security. Without Jim there was no one with whom she could share her worries.

Mae had long toyed with the idea of playing the big hotels of Las Vegas and during this tour she constantly turned the idea over in her mind. She fancied herself Queen of the Gambling Halls, a role she had played several times in her movies. Although she did not gamble herself, there was plenty of money to be made from those who did and she saw no reason why she should not have a cut.

Jim had been trying to set up a deal for years and, on better days, was still working on it. He had backers interested and had virtually clinched a five-year contract during which she would appear at a new casino, to be called the Diamond Lil. She would perform for a minimum of sixty days a year for a fee of $2000 a week. For the other nine months of the year she would be paid a retainer of $1000 per month.

Had Jim been well he would undoubtedly have got the deal off the ground. As it was nothing came of it. She was too busy touring to worry very much and when she returned to California she did not want to burden Jim with business. His health was showing no sign of improvement. They spent their time together quietly as two old buddies who had been through much together.

In 1951 Mae received a writ, filed with the New York Supreme Court, from actress Sara Allen. Miss Allen had an act in which she impersonated Mae as Diamond Lil. Whereas Mae did not object to drag artists impersonating her, she was sour when ladies tried it. The only female who ever had her blessing to do so was Beverly.

Miss Allen alleged that Mae had encouraged her to perform her impersonation and then accused her of stealing her material. Furthermore, Mae had complained to agents and producers about Miss Allen, tarnishing her reputation. Miss Allen was sueing Mae for damages widely quoted at two million dollars.

The matter came to court and in her evidence Mae stated: 'Half the people in the world impersonate me. When I come out of the stage door people put their hands on their hips.' The prosecution tried to put Mae in a flutter by asking her age and weight, two touchy topics. Her counsel, however, leapt to her defence and forbade her to answer.

The hearing was adjourned and Mae turned the court into a theatre by cracking, hand on hip, 'Let the court come up and see me – meet in my flat.' The judge curtly informed her, 'We must meet in dignity.' There was no chance of that with Mae performing her famed Diamond Lil impression.

She was on tour again in the summer of 1952 with *Come On Up, Ring Twice*. She had hoped to introduce a new play that season, *Sextet*, by Charlotte Francis which she had adapted for herself, but stock companies only budgeted for one week of rehearsals which she considered inadequate.

Sextet, which owes more than a nod to Feydeau, is a farce about a movie star. Marlo Manners has had six husbands, all of whom reappear on her honeymoon and prevent her latest husband, an English lord, from bedding her. Mae shelved the play at the time, feeling she could not shape up the men to peak performance in just a week; it was later to reappear in her life.

Jim was in even worse shape when she returned from the tour. He had a heart condition and Mae, in consultation with his doctors, felt that it would be beneficial to remove him from the apartment and expose him to fresh air and sunshine. In order to do this she bought a beach house on Pacific Coast Highway, Santa Monica. It was a magnificent ocean-front mansion of twenty-three rooms plus ten bathrooms, with extensive gardens and a swimming pool. The carpets were cream and the furniture was her customary mix of white and gold French style, a combination of antiques, reproductions and junk. There was a bar, usually unstocked with alcohol, and a fully equipped library from which no one ever saw her remove a book. She adorned it with hundreds of photographs, among which were many of Tillie. One room was devoted exclusively to studies of herself.

There were also photographs of Adolph Zukor. By now Mae was determined to live to a ripe old age while maintaining her perfect beauty and, to this effect, started collecting information on sprightly centenarians. Zukor, who later did become a centenarian, was an inspiration to her. At the time he was a spry seventy-nine. She later claimed, 'I helped keep him alive. On every birthday I would call and tell him to keep on going. "Someone in our business has got to reach 100," I said, and he did, he was 104 when he died.'

An erotic Roman-style frieze of naked charioteers adorned the upper gallery and she indulged herself in her private suite with a bedside table, the legs of which were four sculptured erect phalluses.*

In August 1953 it was announced that Mae was to make a series of half-hour television films based on famous historical romances. This would mark not only her television début but also her first appearance in front of the cameras for ten years.

---

* This description, with others, was given me by an actor who toured extensively with Mae. He has provided information on the understanding he remain anonymous. I do not like using anonymous sources, but must respect his request so I'll call him John Smith. M.L.

Her proposed TV début, as an interviewee, had not taken place because of her broken ankle.

Among the historical romances Mae had toyed with presenting were *Catherine the Great* (naturally) and *Cleopatra*. Based upon evidence that existed largely only inside her own head, Mae had decided that the Egyptian queen had been a nymphomaniac. The project collapsed, however, another of Jim's ventures that never got off the ground.

Mae was not perturbed. She was in no hurry to get back in front of the camera. Her early films had made her a legend, why rock the boat? She was content to wait until a property came along which would be exactly right for Mae West. When that time arrived she would be ready.

The following year it looked as though the right time had arrived. Billy Wilder had not given up on her and was still trying to entice her into a film studio. He offered her the lead in the Rodgers and Hart Broadway hit musical *Pal Joey*. Her co-star was to be Marlon Brando.

Brando, at the height of his fame, was the essence of the primitive American male. His sexuality and unorthodox delivery astonished a repressed world. Tennessee Williams delighted in his style and he had made an enormous hit as Stanley Kowalski in *A Streetcar Named Desire*.* He was partnered in the screen version by the fragile Vivien Leigh, then twelve years on from Scarlett O'Hara and, unlike Mae, possessed of the guts needed to play a fading, deranged woman. When Wilder made his offer to Mae, she was sixty-one and Brando thirty. In John O'Hara's story line of *Pal Joey*, on which the film is based, a substantial age difference is supposed to exist between Joey and the woman who is keeping him. Vivienne Segal and Gene Kelly played it that way on Broadway, and Wilder saw in it a variation of the Norma Desmond theme.

He felt Mae would be ideal as the older woman and this time his idea appealed to her. It looked as though things might start moving since Brando, too, was interested, amused by the idea of playing opposite Mae West. But Mae envisaged the lovers to

---

* The film was made five years after Brando had starred in the part on stage.

be about the same age. So did Harry Cohn, boss of Columbia, the company financing the film. He ridiculed Wilder for even suggesting Mae West could play the part and dismissed the notion out-of-hand, recommending the thirty-six-year-old Rita Hayworth be cast.

Neither party would give way and such was the ill-feeling that Wilder quit Columbia. Cohn had purchased the film rights to *Pal Joey* soon after its Broadway success and had been anxious to make the film ever since. But he had met with nothing but difficulties. His original choice for the female lead had been Marlene Dietrich, who wanted Frank Sinatra as her co-star. But Cohn suggested Jack Lemmon, who was just starting his movie career. Dietrich withdrew from the film.

Cohn was a tough man whom Hedda Hopper described as a 'sadistic son of a bitch'. At his funeral Red Skelton is said to have quipped, 'Give the public something they want and they'll turn out for it.' Cohn decided to teach Dietrich who was boss.

She was enjoying a Las Vegas success and part of the attraction was the stunning Jean Louis gowns she wore. Jean Louis, under contract to Columbia, received notice from Cohn to withdraw Dietrich's dresses. Unfortunately for him, Dietrich was pulling in vast sums of money for the casinos, some of which had mobster connections. Dietrich, not a lady with whom it was wise to bandy threats, informed her employers she might have to cancel some of her performances. In no time at all Cohn reversed his decision.

In 1957 *Pal Joey* was released with Rita Hayworth in the role. Far from playing an older woman, her leading man was Sinatra – Dietrich's original choice – and three years Miss Hayworth's senior.

When Mae received the news that she was not after all wanted for *Pal Joey* she merely stored it up as one more grudge against Hollywood.

Yet another film suggestion was mooted: she was approached to star in *The First Travelling Saleslady*, a parody about two women who set out to sell barbed wire in the Old West. After discussion the parts went to Ginger Rogers and Carol Channing, but the film never gained the success hoped for it.

Mae felt finished with the film industry and got rid of many of her movie dresses which she had moved into storage at the beach house, believing she would never act in front of a camera again. Always family minded, she sent the throw-aways to a cousin who lived near Melbourne, Australia.

A Mrs Hilary Carmody, still living in Australia, remembers the parcels arriving: 'As a very small child I was friends with another little girl whose mother was a cousin of Mae West's. She used to get parcels from America with clothes that Mae West used to wear. We children would get the leftovers to play with and these included spangled shoes, feather boas, silk and lace dresses and a couple of hats.' It is bizarre to think of innocent children in a Melbourne suburb wearing Diamond Lil's regalia.

For want of something better to do Mae started writing a book, jotting down ideas and paragraphs in her dressing room in between appearances. It was not a novel but a serious biography of her hero T. Jack Kelly.

She kept up her psychic studies and regularly attended Reverend Mae M. Taylor's Church of Spiritual Science in Hollywood. Mrs Taylor attracted show business people and was familiar with the vagaries of the profession herself, having toured the country as a child prodigy. In the golden days of Hollywood she had held seances for Valentino in his castle above Sunset Strip. Actor Scott Richards remembers Mrs Taylor talking to him about Mae: 'She said that Miss West had offered to build her a new church there in Hollywood, but she wouldn't allow her to do so. She and Miss West had been friends for many years.'

For all the change of locale Jim was getting no better and Mae prayed for Spiritual healing for him. But he died in 1954 as a result of complications arising from his heart condition. Mae stated, several times, that the only deaths to affect her profoundly were those of her mother and father. Yet, Jim had been her lover and companion for over thirty years and she writes of his death with a restraint that masks a myriad of emotions. He was buried by his family at Holy Cross Cemetery, New York. Mae was not invited to the funeral.

A timely distraction from mourning arrived in the glossily oiled form of Richard Du Bois, winner of the 1954 Mr America Contest. He had stated that he would like to meet Mae West – when the King of England had expressed a similar wish she'd declined but for Mr America she was available.

Not only was Mr America invited to meet her at the ranch, but he was also told to bring along eleven of his muscular colleagues. Mae entertained the dozen regally but Du Bois dazzled her. Her eyes kept returning to him, stunned by his build. She discovered he had a mind as well honed as his body and, when the boys departed at the end of their visit, he returned to keep her company for the next few weeks.

She went to Las Vegas with Du Bois to study the nightclub scene. She was ruminating on Jim's idea of putting on an act at one of the big hotels, then touring with it. Clubs were booming, with big names starring in cabaret. Despite the evaporation of her film career, there was still no bigger name about than Mae's. For all her years of neglect by the industry, her fame remained undiminished. She had, in fact, just received a film offer from the British Rank Organization proposing she play the lead in a comedy to be entitled *Goodness Me*. She accepted but did not believe the film would ever materialize, and her scepticism was justified as it was never made. It is odd that former flour magnate J. Arthur Rank should have solicited Mae's services; he had originally envisaged films as a means of promoting religion.

With the shining example of Dietrich before her, the Las Vegas idea became more appealing to Mae. With Du Bois's help she decided to create a whole new act, just as she had in her vaudeville days when the need arose. Idealistic as this was, she was professional enough to know it would not come about merely by enthusiasm. There was no substitute for hard work.

chapter twenty-one

THE MUSCLEMEN

She had noticed, as who could not, that the club format was based on female eroticism. The few men on show were only there to accentuate the beauty of the girls. The time was now ripe, she believed, to invert the format and present a spectacle at which the women could gawp. To – literally – flesh out her idea Mae decided to put Du Bois on the stage. But she would need more men. She started auditioning. Word spread and she was inundated with hopefuls.

All auditions were personally conducted by Mae who had the men, stripped to their shorts, herded in by the dozen. Sitting at a desk, chewing a pencil, she made notes. Those whom she thought showed promise were then interviewed privately. The auditions were referred to as 'Mae's Cattle Call'.

At some earlier period in her life, Mae had auditioned film star Kirk Douglas. He never forgot the humiliation and writes of it in his autobiography.* He was ushered into her presence, inspected and brusquely rejected.

She selected eight men, all of whom were body-culture title holders. A choreographer was then employed to teach them to dance, but she soon realized this wasn't going to work as the boys remained awkward. So she promptly hired professional male dancers and kept the boys doing what they did best, flexing their muscles.

Steve Rossi, a lead singer, was engaged and he later gave an interview to *Globe* magazine in which he stated that Mae's sexual appetite was insatiable: 'She insisted on having sex every

---

* *The Ragman's Son: An Autobiography*, Simon & Schuster, 1988.

day, otherwise she wouldn't feel right.' She was sixty-one.

She also engaged world heavyweight boxing champion Vince Lopez, and had him squire her about for publicity purposes. When the 'athletes', as Mae termed them, were not working, they were instructed to top up their tans by the pool and perform workouts. Mae, who detested the sun, was inside sweating out routines with her accompanist and writing comedy patter. The only other woman in the show was Louise Beavers, who had played her maid Pearl in *She Done Him Wrong*, and who was to continue in the role in the new act.

Mae was due to open on 27 July 1954 at the Sahara Hotel for a two week engagement for which she would receive a fee of $50,000. But it was clear early on that this amount, and more, would be swallowed up long before opening night. By the time she had paid the musclemen, the dancers, her musicians, Louise Beavers, the choreographer, and expenses for the costumes, arrangements and services of director Charlie O'Curran, she would be running the show at a loss. Her aim was to recoup expenses once she was on the road and the show picked up additional audiences.

The press tried to bait her by asking her opinion about Marilyn Monroe, who had already appeared in *Gentlemen Prefer Blondes* and *How to Marry a Millionaire*, and was being built up by Twentieth Century-Fox in an unprecedented publicity campaign. Mae said she had never seen her. She was told Marilyn was being called another Mae West. She shrugged, and murmured, 'Well, if you want imitations ...' She later conceded that of all the blondes who followed in her footsteps, Marilyn was best. The rest, she said, merely had 'big boobs'.

The Sahara had a reputation for producing glamorous acts. Less than a year earlier Marlene Dietrich had opened there, and Mae knew she would have her work cut out to beat the sensation she had created. But she did her best. On opening night she made her entrance on a divan, carried by four loinclothed stalwarts. She wore a black lace dress with a heart-shaped headdress topped by ostrich feathers. There is in existence a private film of the act and she looks radiant.

The musclemen made their entrances dressed in bathrobes. Each was introduced to the audience according to the title he held. Mae lay upstage on her couch. The men bowed to the audience then turned to face Mae, opening their robes and creating the illusion they were naked underneath. As the first contenders came to her, she yawned a little and buffed her nails, but as the procession progressed she grew more animated. When Mr Italy arrived she gasped, and with the arrival of Mr America she rose to her feet, gasped again and winked in a way only Mae West could do.

Her opening number was 'I Want to Do All Day, What I Do All Night' after which she confided to the audience, 'Tonight I feel like a million, but – one at a time.' She later demanded, 'Why marry a ballplayer, when you can have the whole team?' The boys, wearing G-strings, came into their own at this point when each performed a specialty routine. When they became too energetic she advised, 'Take it easy, boys, last a long, long time.' The act ended with a spirited rendition of 'Frankie and Johnny'. She had the sense not to overdo things and the entire performance lasted just forty minutes. The show was an overwhelming success and received a standing ovation.

'Her material, carefully selected and sharpened by the Westian touch, belies her constant claim that most of her best ad libs have actually been innocuous lines until taken out of context . . . she bares nothing, yet reveals everything.' – *Variety*.

She broke box-office records and the Sahara's owner, Milton Prell, gave her a diamond bracelet as a thank you present. After the act, some of the women in the audience, who had hoped to meet the musclemen in the casino, were disappointed. It was a strict West rule that the casino was off-limits to the fellas. Mae believed that if audiences wanted to see her men (like her clothes and jewels) then they should have to pay for the privilege; there would be no free previews.

Journalists played up her image to the hilt. On one occasion a photographer, Lloyd Shearer of *Parade*, came to take some stills of her. He called while she was talking to some business people and she told him, 'Take your equipment and get into the bedroom. I'll join you later.' The story was told how maneating

Mae West had jumped upon a handsome young photographer and thrust him straight through the bedroom door.

She encouraged journalists to write imaginatively of her sex life and was particularly forthcoming to Hedda Hopper. Flowered hat bristling with anticipation, Miss Hopper breathlessly enquired, 'You had Grant, didn't you?' 'Twice, dear,' lied Mae. 'Had him twice.'

She took the show on the road and in February 1955 played the famous Chez Paree in Chicago followed by the Italian Village in San Francisco, and in May she opened at Ciro's in Los Angeles. All top venues.

Among the celebrities who came to see the show was Cary Grant. Mae told him she was planning to star in a colour version film of *Diamond Lil* and wanted him to recreate his original role. She thought it would be a sensation. As Warren G. Harris says, 'Grant just humoured her. The mere thought of sixty-four-year-old [*sic*] Mae West telling fifty-one-year-old Cary Grant to come up and see her sometime would frighten anyone!'*

Trouble brewed among the musclemen. Mae was stringing two along at the same time. One served as her bodyguard and she visited his room nightly. The other, meanwhile, would let himself into her room and she would join him after she had done with the bodyguard. She tried to keep the two men ignorant of each other's activities but, as happens in hotels, was spotted scuttling through the corridors in the dead of night. The bodyguard was not too bothered but the other was upset. He complained he had been treated like a whore and told her that if not love then at least affection should enter their relationship.

Mae could not deal with this; all she wanted was fun. The emotionally-injured young man continued to complain she had used him so she refused to see him. After several tearful days he could no longer stand the strain and left the company. Improbable as it seems, he joined a monastery.

The *National Enquirer* learnt what had happened and ran their version of the story: 'Mae is forty years older than this

* *Cary Grant: A Touch of Elegance*, Sphere, 1988.

poor, lovesick kid,' it proclaimed. 'He used to walk up and down the corridor outside her hotel room, singing out in a loud voice, "She doesn't love me, she doesn't love me." '

At the end of the run Mae returned to California and moved into the beach house for a while. Because of her auditions she had made friends with several of the habitués of nearby Muscle Beach, an area where bodybuilders gathered to work out. Some of the lads had adopted the habit of calling in on Mae during the day.

One of these was thirty-two-year-old Chuck Krauser, later known as Paul Novak, holder of the Mr Baltimore title. Tall with a quiet manner, Novak was of Polish origin and a former merchant seaman who was never to lose his love for the sea. Neither did he lose his love for Mae. They became inseparable and he remained with her until her death. Without Novak's support her life, particularly towards its end, would have been greatly impoverished.

Meanwhile, she set about trying to impoverish *Confidential* magazine. That notorious scandal sheet which at one time, together with its sister magazine *Whisper*, was the bestselling magazine in the world, specialized in running smear stories about the stars. For years Mae had artfully sidestepped scandal, but word had spread around the bars frequented by the press that there was a juicy story to be had if anyone dared to print it. *Confidential* dared.

Before attacking Mae *Confidential* had gone for other stars, who had suffered grievously at its hands. Notably Mae's friend Liberace, who had claimed damages of twenty-five million dollars over allegations of homosexuality but who wisely settled out of court for the lesser amount of forty thousand dollars. *Confidential*'s success was based on the assumption that most of the sex allegations they served up were true; consequently the stars would be too frightened to take action.

Rock Hudson managed to escape its net. Unlike Mae he was not circumspect in his behaviour, often going to gay bars, holding gay parties and even cruising Hollywood in his powder-blue Cadillac. Of course, in the circles in which Hudson moved, his homosexuality was immaterial. It was only ever dangerous when it threatened to become public knowledge and might jeopardize his box-office appeal.

Confidential had a file on Hudson's encounters and planned to blast the story across its front page. His studio, however, learned of the intended exposé and struck a deal with *Confidential*: Hudson was left unscathed and the popular young actor Rory Calhoun, who had been to jail but was not homosexual, was thrown to the lions.

Rock Hudson had a studio to protect him. Mae did not:

Mae West had 'em rolling in the aisles when she invaded Las Vegas. What made the show so hilarious was the fact that not a soul in the audience believed for a minute that the West wench was as seductive as she acted. But the first-nighters might have roared even harder had they known the behind-scenes story of the 'Empress of Sex' . . .

To get the real lowdown this reporter made the rounds of California's boxing arenas where the name West is as well known as Spalding. Out popped the names of a succession of feather, middle and light-heavyweight fighters who have seen service with Mae, . . . going back as far as Boston's Johnny Indrisano in the early Thirties and rolling right up to California's rugged Negro battler, Watson Jones, in 1954.

A typical example is the adventure of Albert 'Chalky' Wright, a bronze boxer who met Mae one night when he was fighting at the Pasadena Arena . . . Chalky would take his mistress to the fights every Tuesday and Friday, for example, at which times Mae would give him from $100 to $200 for betting money . . . She even came to the rescue when Chalky's brother Lee was arrested for shooting another pug . . .

There have been other tan warriors who followed Chalky and his brother Lee in Mae's esteem, including 'Speedy' Dado, the berry-brown Mexican bantamweight . . .

When she was appearing in *Catherine Was Great* on the New York stage, . . . Mae heard Wright was also in New

York, hanging out in a show business bar. Quicker than a flip of the hip she sent her colored maid out to look him up and invite him up to her lavish suite in the Sherry Netherland Hotel.

Chalky recalls she was delighted to see he was still in shape. He was happy to note she was, too. And he'd be only too tickled to slip back in harness any time.

But Wright's no different than most of the boxing boys along California's muscle row. They all have a stock answer when they hear that silken voice purring, 'Why don'tcha come up and see me some time?'

The reply is, 'How about now?'

Most of the article was true, but it was another thing for the magazine to prove it. Mae had been good to Chalky and both he and his wife (who seems to have liked Mae) signed affidavits denying the report. Neither Chalky nor Indrisano ratted on Mae for all the financial inducements offered them to do so. *Confidential* found itself in possession of a writ from Mae and had to print a retraction.

The death rattle for the magazine came in 1957 when it was sued by the State of California for criminal libel. The case was settled by payment of a $5000 fine and an undertaking from Robert Harrison, the publisher, not to print further exposés of the stars. Who wanted to read a magazine entitled *Confidential* that supplied no confidences?

Private detective Fred Otash investigated the allegations against Mae. She discovered he was prying into her private life and there was an incident when they met face to face. Otash remembers the confrontation: 'She rounded on me,' he chuckles. 'She called me a dirty son-of-a-bitch and said "How dare you invade my bedroom."'

Examples of Mae's generosity to fighters are legion. Robert Duran recalls her telling him she had an affair with 'Gorilla' Jones, so named because of his long arm reach. Gorilla lived rent-free in a house owned by Mae. When Gorilla retired she did not see so much of him, but when they met he would still greet her affably with, 'How's the lady doin' today?' She would reply, as she invariably replied to that sort of question, 'Fine, fine.'

For a time she employed Gorilla's mother, Sally, as a maid. 'Sally was great,' she told Duran, 'pressing my négligées and singing hymns at the same time. I'd say to her, "Why don't you sit down and rest?", but she never would.' Several members of Mae's staff stayed with her for years, some devotedly, and the entire staff of the Ravenswood seems to have adored her. The switchboard operator, Faye Friedland, would nip up the stairs from time to time and have a coffee with her, and Mae passed on to her many of her dresses.

It seems probable that Mae had an affair with the 'Brown Bomber', world champion heavyweight Joe Louis. Mae had a financial interest in Louis as she told Bert Waller, but she does not mention Louis in her writings, but then she would not – Mae never kissed and told. In his autobiography* neither does he mention her. There is, however, a passage in the Louis book that could apply to Mae:

There have always been liberated women. Sometimes you just have to search some to find them. Some are liberated because they demand it, some just because they can afford to be. Well anyway, I found one at the Buick showroom in Detroit ... The salesman ... showed me this car, black with white-wall tires and a mahogany bar built in the back ... while I was fooling around the car this salesman asked if he might be excused for a minute and rushed over to a real good-looking white woman with blonde hair.

He talked with her for a while then came back to me. I told him I liked the car and wanted to buy it. He said, 'The lady has already purchased the car for you.' ... what the hell can you do when the lady is insistent and charming as hell? I took the car and promised her two ringside tickets for the Max Baer fight. I got a new Buick for Christmas for the next five years. The lady was a very important white woman and I was a very important black man. She taught

* *Joe Louis 'My Life'*, with Edna and Art Rust Jr, Angus & Robertson, 1978.

me the word for many of the things I'd been doing all
along. The word was 'discretion'. And we were 'discreet'
the several times we met during those five years.

Elsewhere in his autobiography Louis says, 'I'd see a big,
beautiful movie star and wonder how she is in the bed. We
would find out very easily. These were just one-night stands. But
we both knew to keep it cool.' No one knew how to keep it cool
better than Mae. 'Discretion' was her byword. She was a 'very
important' blonde who would have appreciated a seat at a Max
Baer fight. She also had a habit of buying cars for her lovers.
Few ladies as readily fit Joe Louis's description as does Mae.

In 1955 she made an LP record. She had made various
recordings for Brunswick in 1933 (which have since been transferred to LP), but this was her first custom-made LP. By the
mid-Fifties records had become big business. Nearly every
home had a record player and the radio was constantly belting
out the hit parade. Such singers as Dinah Shore, Frank Sinatra,
Frankie Laine, Johnnie Ray, Kay Starr, Ella Fitzgerald and
Sarah Vaughan were making fortunes from their record sales.
Mae could not allow such a source of revenue to remain
untapped.

Her cabaret act had caused a sensation and her name was
again on everybody's lips. Rumour had it that she was about to
make a new film and start a world tour. These stories were
untrue but there was enough interest in her to inspire Decca
Records to consider her a viable proposition.

She recorded a dozen numbers with the brassy Sy Oliver
orchestra and a male quartet with Tito Coral as soloist. Some of
the items were old favourites, such as 'Frankie and Johnny', 'A
Guy What Takes His Time' and 'They Call Me Sister Honky
Tonk', but they were given sparkling new arrangements with
witty additions to the lyrics. Others were point numbers, seemingly more at home in cabaret than on record, but they came
over well. There is even a concession to the new rock and roll
craze which was sweeping the world, with an up-to-the-minute
version of 'My Daddy Rocks Me'. She liked rock and roll and
included it in her act for the rest of her life; its crude rhythm

suited the grain of her voice. There is also an item titled 'Criswell Predicts', Criswell being an astrologer friend of Mae's who had quite a following in his day.

Timing is everything in this record, particularly in the point numbers where Tito Coral proves an excellent straightman, belting out his Hispanic love songs to a wisecracking Mae ... She pushes the joke as far as she can. Such lines as 'We put our *what* together?' and 'If you want a lot, there's a lot where I've got it' leave no doubt as to her intentions.

Mae's voice is deeper with maturity, the vibrato more uneven than it was in her film recordings, and she has lost a couple of top notes while gaining a chest register. Such signs of wear, however, add character to her interpretations. Vocally, she was in top form as she had recently worked with voice coaches to prepare for her act.

The record was entitled *The Fabulous Mae West** and issued in a glossy scarlet cover with an ostrich-feathered Mae on the front; the back shows her in her day clothes, which look much the same as her evening dress except that the feathers have been replaced by a platinum wig. The photograph was taken in 1955, one of a set she had made to promote the musclemen act. Admittedly it is retouched, but she looks a stunning, well-preserved forty-year-old rather than the sixty-two she was at the time. It is a glamour shot, of the type Jayne Mansfield and Marilyn Monroe made famous.

The record sold well and is still selling.

That same year she took the muscleman show to Lake Tahoe and opened the following year at the Latin Casino, Philadelphia. Paul travelled with her and also appeared in the act under his Mr Baltimore title. By now the show had been slimmed down as the club circuit did not pay lavish Las Vegas-level fees. There were still eight musclemen, but the dancers had been reduced to four. Betty Treadwell had replaced Louise Beavers as the maid.

In one scene Betty would answer the telephone to announce, 'Miss West's suite'. Mae would yell out, 'Don't brag about me,

* Decca DL 9016.

just answer the phone.' Later Betty would tell her, 'Miss West, there are fifty men outside waiting to see you,' and Mae would drawl back, 'I'm a little tired, send one of them home.' It may not be hysterical on paper, but given Mae's delivery the lines brought down the house.

Sometimes on stage Mae forgot a line and would ad lib, causing the musclemen some grief. They were not actors: they either stared uncomprehendingly back at her, or carried on with their scripted responses. When this happened she flew into a tantrum after the show, scolded the offender and yelled that she was working with idiots.

The boys discovered she would also not tolerate sloppy personal hygiene. She would send them back to their rooms to shower if she felt it necessary. One muscleman, with body odour, was told to do something about it or look for another job.

She was fastidious herself. She took several baths a day and never started the morning without an enema. Her hair had to be washed every day despite the fact she wore wigs, and the roots were bleached every three to four days. She liked her wigs always to be set in the same way, not merely to the same style, but with every wave, curl and indentation exactly as it had been the day before. She kept a photograph on her dressing table and her stylist had to match it exactly.

When on tour she had an invariable routine. She would rise about ten o'clock and breakfast on muesli. She would attend to her toilette, apply her make-up, then travel to the club. If rehearsals were necessary they would be held before lunch. After lunch she attended to business matters and made her numerous telephone calls. The first call of every afternoon was to Beverly, who had now given up her attempts at stardom, and lived at the beach house as resident housekeeper. She also regularly spoke to her brother Jack who lived at the ranch.

Before the show Mae would have what she considered to be a light supper, generally a fillet steak and salad. She would then soak in a warm bath, after which she applied full make-up. Make-up was a serious business and she kept an old linen jacket to wear for the ceremony.

She had worn false lashes for so many years her own now looked peculiar. They had been raggedly hacked away when she had had to chop off her false lashes. For the daytime she affixed half lashes, which started about halfway along her eyelid and extended luxuriantly above, from the outer corners of her eyes. She travelled with dozens of pairs of lashes kept in little boxes.

After the show, at about midnight, she would settle down to her main meal of the day; it consisted of three courses including a pudding. When she saw the sweets she would agonize for minutes until she, invariably, gave in. The warning sign came when she found she had trouble fitting into her costumes. As soon as they needed to be let out at the waist she reduced her intake for a few days. This made her grumpy.

John Smith recalls eating with Mae in a restaurant when Mae was at her grumpiest. Her attention focused on a fat lady who was plainly enjoying a pudding. Mae took instant offence. 'She's digging her grave with her fork,' she said loudly. The woman looked selfconsciously across and a piece of food fell from her fork. 'Look,' Mae scorned, 'she's getting food all over herself. And she eats with her mouth open. Never eat with your mouth open, no one should have to see what you're eating.' She addressed her table at large, 'When I was a kid I ate my dinner with a mirror propped alongside my plate. I wanted to chew just right. Not like a cow with a cud.'

She was enraged when a female columnist commented, 'The sands of time in her hour-glass figure have shifted.' She snarled, 'The river's going to be her next address.'

But she was never grumpy when it came to giving autographs, patiently signing every piece of paper or autograph book proffered. One time as she was getting into her limousine, an elderly woman said admiringly, 'You look so young and beautiful, I wish I looked as well.' Mae smiled. In the car she was less winning, and turning to her hairdresser said, 'Jesus Christ, at least I had something to start with.'

Cast changes occurred in the show and Mr America was replaced by Mr Universe, in the form of Hungarian Mickey Hargitay.

THE MUSCLEMEN

Some of the musclemen had enormous appetites and an arrangement was made with the club kitchens that steaks, salads and desserts should be left ready on a counter for them to eat immediately when they came off stage. Since the boys also ate three full meals during the day and this snack constituted a fourth and that taken late at night, some of them began to put on weight. Mae called an emergency meeting.

'Lose weight or quit,' she told them uncompromisingly. 'Keep those muscles trim or you won't be pumping iron, you'll be pumping gas.' She devised a training regime – and personally supervised it – until the lads were sleek once again.

During the act, while lying on her couch and seemingly flirting with the posturing men, she was shrewdly monitoring their performances, looking for bad timing or mistakes in their dialogue. God help anybody who in any way spoiled the routine.

Another of Mae's rules made the living quarters of the musclemen off limits to certain male staff. The hairdressers were mostly homosexual and had offered to massage some of the men after their workouts. Mae did not care what the boys got up to in private but didn't want the press to engineer a smear campaign against the show. By the same token she would not allow male staff members to share rooms with the musclemen. Members of the company were responsible for paying for their own accommodation and to save money many had shared. When she learned of this she forbade it. Again it was the box office that prompted her orders, not morality.

From Philadelphia the company moved east to New York's Latin Quarter. Mae had played there after her stint in Las Vegas and had topped attendance records previously held by Sophie Tucker. At that time her first week's takings had amounted to $97,000; she now improved on this with a staggering $100,000 taken during her first week.

She picked up some new dancers in New York and those with fair hair were told to darken it. Mae was the only blonde in the show.

Among the host of celebrities who came to see Mae were

Liberace,* Truman Capote and stage star Katharine Cornell. Miss Cornell reported in her memoirs that she complimented Mae upon her performance only to be told, 'Thanks, honey, hope I can say the same about you sometime.'

Truman Capote invited her to one of his literary lunches. This was not a success. Mae was taciturn and uneasy, and the gathering intimidated her. Capote wrote in a magazine article that she was observed pacing up and down before the step to his brownstone for a good five minutes before deciding to go in. Capote probably made this up. Mae travelled by limousine and never went anywhere alone because she lived in fear of being attacked. The chauffeur would hardly have dumped her on the doorstep and driven off. And Mae was not the pacing kind: her shoes were too uncomfortable for one thing. Furthermore, once Mae had made a decision she stood by it. If she had made up her mind to go to a literary lunch, grim as that prospect sounds even when hosted by such a dazzler as Capote, she would have strode straight in and not fussed about on the doorstep.

Another visitor to the show was television presenter Steve Allen. Allen also put in the odd appearance in films, including the title role in *The Benny Goodman Story*, which had been released the previous year. It had made him a celebrity. Allen had known Mae for several years, but he had displeased her recently by questioning the tenets of Spiritualism on his television programme. In defence of her beliefs, Mae contacted T. Jack Kelly and held a seance backstage at the Latin Quarter before an invited audience of pressmen and show folk. 'Spectators were astounded,' reported *Chimes* magazine.

Not all Mae's callers were stars. She also saw a lot of her friends Ida and Al Endler. The couple had met her in her vaudeville days and remained friends, visiting her both in Las Vegas and California. Down-on-their-luck vaudevillians were never denied access either.

One of the cast recalls an elderly man whom she greeted like a friend. He was a vaudevillian who was trying to make some

* When Mae's shimmy rival, Gilda Gray, fell on hard times, Liberace gave her a home in his Hollywood mansion where she lived at his expense for a number of years.

money as a songwriter. He had written a couple of songs which, he felt, might suit her. He bellowed these at her in a cracked voice and she gave him $50 even though she knew she would never use them. But she made him sign a release form: she had suffered too much litigation in the past.

While she was in New York one of the papers revamped the story of her romance with Richard Du Bois, who was described as being twenty (he was a little more) and in love with the sixty-five-[sic]-year-old Mae. She was furious, not at the love story, but at the exaggeration of her age.

chapter twenty-two

ACADEMY AWARDS

Mae was uneasy during her New York engagement. Not about the show, which was running as smoothly as any touring show could run, but because she had received a psychic warning that something sinister was about to happen. She feared a gangster might be out to settle old scores or that some member of *Confidential* was hot on her trail. Neither was the case.

One day a cast member heard a scream from Mae's room and rushed in to find her in tears with the telephone receiver in her hand. 'My baby just died, my baby just died!' she cried. He wondered if Mae was a mother and had kept the news quiet. But the truth tumbled out; she had been talking to Beverly at the beach house, who told her that one of her monkeys, whom she had nurtured for eight years, had died. 'I don't know what I'll do without him,' she sobbed, in a manner reminiscent of her hysteria following Boogie's death years before.

Mae now had several monkeys, all quartered in the Santa Monica house. They were looked after by Coco, a new addition to her retinue. He was a punch-drunk Cuban ex-boxer, who acted as co-housekeeper with Beverly. Alas, Mae had scant time to vent her grief, the show had to go on and she had to mop up her tears, go on stage and flirt with her musclemen.

Gossip columnist Walter Winchell had suggested in print that Mae was enjoying a flirtation with her new man Mickey Hargitay. However, Hargitay suddenly shot into prominence courtesy of another beauty. The striking blonde actress Jayne Mansfield was in New York, starring on Broadway in *Will Success Spoil Rock Hunter?* She came to see Mae's show one evening, accompanied by her agent, and was smitten by Hargitay.

Raymond Strait, Jayne Mansfield's biographer, takes up the story: 'When Mickey Hargitay, the former Mr Universe of 1956, walked out on the stage, Jayne's heart told her what she wanted to hear. She must have Mickey.'* She certainly must, and her agent went backstage after the show with a note from her to Hargitay. Jayne came to see the show every night and she and Hargitay plunged into a headline-making affair. They seemed the perfect match – the beautiful Jayne Mansfield and the curly-haired Mr Universe, the jewel in Mae West's crown of Adonises.

Mae was not among those who offered congratulations and one can understand why. The newspapers printed a barrage of photographs showing Jayne and Hargitay entwined. One typical caption read, 'Hello Jayne, Goodbye Mae'.

Mae told Hargitay to forget that 'phoney Hollywood blonde'. Jayne responded in the columns of the press to ask why shouldn't Hargitay prefer a twenty year old to a seventy year old? She later rubbed salt in the wound by adding, 'I wonder when was the last time anybody took a picture of her in a bikini?' Then, confessing she had been brought up to respect her elders, she went on to say that if she looked as good at sixty-four (reverting to Mae's real age) as Mae did, then she would have no problems. Mae refused to be taunted and made no public comment. Privately she could have wrung the necks of both Hargitay and Jayne.

The publicity did no harm to the box office and the four-week engagement at the Latin Quarter was sold out. Her next booking was in Syracuse, in upstate New York. Mae was to make the journey in her chauffeur-driven Cadillac, in which she travelled with Paul. Sometimes she would invite another member of the cast to occupy the spare seat next to the driver, but there was seldom any rush of takers. Mae was never much of a conversationalist. Only three subjects interested her: Mae West, Spiritualism and – to a lesser degree – health. The atmosphere could be strained. There was also no chance of getting an alcoholic drink or lighting a cigarette en route. In addition

* *The Tragic Secret Life of Jayne Mansfield*, Robert Hale, 1976.

Mae had a horror of using public lavatories and refused to do so. She believed it demeaning for a public figure such as herself to be seen entering one. Therefore she regulated herself, and if others were not so disciplined she frowned upon the unnecessary and embarrassing delays. People went to considerable lengths to avoid having to accept a lift from Miss West.

While in New York Mae had taken an interest in Christine Jorgensen, who was born a man and had been surgically transformed into a woman. Miss Jorgensen, then at the height of her fame, had been starring in cabaret at the Café Society. Mae did not go to see her act, but cast members went and came back buzzing with tales. Mae questioned everyone who had seen her and became fascinated by transsexuality. She wanted to know the anatomical details of the operation. When a brief outline was told her she enquired, 'What sort of sex can she hope for?' That, naturally, was the first question that sprang into her mind.

She then came up with the notion that now might be the right time to revive her plays *SEX* and *The Drag*.

The Syracuse venue – the Three Rivers Club – was a little way out of town and Mae, with most of the cast, stayed at the Syracuse Hotel, also a few miles away. They travelled to the club in a convoy of station wagons fronted by Mae in her limo. The papers heralded her arrival with further publicity about Hargitay and Jayne; she still refused to be drawn. 'Without my name, no one's going to print this trash,' Mae carped. Like New York the Syracuse gig was a sell-out.

There was now a week's lay-off before the next engagement, Washington DC, so the cast prepared to leave for their various homes. Mae and Paul Novak were going to stay in New York City as guests of the Endlers. A train left Syracuse in the small hours of the morning, so everyone brought their cases to the club ready for a hasty departure. Mae's props, including her *chaise-longue*, were stacked outside her dressing room, effectively blocking the way and causing several people to stumble while trying to negotiate the corridor.

On the day of her departure a newspaper announced that Marilyn Monroe had hired a former 'tutor' of Mae's to coach her into 'replacing' Mae. 'I don't need any replacing just yet,' she said.

There was a last minute hunt for Mae's vaseline. She lined her nostrils with it before going on stage to trap the dust kicked up by the dancers and prevent it from entering her lungs.

Her feet had to be massaged before she could leave. Now that she was older she insisted on having two people support her when she walked to and from the stage in order that she would not trip. Her lethal shoes had to be tightly strapped and tied over the instep and round the ankle. Wearing them for any length of time brought on swelling and excruciating pain; she would cry out as the weals were massaged to restore circulation.

Finally, Mae's furs had to be packed. In the past her dressing rooms had been robbed several times, so she kept the furs, when not in use, wrapped up and stuffed under the pillows of her dressing-room couch.

Mae opened at the Casino Royale in Washington. Mickey Hargitay arrived late for rehearsal so she ordered the musicians to bypass his music. The press ran a story that Mae had fired him. He had not been fired and she was powerless to do so, for her contract stipulated she had to have a Mr Universe title holder in the cast. While Mickey will always hold the title of Mr Universe 1956, there was, however, a new Mr Universe about to be chosen in a few weeks' time. Mae announced she would be releasing Mickey when the new Mr Universe was named. 'Who wants last year's model?' she quipped. 'If I'm the old model, then what is she?' Mickey was quoted as retorting.

Things came to a head on opening night, 6 June, when Mae broke her silence and gave a press conference between shows in order to staunch the stories that Mickey was leaving her act because of Jayne. The publicity ensured that the Casino was full to the rafters, and the first show went off without a hitch. Then the press started to arrive at the theatre and were conducted to Mae's dressing room for the conference. Paul was at her side.

Her dressing room was guarded against intruders by one Thad Prescot, Mae's hairdresser. Not a very prudent move on

Mae's part, since Prescot, possibly a genius with hair, was too frail to bar the way to any muscleman intent on entering, particularly one as massively built as Mickey.

That was shortly put to the test, as he later informed the *Washington Daily News*: 'Mr Universe crashed the press conference. Naturally, I couldn't oppose him. Naturally, I didn't want to stop him because of the fact he is much bigger than I.'

Naturally . . .

Mickey (who vowed he had been invited to the conference) is Hungarian and inclined to gesticulate when excited. He was very excited now. So was Mae, who for once lost her cool and screamed at him. The press were in seventh heaven, their pencils scribbling like mad. Not to be outdone, Paul stepped forward and socked Mr Universe straight in the mouth. Taken by surprise, Mickey reeled backwards and knocked over a chair. Unfortunately, Mae became involved in the fracas and was unceremoniously sent sprawling, landing on the floor with a hefty bump. 'You can't do this to me,' she yelled. 'I'm an American institution.' She meant it, too.

George Eiferman, another of her musclemen, restored order. Mae's first concern was that Mickey, who had another show to do, was not disfigured. 'Get his face fixed up,' she commanded, but Mickey's place that night was taken by Pete Ganois.

The matter came to court, where Paul pointed out that Mickey had waved his hands and 'I thought he was going to hit me . . . What am I going to do? Wait until he lets me have it? . . . I move quickly. It was instantaneous.'*

The trial went on for three days until the case was dismissed by Judge Armond Scott. Mae attended wearing a pink trouser suit and sunglasses. She told reporter Cordelia Ruffin, 'I don't like this publicity . . . you're just dragged into it.' Actually Mae was flattered by the press implication that two such handsome men were fighting over her. One newspaper account was captioned, 'Defense of the West'.

She took the stand herself and confirmed that her relation-

* *Washington Daily News*, 29 June 1956.

ship with Mickey had never been anything other than professional. She refused to mention Jayne Mansfield's name, only
letting her guard slip once when she snapped at reporters,
'She's a dangerous publicity seeker. Maybe if she went to
school and learned how to act she wouldn't have to do that.'

The audience for the second show had not realized anything
untoward had taken place. Mickey's absence was not explained
and Ganois's appearance was accepted. If the cast sensed ten-
sion in the air, it was not picked up by the audience. Mae
appeared unruffled. However, she hurried through her bows
and seemed anxious to leave the theatre. When Mae had problems she sometimes liked to drive through the night, thinking
things out quietly for herself. She practised meditation at such
times, believing in the power of positive thought, and calming
herself by attempting to attune her mind into the infinite. The
murmur of the car engine and its movement on silky-smooth
springs acted as a solace.

At the end of that long night she seemed to have come to
terms with things. 'It'll all blow over,' she said, but was riled
next morning when columnist Paul Herron wrote: 'Mae has
fought a fine battle with Father Time and, with the aid of her
feathers and the Casino's darkest purple lights, manages to
present a creditable act.' No amount of meditation could calm
her down now. Herron could see her in broad daylight anytime
he wanted, she stormed. Everyone knew she didn't need purple
lights, she could work in the lightest of pinks and still look
great. 'We're going to have to break his writing fiingers,' she
threatened.

Despite these violent outpourings her fears of a personal
attack did not diminish. She never went anywhere alone and
even in the theatre she insisted people were constantly with her.
Once, by a fluke, she was left alone for a few minutes in her
dressing room. As luck would have it, a fan slipped past the
stage doorkeeper and knocked at the door.

All he wanted was a signed photograph, which she gave him,
but after he left there was hell to pay. The man could have been
'some kind of nut', she raged. She brought it to general attention that a similar situation had arisen elsewhere, when

someone knocking at her dressing room door had opened his coat and exposed his genitals to her. Someone laughed and then she laughed too. But her point was made.

With the folding of the act, she accepted a summer tour of *Come On Up, Ring Twice*. (She had hoped to replace this with *Sextet* but her adaptation was not yet ready.) The show was to open at the Capri Theater, Atlantic Beach, and she stayed with the Endlers in New York beforehand. Paul Novak was promoted to the rank of actor and was playing the part of Larkin, the newsman. Of a cast of twenty, seventeen were males. The principals travelled with the show and the bit-part players were hired in whichever town she happened to be playing.

Rehearsals started without Mae, who knew the piece backwards, but by the time she arrived there were only two days to go before opening night. This was cutting things too fine, leaving insufficient time to tighten the show to the necessary degree. She became bad-tempered again and snapped when the show did not gel as she felt it should. If a scene lagged she would impatiently click her fingers to quicken the pace.

There were eight performances at the Capri given over a period of six days. The critics were kind although it was noted that the cast would have benefited from extra rehearsals. Mae called a meeting to reprimand the actors.

Once the show was rolling, the director, Howard Miller, took off to the next venue to cast the smaller parts for the following week. Occasionally, an audience member would ask Mae why a star of her stature was playing repertory. Her standard reply was that she wanted to give the 'little folks the thrill of seeing a great star in person'. Some of the 'little folks', of course, were sophisticated professionals, but to hear Mae talk it might be imagined they all had straw in their hair.

She was on tour because she would have rotted away living quietly. She needed the lights, the paint, the excitement and – above all – the sound of applause.

Once again the journeys to the venues were made by car, and as before the cast fell over each other to avoid being chosen to accompany the living legend. Small talk was now banned altogether in the vehicle. She informed the chosen few that she must have quiet as her mind was always working, thinking up ways to improve the play.

She could be persuaded out of her reverie by mention of the sacred enema. High colonic irrigation, she believed, coupled with a regular intake of carrot juice and sex with multiple partners was the secret of good health. She told how she had seen people 'bent over, lazy and lifeless' until they adopted this invigorating regime.

She often talked people into buying enema kits, then asked if they had used them. If the answer was no, they would be sent away and told to return when they had done so and tell her the results.

The next stop on the agenda was three hundred miles north at the Lakes Region Playhouse, Gilford, New Hampshire. Mae stayed at the Chanticleer Inn on Lake Shore Road.

There had been trouble at the last venue when a cast member had had a row with his girlfriend, who spitefully hurled a rock through his bedroom window. The press wrote up the incident, but happily did not link it with the Mae West show. Nonetheless she was furious and issued a ukase that any cast member who allowed his or her private life to disrupt the smooth running of the show could expect instant dismissal. This from the lady whose name had recently been splashed across the papers over the Novak/Hargitay punch-up.

At each new theatre she ensured that her dressing room had a private lavatory. If not, then special arrangements had to be made to move her into a room that did contain one. After that she would greet the theatre owners and meet new cast members, impressing upon any trembling newcomers the importance of being perfect in word and movement. Her lighting cues would be personally inspected – she insisted on a pink spot following her every move, just as she had done in London. Then her exits and entrances were thoroughly gone over. Mae's eyes were not too good and woe betide any stage manager who left an item of furniture where she could bump into it.

The *Laconia Evening Citizen* gave the show a handsome review under the heading, 'Mae West wows 'em at Playhouse'.

Reviewer Ed Lydiard noted that women as much as men seemed to be amused by her.

It was while Mae was in Gilford that she developed a new obsession. White was one of her favourite colours and she now for some reason insisted that her dressing room must be entirely white. Batches of sheets had to be obtained and tacked to the walls and floor.

The weather was unseasonably hot. One particular night Mae told Joe, her driver, to get some bottles of beer and to park the car by the lake while she cooled off. In one of her reflective moods she drank the beer from the bottle with the car windows open to enjoy the breeze. Then she seemed to realize that if another car came along she might be spotted. Dumping the empties unceremoniously on the shore of this renowned beauty spot, she gave instructions to be driven back to the Inn.

From Gilford the company moved to Camden, Maine, where she appeared at the Camden Hills Summer Theater. She stayed at the Whitehall Inn in a suite recently vacated by Tallulah Bankhead. Miss Bankhead had just concluded her run of *Welcome, Darlings*.

Mae found a tube of a substance called 'nupercainal' in her bathroom; Miss Bankhead had obviously overlooked it. Mae murmured, 'Tallulah must be opening up new canals – the old one must be worn out.'

On the way to the theatre she discovered not enough posters were about advertising her appearance. She informed her publicity representative, 'I'm like a circus performer, you've got to ballyhoo me to get the people to come in.'

She refused to accept any invitations offered by civic authorities, the Chamber of Commerce, or lunch clubs. She referred to them as the 'creamed-chicken and green pea circuit'. 'If people want to see me, they've got to come to the theater,' she said. That was one reason. Another was that she was uneasy in the company of strangers.

She was never interested in sightseeing. One cast member told her he was going to look around town. 'What for?' she asked in surprise. 'We rode down the main street when we came in, dear, what more is there to see?'

She broke a ten-year attendance record at the theatre.

From Maine the company moved across the border to the Princess Theater, Niagara Falls, Canada. Again, she received excellent reviews. But one of her dresses was mislaid on the way to the theatre and she construed this to be the sign of an evil force at work. She burnt incense and made an incantation which she believed would drive it out. She wanted to pray, but in suitable surroundings, so she sent an actor to find a church she could visit after the show. Its denomination did not matter. The magic name of Mae West produced a minister willing to allow his church to be used at such a late hour. At about eleven in the evening Mae and her party slipped into the church. She prayed for several minutes and quietly left, making a point of thanking the minister for his consideration and donating $100 to church funds.

On the way home she announced that she had always given a donation to the Salvation Army in whichever town she had played, but had forgotten, of late, to do so. This was the reason the evil forces had been permitted to approach.

She was obviously in a religious frame of mind at Niagara Falls, for she telephoned T. Jack Kelly and asked him to come to the hotel and hold a seance for the cast one evening before the show. Kelly came and, as was his rule, insisted upon being blindfolded before answering written questions, rather as he had at his initial seance with Mae.

It was as well she did not witness the scene that later took place at the theatre before her arrival. Some cast members had not been as impressed with Kelly as Mae had hoped. One of the actors had a towel wrapped round his head like a turban and was feigning to be in a trance, while another ran about squeaking in falsetto pretending to be a spirit. The fun was quickly abandoned when a look-out announced Mae was at the stage door. When she asked the actors their opinion of the seance she received respectful replies. But she was not gullible and had her spies. She looked the man, who had worn the towel, in the eyes and told him, 'There will always be doubters.' He had the grace to blush.

The show was also visited by a troupe of men from the nearby Jewel Box Revue, which specialized in female impersonation.

There was a Mae West impersonator among the company, so naturally everyone was curious to see the real thing. Word spread and a lively party of about fifty made their way to the Princess Theater.

Mae asked for and was told the names of some of the drag artists. During her performance she substituted their names for the character names in the play. She added a couple of her classic one-liners for luck and threw in, seemingly off-the-cuff, the line, 'You watch out for those Jewel Box boys.' She received a standing ovation.

The Jewel Box company called backstage afterwards and, as the original fifty seemed to have swelled in number, Mae received them on stage, giving everyone a signed photograph, 'Sex-sationally yours, Mae West'.

Her next venue, the Grist Mill Playhouse, Andover, New Jersey, was the last port-of-call before the show folded. She booked into the Andover Hotel, just a block from the Playhouse, which meant she could cut down on travelling time. The run turned out to be as successful as the rest of the bookings and, when the time came to close, she could congratulate herself on a successful three-month tour.

Mae was not sentimental about goodbyes. There were few kisses and embraces. She took the details of those whom she thought she might use again, mentioned to one or two whom she liked to give her a ring if they were in Los Angeles, tipped the theatre staff and went home with Paul.

Mae now spent a lot of time at the beach house. She had hired a handyman-cum-butler, Larry Grayson, to run things and when Mae was in residence Beverly came over from the ranch, where she now lived, to cook for her. She stayed mainly in the kitchen where she kept a bottle of vodka as Mae seldom ventured into the room.

Any visitor who went to the kitchen was likely to be offered a drink by Beverly. Although sometimes she and Mae ate together, Beverly spent most of her time alone. The strain of her life had left its mark on her looks and, six years younger than Mae, she looked older and in poorer condition.

The sisters contrasted in their social demeanour. Mae never

swore in public, but foul-mouthed Beverly did not care who heard her. Mae's shyness was hidden by an aloofness, but happy-go-lucky Beverly exuded a fawning need for company. Beverly was tactile in conversation, reaching out to touch whomever she was with. Mae spoke with little animation.

Beverly had been married, but her marriage remained childless and ended in separation. She had no career and no one to whom she could turn apart from Mae and her brother John. John was a comfort. He shared a drink with her and was good company.

Mae spent a lot of time in her own bedroom. It was a big room, overlooking the ocean, dominated by a huge circular bed. Her fifteen foot square, private bathroom, marbled and mirrored, adjoined it. Often the bedroom looked in need of tidying but she gave orders it was to be left as it was. She knew where to find everything.

Her secretary, Larry Lee,* was also based at the beach house. Mae had a project in mind that was soon to occupy a lot of his time. In 1957 she decided to write her memoirs. This was not an overnight decision but something she had thought about for a long time. The idea had been broached before by publishers, but she had always declined. Now she received an enquiry from Prentice-Hall and decided to go ahead.

One reason for her previous lack of enthusiasm was that there had been a flood in the basement at the Ravenswood and records she had stored there had been destroyed. Other documents, which she had entrusted to Beverly at the ranch, had been eaten by rats. She had only the haziest idea of what had happened, when and where.

Friends, however, assured her they would be happy to research the book. Her life had been fairly well documented – since her arrival in Hollywood in any event. She herself could provide her version of what happened before that. Mae loved to talk about her days in vaudeville.

Larry Lee suggested they try a couple of chapters to see how it went. Also Criswell, who was enjoying success with his TV

* Lawrence Liebman.

show *Criswell Predicts*, encouraged her and did, in fact, do considerable research, but she supervised everything. 'Nobody can write about me, except me,' she said.

One thing goaded her into activity: it was pointed out to her that someone else might write an unauthorized biography. Much of her life had been spent in the public domain and there would not be a great deal she could do about it if someone wanted to cash in on her fame. If she wanted things to be depicted as she would wish and collect the revenue that came from the undertaking, then she had better get on with it quickly. Still she hesitated: 'I've got a lot more life to live, and things to do,' she wavered. 'It's too early.' Someone told her there could be a sequel.

Another helper suggested she should speak into a recording machine but she refused, nervous someone would get hold of the tape and use it against her. She insisted on dictating her thoughts to Larry Lee. Once she got going, however, the autobiography became important to her. It became a monumental part of her life and she spent hours poring over the typescript, fighting to find exactly the right words.

Authorship, however, had to be interrupted when she received an offer she could not refuse from Jerry Wald of Twentieth Century-Fox. He was producing the 1958 Academy Awards Ceremony. Mae was not a nominee (she had never been recommended for an Academy Award though *She Done Him Wrong* had received a nomination for Best Picture in 1933). For the 1958 season Wald planned a surprise. The ceremony was to be televised and he wanted Mae to make an unadvertised appearance with Rock Hudson, singing the duet 'Baby, It's Cold Outside'.

It would be Mae's first television appearance and was to be transmitted in colour – by no means an everyday occurrence in 1958.* She was stunned when Wald told her that her spot, of two and a half minutes' duration, would be seen by about twenty million people. She saw herself topping a cavalcade of

---

* Full-time colour transmissions did not become readily available until 1964–5.

stars and was determined to make it an evening to remember.

Special lyrics were written for 'Baby, It's Cold Outside' – 'to match my personality', and a rehearsal pianist summoned to the beach house. Hudson, at the peak of his popularity, willingly rehearsed until they were word and note perfect. He flattered her vanity by pretending to flirt with her even though he knew that she knew he was homosexual.

The ceremony was to take place on 26 March at the RKO Pantages Theater in Hollywood. The *chaise-longue* was again hauled out of storage for Mae to make her entrance upon. She wore a black, spangled gown designed for the occasion, which flared out to a fish-tail beneath the knees. Yards of white fox and a towering, plumed headdress completed her ensemble.

The number went off without a hitch. 'The audience got a rise out of Rock's offering Mae a cigarette and saying, "King-sized". Mae's retort: "Uummmm, it's not the men in your life, it's the life in your men." Their duet ended with a long and realistic kiss as the audience clapped and howled like the Saturday night crowd at Minsky's.'*

What the television viewers did not see was that after the song had finished Mae brought up her knee and gave Hudson an unrehearsed joke kick in the crotch. Which explains the delightful end close-up where he suddenly explodes with laughter. It also explains why Bob Hope – the MC for the evening – who walked on immediately afterwards was also convulsed.

The audience rose to its feet in delight. The legend, so long absent from the silver screen, had once again stolen the show. Among the celebrities present that night were Ronald Reagan, Cyd Charisse, Ernest Borgnine, Anthony Quinn, Gregory Peck, Joanne Woodward and Paul Newman, Anita Ekberg, Vincent Price, Joan Collins, Fred Astaire, Doris Day, Clark Gable, Sophia Loren, Cary Grant, Maurice Chevalier, John Wayne, Gary Cooper, Bette Davis, Vic Damone, Johnny Mathis, Dean Martin, Tab Hunter and Debbie Reynolds. Not a bad gathering for an older lady to upstage.

* *Inside Oscar*, J. Mason Wiley and Damien Bona, Columbus Books, 1986.

Lana Turner, never more luscious, was also there with a party that included her mother and daughter. Also seated at her table was a burly young Scot who had been a runner-up in the 1952 Mr Universe contest. Within five years Sean Connery was to become the definitive James Bond.

Later, when the press asked Mae how she kept her figure, she told them, 'Dumbbells, dear'. For a while, the hottest property on the underground market was a sound tape of Rock and Mae duetting 'Baby, It's Cold Outside'.

But, as in the early days of her film career, although the audience was cheering not everyone was pleased. There were certain influential people in television who thought her knee to Hudson's groin was in poor taste. 'That old broad will never learn,' someone was heard to mutter.

For the moment all that concerned the old broad was the hit she had made. She was delighted when she read the leader for the critique printed by the *Los Angeles Examiner*: 'Mae West and Rock Hudson Stopped the Show Cold'. Congratulatory letters came from all over the world, and with them an enquiry from a television company: would she consider doing a fifteen-minute daily transmission in which she would give advice to the lovelorn? Mae West as an agony aunt.

On the face of it this seems smart thinking. The empress of sex advising on sexual and emotional problems. The negative factor was that Mae claimed never to have had a sexual or emotional problem in her life; hardly the qualification for a dispenser of advice. Her marriage and Jim's death had, of course, brought sleepless nights, but she had overcome these singlehandedly, without advice from family or friends – or help from Hollywood's remedy for all ills, analysis. The only help Mae ever sought came from Spiritualist mediums.

The thought of Mae giving advice to the lovelorn was a novelty. How long the novelty would have lasted is another matter, but it was never put to the test. She went to the studios and made a pilot. It did not go down well. Mae's advice to teenagers was 'grow up' and such bluntness imbued everything she said. She relied heavily upon her tried and tested one-liners but by now they were far from original, having been bandied about across the world for over twenty years.

The television producer discovered something that Mae's intimates already knew. The mistress of the wisecrack was no consistent ad-libber. In her vanity she did not realize the unsatisfactory impression she had created, and called a press conference, telling Ronald Singleton, 'Dear, they need me. They need my positive thinking. I shan't be vulgar, I'll make fun of vulgarity. We'll take sex out in the open and maybe laugh at it.'

Unfortunately the effect of the West audition on the TV moguls was not laughter but boredom. The great shocker had not only failed to shock, she'd sent everyone to sleep. The distrust she had aroused by kneeing Rock Hudson in the groin must also have gone against her. This was the era of live television and Mae could not be trusted to behave with decorum. The lovelorn would have to struggle along without her. Another slap in the face which the triumphal parade of her memoirs fails to record.

chapter twenty-three

THE SWINGING SIXTIES

She persevered with her autobiography and by 1959 the manuscript was finished. The publishers decided to take stills of Mae in the Ravenswood for the cover. Before an important session, she'd always taken days to prepare herself and an army of beauticians now bumped into each other in the apartment. Her hair had to be bleached days beforehand because she had begun to intertwine it with her wigs to create a more natural effect.

On the day of the shoot the crew set up in the bedroom. Conditions were cramped; Mae lounged on her mirror-canopied bed wearing a négligée, slithering about for the camera, under a pool of fierce light. But the session did not work out, she looked stiff and uncomfortable. So she agreed to be photographed in bed, under the quilt, with only bare arms and shoulders showing. This looked better.

Within a few days she had to go to Las Vegas to revive the musclemen act. She had a return engagement at the Sahara Hotel five years after her initial opening. It was suggested she might like to incorporate some new ideas into the act, and with this in mind she met with choreographers and a costume designer. New songs were brought in, including a hot-blooded version of 'Temptation'.

Then she discovered how expensive this exciting new look would be and decided it was not worth the money. She dismissed the choreographer and costume designer, cast aside the new songs and reduced the muscle line-up from eight to six. To suit the more racially conscious times the black maid was exchanged for one who was French, but the gags remained the same.

The show opened for a week's tryout on 15 March 1959 at the Palm Springs Chi-Chi Club. In spite of the economies the reviewer for the *Desert Sun* was enthusiastic, commenting that she was ready to conquer a whole new generation just as she had conquered generations in the past.

Mae was booked for a month at the Sahara. An influenza epidemic was sweeping the town when she got there and many of the hotel employees were down with it. She insisted that her personal retinue wear muslin masks, like operating surgeons. Nevertheless she caught flu. A doctor gave her an injection of vitamin B, but warned that it might be ineffective. She was full of aches and pains and tried to alleviate her distress by spending long periods in meditation.

For all her sorry condition she opened on schedule, but her flu had taken its toll. She was not herself and as her illness worsened attendances dropped. Word spread that she had lost her magic. A reputation is a frail thing – after two bad weeks people were ready to write her off.

By the third week she found it difficult even to stand unsupported but she refused to cancel. A chair was placed on stage and she remained seated throughout her act. She could not stand even to take a bow at the end of the performance. Not that there was now much to bow for – applause was barely polite. She was helped to her feet, drenched in sweat, at the end of the last performance of her third week. Her voice was merely a croak. She had to cancel the final week.

Her fee was $50,000 per week, but since she had cut short her engagement a week's fee was forfeited. That $50,000 amounted to the profit she would have made after expenses were deducted. In real terms she had done the whole, miserable stint gratis. She blamed the hotel staff for giving her a cold and losing her the money. She blamed anyone who came near.

When she had left the Sahara in 1954 she had been given a gala farewell plus a diamond bracelet. This time she left at six in the morning with no one to wish her goodbye, apart from the bellhop who lugged down her many cases and packed them into the Cadillac and then waited for his tip. Six a.m. is about the only hour when Las Vegas is dead; most revellers have finally made it to bed. The huge neon lights advertising her name still glowed, their bulbs winking to each other, as she made her way home in the early morning light through an already shimmering desert. 'Some maid gave me a $50,000 cold,' were her last words as the big car silently bore her back to Los Angeles.

Her memoirs were published in October 1959 and launched her on another round of personal appearances. She had originally opted for the title of the book to be *Empress of Sex*, then *Come Up and See Me, Sometime?*, but eventually settled for *Goodness Had Nothing To Do With It*.

The book received universally good reviews and, indeed, is Mae at her best. Wittily and concisely written, full of anecdotes and well-turned phrases, this is not a run-of-the-mill autobiography of a movie star, but a literate and entertaining document. Her story is synonymous with the history of American vaudeville since Victorian times. Her love for the genre shines through, as does her contempt for the movie people who made her life unbearable.

A press launch for the book was given by her publishers at the Beverly Hilton hotel, presided over by Myron Boardman, then vice-president of Prentice-Hall. During the speeches Mae, attired in floor-length white satin, ermine, diamonds and emeralds, was presented with a copy of the book bound in gold.

She announced that she was about to write more books, including a novel based on *The Drag*, and delighted her audience with a potted history of how the police had closed *The Drag* for anyone present who might have been ignorant of the matter. She added: 'This book was originally 559 pages, but they cut it down to 270. They left out a lot of good men.'

Part of her publicity tour included a television interview for CBS on *Person to Person*. This was pre-recorded at the Ravenswood but not transmitted. Some of Mae's wisecracks raised objections: she pointed to her bed, for example, and said: 'That's where I do my best work,' adding that the mirrors were there so that she could see how she was doing. Lines she had been using for years, but not on television, and lines television wasn't about to allow her to use.

She made a public appearance of another kind in October 1959 in San Francisco when she faced actress Marie Lind across a court room. Miss Lind had been appearing at the Gay Nineties Club, where part of her act was an impersonation of Mae's Diamond Lil character. In her defence Mae stated that she, and she alone, had the right to be billed as Diamond Lil. She proved that she and Lil had been synonymous for over thirty years and that she had written both a novel based on the character and a play which had first been produced in 1928. There had even been a movie – although in *She Done Him Wrong* she was billed as Lady Lou. Mae stated she had spent a million dollars advertising and exploiting Diamond Lil; the name was so associated with her that, on one occasion, a letter had been delivered to her which was simply addressed 'Diamond Lil'. Presiding Judge Alfred Gitelson ruled in Mae's favour.

Mae spent much of 1960 working on her script for *Sextet*. She had hoped to place it with the Shuberts but they were not interested. There were dark mutterings from Mae about ingratitude and concrete boots when that comforting piece of information was passed on to her. She had hoped for a Broadway opening but, as it was, had to settle for the Midwest, an area that had always appreciated Mae West on stage.

Sextet was to open on 7 July 1960 at the Edgewater Beach Playhouse, Chicago. As before, a nucleus of leading players (including her old friend Jack LaRue) were to travel with her and the small parts were to be picked up on the road. As *Sextet* was a new production she could not very well avoid attending rehearsals, but she caught a cold which affected her throat. She went into an extensive period of meditation but to no avail, by opening night she had laryngitis. This affected her concentration and, when the show opened, she did not know her lines and required audible prompting. The audience was indulgent, however, and awarded her her usual standing ovation. The critics were not so kind:

Miss West wrote the play herself – quite possibly during costume changes last night. *Chicago American*

I will not review this play because there is no play; nor the acting, for there was no acting ... When she [Mae] arises it is as though a Wagnerian heroine were emerging out of a mountain of marshmallow (this, a reference to her specially designed bridegown) ... only two lines have any merit. 'Tact is knowing how far to go too far,' borrowed from Jean Cocteau without credit. 'He is every other inch a gentleman,' borrowed from Rebecca West without credit.

Chicago Daily News

Mae never read books so could not have picked up the quotes first hand. But she was an avid listener and remembered, 'borrowing' secondhand any quotes she felt appropriate. She collected witty remarks as a magpie collects bright objects. Larry Lee, however, was a keen reader and he often supplied her with material. For a lady who was quick to defend things she considered to be in her province, she was lax in crediting others when she used their material.

The play ran into trouble on the Saturday night. Two shows were scheduled but Alan Marshal, the actor playing Sir Michael, became ill. He struggled through the first show but was unable to continue so the second performance had to be cancelled. Marshal was a Christian Scientist and in keeping with his religious belief refused to see a doctor, telling an empathic Mae that he would will himself better. He did not succeed and that night died of a coronary.

His son, Kit Marshal, was also in the cast and in good trouper tradition announced that his father would have wished the show to go on. So Henry Guettel, the manager, read from a script for the following performances until a replacement could be found. The audience, having learned of the tragedy, was supportive.

Tom Conway was eventually hired to take over the role. He had enjoyed a successful television series during the early 1950s, entitled *Mark Saber* (not to be confused with the British series of that name which starred Donald Gray). Conway was the brother of British-born star George Sanders and, like Sanders, had considerable charm. But he was fifty-seven when called on to replace Marshal – and looked older – far too old to be acceptable to Mae.

It has been said that Conway took one look at the script and immediately walked out but, according to a cast member, the truth is different. Film writer Leslie Halliwell put his finger on the problem when he noted that Conway's career 'declined very suddenly'. Perhaps a reason for this was his heavy drinking. He arrived in Chicago drunk and remained that way during his brief stay with the company. Guettel knew that Mae would not work with a heavy drinker and Conway was put on a plane, still drunk, the following day. He had not even said good morning to her.

Conway's replacement was Francis Bethencourt, a classical player from Britain who had acted in both Shakespeare and Pirandello. He was thirty-five and had an Errol Flynn charm about him which Mae adored. He was seldom at a loss for words except once: when Mae asked him directly what he thought of the play. Mae called extra rehearsals, tightened up the script and added another song for herself – one that was in the public domain so she would not have to pay a royalty.

Nothing could save the Chicago run. What with the bad reviews, death of the leading actor and producer/actor substitute in his stead, audiences stayed away. The Edgewater Beach Playhouse underwent one of the worst financial disasters in its history. Mae had never played to such empty houses since her earliest days in vaudeville.

On 18 July the show trailed on to the Northland Playhouse, Detroit. This meant drastic restaging was needed as the Playhouse had an 'apron' stage instead of the usual proscenium arch. Mae's nerves were shaken, making her tetchy. The unkempt 'star' dressing room did nothing to sweeten her disposition. She instructed that sheets be pinned to the walls and, as there was no en suite lavatory, a chamber pot had to be placed at the ready. She took care of the more drastic needs of nature with her daily enema. There was no way she was going to share a lavatory with anyone.

While leaving for the theatre on the first night she was accosted by fans. She was courteous and gave them postcard-sized, autographed photographs, a stock of which she always carried. One of the fans remarked, jocularly, that now they had met her they would not have to see the show. She was furious and, once in the sanctity of her limousine, tore into her escorts for not keeping her from public view.

There was further trouble at the theatre. One of the bit-part players did not show up. Never at a loss in an emergency, Mae ordered her hairdresser to deputize. Eventually the real actor arrived, the worse for drink. He was dismissed.

Although the critics were no kinder in Michigan (one writing, 'Read her autobiography, it's cheaper and probably more fun'), business improved and she played to fair houses.

From Detroit the company moved to Warren, Ohio, where it followed Martha Raye, who had just finished a run in *Separate Rooms*. The highlight of the evening came when Mae sang. There was no logical reason in *Sextet* as to why Marlo Manners should suddenly burst into song, so Mae never bothered to fabricate one, merely walking centre stage to announce 'I feel like doing a song.' To enthusiastic applause she would plunge straight in, after which she would take her bow and resume the action.

As always, with Mae, the female critics were the deadliest.

Sextet was saved by short acts and long intermissions . . . She's a good ad for compulsory retirement.

ANNA JEAN CUSHWA

But the picture was not entirely black. Among the poison darts were a few sops of encouragement:

. . . the play is a West-ern, a Mae West-ern, not loaded with the gunfire of a TV western, but with the machine gun staccato of the West wit.   *Cleveland Plain Dealer*

August saw the show in Columbus, Ohio, at the Veterans' Memorial Auditorium. In an attempt to staunch the bad reviews Mae gave a press conference in which she mentioned everything from diet to Khrushchev. It did the trick. Rather than publish reviews, the papers merely printed their interviews, which were largely favourable.

The last port of call was the Cocoanut Grove Playhouse, Miami Beach, Florida. As this was a long journey Mae reluctantly agreed to fly. Having benefited from her press strategy in Columbus, she decided to pull the same stunt again and held another conference, this time in the airport lounge.

She remained on the plane until the rest of the passengers had left, then, make-up freshly applied and the torture-shoes strapped on, she faced the barrage of flashbulbs that greeted her. Clutching Paul's arm she made her precarious way down the portable steps. A microphone had been set up in the lounge and standing in front of it she did her act for the reporters. 'Miss West, how do you like it in Miami?' 'Boys, I like it anywhere.'

Inspired by the hullabaloo she announced, purely on whim, that she was in the midst of discussions to take *Catherine Was Great* to Russia.

Miami was at the height of its tourist season, and Mae dared not venture out of her hotel. As soon as she showed her face she was mobbed. Even in the dining room she was badgered; all her meals had to be sent to her suite.

Backers, who had the power to extend the tour or perhaps offer a further tour, were expected to attend, and Mae wanted an outstandingly enthusiastic public reaction. To this end she added a further song, her old stand-by 'Frankie and Johnny'.

Suddenly – in Miami, the most important date in the tour – things clicked into place. The press-hype helped and when Mae stepped on stage she was greeted by a storm of applause. Press reports later stated that not even Bankhead or Katharine Cornell had received such homage. She grew radiant, her famous slouch became a strut. The audience laughed at every gag and she received a terrific ovation after her songs. What with the addition of 'Frankie and Johnny', plus the audience reaction, fifteen minutes were added to the running time, which benefited the show for it had been rather short, another feature complained of by critics earlier in the tour. In Miami even the critics seemed happy:

'Mae West Wows 'Em As She Always Has'
Miami Herald

'Mae West Oomph Creates New Interest in Theater'
Miami Beach Sun

Among these pleasantries was an article that did not please her. Myrna Odell of the *Miami News* had interviewed certain members of the cast. All knew their jobs would be on the line if anything detrimental to Mae appeared under their names; great care was thus taken during the interview to ensure anonymity. But buried in the middle of the article was one reference to Mae as a 'tough old lady'. She summoned the cast and no amount of pleading innocence was accepted. She said they should have known better than to speak to 'those bitches' of the press in the first place. She was so incensed she hired a private detective from the Greater Miami Detective Agency to track down the culprit who had supplied such an unflattering description to Miss Odell.

Eventually a source was located which seemed to place the blame not on a member of the cast, but on a woman who had been working as a Mae West impressionist whom Mae had threatened with legal action unless she ceased the practice. The abrupt loss of a substantial amount of her act had caused the impersonator to utter a few strong words. Some of them had been picked up by the press. There were those, of course, who considered 'tough old lady' a pretty gentle remark and pretty close to the truth.

On the last day of the run Mae joined Governor Bryant, Mayor Tom Harris and a band of Seminole Indians for a ceremony which opened a new motorway. This stretch of road included a section which had a 45-degree bend, and the mayor suggested this should be called the 'Mae West Curve'. She spontaneously took the mayor's hand in both of hers. When asked how she kept her curves she said she did a great deal of bicycling. No one had ever seen Mae West go near a bicycle.

Before leaving Florida she visited a monkey farm and bought

two woolly monkeys, cooing over their cuteness. Sadly, one died before reaching California.

Despite her Miami triumph, the tour as a whole could not be described as a success. She was becoming tired of the road and her agents were seeking new avenues for her. Television was booming, and the William Morris Agency was trying to generate interest in a situation comedy in which she could star. Mae let it be known, however, that any role which cast her as a mother was out of the question. Motherhood was not in the Mae West tradition. Various ideas were put forward, including a pilot which cast her as the proprietor of a boarding house for vaudevillians; another had her as a detective, a role she had always fancied; yet another made her a saloon keeper in the Klondike of the 1890s. All of them failed to get off the ground. The hitch was that Mae did not like the idea of being available in people's homes at the turn of a knob. She felt a Mae West appearance should be an event, not something freely available.

In 1962, however, CBS expressed interest in making a colour version of *Catherine Was Great*. Mae had always wanted to see herself in colour and was excited by the proposal. But CBS stipulated that the budget should not exceed $15,000 inclusive of her fee, and that she would not be required to adapt the script as the company had its own professional writers. Mae had already taken her script out of storage and, with spectacles perched on the end of her nose, had started to pencil in her rewrites. Her hackles rose and she backed out.

She recorded three numbers for Plaza records which were issued as singles. These were 'Am I Too Young?', a dialogue with a teenager; 'He's Bad, But He's Good For Me' and 'Peel Me A Grape'. None of them sold well.

She spent much time in the beach house. Now and then, Beverly would limp in with some jasmine tea and some of her homemade chocolate biscuits. If her breath smelled of alcohol she was shot a hostile glance, to which she had become immune. When at home Mae slopped about in Dr Scholls sandals: her feet needed all the rest they could get.

This was the Swinging Sixties and quite inexplicably Mae decided to become a part of it and abandon her Gay Nineties image. She took to wearing miniskirts and had her hair styled in two stringy plaits. A dance teacher was hired, together with a three-piece combo, and she learned the frug, bugaloo, twist and the swim.

Plaits looked fetching on folksingers such as Joan Baez, but Mae felt on reflection they were not quite her style. She decided to replace them with some of the new beehive wigs that were all the rage. A wig-maker arrived at the mansion and fitted her out with a lacquered blonde structure, but that did not please her either. 'Jesus,' she complained, 'It looks like a rat's nest.' Grayson was instructed to drive her to a department store on Sunset Boulevard which sold ready-made wigs. When told she would have to take the elevator to the wig department, she was horrified to see it was made of transparent plastic. 'A person could get shot in that thing.' she quailed.

Upon arrival at the salon she was served by a young man who evinced symptoms of disbelief when she started to flirt with him. He had no idea who she was. Her appearance, at nearly seventy, in a miniskirt, fishnet stockings and plaits, made her look decidedly batty. His opinion of her did not change when she lost a contact lens and the place had to be searched. She spent an hour trying on the wigs, some of which were made of plastic, and eventually bought nothing. Mae did not stick to the Swinging Sixties for long and was soon back in her long gowns.

When not working Mae's excursions from home were rare, so Beverly and Jack, who was visiting, took advantage of one infrequent absence to celebrate their freedom for a few hours. After a drink or two, Beverly slipped back to her room for a rest, forgetting she had put some television dinners in the oven to warm. When Mae returned she was greeted by incinerator-like fumes. Coco, now acting as housekeeper, was rushing about, wringing his hands and flapping towels. Mae roughly shook Beverly awake.

She was asked to be guest of honour at the Friars Club, the Friars being a male organization comprised mostly of entertainers. The occasion was a testimonial dinner for Harry

Richman, Mae's sometime accompanist and a celebrity in his own right. For a woman it was something of an honour to be invited, mostly on account of the hearty 'stag' atmosphere that predominated. Guests that night included George Burns, Milton Berle and Bob Hope.

Mae West at a stag night was guaranteed to bring down the house, and she loved the whistles she received as she swayed her way through the cigarette fumes to the microphone. She elicited further cheers when she opened her number with, 'My favourite audience, wall to wall men.' She went on to say, 'I don't remember, Harry, whether I discovered you, or you discovered me, but what I do remember is that you always had a great touch . . .' Then she added, patting her hair in the famous West gesture, '. . . even at the piano.'

It was no secret that she and Richman had been lovers. He convulsed at his table and the audience went wild.

chapter twenty-four

THE DOUBLE THYROID

A description of Mae as she was at this time in her life is given by Alexander Walker, writer and movie critic for London's *Evening Standard*. In 1963 he was visiting Christopher Isherwood, who lived near Mae's beach house in California. Isherwood rang Mae, on Walker's behalf, and explained Walker was a British film critic. She agreed to see him. Upon arrival he found the beach house unkempt: 'I got the impression that the inhabitants did not receive too many callers so were not very houseproud.'

Then Mae made her entrance: 'I was quite unprepared for how small she was,' he relates. 'She was like a little infanta. I knew she was around seventy but she looked about thirty, a plumpish thirty. The reason for this was that she had painted a kabuki mask on her face; it was thick with plaster and simulated that of a thirty year old ... She sat beside me. She wore several layers of false eyelashes and her eyes travelled slowly up and down my body. I realized she was giving me her interview treatment as she expected me to write about it. The silence mounted. "It's a hot day," she said slowly ... Everything she said was full of sexual innuendo, everything she said seemed to have *double entendre.*

'I was with her for about three-quarters of an hour and, really, she did not say much. She just kept repeating what she said in various ways, the way old people do. They forget they've just told you something and tell you again. I felt a slight uneasiness with her, but I was fascinated to watch her going through her act. It was eerie rather than having a sexual feel to it. I asked if she still had love affairs. "Honey," she replied, "the day isn't long enough for them all." '

Be that as it may, she turned down yet another film offer from a top Sixties director. Federico Fellini was winging his way to Los Angeles to attend the 1963 Oscar Awards. His films, such as *La Dolce Vita* (which precipitated Anita Ekberg – truly a Goddess come to life – to fame), had won universal acclaim, making him one of the most influential directors of the time. Another of his films, *8½*, was just being released in Europe. However highly the Europeans might think of it, the morally staid (albeit poisonous) Hedda Hopper denounced it as 'beneath contempt'.

Fellini's presence at the Oscars concealed an ulterior motive. He was casting his new film *Giulietta of the Spirits* and hoped to induce two old-timers to take part in it, namely Groucho Marx – a friend of Mae's since their days in vaudeville – and Mae. Despite its attractive Spiritualist theme, the story concerned a bored, middle-aged woman and, plead as Fellini did, Mae would have none of it (neither would Groucho).

Fellini tried again to entice her before his cameras in 1967 when he was planning *Satyricon*. He wanted her to play a sorceress, versed in erotica, who would guide adolescents in their first halting steps on the path of sexual adventure. This was more up her street. But she found out that the sorceress had children and not even in a mythical role would Mae West consent to being cast as a mother. Another project went out of the window.

So did the proposal that she play the role of the older woman in the Elvis Presley film *Roustabout*. It finally went to Barbara Stanwyck.

Although she turned down *Giulietta of the Spirits*, her real-life fervour for Spiritualism remained undiminished. T. Jack Kelly continued to be a regular visitor to the beach house and she sponsored many soirées there for his benefit. She would sit in a separate room while he gave his demonstrations so as not to deflect attention from him. She knew that most of the guests would be more fascinated in catching a glimpse of her than listening to what the spirits had to say. Sometimes there would be as many as fifty people attending these seances and, on these occasions, she would charge a $5 entrance fee per head. Not for herself, but to ensure Kelly would not be out of pocket.

Through studies in meditation Mae claimed to have mastered control of her bodily mechanisms and that this would lead to longevity. She could, she said, slow her heartbeat by limiting the number of breaths she took per minute, and reducing the expansion of her lungs to a mere one-quarter of an inch.

For all this fending off of death, it held no special terror for her. The ageing process itself was the enemy, not the final adventure. She believed she would continue to live after death in a form not too different from the one she now had, and that when that state arrived it would be heralded by a glorious reunion with Tillie. There was much spiritual work to do, she said, and the world needed someone of her quality to undertake it.

Houdini, she claimed, had been a lover of hers. After his death in 1926, his widow had conducted a series of seances in which attempts had been made to contact him, but so far no evidence to the satisfaction of the widow had been forthcoming. Mae remained convinced of Houdini's survival and felt that Mrs Houdini was being obdurate. Mae had, she said, received Houdini at several seances, and was certain from personal evidence that it was indisputably him.

Forces of darkness, as well as good, she believed to exist and the dark forces were blocking the world from spiritual knowledge. She believed she was a 'vessel' for the 'good forces'. When asked if she could see into the future she admitted she couldn't. 'Maybe next time round,' she said. But she was a firm believer in reincarnation – how else, she expostulated, could a brain such as Einstein's or Freud's be explained? Not to mention her affinity with Catherine of Russia, of whom, she was sure, she was the living incarnation. 'I've got to come back,' she said. 'I've got too much to do.'

She had, so far, received no contact from the hereafter from Jim. He had tried to reach her, she was certain, but the dark forces were blocking his way. She held his family responsible for this. Jim came from Catholic stock and certain family members had disapproved of his connection through her with Spiritualism. With a touch of classic Westian megalomania, she lamented one time that 'It's a pity Jim can't get through, he might have something to tell me to help me with my career.' Apparently, Mae West was as revered in the hereafter as she was on the physical side of the great divide.

Various deceased stars came to visit her through Kelly's good offices. On one memorable night Mario Lanza, who had died in 1959, apparently tuned in. Presumably the late Grace Moore was still a regular caller, too, in which case, had they run into each other, they would have had their music in common and may even have sung a duet.

Mae also conducted experiments in telepathy. A group of people would sit in silence while one of its members tried to establish contact with someone in an adjoining room. ESP became a particular interest.

She had always had strong willpower and now developed this capacity even more. Recently she had been diagnosed diabetic and, as a result, had to have insulin injections. She blocked the illness from her mind, just as she had blocked her marriage from her mind when she had been eighteen. It never became public knowledge.

Television producer Arthur Lubin came to see her on one of the evenings Kelly was present. He was producing a show called *Mr Ed*, which concerned the adventures of a talking horse, rather like the famous *Francis* series of movies starring Donald O'Connor.

Lubin suggested Mae make a guest appearance on one of the *Mr Ed* shows and Kelly, whom she consulted before accepting, recommended she go ahead. So, she, who had turned down Fellini and Billy Wilder, agreed to co-star with a talking horse. It was a great success. In the story she 'adopts' *Mr Ed* and pampers him, filling his stable with French furniture and spraying him with perfume. He is glad to get away and settle for the more homely comforts of a normal stable. A couple of musclemen were worked into the episode as grooms at Mae's suggestion.

Mae's television appearance set Hollywood talking. Hedda Hopper, attending a formal dinner, demanded that the television be turned on to watch, as did many others. Mae had always insisted that her television appearances must constitute a special occasion, and *Mr Ed* certainly did.

She recorded the show under the handicap of impaired sight. Her vision, never good, had become restricted by cataracts. Shortly after recording *Mr Ed* she had the cataracts surgically removed. Again she succeeded in keeping the story from the press.

She spent most of her evenings either in pursuit of spiritual knowledge, or watching television, but would sometimes go out if the object of the sortie were of sufficient interest. One reason for her seclusion was that she would not leave the house until she looked like Mae West. Grooming for this took up most of the day.

She ventured out, one evening, when she was told of a night-club on Ventura Boulevard which featured a puppet show. The puppets were effigies of theatrical ladies such as Dietrich, Eartha Kitt and Mae; they 'mimed' to recordings. With a friend for company she swept in. She loved the Mae West doll, swathed in furs and diamonds, and seemed to be enjoying the club. The other diners were not intrusive.

During the evening, however, a young Italian approached and asked if he could join her. As he was easy on the eye she gave permission. She had been drinking mineral water but now augmented this with a glass of white wine. The Italian monopolized Mae and told her of his hot Latin blood, of his need for sex and how difficult it was to keep himself in check when seated next to such a beautiful woman. It was clear he was drunk. For once this did not offend her. She encouraged him in his sexual advances and, eventually, he smashed his fist on the table in an outburst of frustrated lust. Mae took refuge behind her napkin, using it coquettishly, rather as Restoration ladies used their fans.

While the Italian was plighting his troth another young man, engaged by the restaurant to entertain the diners with an electric guitar, began taking an interest in her. He sang for her, and moved as close to her as he could get, allowing for the restrictions of the plugged-in cable attached to his instrument.

Mae took a few sips of wine and announced it was time to leave. The combination of the torture-shoes and the sips of unaccustomed alcohol meant she had to be supported out by both her friend and the Italian. She left with impeccable dignity, the diners bursting into spontaneous applause, which she acknowledged as best she could, precariously lifting an arm from the Italian's shoulder to wave.

Grayson was waiting in the limousine to float her away. The Italian followed her inside. Mae's original escort was affronted when he received an unceremonious shove on the chest from Mae, who told him to get a taxi back; he had no option other than to withdraw. He was left watching the diminishing number plate as Mae and the Italian sped into the darkness.

He was not alone for long. The guitarist had followed the trio out. Disappointment registered on his face when he was told she had left with the Italian.

'Say, man,' he said to the friend, 'what turns that West broad on? Would she go in for more than one guy at a time?'

The friend shrugged his shoulders, but the guitarist produced a pen and wrote his number on a scrap of paper, pleading to be put in touch with her. It was duly passed on.

Kelly died that year. He and Mae had been loyal friends and good for one another. Kelly had not only given her a meaning to life, he had brought her in contact with Tillie. For that alone she could not thank him enough.

Mae retained a spiritual counsellor. Before his death Kelly had introduced her to another psychic, Richard Ireland. Although he could not replace Kelly, she was able to gain comfort and encouragement from him.

Her brother John also died that year. He was sixty-four. Although he had not been as big a part in her life as Beverly, he was nevertheless family and his death was a further erosion of her security. It left her with even less contact with the outside world.

People who met John had liked him, as indeed they had his father. The West men, good-looking and charming, seemed to generate popularity. John married and his wife Selma still outlives him. She bore him a son, John West III.

John II died from a stroke complicated by heart disease, the same combination that had killed his father. Mae had his body laid to rest at the Abbey of Cypress Hills where he joined Tillie and Battling Jack.

John's death frightened her. She thought that she, too, might go as a result of a heart attack since heart conditions tend to run in families. She became listless and withdrawn. As her current frame of mind seemed to suit the project, she took out the discarded manuscript of her biography about Kelly and, with help from Larry Lee, renewed work.

In order to cheer her, a few friends, with Beverly and Paul's connivance, gave her a small party to commemorate her seventy-first birthday. Her age could not be acknowledged, of course, merely its anniversary as a good excuse to celebrate her continuing youth and beauty.

A cook was brought in for the day. In addition to Beverly and Paul, the gathering consisted of Larry Lee, Criswell, and a sweet old lady, Dolly Dempsey, who had been a founder of Mae's fan club in 1935 and had since become a trusted member of her coterie.

It was a subdued evening and the general consensus, although nobody admitted it, was that it had not been a good idea. Mae was simply not in the right mood. A bonus, however, was that everyone had had a decent meal. With Beverly alone at the helm, meals at the beach house were pretty haphazard.

Much more fun happened the night the University of Southern California realized Mae was worth honouring and decided to devote an evening to her. George Cukor chaired the celebrations, and among the guests were Billy Wilder, Jack Lemmon and Gloria Swanson. Mary Pickford agreed to act as Mistress of Ceremonies.

Miss Pickford seems to have been an odd choice as she did not approve of Mae and had voiced her disapproval publicly several times. But her mental health was capricious at the time and she possibly did not know to what she was agreeing. On the morning of the scheduled day she casually sent a message that she would not, in the event, be attending.

Cukor nearly had apoplexy. There was enormous press interest in the evening. To secure Mae was a coup, and hardly less
prestigious was the anticipated presence of Miss Pickford.
What, now, was he to do?

Miss Swanson responded magnificently to the challenge, as
she had been responding magnificently to challenges all her
life. She calmed Cukor by assuring him she would undertake to
be Mistress of Ceremonies. Unrehearsed, but in command, she
saved the evening. Moving among the celebrities, microphone
in hand, she was graciousness personified.

As the months slipped away various projects were offered to
Mae. One such was an operatic version of *Diamond Lil*. Mae
knew nothing about opera, and cared less, but she like the idea
of *Diamond Lil* being elevated culturally so she agreed to lend
her support. But, like so much else, nothing further came of it.

Throughout most of 1965 Mae had felt below par. Her
diabetic diet depressed her and she felt deprived without the
many sweet things she had enjoyed. She thought she might
write another book, and planned a volume of recipes for raw
food dishes – something fashionable today but in advance of its
time; publishers were not interested.

She had never encouraged visitors and now hardly any
called. An air of neglect hung over both the Ravenswood apartment and the beach house. The ranch was in a state of
decomposition as Beverly had developed a neurosis about
workmen, fearing they might molest her; when Mae bestirred
herself to hire carpenters to repair the broken barn doors,
Beverly sent them away before they could start, hobbling
drunkenly out of the house, her mouth full of abuse.

Mae's lethargy, however, was abruptly swept away when she
learned that Joseph Weintraub was preparing a book about her.
This was to be a slim volume, illustrated with stills from her
shows and movies, which listed biographical details plus some
of her famous sayings. A tribute to her art, but all she could see
was that someone was making money out of her and she was
not getting a cut. She did her utmost to prevent publication but
finding that was impossible, tried to ensure she was financially
involved with the deal. There was nothing she could do,

however, and the book was duly published under the title *The Wit and Wisdom of Mae West*.*

Other 1960s figures were encroaching on her fame. The Beatles had arrived, and were preparing their world-famous LP, *Sergeant Pepper's Lonely Hearts' Club Band*. The record sleeve is a montage of photographs of famous personalities and permission was sought from Mae to feature her photograph among those on the cover. At first she was affronted. 'What have I to do with lonely hearts' clubs?' she wanted to know. It was explained that this was the title of a pop record. She still withheld permission until all four Beatles wrote her personal letters, then she melted under the onslaught and conceded.

She made another LP herself in 1966. This came about because some of her movies had been shown on late-night television and youngsters, to whom she had been only a name, realized, as does everyone who has seen Mae in action, that she is fun.

She always liked rock and roll and murmured from time to time that she would like to turn *Catherine Was Great* into a rock opera. This did not happen, but she was approached by Tower Records and invited to make a rock album. Four shaggy-haired young musicians were brought in as a backing group, and Mae gave torrid renditions of eleven items, including Lennon and McCartney's 'Day Tripper', Bob Dylan's 'If You Gotta Go', and the Percy Sledge hit 'When A Man Loves a Woman'.

Mae was on home ground here. Always an able singer, her rough, belting voice, still well – some might say miraculously – preserved, did not let her down. What may have started out as a gimmick ended up a valid rock anthology. *Way Out West*, issued with a selection of photographs from her films and sporting a stunning, air-brushed cover still of Mae, sold a creditable 100,000 copies.

As part of *Way Out West*'s promotion, reporter Glenys Roberts went to the beach house to interview Mae for the London *Evening Standard*, and found Mae in the company of record producer David Mallet, who was teaching her how to play an electric guitar.

* Known in England as *Peel Me A Grape*, Futura, 1975.

'She is still a statuesque blonde with an Edwardian hour-glass figure,' she reported, 'and she received me in a peach satin négligée, with a décolletage which would put a lesser woman to shame. She had bright red finger nails and a bright red rose-bud mouth . . . and the good facial structure which age only improves. Her hair tumbled on her shoulders and she had a look of contained amusement and, best of all, she still had that marvellous voice which seems to have come from Brooklyn via New Orleans and rasps with innuendo even when it is offering you tea and toast.'

During the proceedings the ever-accommodating Paul served tea. Beverly had orders to remain in the kitchen while Mae was conducting business. The prospect of Beverly lurching through the doorway was too horrifying to contemplate.

Miss Roberts continued in her article, 'fans of Miss West . . . are, to judge from her mail, largely between fifteen and thirty . . .' One of the young fans who wrote to her was Robert Duran, aged eighteen. He had seen her on *Mr Ed* and sent a congratulatory letter. She was intrigued to meet such a young fan and asked Craig Russell, a famous drag artist and friend who ran her fan club, to bring Duran to the beach house to meet her. He duly presented himself at the appointed time, wearing his best suit: 'I was told by Craig not to spend more than five minutes with her,' Duran recalls. 'That five minutes turned into eight hours. "She likes your dark, good looks," he told me. I was about to leave, when she said, "Oh no, dear, you're going to stay to dinner, aren't you?" '

Dinner was served in the formal dining room, which was furnished with the antique Chinese furniture Mae had purchased as a job lot with the house. From that day, Duran spent numerous hours with Mae and he often witnessed the kindly side of her nature.

'She had such a hearty appetite,' Duran recalls. 'Sometimes we'd be in the car and she'd grab my leg and ask, "Where do you want to eat?" She liked Italian food and we'd often have pasta.

'We were in a restaurant once and the *maitred d'* asked her to sign the menu, then offered us a complimentary drink. She ordered a Cointreau so I said I'd have one too. I had a cold and was frightened of giving it to her, so I told her the alcohol might prevent that. "Don't worry about it," she told me. But I was so nervous when the drink arrived that I spilled it. "Dear," she said, "I guess you weren't meant to have that." She had only taken a sip from her glass and passed it over to me. "It'll be good for your cold," she said.

'She liked Madame Woo's restaurant. No one bothered her there and she could drift off quietly into a world of her own. You didn't have to talk to her all the time, we'd just sit and she'd tap her fingers, a habit she had; after a while she might make a comment, then be quiet again. She loved the fortune cookies there and always kept the slips with the fortunes on them.

'We were in Madame Woo's one evening – she liked to dine early, between five and six, to avoid the crowds – when Madame Woo came up and told her Carol Burnett was in the next room and would Mae like to say hello. Miss West refused to budge. "I think she should come and say hello to me," she said sternly.' Madame Woo, trying her best to keep everyone happy, had misjudged that one.

Duran also remembers an incident at yet another restaurant, the Smuggler's Inn: 'We were sitting at a table when the waitress asked us if we could move. Miss West asked why, and the waitress said because it was less distance for her to walk. Miss West stayed put. Later the waitress came up and said, "You look like Mae West." Miss West did not answer, so the waitress asked, "Is that good or bad?" Miss West told her, "I should think it would always be good to look like Mae West." '

Mae was unyielding when it came to protocol. She was always prepared to talk to her fans but would brook no familiarity, noticeably tensing if any of them failed to treat her with the courtesy she extended towards them. None but her closest friends addressed her as Mae.

Since *Way Out West* had done so well she recorded a follow-up album. This was a Christmas LP entitled *Wild Christmas*, but it did not sell as well.

She received further film offers – 'cameo' guest roles – and she rejected them all on the grounds she was being asked only to prop up talentless younger stars. Her own ego got propped up in other ways.

Mae's film career had ended in 1943. Since then, a market for West memorabilia had developed. Fans sometimes went to extraordinary lengths to purchase rare photographs. Sometimes they would bring their treasures to the Ravenswood and ask her to autograph them. She was happy to do so, providing the pictures were of her Hollywood or post-Hollywood era. If any pre-Hollywood photographs turned up she would do her best to have them destroyed. Her appearance had altered drastically since she had become a film star and it was that image she wished to perpetuate. She wanted no brown-haired upstart from the distant past to intrude.

Robert Duran recalls that he was once sent down to the foyer when a fan arrived at the Ravenswood with an early photograph of Mae with a request for it to be signed. 'Jesus Christ!' she exclaimed when she saw it, 'I'm not going to sign this. Tell him I'll give him a colour picture for it.' But the early still was so rare the fan refused to swap. Duran was again delegated to go down to the foyer with the message that Miss West would love to own the picture. Could she buy it? The fan was sorry but he would not part with it.

'Who needs fans like that?' she exploded on his return. She had no option but to return the picture, but she did so with ill will. She refused to sign it and autographed instead a more recent photograph.

Sometimes fans were tempted to make a repeat visit. This was tolerated providing they were male and handsome, but if they veered towards the plain side, they were refused a second visit. 'I've already seen him, why would I want to see him again,' was the message relayed to one unremarkable youth.

Robert Duran fared better. When he decided to move to Los Angeles from his previous address in Palm Springs, Mae suggested he stay at the beach house as her guest. He stayed for a while but was not entirely comfortable, because he was conscious that Mae felt an obligation to entertain him. Sometimes she would drive to Santa Monica from the Ravenswood rather than leave him alone. He felt this placed an unnecessary strain on her ability to cope.

'Jesus Christ,' she remarked upon arrival on one occasion, stopping dead in her tracks and her hand flying to her face. 'I've got no eyelashes. The only time in sixteen years I've got no eyelashes on. That goddamned son-of-a-bitch was rushing me.' She did not specify who the son-of-a-bitch was.

Mae always drove up in her big, black 1959 Cadillac Fleetwood, but never drove herself. She had given up driving in the 1940s when, according to her own account, she had hit a policeman on point duty. She had been going slowly so he was not hurt: 'I ought to give you a ticket for this,' he had reprimanded her. 'No,' she answered. 'I'll give you two – for my show tonight.' The policeman accepted the tickets but the incident unnerved her. She was never a happy traveller and never rode without her seat belt fastened, even before it became illegal not to do so.

From time to time Duran went with her to the ranch. On the first visit Mae, who had not seen the place for a while, was horrified by its neglected state. She shouted at Beverly, who took no notice. In disgust Mae asked Duran to help her move some furniture. While he heaved it about he came across some original crayon caricatures of Mae and W. C. Fields, obviously early publicity materials for *My Little Chickadee*. 'You can have them, dear,' she said. 'Take them with you.'

Another time, while he was rummaging through a curio shop in the Hollywood area one day, Duran came across another piece of West memorabilia – a very recondite item. It was an expensively produced leather-bound booklet which, to his amazement, contained a sequence of pornographic cartoons of a beautiful blonde film star called Lotta Leadpipe, who was engaged in explicit sexual encounters with Popeye the Sailorman. Miss Leadpipe was unmistakably based on Mae.

Duran mentioned what he had seen to Mae when they were motoring one day. 'Oh, yeah,' she said. 'They did that in the Thirties. When we get back I'll show you something.'

'The minute we got in,' he says, 'she went to a trunk she kept in the hall. There were six immaculate copies of the book there.' When issued in the 1930s the booklets had sold under the counter for $1000 apiece. Mae was amused by the whole concept, but she explained, 'I had to get the DA to stop them, so I put them out of business.'

The books are worth a great deal of money today, but she gave one to Duran. An odd choice of gift for an elderly lady to pass on to a young man, some might think, but not if the lady was Mae West. When talking of the booklet, Mae referred to it as 'the bible'.

Some time before her seventy-fourth birthday, Mae had a long look in the mirror and decided something must be done to maintain her youthful appearance. She decided she must have some longer style wigs made, which would fall gently over her face and mask her neck and jowls, hide everything, in fact, except the tip of her nose and mouth.

A wig-maker was summoned, but in the interval between Mae making the decision to consult him and his arrival she had changed her mind. 'What's all this wig business,' she snapped at him. 'People tell me I don't look more than thirty-six; any fool can see that. What are you trying to do to me?' A couple of weeks later she again contacted the wig-maker. She had changed her mind once more.

Once again he made the trek to the beach house, not quite sure what sort of reception to expect. He discovered Mae sipping a glass of wine. She made a down payment of $600 but insisted only the finest, baby-soft hair would suffice. She then approved styles similar to those she had worn over half a century earlier, and insisted there had to be a topknot of some description to give height, and tendrils of hair down her face to cover any signs of a potential dewlap.

Her real hair was now shoulder length and she gathered it in a little knot at the nape of her neck when at home. For emergencies she had a multitude of mantillas and silk scarves which she could throw over her head.

She explained she needed wigs because Warner Brothers were about to film *Sextet*, a wishful thought. Warner Brothers had expressed interest, and even provisionally cast Rock Hudson, Cary Grant and David Niven but, like so many things in the movie business, the idea never got off the ground.

The University of Southern California approached her again. The national film fraternity – Delta Kappa Alpha – was holding a thirtieth honorary awards banquet and invited her to be guest of honour. James Stewart and director Mervyn LeRoy were to be present.

The USC dinner soon became the hottest ticket in Hollywood. 'We're sending back money for tickets from some of the biggest names in town,' reported a member of the committee. 'We've been sold out since the first week.'*

It was to be Mae's evening from the start. Neither James Stewart nor Mervyn LeRoy attempted to upstage her. Before her entrance, a montage of film clips was shown, then the lights came up on a white fur rug and three footballers in a huddle. The men parted to reveal Mae draped on her famous couch, which had again been refurbished and in fact rescued in the nick of time from the gnawing appetites of the rats at the ranch.

She was dressed in white and diamonds. Her face glowed from the joy of being once again in front of an audience. She quipped, 'I could have been the sweetheart of Sigma Chi . . . could have been the sweetheart of Sigmund Freud, but I reclined, . . . er, declined.' She spoke about *SEX*, and *The Drag*, then sang a chorus of 'Doin' the Grizzly Bear', with which she had enjoyed a success around 1910. If only Battling Jack could have seen her now. She then slung a boa over her shoulders and performed her monologue about *Diamond Lil*, climaxing with a rendition of 'Frankie and Johnny'.

She was made an honorary member of the fraternity, the highest distinction the university could accord. As James Powers of *The Hollywood Reporter* wrote:

Miss West has outlasted her niggling critics, those who once professed to find her talents naughty or even unlawful. Miss West has known the censor's steamy breath. She has fought the good fight from the end of a ride in the paddy wagon. And where are her tormentors today? Scat-

---

* *Hollywood Reporter*, 7 February 1968.

tered, as the Philistine host was dispersed. Miss West, who
has defied age as she has defied everything else that stood
between her and her art, still is unmatched . . .

Once again a flutter of interest in her emanated from various
television companies. She took part in the *Red Skelton Show*,
but other sponsors worried that she was too specialized a performer for general advertising. Only sophisticated products
could be marketed around her; anything to do with domesticity
would be unsuitable. That, at least, was the answer she received
when she queried why the offers were not followed up.

Not only television companies were taking notice of her. The
anchoritic Garbo expressed a flicker of interest and told her
friend George Cukor she would like to meet Mae. Cukor
needed no further encouragement and threw a soirée where
both Hollywood legends could meet, perhaps even converse.
The latter was by no means a certainty since both ladies were
known to be temperamental: Garbo was renowned for her
silence and Mae could become monosyllabic if upstaged.

Mae did not trouble herself too deeply about what conversa-
tional gambits she'd employ at the party; she later told a
reporter, 'Before I went I said to a friend, "Let's see, what will I
talk about? Oh, I'll talk about myself." '

According to the *Los Angeles Times* Mae ended up telling
Garbo about her musclemen, naming a dozen or so whom, she
said, had been in love with her. Both ladies claimed they
adored each other's films. Later, Mae declared to *Life*
magazine, 'I admire her because she's always conducted herself
well; didn't cheapen herself. She looked very good. I'd like to
see her make more pictures.' The evening had been a success.

The *Life* article was written by Richard Meryman and her
friend, the actor Roddy McDowall, took the photographs. Mae
had been nervous before Meryman arrived. Robert Duran was
with her and had put on a suit and tie for the occasion. 'Jesus,'
she told him, 'you look like an undertaker.' She was yelling at
everyone, reminiscent of the scene in *Goin' To Town* when she
rehearses her aria. Her wig worried her; she had arranged it in
a new style, a sort of ponytail curled over one shoulder. Now

she thought this might be wrong and, at the last minute, draped it over the other shoulder.

In Meryman's article Mae mentions her 'double thyroid', a condition which was to crop up in her interviews from now on. She explained: 'I've always had this tremendous energy . . . One time they X-rayed my chest and found I had double thyroid glands and that's where you get your energy, you know.' The author is grateful to Dr William Russell MB MRCGP who elucidates such arcane anatomical conditions: 'The symptoms of overactivity are those of progressive loss of weight, protruding staring eyes and profuse sweating, none of which are terribly glamorous and could not be attributed to Miss West. She may well have had a double thyroid gland but she would undoubtedly have had treatment if she did have overactivity. Overactivity of the thyroid could not have been the cause of her phenomenal energy.'

Whatever the cause, she was about to need all the energy she could muster.

chapter twenty-five

COMEBACK

There is no mystery as to why Mae made a film comeback after an absence of twenty-six years. The spirits told her to do so. She confided as much to director Michael Sarne soon after they had started working on *Myra Breckinridge* together. It happened in the following manner.

One day, early in 1969, Mae was rolling through Hollywood in her limousine in the company of one of her psychic advisors. She held some mail in her hand which she had collected on the way out of the Ravenswood and, as they chatted, she opened one of the letters. It was from Sarne, offering her the role of theatrical agent Letitia van Allen in his forthcoming film based on Gore Vidal's satirical novel *Myra Breckinridge*.

She seldom made any major decision without advice from Spirit, so passed the letter to her psychic who told her, 'Mae, this man is so determined, so determined.' Later, Mae told Sarne, 'He told me to do the picture, he said I had to do it.'

She telephoned Sarne, inviting him to call and discuss the project. Sarne, a former pop star, was thirty years old, blond and sexy which, doubtless, smoothed the meeting. 'She was a terribly sweet old lady,' he says. A description that would have elicited anything but sweetness from her had she heard it.

But, as always before Mae would commit herself, she made stipulations. The first was that she must have star billing. Letitia is not the central character and when Mae glanced through the book she had not been impressed. She was mollified by assurances of star billing, control of her script and the expansion of Letitia's part. Then there was the question of her fee, which had to be commensurate with her star status. If she was returning to the movies, then Hollywood must know it was on the right terms. She wanted $300,000.

This was a hefty sum and there was some delay in Fox agreeing the amount. Mae was insulted and phoned Sarne to complain: 'They won't pay me the money,' Sarne recalls her saying. 'I told her to go for $350,000,' he said, adding, 'and tell them the director won't do it without you.'

Sarne had been asked to do the film by Richard Zanuck, vice-president in charge of production for Twentieth Century-Fox. But Sarne was beginning to have his own reservations about the project. He recalls, 'I really thought that if Mae did not get the money and abandoned the film, then it would give me a good excuse to opt out. Someone else could do it. There are, after all, a million directors in Hollywood. But Mae rang the next day: "Well, dear," she said. "I did what you said and I got the three-fifty." So I went round to the Ravenswood and we went out for a meal to celebrate. She was into health foods and drank herbal tea.'

The press were excited by Mae's proposed return to the screen. Far more excited than she, who took it easily in her stride. Once the official announcement of her signing had been made, reporters flew to Hollywood from all over the world to interview her.

The story was particularly newsworthy as Mae was returning to the screen not as a character actress, but, at the age of seventy-six, as a sex symbol. Letitia's need for sex is impossible to assuage; it is the key to her nature. As a Hollywood agent catering for young men, the only way her clients get parts is by servicing her.

Cast opposite Mae and playing the title role was the twenty-nine-year-old Hollywood sex symbol Raquel Welch. Rivalry between the ladies was anticipated. The reporters licked their lips.

Sarne was British and his task was to give the film a Swinging Sixties look – it was still the end of the Sixties and London and the Beatles led the pop world. Zanuck had seen Sarne's film *Joanna*, starring Donald Sutherland, and it had seemed to epitomize the new look. Now Sarne had to bring 'Carnaby Street' on celluloid to Hollywood.

Twentieth Century-Fox was still basking in the success of its 1965 release *The Sound of Music*, which had netted a profit in the region of ninety million dollars. Despite a number of expensive musical flops in the interim, the company decided to speculate a little, and Vidal's story was certainly different from any other Hollywood had yet tackled.

Myra Breckinridge tells the story of the homosexual Myron, who through surgery becomes transsexual Myra. Most branches of sexual exploration are covered, and the highlight is a spectacular scene in which a young man is anally raped by Myra equipped with an artificial penis.

As the above indicates, the novel was a daring, not to say reckless, choice to film. On publication in 1968 it had caused outrage. *Time* enquired, 'Has literary decency fallen so low?' But other critics acclaimed it as a masterpiece and it has been a consistent bestseller ever since.

Sarne recalls, 'Originally, I was simply interested in writing the script. I thought I might make $75,000 from this. But Zanuck persuaded me to direct it. *Myra* is a crude but funny book. I tried to look at the funny side of it. It was virtually unfilmable, you had to be there to understand the full implications. I had a million discussions with people over it. For example, how were we going to do the dildo scene?'

Not surprisingly, Sarne had a premonition that things were not going to go smoothly. 'I had my reservations about Hollywood,' he states. 'I had been in a film with Brigitte Bardot called *Two Weeks in September* and she warned me, "Don't go to Hollywood, they eat people like us alive." I remembered Brigitte's words. Initially I had hoped I could just knock off the script in three weeks, take the money and run. I told Zanuck of my reservations and he asked me, "Why don't you want to direct your own work?" What can you say to that? I couldn't tell him that a camp story about a sex change was not at all what I had envisioned for my career.'

Gore Vidal was scheduled to become involved with the adaptation of his book but he soon disassociated himself from the project. Joyce Haber noted in the *Los Angeles Times*, 'Sarne's interjections after Vidal's initial drafts, made Vidal run off to

Italy in a huff.' After many incarnations, the script was eventually co-written by Sarne and David Giler.

'At the back of my mind,' Sarne continues, 'I was also thinking there's a fifty-fifty chance this could be a great film. It was the era of Andy Warhol; the underground movement was fairly strong and I was involved in "pop culture" as such. I thought I would turn everyone into cartoon characters and shoot it all in red, white and blue.'

Commenting on the casting of Raquel Welch and Mae, Sarne recalls, 'Raquel Welch was under a three-picture deal to Fox, so we had her under contract, and I thought that was wonderful. If any man wanted to turn himself into a woman, Raquel Welch is the sort he'd choose to be. Then we had to cast this maneater, Letitia van Allen. I got Mae West probably as a result of my ignorance. I was new to Hollywood. I wrote to her and, I can't remember now, but I'm sure I didn't even send a script.'

According to the *Los Angeles Times*, Giler and Sarne did not get on. The paper reports that Giler had found some bad reviews of *Joanna* and tacked them up in his office for all to see. The same source records a remark made by Giler at a press conference: 'I don't understand it,' he is alleged to have said. 'Bobby Kennedy and John Kennedy were both assassinated. But no one touches Sarne.'

Mae, on the other hand, oozed confidence. She gave numerous interviews and was photographed by the finest photographers; the pictures were featured by every major paper in the world. She was as elegant as ever, with a whole new wardrobe of Edith Head gowns, new wigs and a new face. Some time before the shoot of *Myra Breckinridge* she had had a face-lift. It could only have happened in 1969, for Robert Duran categorically states, 'I was around constantly between 1964 and 1968 and there was no lift.' He does, however, acknowledge that there had been a lift sometime.

Jon Tuska, who wrote *The Films of Mae West*,* is of the opinion that Mae had no less than six face-lifts. He told her he

* Citadel Press, 1973.

planned to include this information in his book and received a telegram threatening legal action. All references to face-lifts were removed. Six does seem excessive.

Yet the proof of at least one is on the screen. The wrinkles and flaccidity have been replaced by a tight and glowing face. She took care how she was photographed, but there are inevitably give-away angles where a distinct line can be seen around her jaw where the new face begins and the neck remains loose.

The 'lift' was a success in that it made Mae look younger, but the scalpel, in rejuvenating her looks, took away that prettiness which so characterized her appearance earlier in her life. From *Myra* on she remained glamorous, in a movie-star way, but her image has lost its individuality. There is a plastic look to her. Apart from her grooming, she could pass unnoticed as any other Beverly Hills matron with money to burn in the fight against Father Time.

Ultimately Raquel Welch and Mae would have to meet. It was felt better for the meeting to take place before the cameras started rolling. Mae was apprehensive. In Raquel Welch she was competing with an outstandingly beautiful woman, almost half a century her junior. But the meeting was a model of decorum on both sides. Miss Welch came to the Ravenswood and presented Mae with a bouquet of red roses. 'Pleased to meet you, honey,' smiled Mae. 'I've admired you for a long time,' responded Miss Welch. The roses came in handy for Mae during the photo session. Miss Welch had a svelte waist whereas Mae had no waist at all; so, while the cameras clicked, Mae held the flowers to her abdomen to mask her figure.

Mae had to pass a medical for insurance purposes before her contract could be signed. (No film is undertaken without such precautions, for the liability, if a film is not completed because of an actor's illness or death, can run into millions of dollars.) Both Sarne and Robert Fryer, the producer, were fearful the insurance company might not grant her cover. In addition to her diabetes, it was known that she had a slight fluctuation in her heartbeat. As a back up, Shelley Winters was asked to take over the part (which would have suited her) if Mae was denied the opportunity. But, although Mae was found to have moderately high blood pressure, she passed her medical.

Some of Mae's music for *Myra* was written by John Phillips. He arrived for an appointment with Mae shoeless and in hippy clothes. She was horrified by his lack of respect. 'I hope my carpet doesn't dirty your feet,' she said witheringly.*

One of Phillips's numbers was 'Hollywood Was Always a Honky Tonk Town'. Mae objected to this title on the grounds that she was a movie star, and consequently the emblem of Hollywood. It was changed to 'Hollywood Was Never a Honky Tonk Town'.

One of the many journalists who contacted her was Victor Davis, today showbusiness editor for the *Mail on Sunday*. When he had learned of her comeback he had asked her press representative, Stanley Musgrove, to set up an interview. Like many Americans connected with the entertainment industry, Musgrove could sometimes be a touch discourteous. The world was clamouring for Mae West, what interest was Davis to him?

Davis was not going to be fobbed off and he rang Mae direct. 'I really gave her a sob story,' he remembers. 'I said to her, "Miss West, I've travelled over 6000 miles just to see you and your agent says you're too busy."

' "Honey," she said, "then you'd just better come up and see me." I later learned she had a soft spot for Englishmen.

'I went to the Ravenswood and the door was opened by a man with very broad shoulders [Paul]; I gathered this was the lover. It was an incredible household, the whole place was a riot of white and gold. There were nude paintings of her, some quite explicit, and the famous nude statue of her.**

'I was shown in and waited for about a quarter of an hour, then the old dear came toddling in in a tea-gown that swept the carpet, a great blonde wig and eyelashes like black steel hawsers. There was no way she looked like a normal mortal. She looked peculiar, I suppose, and when you got close, you could

---

* *Mae West: The Lies, The Legends, The Truth*, George Eells and Stanley Musgrove, Robson Books, 1989.
** By Gladys Lewis Bush. Mae was proud of the statue and it stood on her piano.

see it. She walked like a little Chinese woman whose feet have been bound too tightly.

' "Honey," she said, as she had no doubt said to three generations of journalists, "is that a notebook in your pocket, or are you just pleased to see me?"

'She had a rounded figure, not a bit like a sex symbol, but a flawless skin. I've only seen one other person with a skin like it, and that was Gloria Swanson, who followed rigorous food fads. Mae told me she only bathed in spring water. I thought that was the usual publicity but, as I was leaving, I saw boys carrying up huge carboys of bottled water, so it must have been true.*

'Stories of her rivalry with Raquel Welch were already circulating and, when we started to talk about *Myra Breckinridge* she asked, "Tell me, honey. What's this Rock Walsh like?"

' "You mean Raquel Welch, Miss West?" I said.

' "If you say so, honey."

'She told me she loved England, and was thrilled to have the Mae West jacket named after her. Then she told me how the police had raided her shows and of her property deals, and how she had invented herself. She showed me round the apartment. We sat on the bed and she brought out what she called her "picture album". It was full of pictures of musclemen, Mr Minnesota, 1954, Mr Myrtle Beach, 1948, and the like. They were all in jock straps and trunks. The implication, although she did not say so, was that they had all been her lovers.

'As I sat browsing through them she sat beside me, humming happily, obviously enjoying old memories. She was very likeable and I was having a wonderful time, laughing with her. I pointed at one photograph and said, "Well, Miss West, he seems a handsomely set up young man."

' "Yeah," she said. "He wanted to marry me. I said no and he went off to India." I was rolling over the bed laughing. It struck me that if you were a good audience then you got a good interview. She had a good audience that day.

---

* It was true. Mae's apartment could easily be located as carboys awaiting collection were always piled outside the door.

'She sized me up. "Honey," she said, "how would you like to be in the movies?" Those magic words for which we forget all other trades. She told me she was working on a scene with young male actors. "You want to be one of the studs?" she asked.

'By this time I had tears of laughter rolling down my face. I thought, "This is Mae's casting couch." She was loving it. I thought it might be a good wheeze for the paper if I accepted, but the timing was not practicable, so I gratefully declined. I received a kiss on the cheek when I left. She was an absolute delight and extremely nice.'

Davis wrote an enthusiastic and entertaining article based on his visit, which was published in the *Daily Express*. But not all the journalists who called to interview Mae were as honourable. One piece which upset her was written by the photographer Cecil Beaton, who had managed to secure a commission from *Vogue* for $750 to photograph Mae and write an accompanying article. As a gimmick, Twentieth Century-Fox arranged that Mae would pose with one of the studs from *Myra Breckinridge*, the twenty-five-year-old Tom Selleck, later to achieve fame in the television series *Magnum, PI*.

Mae became nervous as the date of Beaton's arrival approached. She was frightened of what his camera might reveal and insisted upon picture approval before anything was released. Beaton wanted the commission and had no option other than to agree. Perhaps this soured his feelings, for the following is part of an article that appeared in *Vogue* in June 1970:

I was surprised to find how small her personal quarters are. To begin with I was fascinated; white carpets, pale yellow walls, white pseudo-French furniture with gold paint, a bower of white flowers, huge 'set' pieces of dogwood, begonias, roses and stocks – all false ... There was a great display of photographs of Mae West retouched beyond human likeness all in silver frames. Dust was covering everything. In a nearby lavatory, for instance, a discarded massage table looked grey and it was only when

I put my finger on it that I discovered the dark red, artificial leather underneath.

Perhaps Miss West likes to preserve every dollar she has earned. She seems quite contented, or so it appeared from my short glimpse of her during the afternoon photographic session. Miss West's entourage consisted of about eight people from the studio, her own Chinese servant, and her bodyguard, Novak, an ex-muscleman ... She was rigged up in the highest possible fantasy of taste. The costume of black with white fur was designed to camouflage every silhouette except the armour that constricted her waist and contained her bust. The neck, cheeks and shoulders were hidden beneath a peroxide wig. The muzzle, which was about all one could see of the face, with the pretty capped teeth, was like that of a nice little ape. The eyes, deeply embedded and blacked, were hardly visible. She smiled like an automaton. She gurgled at the compliments. She seemed shy and nice, and sympathetic. When I told her that Lady Sitwell had seen her at a party dressed all in white looking like a vestal virgin, she pretended to be shocked.

She moved very slowly into the living-room and stood – she could not sit – on very high heels. She stroked her yellow fronds of borrowed hair with fat, pointed fingers on which a dozen false diamond rings sparkled: her fingernails grown to several inches in length. She preened and her audience gasped with admiration.

'Oh, Miss West, you have never looked so beautiful – the lighting is so soft.' Miss West chortled.

As a prop, a young Adonis, a former athlete from the local university, Tom Shelleck [sic], had been corralled from the film studio to be included in the photographs; a more outrageous combination could not be imagined, this beautiful, young, spare, clean, honest specimen of American manhood, and the *pourriture* of this old 'madame'.

She has a sense of humour and is able to laugh at herself. I liked her twinkle; and her vulnerability.

When the whole thing was over she started to walk, but

teetered and I caught her just in time. By now, the apartment had become too cloying and airless and I escaped.

To describe an elderly lady, a former beauty, as *pourriture* is not
only ungentlemanly but unforgivable. As is his breach of
etiquette in describing her lavatory. He had been invited to take
snaps, not poke about her bathroom and write of it. Noël
Coward, no stranger to bitchiness himself, with justification
dismissed Beaton as 'mean, malicious, full of untruths and
utterly superficial'. Beaton's article about Mae bears him out.

When Mae saw *Vogue* she was deeply hurt. She had behaved
cordially towards Beaton and trusted he would behave decently
towards her. Beverly summed him up succinctly by downing a
glass of vodka and dismissing him as that 'English faggot'. One
of her more accurate observations.

Mae started filming *Myra* on 16 October 1969. It was a red-
letter day for transsexuals as filming also started that day at
United Artists on *The Christine Jorgensen Story*. (Miss Jorgensen was the lady whose story had so fascinated Mae when they
had both been appearing in New York, and who had since
become a friend after they had met at the USC gathering.) In
order to make Mae feel welcome she had been given a sixty-
five foot long trailer, parked off the set, in addition to the star
dressing room, which had been redecorated in white and gold.
But someone made the mistake of telling her that this was Bar-
bra Streisand's 'old room' and she took offence.

Reporter Steven Roberts was there, and wrote for the
Observer that her voice 'took on a tense shrillness'. She yelled
how she had saved Paramount single-handedly, and added, 'I'd
like to see someone break records like that and I'll respect them
as a star. Till someone can do that I feel I'm in a class by myself
. . . So don't say they put me in someone else's room.'

The reason for the shouting, of course, was that she was
nervous. She was about to face a film camera for the first
time in twenty-six years, against such seasoned professionals as
John Huston and Raquel Welch, and a beautiful newcomer,
Farrah Fawcett, who was also in the cast. Mae's ego was
enormous and she intended to see off the opposition like a

feisty old bull terrier bitch, but the fight would not be easy.

She had not read the script, although one had been delivered a long time ago, but had merely learnt her own part. Obviously she did not intend to change the habit of a lifetime. She did, however, change the spelling of the name of her character to Leticia, as opposed to Letitia, in order to avoid any possible crude connotations.

The first morning Mae walked on the set everyone stood and applauded. The crew were plainly delighted to be working with her. Sarne soon got her measure. 'Mae knew what she wanted. "What I do works," she would say. "People like what I do. If it's not done that way it doesn't work. Get someone else." '

Rumours quickly flew around that she and Sarne did not see eye-to-eye and how they fought on the set. In Sarne's memory, none of this was true, but merely press hype and the result of behind-scenes gossip. 'In all the time we worked together,' he says, 'I never knew her to be a bitch, and I remained in contact with her for years after we finished *Myra*.'

'She was a wonderful writer of dialogue,' he adds. 'She would read me things she had written and I'd say to her, "That won't work, we can't do that." She'd look at me with those blue eyes of hers and say, "You do what I say, dear, and they'll laugh." And she was right. She knew the business inside out, and what she was trying to do was make a successful movie for all of us. She wrote some scenes which didn't survive the movie, great stuff. There was an airport scene which was superb.

'With a great artist, like Mae West, it's not a case of acting, it's a case of her doing her own thing. As director, I was trying to help her to do it as well as possible.

'A certain amount of patience and consideration were required to get the best out of her, however, and an artist is at her most vulnerable when trying to create a role. That's why she was so upset when the press started getting vicious, and people were saying she was too old and that she wore too much make-up, and was difficult. She was really hurt, and she'd ask, "Why are they doing this to me, dear?" She could not understand. Sometimes she'd be in tears because of what the journalists had written. She was not a bit hard, a great big baby.

'The gossip columnists were out to get her, and she suffered terribly because of it. I tried to defend her. I had not realized the impact gossip columnists have before I went to Hollywood – how they invented studio policy, but they do.

'She would sit in her dressing gown, in her room, with her hair tied up in a little knot. She was a complex person. She loved to chat, but not to everyone. There were not that many people who were allowed to get close. There was a secret Mae West that she did not want to escape, it would take away from her persona.

'In America, the message is to survive. And she had been a victim before the creation of Mae West. Her husband had exploited her at eighteen, she had been exploited all her life by theatrical managements, and she wasn't all that young when she created the mixture that became *Diamond Lil.*

'It doesn't matter whether you're creating Coca-Cola or Levi jeans, you've got to create a product. She invented something, and it worked. She would come in some days and say, "Here, come and feel my hands, I've got a great skin." It was part of the persona. She referred to herself in the third person. In discussion she would say, "Mae West wouldn't do that," or "Mae West can't play someone over twenty-five years old." But that was the character, it made the joke work.'

It took Mae a long time to get ready for filming nowadays. In addition to her make-up and wardrobe demands a degree of 'taping-up' was now required. This is a process where the facial skin is gathered by tape at the hairline and nape of the neck and tightly bound so that nothing sags on the face. A wig hides the handiwork. It works like an improvised face-lift. A side-effect is that it is quite painful and makes it difficult for the face to register expression.

Mae was pleased with the effect of her taping-up. So much so that she remarked to producer Robert Fryer when stepping from her trailer one morning, 'Tell everyone to relax because when I come on they'll all get sexy.'

Paul was on the set with her the whole time. Sarne noted, 'He was absolutely devoted to her, a lovely guy.' Joyce Haber wrote, 'Paul's obviously very much in love with her. He protects her with regard to her diet, keeps bores away from her, and she couldn't function without him.'

On a more general level Miss Haber reported:

Myra Breckinridge might as well be called *They Only Kill Each Other*. The *Myra* company seems to consist of antagonists. There's director Mike Sarne on the one hand, producer Robert Fryer and most of the cast on the other. In the midst of it all, like a totem pole claimed by squatting squaws, is Fox president Richard Zanuck. 'I've never seen so many personality conflicts on one picture,' Zanuck said candidly. 'Fryer has quit three times. I don't think there's anyone on this movie who hasn't been fired . . . including me.'

Reading through the mass of publicity concerning the making of *Myra Breckinridge*, an element of xenophobia seems to be present. Sarne was a 'flash' pop director. An Englishman in charge of an essentially American art form. Ivor Davis of the *Daily Express* did not help matters when he wrote, 'Sarne is openly contemptuous of the Hollywood establishment.' In 1990, Sarne reflected, 'I'd always thought film-making had something to do with art. But I've got a director friend who views it all as a boxing match; now I think he's got something.'

Mae was doing her share of sparring. Edith Head had created her wardrobe, although the rest of the cast were outfitted by Theodora Van Runkle. It was decided that Mae should stick to a main colour scheme of black and white. At first this did not please her. *Myra Breckinridge* was her first colour film, something she had always wanted, and she saw herself in a riot of lilac and pink. Tests were made, however, and she had to acknowledge the absence of colour was flattering to her figure. Once the black and white motif was established she took to the idea, using it as a symbol of her exclusivity.

In the story Rusty (the rape victim) has a girl friend but Mae objected to this. Mae West never took a woman from another man. Overriding all was the commandment that Leticia was never to behave as though she were more than twenty-six years old. Writer David Giler queried this, but got no joy. 'When I suggested that Leticia must have known Buck Loner back in the Thirties and must be around his age, Mae just looked at me in silence,' *Premier* magazine reported him saying. 'So she won't be what Vidal wrote. There's little of his book left anyway.' Mae revamped much of her old material for Leticia. Routines she had been using in the theatre for years. Since the majority of the film-going public had not seen her on the road, it worked well. Her lines are still being quoted.

She sets the pace for her entire performance by her power-packed first entrance. With all the old West panache, she strides into her office through a group of young men, disproving Beaton's claim that she could not move unaided. 'Boys, get out your resumés,' she commands. A prime example of an innocent line becoming pregnant with meaning when delivered by Mae.

Her entrance is followed by the camera panning along the men, mirroring Leticia's gaze. It rests on a crotch shot and, without raising her eyes, Leticia asks the man, 'You're new here, aren't you?'

As she is about to enter her office a dozen men clamour for her attention. 'I'm feeling rather tired today,' she says. 'One of you had better go home.' Perhaps the most famous line is: 'How tall are you, young man?' He squares his shoulders and answers, 'I'm six feet seven inches, ma'am.' 'Never mind the six feet,' says Leticia. 'Let's discuss the seven inches.'

All were sequences she had used in *Catherine Was Great* or her cabaret act, but there were new lines, too. While driving through Beverly Hills in her Rolls, Leticia stops a policeman. She points to a motorcyclist behind the car. 'Officer,' she says, 'that young man has been following me all day.' The policeman asks, 'Shall I arrest him?' 'No,' she replies, 'give him my card.'

She explained the origin of one of her best-known lines to *Premier* magazine:

> I was going on a personal appearance tour for one of my pictures, see, and the D.A., here in L.A., he'd given me these plainclothes policemen to protect me ... But they

couldn't come with me on the tour ... When I came back they were at the station. I got off the train and they came up to me and this one – very good-looking guy with big shoulders, wavy blond hair and a thin moustache, I remember – had these flowers for me. And he said, 'The D.A. asked us to welcome you back, cause we really missed you.' ... And he told me the chief said to give me a big hug from him. So he comes over and takes me in his arms to hug me. He was a strong guy and was holding sort of tight, see, dear ... Cause he was so passionate, I said to him, jokingly like, 'Is that a gun in your pocket or are you just glad to see me.' ... It got around town what happened and everybody was quoting. And that's the story, dear.

She had been using a variation on that line since her touring days with Mike Todd.

Although much trusted material was used for *Myra Breckinridge*, a new facet in Mae's character appears in the film, a facet that does not display her to advantage. Her dialogue is cruder: instead of being the mistress of innuendo as of yore, she becomes downright coarse at times. Much of the new coarseness came from consultants; they advised her that stronger medicine was needed in 1970. It was poor advice.

Mae was at sea when she accommodated trends, infinitely better when she simply did what she knew she did best. Rightly she refused to include the sequence in which Rusty puts Leticia, after a bout of sadistic sex, into hospital. No man could put Mae West in hospital as a result of sexual play; she reversed the process and in the film it is Rusty who is hospitalized, and the scene is much funnier.

In February 1970, to scotch talk of on-set fighting, the company took a full-page advertisement in *Variety*. It bore a pack shot including Mae, Raquel Welch, Sarne and Fryer: the shout line printed underneath read 'Togetherness'.

During the pre-release hype, the *Los Angeles Times* ran an item on whom famous people would choose to be if they were not themselves. Phyllis Diller wanted to be Raquel Welch, Jean Simmons saw herself as Carole Lombard, Richard Brooks pre-

ferred Beethoven, Gore Vidal saw himself as US President
Warren Harding, but Mae had other ideas: 'I have never wanted to be anyone other than me. Why would I? When half the
world was trying to imitate me? There was the time when my
fans, from eight to eighty, tried to look like me, to walk like me,
act like me, even feel like me. Too bad everybody just can't be
themselves and be happy about it. I am. Remember that once
popular song, "I love me, I love me?" Baby, that's me.'

The film had two sneak previews before its official première,
one in Orange County and the other in San Francisco. In ultra-
conservative Orange County the audience 'sat stunned and
silent'.* In hippy San Francisco a house crowded mostly with
the young adored it.

On 23 June 1970 *Myra Breckinridge* premièred at New York's
Criterion Theater. The press referred to the event as 'Mae Day',
and a reluctant Mae had been persuaded to fly to New York for
the opening. The entrance to the theatre was jammed by a
throng of 10,000. Joyce Haber covered the event for the *Los
Angeles Times*:*

> Mae West arrived, surrounded by musclemen. She wore a
> regal $3800 white evening sheath with boa by Edith Head.
> The police could hardly contain the mob's enthusiasm.
> Two officers suffered minor injuries as Mae was hustled
> inside, amid screaming fans and wild applause and posters
> and banners and placards ... In the foyer, Mae raised her
> arms, like the Goddess she was, and received her
> accolades. Acres of roses were aimed at her. Afterwards
> she was quoted as saying, 'Too bad I didn't get all the
> policemen's names.' ... A Mae West entrance, then, is
> always a happening ... Mae West is the last of the female
> living legends, except for Garbo. Wherever she goes, she's
> surrounded. Where do the fans come from? What is the
> mystique of Mae West?'

Unfortunately, the audience was not so dazzled by the mystique
of the actual film. Many were perplexed, others booed, some

* *Los Angeles Times* (undated).

walked out. As Same explains, 'The film opened at a time of moral backlash. At its conception marijuana, pop and flower-power were "in", but by the time it was shown, the things I had been chosen to depict were no longer popular. The Manson murders had taken place and, after the killing of Sharon Tate, the whole Hollywood community was terrified, scared of getting killed by drug-induced madness. By the time *Myra* was finished the joke of sexual promiscuity went sour. What had seemed funny six months before now seemed immoral.'

'*Myra Breckinbridge* opened last week in New York and Hollywood,' reported the *Los Angeles Times* for 29 June 1970. 'The principals were topping themselves for sheer venom. For example, when star Mae West said she was going to the East Coast for the première, star Raquel Welch decided, at the very last minute, that she'd go too. When the two arrived at Times Square, Raquel got only a "moderate" welcome from fans, but Mae was mobbed by 10,000. Mae West, nevertheless, refused to sign autographs or to pose with Raquel Welch for pictures. In turn, Raquel Welch refused an invite to the party *Time* magazine gave in her honour.'

Mae refused to sign autographs because she was terrified of crowds, always convinced someone was out to get her or, a more recent phobia, that someone on drugs might attack. Naturally she did not want to be photographed with Raquel Welch; it might invite harsh comparison. Anyway, there was only one star of the film as far as Mae was concerned, and she was it. Later, when Raquel Welch was mentioned, she told *Sun* reporter John Sampson, 'I guess she had a couple of lines.'

After the première, Fox gave a party for Mae, and among the guests were Shelley Winters and Joan Bennett. Next day Mae gave a press conference at her suite in the Sherry Netherland. The reporters could not wait to ask her about Raquel Welch. Joyce Haber reported her response: 'I wonder how any actress, with any following, could have played Myra ... they only signed her because they couldn't get anyone of stature to play the lead' – an unfortunate lapse since she, herself, had insisted she was the lead to begin with.

On the first day of screening *Myra* broke box-office records.

It took $9000 at the Criterion, whose previous record holder
was *Valley of the Dolls* with $5000. Records in Hollywood were
also broken with $86,000 a week taken at Loew's, where *The
Dirty Dozen* had earlier topped at $56,000.

At about this time the British journalist John Sandilands met
Mae and reported his reaction in these words: 'I had been
around. I'd just interviewed Warren Beatty, but in the presence
of Mae's worldly knowledge I felt myself eleven years old. I
liked her immensely.'

Not everyone was ecstatic about Mae. The following charming letter was published by the *Los Angeles Times* on 30
September 1970:

Mae West has become a tiresome old bore forever talking
about how wonderful she was and thinks she still is ...
She needs to be straightened out that she was, or is, a sex
symbol. She was never anything of the sort. She was a
comedienne, vulgar as they make 'em ... No man in real
life ever gave much thought to Mae West being the girl of
his dreams ... an old lady, who thinks of herself as a sex
symbol is sad and somewhat revolting.

The critics were also unequivocal:

Myra Breckinridge is about as funny as a child molester.
Time

The most flamboyant celebration ever of the silliest, most
meandering and sickest of nocturnal, sex-sprung fantasies.
Herald Examiner

Gore Vidal, when asked to contribute to this book, sent a message care of his agent: 'He asked me to advise you that he has
never personally seen the film *Myra Breckinridge* and never
ever met Mae West.' He had been more expansive in 1985
when, in a new introduction to the novel, he wrote, 'Twentieth
Century-Fox bought the film rights as a vehicle or, to be more
precise, a hearse for Raquel Welch, John Huston, Mae West

and an assortment of other exciting nonactors ... For the first time in the history of paperback publishing, the film of a book had proved to be so bad that the sale of the book stopped.'

Viewed today, the film comes over as bawdy, witty and well shot; both Mae and Raquel Welch are superb. Although the film was slated, Mae came off well with the critics and Miss Welch, who looks stunning, acts with swaggering ostentation. Mike Sarne says he is sure she is proud of her performance. She has reason to be.

chapter twenty-six

IN DEMAND AGAIN

Myra Breckinridge marked a new chapter in Mae's life. Whatever may have been said against the film – and there were some fine things in it – she had enjoyed a personal renaissance and was back in the Hollywood mainstream. She had plans for several more movies and remarked that the time for her to give up films would be 'when I make my first lousy picture'. It was as though the twenty-six-year gap in their production had never happened.

The Ali MacGraw/Ryan O'Neal film *Love Story* was being premièred and she accepted a promotional gig for it where she judged a kissing contest. Unfortunately a female fan came rather too close for comfort and reached out to touch her hair. Mae was for looking at, not for touching, and she cried out in fear, 'Oh, please, please.' The fan was hustled away.

No plans for the future in Mae's eyes could be complete without a revamp of *Diamond Lil*. She planned to remake this as a colour film, directed by George Cukor. 'It would be the same story, but kickier,' she told Joyce Haber. 'All the things I couldn't do in the Thirties I'll put in now. There's white slavery – it's basic – and drugs.' Someone was rash enough to ask whom she had in mind for Lil. 'Why me, of course,' she replied, 'who else could play Mae West? I still look like her.'

She saw the Ryan and Tatum O'Neal film *Paper Moon* and planned a sequel starring Burt Reynolds. 'You know what irritates me?' she asked William Scott Eyman. 'All this talk of Hollywood being dead. Hollywood isn't dead, it's just taking a siesta. Right now I've got four great projects that I want to do.' The premise being that Hollywood had woken up because Mae was back on the movie lots.

She was keen on Burt Reynolds. At the time he was making a television spectacular and called on Mae to try to interest her in appearing on it. Mae could be haughty with visitors and keep them waiting in the foyer at the Ravenswood, but she did not keep Reynolds waiting at all. As soon as he arrived in reception he was told to go straight up.

'She wouldn't do the show,' Robert Duran recalls. 'She told him she wasn't going on television for no specific reason. He was wearing buckskin trousers, and when he left she grabbed my arm and said, "Did you see that crotch? It seemed endless." '

Another of her plans was to record a new LP, with the tongue-in-cheek title, *Bedtime Stories and Fairy Tales*. She also resumed work on her biography of T. Jack Kelly, which had progressed inasmuch as it now bore the title *The Amazing T. J. Kelly*. Neither of these projects came to fruition but she did succeed, with the help of Larry Lee, in turning *Pleasure Man* into a novel. For the first time, his considerable assistance was acknowledged in print.

She continued with her ESP studies and called upon this skill when there was a personal problem to solve. When troubled, she would get her dictionary, open it, and jab at a word. Whatever word her finger happened to alight upon bore the key to solving the problem. She then had to work out the best way to do this.

She invited Dr William Banowsky, chancellor of Pepperdine University, to be present during certain Spiritualist seances she held at the beach house, and encouraged USC to open a department of parapsychology.

Joyce Haber has a daughter, Courtney, born a month prematurely on 17 July. Since Mae's birthday was 17 August, she believed that she and Courtney were meant to have been born on the same date. This, she considered, linked them. Every birthday she sent Courtney a small diamond, mounted in either a ring, a bracelet, or some other ornament. She even held the child, though plainly without much glee: 'She was very awkward with her,' says Miss Haber.

Mae had accepted an invitation to dine with Miss Haber at

her home, but on the evening in question Mae cancelled. She had learned that Lucille Ball was also expected. 'She thought Lucy was competition,' Miss Haber says. 'She wanted to be the star. This marvellous, legendary lady was terrified of meeting another comedienne.'

Miss Ball was informed of the situation. 'Lucy was one of the few people in Hollywood who did not have a mean bone in her body,' says Miss Haber. 'That's ridiculous,' she recalls Miss Ball saying. 'Why, I'm dying to meet her. Tell her I said I'm nothing compared to her. Tell her I'll be devastated if she's not there.'

This information was relayed to Mae and her toilette was resumed while she was further assured Miss Ball had promised barely to utter one word all evening. The powder puff was allowed on to the countenance again, the wig dressed and she was stitched into her frock.

Mae arrived with her muscleman before Miss Ball and settled herself on a chair. Miss Ball arrived shortly afterwards. 'She walked straight over to Mae's chair,' remembers Miss Haber, 'and flopped down on the floor next to her, despite the fact she was wearing the most beautiful dinner gown. She said, "I can't believe I'm meeting you, you're so wonderful." She reached out and took her little hand. It was a tender and touching moment, spoiled only, I might say, by some producer who was in the room who yelled out, "You two ladies look wonderful together. Why don't you do a special for me?"'

Mae made no attempt to duck out of a further invitation extended by Miss Haber, as this involved Spiritualism. Miss Haber lived at the foot of Coldwater Canyon, Beverly Hills. The house had previously belonged to actor Clifton Webb, who had shared it with his beloved mother, Maybelle. It was a one-storey home purchased when Maybelle became too frail to climb stairs. Webb had died there in 1966. During Miss Haber's occupancy, the Coldwater Canyon house gained a well-known reputation for being haunted by Webb. Mae couldn't wait to get inside. She arrived, in a business-like mood, accompanied by her psychic consultant.

The real reason for the visit was not to investigate the haunting, but to attend the screening of a new film, *The Legend of Hell House*, a ghost story which starred Mae's friend, Roddy McDowall. Mae did not normally attend screenings but the showing of a ghost story, in a haunted house, was too much to resist. She listened intently as Miss Haber revealed the psychic history of her house.

'I didn't believe in the supernatural,' says Miss Haber, 'but I have to now. I was standing with my mother by the pool one morning and saw a figure standing in the blue bathroom. There was no one in the house but us, and it was a corporeal figure, we both saw it. On another occasion I woke suddenly in the night and Clifton was standing over me. I plainly saw his face and he was pointing his finger at me. He was trying to tell me something, but I still don't know what it was.

'When we bought the house there had been a picture of him in an alcove which we removed. Howard Koch, a nephew of Walter Winchell's, was visiting us. When he passed the alcove he involuntarily shuddered and said, "My God, it's cold". He knew nothing about the picture.

'Out of curiosity we borrowed a film of Clifton's called *Sitting Pretty*. When we ran it our dog rushed at the screen barking, and she was used to movies, which usually had no effect on her. The cats also behaved strangely and would not cross a certain spot – where Clifton was standing, I suppose. Lots of people thought Maybelle was also there.'

'You really should get into this, dear,' Mae urged Miss Haber. 'It could help you.' Miss Haber was already in it, right up to her neck, and did not find being there at all helpful. 'Eventually,' she says, 'the place was exorcized by medium Sybil Leek.'

Mae later claimed to have contacted Clifton Webb herself, at a seance also populated by the spirits of both Noël Coward and Tallulah Bankhead. Webb told Mae he wanted someone to write his life story, he wanted the truth told. Alas, she was too busy with her book on Kelly to give the matter her personal attention.

Miss Haber admits she was never able to get close to Mae. 'She kept her distance,' she says. 'It was a defensive mechanism, of course, and an attempt at dignity.' She seemed closer to the staff at the Ravenswood, who unreservedly adored her. She trusted them as they were not in the entertainment industry so not about to try to make money from her.

Switchboard operator Chris Basinger remembers that when he took the Ravenswood job he was agog to meet the great star. He thought he had done so on one occasion when a blue and white Cadillac drew up and an infirm, elderly blonde was helped out by a chauffeur. She was walking with the help of a zimmer frame, and he thought Mae had injured herself. But co-operator Faye Friedland explained it was only Beverly, whose limp had worsened, on one of her regular visits in from the ranch. Mae had given Beverly one of her old Cadillacs – she dispersed them like confetti.

Basinger did not have to wait long to see Mae, however, as word soon came for Miss West's limousine to be brought round to the entrance. 'She walked out of the elevator with several men,' Basinger remembers. 'Her hair was shining and cascading down her back. She was gorgeously dressed. I was staring at her through the glass panel of the switchboard room and she turned round and looked at me with those beautiful blue eyes. When she saw me, she did a double take, as I was a new face. She smiled.

'Shortly afterwards one of the men asked me my name, and told me, "Miss West has asked me to tell you how nice it is to see a good-looking feller at the switchboard." I was in love with her. She could compliment you and make you feel wonderful. "Everyone should have a friend like you," she told me once. She was something else, not a bit like an old lady.'

She told Basinger to visit her 'any time at all' as she was often by herself. He took her up on the offer and frequently nipped up during a break or after he had finished his shift.

'Her apartment was like another world,' he remembers. 'She used Joy perfume and its scent was everywhere; the French furniture and the hum of the air-conditioning' (Mae insisted on her air being filtered – whatever the conditions outside the air-conditioner was always on and the blinds firmly drawn against the detested sunlight). 'It was always the same and always so peaceful. She loved flirting. When she came in sometimes, she would come up to me, and she would look at me with those eyes and slap her gloves and purse on the desk. "Any messages, honey?" she'd ask.'

Basinger experienced other examples of how sweet Mae could be when she did not feel threatened. 'You like carrot cake, honey?' she asked him once out of the blue. 'I've never had it,' he told her. 'Oh,' she said, 'we've got some upstairs.' Paul came down with a slice on a cardboard plate. 'She was always giving me things,' Basinger remembers, 'wonderful shoes and shirts.'

One day Mae had to go to MGM for a meeting and she asked both Basinger and Robert Duran to accompany her. When she arrived she seemed preoccupied and they walked along the corridor in silence. 'Suddenly,' Basinger recalls, 'Elvis Presley came out of an office. He saw Mae and just stared. "Miss West," he called out, "I'm your greatest fan."

' "Oh, er, fine, fine," she said distractedly. She would not stop, she just wanted to get to her meeting. Presley was appearing at the Inglewood Forum that evening and he called up, later in the day, telling her he had arranged tickets for her and a limo to collect her and bring her back home after the concert. She liked Elvis but she would not go. "They'll all want to look at me," she said.

'One day a call came through the switchboard from Elizabeth Taylor,' Basinger remembers. 'I told Miss West. "Who, dear?" she asked. No matter who it was she always asked, Who? If it had been the Queen of England it would have been the same; it gave her time to think what to do. "Elizabeth Taylor, Miss West," I repeated. "Oh yes, now I remember," she said. "I met her at a party. Yes, I'll talk to her, dear." '

'Bette Davis and two guys came into the building once,' Basinger continues. "We're here to see Miss West," said Miss Davis. So I rang up. "Bette Davis is here, Miss West."

' "Who, dear?"

' "Bette Davis, Miss West."

' "Oh, yeah. How many in her party?"

' "Three, Miss West."

' "How many of them men?" '

' "Two." '

' "I'll call down when I'm ready. Get them to wait." So they sat down and waited in the lobby for over ten minutes. I knew she was fixing herself up for the men. "You can tell Miss Davis and her party they can come up," she rang down and said after a while.'

Another day Marlene Dietrich telephoned. She had been visiting her husband who lived in the San Fernando Valley. Robert Duran was with Mae, and answered the telephone.

'Tell her I'm not here,' Mae said. 'But say Beverly's here.' Miss Dietrich said she would talk to Beverly. Mae then took the call on the kitchen phone. 'She always leant with one elbow on the table,' Duran remembers. 'She started off as Beverly, then she'd forget and answer as herself, then she'd go back to being Beverly again. Marlene Dietrich must have known it was her. She asked if she might call at the Ravenswood the following day.

' "Well, I dunno," said Mae. "I'll have to ask my sister." '

'After the call Mae said, "Well, we'll see if she shows up." '

She did not.

Friends of Veronica Lake were themselves hoping Mae would show up at a house-warming party they were giving. Miss Lake, then rather on her uppers, had recently moved into a new apartment, and her friends were rallying round. They knew it would be a tremendous ego boost for her if an artist of Mae's stature came. But they also knew that, in the normal course of events, Mae would turn down the invitation, so she was told the party was for journalist Rona Barrett, whom she liked.

Mae agreed to go and bought a crystal vase as a present. Although gracious at the party, she was indignant when she learned of the deception and later denied she had ever been to visit Miss Lake. 'Why would I go there?' she demanded.

She was pleased, however, to see her old boss Adolph Zukor, who came to visit her at the Ravenswood on his 100th birthday. It gave her a boost to see him still in good condition, supplying hope for her own immortality.

She was less pleased in 1973 when Jon Tuska published his

book *The Films of Mae West*. He had communicated with her throughout its preparation and had found her difficult to deal with, as she always was when an attempt was made to unravel the facts of her life. According to Duran, she came to accept the book, but refused to forgive Tuska for his suggestion that she had appeared in burlesque. This she considered demeaning. She lashed out at everyone close to her, accusing them of treachery, and of having betrayed her to Tuska.

'Mae West and I only had one blow out,' says Robert Duran, 'and that was when that book came out. She accused me, "You told him I did burlesque!" I told her I didn't even know the guy and how the hell could I know whether she had done burlesque or not. I didn't meet her till 1964! She didn't believe me. "Well," she said. "Someone told him."

' "Listen," I told her. "I'm leaving." '

'She rang me later at my apartment. "Come on," she said. "You're my right hand man." '

' "I don't appreciate being called a liar," I said.

' "Oh, I know, dear," she told me. We were OK after that.'

That same year Decca came up with the idea of issuing an album of soundtracks from her films. A function was arranged to promote it and Mae arrived with muscleman Cal Bartlett, an athlete and actor in his early twenties, who accompanied her now and then on public appearances.

In the autumn, MGM issued an album of more rock songs, *Great Balls of Fire*, which included 'Rock Around the Clock', 'Happy Birthday Sweet Sixteen', and 'Whole Lotta Shakin' Goin' On'. It was recorded at a studio on Hollywood Boulevard, and the instrumental tracks had already been laid down by the time Mae arrived to provide the vocals. She sat on a stool with the lyrics to the songs held up in front of her on idiot boards. She was not in good form at first and found it difficult to get the right rhythm for 'Rock Around the Clock', but ultimately it clicked into place. 'Love Potion No. 9' was also recorded but not included on the album.

A celebration was arranged to launch the new record at the Masquers Club, and Mae sang two songs, a rock version of 'Frankie and Johnny' and 'Whole Lotta Shakin' Goin' On', which came from the album. The Master of Ceremonies was Hal Kanter, executive producer of, among other successes, *All in the Family*. Kanter's introduction included the following description: 'She is one of those rare and fortunate people who knew at an early age what she wanted and she went out and got it . . . I understand she's still getting it . . .'

Among those who interviewed her at the *Great Balls of Fire* conference was Roderick Mann of the *Sunday Express*. He paints a powerful portrait of the great lady at this time:

> In comes Mae West. Sashays rather. She is wearing a white robe, trimmed with white fur. Her hair, movie-star blonde, is piled up on her head. A wig? Who knows? She walks carefully, as though balancing it, like a book. The bottom half of her does not seem to be attached to the top half. Odd. Both are going in more or less the same direction, though. Towards me.
> 'Miss West,' I say, riveted.
> 'You bet,' she says . . . The indestructible Mae West . . .

They sat and sipped orange juice brought in by Larry Grayson. She explained she kept herself fit by lifting barbells, invited Mann to feel the muscles in her arm, and to examine her skin and note its baby-fine texture. She mentioned her double thyroid and added a new exclusivity to this fictitious gland by stating that she was one of only twelve people in the world to be blessed with one. She had so much energy, she said, that she sometimes arose at 6 a.m. (The switchboard at the Ravenswood had strict orders on no account whatsoever to call her before noon.)

She spoke of the care she took over her diet and warned against using canned food. 'Never eat anything canned,' she told Mann. 'Remember that. All that preservative they put in. It may be great for the can, but it's no good for your stomach.' This was advice she had received from Tillie when a girl. The process of tinning foods was, at the turn of the century, more hazardous than it is today, but Mae had not caught up with the times.

As her latest project demonstrated. She went to the theatre to see *The Boys in the Band* and was convinced *The Drag* had been plagiarized. There was a spate of homosexual plays produced at the time and Mae believed every one was a rip-off of her script. She set Larry Lee to work, under her supervision, adapting *The Drag* into a novel, which he was then bidden further to convert into a screenplay. She believed the time was ripe to present homosexual themes openly. Naturally, in her scheme of things, she would star in the movie: she envisioned herself in Busby Berkeley-style production numbers, in the midst of a group of gorgeously attired transvestites, she in the most glamorous costume of all.

Stupidly, producers to whom she showed the work did not share her breadth of vision. The film never got off the ground (neither did the novel for that matter). A few years later *La Cage aux Folles* was to feature exactly such a chorus line, to standing ovations throughout the world.

MGM had expressed an interest in filming *Sextet*, a prospect dear to her heart. She held a conference to announce that she would choose her six husbands from the members of the USC football team. And a bevy of the players, attired in kit, good-naturedly assembled to cheer her on at the conference. For all their support, that project too failed to get off the ground, but no one could accuse her of indolence.

A wax effigy of her was unveiled at the Movieland Wax Museum. She appeared at the unveiling ceremony with George Raft. The cheers nearly raised the rafters. He was seventy-seven years of age to her seventy-nine. She never forgot that he had got her into the movies and, later, when he became ill, she invited him to stay at the beach house.

In March 1973 Mae rejoiced in a psychic revelation. She was alone, watching television at the Ravenswood when, she told the *National Enquirer*, 'I glanced sideways and saw Jack Kelly sitting right next to me on the couch.' Mae jumped up in surprise, for Kelly had died ten years ago, and despite her desire to contact him had disappeared. 'When you're sitting in a room alone,' she continued, 'and suddenly here's a guy in a tuxedo who's passed on, sitting next to you with his arm over the back of the couch ... well, I was really startled.'

By now she had seen other visions. Jim Timony, after apparently experiencing difficulties, had eventually managed to visit her and she had reached out to touch him. Her arm had passed through his spectral form. Tillie had also appeared again, and had floated serenely before her, which promoted in Mae a feeling bordering on ecstasy.

She decided to make her eightieth birthday a gala day. So, it seemed, did the rest of the world. Her telephone rang constantly with congratulatory calls, many from foreign countries. Flowers were delivered non-stop until the Ravenswood seemed too small to hold more. Beverly had Grayson drive her up from the ranch to spend the day with her sister. It would be a dry day for Beverly, despite the fact the sisters had been invited to three separate functions, all of which they hoped to attend.

Beverly's arrival heralded a drama. After safely delivering her at the Ravenswood, the great blue Cadillac (which had been Mae's) performed a U-turn in Rossmore Avenue and was hit broadside by another car, the impact swooshing the vehicle across the road. Chris Basinger remembers: 'It was as though the occupants of the whole building drew their breath at the same time.' Word went round that Mae was in the car and had been killed. This was commuted to Beverly having been killed. It seemed rather disappointing when the truth was discovered – only Grayson was in the car and he was unhurt.

Among the dozens of birthday callers were several journalists. Mae had risen uncharacteristically early to be in a fit state to receive them. She spoke of her double thyroid gland. 'I wish it ran in the family,' quipped Beverly to John Sampson. She was sitting on the couch and Mae had forgotten she was there.

As she did not get the forbidding glance from Mae that she expected, she further added that Mae had two current lovers, a muscleman and an 'intellectual in his twenties'. 'She has to keep them apart,' continued Beverly, 'but there's never been a fight yet.' This was the sort of stuff of which Mae approved. Beverly was allowed to remain on the couch.

Sydney Edwards asked Mae the secret of a happy sex life and she responded, 'There's no secret. Just keep on with what you're doing. It's dangerous if you don't get enough.' She told him she had just finished writing a new book called *Sex Drive*. Edwards marvelled, as had others before, at how much younger than her years she looked, and described her as 'something like a Brunnhilde with a sweet nature'.

Although Beverly was in good form on Mae's birthday, this was an exception. By and large she was now in a sorry state. A friend who visited her at the ranch was appalled by the squalor in which she lived. When Mae's films came on television she would derisively heckle the image then inevitably start to cry, only to forget why she was crying. The once splendid interior of the ranch house was covered in dust; the white piano ringed with bottle and glass marks; half the furniture broken where Beverly had crashed into it; the garden a jungle.

Mae did the best she could, but she did not visit the ranch much, and was not fully aware of the extent of Beverly's plight. She saw her regularly, telephoned her, gave her money, housed her, clothed her and left instructions her sister was not to have alcohol. The latter was a doomed cause.

Beverly had never had many friends, and did not know where to meet them now. She was not the tupperware party type. She had so much wanted to be a movie star like her sister; her mother had wanted it too, and Beverly was conscious of having let down the side.

When Beverly was in the greatest need Mae would send her to a home for alcoholics. She responded to treatment for a while but always reverted to drink. It was a tragedy for both Beverly and Mae, as despite their disagreements, the sisters loved each other.

But Mae had learned to live her own life. Shortly after her birthday she agreed to see an officer of the Republican Women's National Committee over some charity matter. 'Why, Miss West,' cooed the woman, 'you look like a woman half your age.' Robert Duran noticed Mae's face cloud. 'I knew what was wrong,' he said. When the officer had gone Mae rounded on him. 'Can you imagine that?' she said. 'Jesus Christ, she thinks I look forty years old? She said I look half my age, that's forty. Why would someone say that?'

'She meant it as a compliment to you.'
'What a vicious bitch. What a thing to say.'
'It's not what you think.'
'Yeah, but it is.'
Duran had been with her on her seventy-fourth birthday, when she had insisted she was seventy-three. Her logic, from which she refused to budge, was that she could not have been born at one year old therefore she was a year younger than her actual calendar age. No arguments would convince her otherwise, not that anyone bothered much.

The novel, *Pleasure Man*, was published in 1975. It did not cause the sensation Mae had hoped for. She had banked on her castration scene scandalizing the world, but long before the novel appeared, Tennessee Williams had written *Sweet Birth of Youth* and *Suddenly Last Summer*, the latter dealing with cannibalism. Nobody any longer turned a hair at mere castration.*

That same year, W. H. Allen published *On Sex, Health and ESP*, the sequel to *Goodness Had Nothing To Do With It*. Sadly *On Sex, Health and ESP* is not in the same league as *Goodness*. The only good lines in it are the ones she had been using for years. She offers coy advice on sexual problems, and it is easy to understand from this why television declined to give her the series as an agony aunt.

The dreadful truth was that the old lady had nothing new to say. When it came to shock value the world had overtaken her. The book, so eagerly awaited, is a sad testimony to Mae's clouding judgement. In her heyday she would never have permitted it to be published.

But if Mae had nothing new to say, she still said the old stuff well. Maybe the rehash did not work between covers but it still paid off on the screen, and in personal appearances where she gave her material the inimitable West touch. The lines may not

---

* In 1959 she wryly commented, 'After Tennessee Williams's sexual hullabaloos the audience are now free to face the lower half of man's aspirations on earth without arrest.' She did not have time for the majority of playwrights but appreciated Williams and once asked, when evaluating contemporary writers, 'Who's left now, but Tennessee and me?'

have been new, but the concept of an octogenarian nympho-maniac was. Not new to history, of course, but new to the Seventies generation. She was considered a riot.

In April 1976 she agreed to appear on a television special, *Back Lot USA*, mounted by CBS for Dick Cavett. At first Mae was not keen on the idea, for her usual reasons, but was enticed by a fee of $25,000. She agreed to sing two numbers and be interviewed by Cavett. Mae wanted to know beforehand what questions Cavett would ask, so that she could prepare 'ad-libs', but Cavett would not have it, insisting that the interview be conducted spontaneously. She had to back down.

The two songs she chose were 'After You've Gone' and 'Frankie and Johnny' – both to be performed in a set which could have come straight from *Diamond Lil* – so much for Mae's concessions to 1976.

She decided she would be costumed in the style of the Gay Nineties, and Edith Head was again commissioned to supervise her wardrobe. 'Hi, Edith, how ya doin'?' she greeted her. Miss Head designed for Mae a clinging black gown with a plumed headdress.

Mae's songs were to be pre-recorded. She would mime them on the show.

There were a few tense moments during rehearsals. It had been planned for Mae to make her entrance at the top of a grand staircase and walk down while performing her first song. She agreed to this, but it became apparent her shoes exposed her to risk of falling. The insurance company would not allow it. So it was decided she would open her routine at the foot of the stairs and then wander about the tables of the set on the arm of Lou Zivkovitch, contender for the *Playboy* 'Man of the Year' title.

Those who had worked with Mae before noticed something new, her loss of concentration. Edith Head remarked that she seemed, at times, confused as to what exactly was going on. But what fluffs Mae made she quickly recovered from, by laughing at herself. Paul was with her all the time, and impressed the crew, as he had impressed Mike Sarne, by his tenderness towards her.

Mae was given a trailer on the set, and when she stepped on to the floor in costume, the whole crew – grips, scenes, props and Cavett himself – gave her a standing ovation. Even the producers cheered. Miss Head trailed behind Mae, her lady-in-waiting, primping and smoothing her dress, and carrying extra ostrich feathers in case they were needed.

The welcome was touching but Mae, as always in a new venture, was nervous. Perhaps, because of her worries, things worked out. Richard Hack of the *Hollywood Reporter* covered the event: 'There she was camping and vamping her way past the crap tables, the Victorian bar, the guys playing roulette and the ones just staring in disbelief. Nothing had changed. The movements, the timing were all true. Her voice sounds just the same as it did in her old Paramount days . . . Through take after take, her lip synching was perfect.'

The interview with Cavett was transmitted live. Cavett mentioned her famous mirrored bed and she cracked, 'Yeah, I sharpen a lot of pencils there.' She spoke of censorship, W. C. Fields, and delivered his famous line, 'Somebody stole the cork out of my lunch'; she told of her jail sentence and how she had worn her silk lingerie in prison.

In Hollywood a fan hired the Oriental cinema on Sunset Boulevard for the evening of the broadcast, and advertised across its marquee 'Closed Tonight To Watch Mae West on Television'.

The *Los Angeles Times* headed its review 'What is so rare as Mae in April?' When Mae saw the video of the show, however, she was disappointed. She felt it unnecessary for the director to have taken so many close-ups.

Many offers came in as a result of the Dick Cavett show, but Mae would consider only those that could be done in Los Angeles. She had given up travelling. She had not taken a holiday since arriving in Hollywood, apart from a few days in La Centa. 'I have three environments,' she would say, 'Hollywood, Santa Monica and the ranch.' But now she only had two environments, as the beach house was sold. It was difficult to maintain and she had always preferred the Ravenswood.

She considered an offer from an Australian chat show host.

She had no intention of going to Australia, but agreed to discuss the possibility of being filmed at the Ravenswood. Robert Duran was present.

'During the interview,' he recalls, 'the guy asked, "Miss West, can you tell me how you taught Cary Grant to drape himself over you when you filmed together?"'

' "Oh," said Mae. "Stand up a minute, I'll show you." '

She told the man to hold her while she pressed herself close to him and placed his arms about her, giving him the full Mae West treatment. When he had left she said to Duran, 'He got excited, you know, when he was holding me. I could feel his thing, right here.' She pointed to her abdomen.

Mae still had a fondness for circuses, and Duran accompanied her to the Shrine auditorium one day, where she sat in a box throughout the performance and went backstage afterwards to see the animals. She doted on the chimpanzees and posed for Duran as he took a picture of her nursing one.

Paul drove her on these excursions, and she would sit beside him, firmly buckled into her seat. She enjoyed a detour through Wilshire Boulevard, as she liked to window shop. If she noticed obvious homosexuals in the street – and they usually noticed her – she would wave to them. 'Oh, there's a couple of the boys,' she would murmur.

Duran was driving with her on one occasion when she asked, out of the blue, 'How's your mother doing?' Duran replied that she was not doing well. His father was out of work, his mother was pressed to make ends meet, and there were difficulties at the bank.

'Oh, those banks, aren't they terrible?' he recalls her saying. 'Remind me, when we get back, I'll write out a cheque, and she can forget the bank.' She gave him a generous cheque as soon as they returned to the apartment. She had never met his mother.

Sometimes these outings exhausted her, and when she got back to the Ravenswood she would lean against the wall of the lift and mutter 'I'm all in.' But the exhaustion seldom lasted long. After a cup of herbal tea or a glass of mineral water, she would recover.

The stars still came to see her, when they were granted permission, and both Jennifer Jones and Ricardo Montalban called, as did Marjorie Main, a devout Spiritualist, now best remembered as Ma Kettle in the long-running film series.

Mae had known Miss Main since they had played together on stage in *The Wicked Age* in 1927. Miss Main had come in as a last-minute substitute and she and Mae had remained friends throughout the years.

Not all the stars were from the Golden Era. Duran recalls her asking Grayson one morning:

'Who's coming today?'

'Elton John, Miss West.'

'Who, dear?'

'Elton John, you know, that singer.'

'Oh yeah. When's he coming up?'

'Three o'clock.'

'Umm. That'll give me time to get fixed up.'

When she was preparing for John, Duran remembers the old jacket she wore while applying her make-up was ripped. 'Some people said she was really a man,' he says, 'but I knew she wasn't. The apartment was full of mirrors and I couldn't help seeing everything. Often the first thing I had to do, when I arrived, was zip her into her bra. She would come to the door with just her slip on and her bra hanging loose. She would breathe in as I did it.'

As her cheque to Duran's mother illustrates, she was often generous, but she hated to be bettered in a business deal. Duran recalls an occasion when he called into a bar in Santa Ana and saw displayed some pastel portraits of Mae. He spoke to the artist and received permission to show them to Mae. She wanted to buy them, and Duran told her the artist wanted $65 apiece. She shook her head. 'Give him $60,' she said. 'He'll be happy with that.' 'That's a lady who doesn't pull the punches,' the artist remarked when the message was delivered. She bought the pastels at $60 each.

For Christmas 1975 Mae decided to have a Christmas tree. Not a real one, but one made of silver and tinsel with shining balls. She was riding in the car beside Paul, with Duran in the back, when she saw some displayed on the pavement, and that gave her the idea. She stepped out of the car to inspect them. There were not many people around but a few gathered about her. She was unmistakable with her blond hair and furs, every inch a star. As the crowd was small and thrilled to be meeting her, Mae did not panic but chatted.

She paid for the tree and, while it was loaded into the boot, resumed her place in the car, waving goodbye to the crowd.

On the way back to the Ravenswood they passed an advertisement for a Diana Ross concert. Duran mentioned he would like to go. 'What do you want to see her for?' demanded Mae. 'You can see her on television anytime.' She had reacted similarly when he had mentioned he would have liked to have met Bette Davis when she had called. 'What do you want Bette Davis for,' she had asked, 'when you've got me?' He learned it was better not to mention other stars.

She loved to hear praise of herself. One of the Hollywood movie houses ran *Belle of the Nineties* and Duran went to see it. He telephoned afterwards to tell her how the audience had laughed at the scene where the hotel is burning. Mae rings the fire brigade, yelling, 'There's a fire!' Then she repeats what the operator has said: 'Can you hold the line? . . . No, I'm in a burning building.' As Duran babbled, she was laughing delightedly, repeating his words to Paul.

When she was in the mood she would occasionally knock out a song in her apartment for Duran. Now that the beach house was gone, she kept her gowns at the Ravenswood, and would bring one out and hold it up against her as she sang.

She would, sometimes, lend frocks to friends to wear at drag functions. Duran recalls a friend telling her he was going to perform an impersonation of her in some Los Angeles bar. 'Take the gold dress,' she said, motioning to the wardrobe, 'it'll look better.' It was a Travis Banton original that had cost $1600.

Mae had business interests in a gay bar herself. The establishment was on Ventura Boulevard and, although she had no say in the management, she owned the property.

Chris Basinger remembers an occasion when Mae became worried that Paul was seeing another woman. 'He would come down about seven in the morning,' he says, 'and ask me to tell Miss West, if she rang down before 10 a.m., that he left just an hour ago. Well, she did ring down. I found out later that she had had him followed.'

Mae discovered that Paul did have interests elsewhere. Being a former sailor, he had bought himself a boat and was spending his time at a marina.

chapter twenty-seven

SEXTETTE

For years Mae had been trying to interest film companies in *Sextet*. MGM had chewed at the bait for a while, but a change of policy made *Sextet* one of the casualties. Warner Brothers had also explored the possibility but taken the idea no further.

Periodic announcements appeared in the trade press stating the film was to be made, and cast names were given. Mae had frequently said that she'd engaged Christopher Plummer; Peter O'Toole ('I like him. I don't know which number husband he would be, but I like him.'); Paul Newman (whom she had 'considered'); Elvis Presley and Tom Jones. She stated that George Cukor, with whom she had long wished to work, was engaged to direct. Cukor had indeed read her treatment but had declined. Even Marilyn Monroe in her prime, he felt, was not beautiful enough to fulfil the part Mae had written for herself.

It seemed the project was doomed until private backing fell from the sky. The backers were two young men, Robert Sullivan, twenty-three, and Daniel Briggs, twenty-one. Briggs is the son of Mimi Stauffer, a sometime major stockholder of Las Vegas's Tropicana Hotel.

The trade press broke the news that Irving Rapper was to direct *Sextette* (Mae changed the spelling to the feminine version for the film). At seventy-nine, Rapper was a movie legend himself, having directed Bette Davis in *Now, Voyager*. He had also directed *The Christine Jorgensen Story*. A dinner, which Mae attended, was given in the Escoffier Room of the Beverly Hilton to mark the occasion.

There was an embarrassing moment when Mae had to use the public lavatory: she surreptitiously crept between tables during the speeches but, to her annoyance, someone trained a spotlight on her as she was entering the ladies. This caused a great laugh. She did not join in.

Simultaneous with the news that *Sextette* was to go into production, came an announcement from Tom Bradley, mayor of Los Angeles, that he was creating a special Mae Day and issuing a proclamation in her honour.

Her leading man was to feature prominently during the Eighties. Timothy Dalton was chosen after Mae had seen him in a film and, just as Cary Grant had soared to stardom after she had chosen him, so Dalton coincidentally rose after *Sextette* to become the new James Bond. In addition to Dalton, a distinguished cast was assembled – Tony Curtis, George Hamilton, Walter Pidgeon and George Raft. Representative of the Seventies were pop figures Ringo Starr, Alice Cooper and Keith Moon. Edith Head would again attend to Mae's costumes. On paper everything looked good.

Mae told her friends that, as she was about to start filming again, she must lay off sex for a while. Like the boxers she so admired, she had to go into training.

Again the press arrived in droves, more incredulous than ever. Was she really going to play a sex symbol whom six virile men spend the entire film trying to entice into bed?

'What can a star aged eighty-five, even if she has a new film on the way ... say to us in the post-permissive Seventies?' enquired the *Evening Standard*. 'Well, let the lady speak for herself. "Sex and I'', she once said, "have a lot in common. I don't want to take any credit for inventing it – but I must say, in my own modest way, and in a manner of speaking, that I have rediscovered it ..." '

She was interviewed by Michael Roberts of the *Sunday Times*:

This summer Miss West plans to make a new film ... in which she plays a woman who has six husbands. 'Not all at once, dear,' she says. She says she writes a lot, although nowadays she does tend to forget what she has written. 'I should write my autobiography,' she says to Paul. 'You already did it,' says Paul . . . Does she still get fan mail? 'Oh yeah, but nowadays the men include nude pictures of themselves.' She puts her hand on her hip and rolls her eyes . . .

As she drifts off into the story about Ziegfeld discovering her again, Paul coaxes her back to the question. What did she think of Marilyn Monroe? Miss West looks blank. 'You remember Monroe,' urges Paul. 'Oh yes. She came to see me with her mother once. They queued up for hours and . . .' 'That wasn't Monroe,' sighs Paul, 'You're thinking of Jean Harlow dear.' 'Well, which one was Monroe?' snaps Miss West . . .

As we leave Miss West delays our exit by showing us the pictures of herself stacked in dusty piles in the hallway. Mae West caricatures, Mae West as the Statue of Liberty; idealised pictures of Mae West in the nude; stills from her famous films of the thirties.

She says that in her new film 'Every time I come out I'll have a different gown on – and I'm doing *four more pictures.*' She has been standing in the hallway talking for 20 minutes. Slowly she slumps against the wall, feebly trying to find her pockets so that she can put her hands in them. She looks defiant. Paul opens the pink-and-gold front door and whispers, 'She's a wonderful old lady really – so much energy.'

Gerald Clarke of *Time* magazine noted: 'There is . . . none of the pathos of the ageing star about Mae, none of the desperate anxiety of the character played by Gloria Swanson in *Sunset Boulevard.*'

The *Evening News* ran the caption: 'Manhunter! Mae West looks for a Lord.' This harked back to the pre-Dalton announcement when Mae was auditioning young men for roles for publicity purposes. Mae was asked why she was again returning to the screen and coolly responded, 'Public demand. They'll see me as they always like to – as myself. You know, sort of sexy.'

In addition to the leading men, *Sextette* was to feature a large cast of beefcake. Mae insisted on being present at all auditions, for which queues stretched for blocks.

Jean Rook of the *Daily Express* went to meet Mae and the two old war horses got along fine. Miss Rook wrote of the men queuing for the auditions:

> Once on the sacred ground, they sat, herded on long benches, like beef waiting for the slaughter. A man who turned up too late for the audition was pressing himself against the locked gates, like a creature barred from heaven. 'I missed my chance, oh my God, I missed it,' he said, wringing his hands and mine. 'What do they look like in there? How do I compare? Do you think I'd have made it – no don't tell me. If I thought I could, I can't bear it.' He frightened me more than Miss West.

Costume fittings were held at Western Costume, where Miss Head awaited Mae. Again Mae's weight fluctuated and she was liable to be several pounds lighter or heavier at each fitting depending upon how her diet was going. If the costumes did not fit, the fault was put down to Miss Head.

Miss Head had designed a trouser suit; when Mae tried it on she announced it made her 'arse look too big'. 'Let's face it,' said a member of the staff afterwards, 'her arse was too big.' Miss Head, however, whatever she thought, could not voice such sentiments and burst into tears. Mae was unmoved and continued to complain about the feathers in another gown, the fabrics, and most other things.

She was in no better mood for her fitting for hairpieces, and the wig-maker received a roasting: the hair he had used was not fine enough. During this abrasive meeting she asked Paul, who had driven her all day, to knot something for her. In a successful attempt to soothe her, he asked if she wanted a lover's knot or a sailor's knot. 'A sailor's knot,' she told him. 'That means you'll never leave me.' He was the only one who received a smile that day.

During one of the camera tests, which Mae performed with

actor Dennis Cole, a keen, young make-up man told Mae her eyelashes were too heavy, launching into a complicated argument about the demands of filming in colour. Mae listened in silence, then told him, 'My fans want to see me looking the way I always looked.' The lashes remained intact.

She was in form for the test, a copy of which was sent to her medical insurers to illustrate her prime physical condition. She made several changes of costume for the camera – involving lengthy lighting changes – and even strutted across the set in time to the beat of a drum to demonstrate the famous slouch.

When it came to acting a scene, though, she was not so good. Her memory let her down and she forgot her words. She made the excuse that there was too much noise in the studio and went to her room to rest before returning; it was clear she had been boning up on her lines. The effort paid off and this time she remembered them, but delivered her dialogue like an automaton. The fabled West timing was off. Her pride was saved by applause from the floor staff and their presentation to her of a bouquet of two dozen white roses.

Meanwhile a change in personnel had occurred. Director Irving Rapper had disassociated himself from the film and was replaced by Liverpudlian Ken Hughes. Mae liked Englishmen and Hughes had an impressive record including the direction of *Chitty Chitty Bang Bang* and *The Trials of Oscar Wilde*. In addition he had already directed her leading man Timothy Dalton in *Cromwell*. His name began with an H, the eighth letter of the alphabet, another point in Hughes's favour. Eight was her lucky number.

Hughes had accepted the engagement as the result of a telephone call to his London home: 'I was asked to make a film with Mae West,' he remembers. 'I think it was some London agent calling. Naturally I questioned it. "Is she still alive?" I asked, not facetiously, I really didn't know. "Oh, yes," they assured me, "she's running around, playing tennis and cheerful as they come." '

Hughes flew to Los Angeles to meet Mae and was received at the Ravenswood. 'We carry an image of the first time we see someone,' he says, 'and I remembered her in films, blonde and witty, and then suddenly I was talking to this old lady. She was a totally old person, she didn't understand what was happening, she was talking about some other script, she wasn't even with us. But she was awfully nice, and that's important.'

Filming started on 2 December 1976 at Paramount, her old studio, and to mark the occasion a banner was slung across the gates proclaiming, 'Welcome Home Mae West'. At one o'clock the Cadillac purred up with Grayson at the wheel and Mae and Paul in the back. She was dressed in white and ablaze with diamonds. The crowd that had gathered round the gates applauded her.

Hughes, however, now found his problems starting in earnest. 'On the very first take she couldn't remember a single line,' he recalls. 'Two lines at a time were out of the question, and if she had to speak she couldn't move, to do both at the same time was impossible for her. Mae tried very hard, poor old lady, but just couldn't do it.

'I called an emergency meeting. I pointed to a chart on the wall which listed the shooting schedule as six weeks. "You'll never get through in twice that time," I said, "and as for the budget (which was three million dollars), double it." I ripped the schedule off the wall and tore it up. But I stayed. After years of tradition you don't just walk off a film.'

Tony Curtis, who played Sexy Alexei, commented, 'I did the film because my old friend, Cary Grant, whom I so admired, had worked with both Marilyn Monroe and Mae West, and there aren't many who can claim that. I had worked with Monroe so now I wanted to work with Mae West. But we really had to shoot one line at a time, piece by piece. Perhaps that was how she'd done it in the old days. I don't know.'

'As long as you were talking about the old days and her old films, she was fine, but when it came to what was happening today – no. She told us that she wanted no mention of age on the set and, I think, that's how she coped with it all. She just refused to acknowledge that time was passing. She was nice enough, we went out to dinner a few times.'

She also went out to dinner with Ringo Starr, who was amused that she insisted on getting to the restaurant early in order to arrange the seating so that she was in the most advantageous lighting.

John Russell Taylor observed in an article in *The Times* that Mae seemed to glide as she walked. This puzzled him. 'Closer study shows how it is done. Miss West appears to glide because she does glide: always in public flanked by two of her more substantial gentlemen friends ... she is clearly lifted bodily by them an inch or two off the ground and conveyed effortlessly wherever she wants to go, her habitual floor-length dresses concealing the mechanics of the operation.'

Taylor regretted the fact that Mae censored her photographs, claiming, 'Mae West has the most charming, spontaneous smile in the world, feminine and infectious, which in pictures we never have a chance to see. But, as ever, right or wrong, she decides for herself.'

'She lived in a dream world,' Hughes confirms. 'She had performed her original play, and that's what she knew. They hired a very good writer who wrote some dialogue, but all the jolly jokes were wasted. I tried to salvage the good lines and give them to other people.

'She couldn't handle the simplest moves. In one scene she had to go to the elevator, push the button, and say a line. Getting all three things together was difficult. If she remembered to push the button then she forgot the line. If she remembered the line then she forgot to push the button. That was how it went on; we spent the entire day on that one scene. Finally she got it right, and I just yelled out, "That's it, it's a wrap." We were so relieved.

'To help her, we tried putting marks on the floor, but this was useless as she would forget all about them and just carry straight on. We tried putting sandbags on the floor to remind her to turn, and shooting from above her waist, but she would forget they were there and stumble over them. We had to use an actual assistant as a marker. He would lie on the floor and grab her knees as she walked, and gently turn her.'

Because of Mae's trouble memorizing lines Hughes, a former sound engineer, devised a system. He ordered a wooden booth to be constructed, like a telephone kiosk, in which he would stand. In front of him were three microphone systems, one connected to the cameraman, another to the floor, and the third to Mae. She wore a small receiver in her ear, hidden by her wig, the aerial taped down the back of her dress. Hughes would say her line into her microphone, which she would then repeat. This somewhat hastened the filming.

'I directed the whole movie from inside this sweatbox,' recalls Hughes. 'As I was giving her her lines I had to be ahead of her – my timing had to be impeccable – she would stand there, waiting for me to speak. While she was saying one line I would be telling her the next. The defect with the system was that the other actors could overhear my voice coming from Mae's earpiece. And they were having to talk over me while I was speaking to her. Somehow, we actually got through.'

Exaggerations of the bizarre happenings on the *Sextette* set spread through Hollywood. Since few knew her real age, it was said that she was past ninety, nearly one hundred. It was even whispered that she was really dead and was being impersonated by Beverly in the film. It seemed the only rumour not circulating was the truth: she was an elderly diabetic determined to hang on to her legend whatever the cost. Unwise, perhaps, but undeniably brave.

Overstatements about her difficulty with the microphone system proliferated. One yarn still current has it that short wave radio transmissions from cab drivers became intermingled with Hughes's lines, and while enacting one scene, Mae gave directions for a taxi to be sent to the lot. Another version of the story maintains she talked down a jumbo jet at Los Angeles airport. Hughes is adamant that no such things occurred. 'They never happened,' he says. 'She did once repeat something I said, but she knew what she had done, and laughed herself.'

In order to bleach out any signs of facial lines, Mae's lighting was augmented by pink 'baby' spots, placed low to shine directly on to her face, which provided the same effect as stage footlights had done in the past. The heat in which she had to work was great, made worse by her elaborate costumes.

Miss Head's modern designs were gradually dumped by Mae. The wedding gown, she decided, made her look bulky and she brought in the dress she had worn in the stage version of *Sextet*. She also renovated the gown she had worn for the Academy Awards ceremony with Rock Hudson. Miss Head, the recipient of eight Oscars, was philosophical about Mae's conduct. Over a comforting glass of mimosa taken with a crew member in the Polo Lounge of the Beverly Hills Hotel she stated, perhaps a shade too brightly, 'I don't care what she does. I've already been paid.'

Like a phoenix, Mae arose from the ashes of this 1977 project to become the Diamond Lil she had created in the 1920s. The swan bed from *She Done Him Wrong* was reconstructed and she used lines she'd written years before.

New lines were in evidence, too. Timothy Dalton says, 'I'm British, we've a stiff upper lip.' 'Well,' answers Mae, 'you've gotta start somewhere.' Elsewhere a young athlete tells her, 'I'm a pole vaulter.' 'Aren't we all?' she responds. To another, she remarks, 'I'd sure like to see your javelin.'

'Timothy Dalton was the Rock of Gibraltar,' remembers Hughes. 'If we had to do lines again, he was always there.' So was Mae, even if it took her many takes to get it right. 'There was no trouble ever with this dear lady on that score,' says Hughes. 'She'd do it over and over again. "That's all right, dear," she'd say when I apologized for doing another take. There are worse monsters in Hollywood than Mae West . . . you want a list?'

But she could drive the service departments wild by insisting on her make-up being constantly retouched. On one occasion one of her eyebrows had to be repainted six times before she was satisfied. By and large, however, the crew seemed fond of her, although some of the younger members were nervous. Once a new make-up man was so sweating with fear that drops of his perspiration fell on Mae's arm and made her jump. He wiped off the moisture with a tissue, apologizing because he was nervous. 'There's no need to be,' she told him. 'I won't bite.'

Management threw a Christmas party for the cast and crew, but Mae did not attend; she was too tired. An old security guard at Paramount recalled the days when Mae had been shooting *She Done Him Wrong*. She had often worked until after midnight and on Christmas Eve had stayed until two in the morning. Everyone connected with the film had received a present from her. He, himself, had been given $150.

An extensive publicity campaign was unleashed for *Sextette* in 1977, which involved Mae in hours of posing. She did everything asked of her and did not complain, but was frequently exhausted by the end of the day. Attempts were made to boost her morale. Her trailer was redecorated in Victorian style with flocked wallpaper and gilt cupids. Every morning a single white rose was delivered to her with the message, 'Good morning, Mae'.

One day she moved several of her old costumes into the trailer. She explained that she had used them for years and felt more at home surrounded by them. It was as though she was reaching out for the security of the past. She told one of the cast that a spirit had told her that she must surround herself with things that had brought her good luck. Now and then the smell of incense, issuing from a small oriental burner, would waft from the trailer as Mae practised meditation.

Rock star Alice Cooper was kind to her. A man with the wildest of public images, the script dictated he was to perform a song entitled 'No Time for Tears', while Mae wept. Mae West, of course, cried for no man and she refused to do it now; she swept off to her trailer until the situation was resolved. Cooper took in the circumstances and merely said, 'No sweat,' before coming up with another song, 'The Next Time', of which Mae approved.

The strain told on her health and she was plagued with a series of sore throats, high temperatures and stomach upsets. Her insurers, Lloyds of London, had stipulated she should work only four hours a day, but what constitutes four hours? The application and removal of make-up took nearly that amount of time. Added to which was the amount of time she spent wrestling with new lines introduced into the script daily.

She began suffering moments of disorientation. When someone came to fetch her one day, she asked, 'What time's the matinée?', obviously believing she was working in the theatre. She began to take days off. Over a three-month shooting schedule she was absent for a total of nearly three weeks and her stand-in was used for long shots.

However, she did not entirely lose her sense of humour. When rumours reached her that people were now saying she was stone deaf because of the ear-piece, she would move her wig to wiggle her ears. Her spirit remained dauntless as well. She announced that when *Sextette* was completed she was planning to make two further films, *Catherine Was Great* and *Pleasure Man.*

By April *Sextette* was eventually finished and she gave Hughes a gold watch as a thank-you present. Hughes recalls, 'She was eighty-four and what she did was a miracle. How many people of that age are still doing it? But I think that by appearing in that film a terrible disservice was done to an image that would have been better left alone. I respected and admired her. She was a great and a sweet old lady. She would do anything I asked of her. She would have worked days and nights if necessary, way after midnight . . . but I have never been through anything like *Sextette* in my life. I was a trouper, I carried on and was professional and, in the end, saved the day. I came in with a film, which is what I'd been paid to do. No one, in those circumstances, could have done what I did.'

chapter twenty-eight

DEATH

By some appalling oversight Edith Head, who had already been insulted by having her costumes rejected, was not invited to the wrap party. She had, it is true, remarked that she would gladly return one of her eight Oscars to get off the film, but it is unlikely that that would have been the reason. Inefficiency on the part of the organizers was more likely. To show she was not bothered she gave a party of her own on the same night at her home off Coldwater Canyon. There, in a shower of mimosas,* she let off steam.

After Dark magazine named Mae as the recipient of its Ruby Award, and she received the trophy at the Beverly Wilshire Hotel, escorted to the stage by seven strapping marines. Clips from her films were shown and friends paid tributes. 'Everything good happens after dark,' she said in her acceptance speech.

A few days after this, *Sextette* was given its first screening at the Directors' Guild Theater. The selected audience wrote their opinion of the movie on cards which they had been issued. The consensus was positive. Mae telephoned friends to tell them the film was going to be a smash hit.

Billboards were pasted up all over town, depicting a caricature of a timeless Mae reclining in a sheath frock, sporting a cigarette holder. 'Mae West Is Coming' screamed the pink caption. This was a bit premature, at least in reference to the general release of *Sextette*. The major companies were cautious and wanted further audience reaction.

To test the water further, Warner Brothers hired the Bruin

* The American equivalent of Buck's Fizz.

396

Theater in Westwood for an evening. On the bill with *Sextette* was *Outrageous*, starring Craig Russell, the female impersonator who had once been president of Mae's fan club. The UCLA campus is in the heart of Westwood and the students went along with the mood of the evening, spiritedly supporting the event. Ken Hughes was also there.

'You couldn't get near the theatre,' he remembers. 'The whole area was packed. I drove up in my car but I had to park some way away. When Mae arrived there was a riot. I should think every queen in Los Angeles was there that night, some even dressed as Mae West. It was like a carnival.

'It was the same during the screening. Every time she came on the fellers cheered, every gag was greeted with whoops of delight. I'd made sure that nearly every famous saying she'd made was in that film. They stood up and applauded at the end. As I drove away, I thought, "God damn it, we've made a money maker." '

Despite this, Warners did not pick up the option and neither did any other major studio. 'She was so disappointed that it didn't get distributed right away,' recalls Robert Duran. 'She told friends she could not understand why. Everyone had loved it during its two showings.'

The reviews were muted, but there was some acclaim for Mae. Jim Bacon wrote, 'Mae . . . can still deliver a G-rated line with those hips in pelvic gyration and make it sound like hardcore porn.' And *Time* magazine supported his view: '. . . a work so bad, so ferally innocent, that it is good, an instant classic . . . Mae West is her own best invention.' But *Playboy* was savage: 'The production almost embalms the myth they set out to revive. She seems an antique, wind-up doll wheezing her innuendo.'

Sextette is, in fact, a fascinating film. It is a wild, over-the-top extravaganza, and whereas Mae does not pull off every scene, there is still enough magic for much of what she does to work. In a way *Sextette* is the ideal vehicle to watch Mae's art for she works so much slower than in *Myra Breckinridge*, for example, that her technique can be observed. The one-liners are studied and her movements, still aggressive, have become more liquid. She represents the preservation of a mannered school of acting

now no longer fashionable yet none the less valid for that. The
Seventies pop figures who appeared alongside her are, by
definition, ephemeral and she timelessly upstages them. After
all, when watching Mae one is watching eighty years of American vaudeville come to life.

Ken Hughes's direction, when concentrating on Mae, is sensitive and refined. His sheer professionalism gives the film a
gloss. He is gentlemanly and ensures she is shot as she would
wish – indeed, as she insisted. In the scenes not dominated by
Mae he has a freer rein and the comedy sparkles, particularly
when focusing on Tony Curtis or Dom DeLuise.

Sextette has been too harshly treated by the critics. It is time
for a reappraisal. It is eccentric – how could it not be with an
eighty-four-year-old sex-mad heroine – but remains an encap-
sulation of Mae's art. Perhaps not Mae in spring, more Mae in
autumn, but even this autumnal Mae is a treat. Her original
style, so often copied by lesser artists, still shines true.

Her last film in her Hollywood heyday was *The Heat's On*; it
finished off her film career for nearly thirty years. She was
unhappy making it and her leaden performance reflects her
state of mind. Yet there are times in *Sextette* when she sparkles.
Off camera, she did momentarily lose her orientation but
nonetheless she was happy in her work. For all her frailty she
was happy being where she belonged – in front of a movie
camera – and it shows.

As 1977 melted into 1978 there were still no takers for *Sextette* and Mae was mortified to think that, for the first time in
her life, one of her films was going to end up in a vault, unseen
by her public. No one could fault Briggs and Sullivan for not
persevering, for in March 1978 they hired the Dome Theater
for a month and decided to launch the event with a real Hollywood première. Mae arrived in a white limousine, accompanied
by the obligatory muscleman and her faithful Paul. A roar went
up from the crowd as she alighted and waved.

But the run ended with disappointing receipts.

Not until the autumn of 1978 was *Sextette* shown again. The
release rights were purchased by Crown-International and a
première was announced for 16 November at the Warfield

Theater, San Francisco, at which Mae would make a personal appearance. The theatre was sold out the same day as the announcement appeared. Paul drove Mae to San Francisco, as she did not want to fly, and they stayed at the Mark Hopkins Hotel.

According to the *San Francisco Chronicle* over 2000 fans clogged the street waiting for a glimpse of her. These were not elderly fans, but mostly teenagers, as video coverage of the event proves. Mae appears, dressed in white satin, and enters the theatre to a storm of applause. The crowd mills around her in a way that clearly unnerves her, although her fixed smile only wavers briefly. She clutches Paul's arm as she slowly but determinedly ploughs forward. A reporter asks her, 'How do you like your films, Miss West?' 'They're all good,' she replies. The coverage focuses on her feet – she is having trouble with one of her shoe straps which has come adrift – but she still moves resolutely on backstage, to the wings.

As her introduction is roared over the loudspeakers, half-a-dozen musclemen in swimming costumes parade on to the stage and strike attitudes, awaiting her entrance. Mae then moves to the microphone, Paul by her side, her little beaded bag clutched tightly in her free hand. The audience leaps to its feet roaring approval. As the applause dies down she makes the shortest speech of her life, gesturing to the men behind her: 'I hope you are enjoying my demonstration of progressive education,' she says. With that she leaves the stage, muttering like some sort of mantra, 'fine, fine', in answer to the well-wishers who crowd round her. Paul is grim-faced, clearly worried about her.

Given the pressure of crowds, the police had to guard the hotel for the three days of her stay. But, without Mae's presence, the film continued to flounder at the box office and receipts once more did not live up to expectation.

She, however, returned to the Ravenswood happy. The magnificent audience had reassured her that Mae West was still a star. By now, the apartment was looking distinctly cluttered. Several items from the beach house had come to rest in its already cramped quarters. There was an additional ormolu clock and, most prominent of all, yet another nude statue of Mae, this time one that was three feet high. As Mae preferred bathing to a shower, the unused shower stall was filled with files, hats, props and the like.

Her wit was unimpaired when she was on home territory, as Chris Basinger was continuously discovering. One day a black lad of around seventeen approached him at the Ravenswood. 'He asked if he could just sit on the settee in the lobby in the hope that Miss West might pass through so that he could see her,' says Basinger. 'He came for several days and quietly sat down and waited. As he was so quiet, I didn't mind.

'Sometimes, Miss West would ring down if she wanted to know something, and sometimes she just rang down for a chat. "How you doin'?" she'd say. She'd talk for a while and when she wanted to go she'd just say "All right" and the phone would go down with a click. She rang me one afternoon and I told her, "Miss West, there's been a boy sitting down here, hoping to see you. He's been here several times."

' "Boy?" she said.

' "Well," I told her, "he's very young, about seventeen, and very handsome, a black guy."

' "Oh," she said. "Well, the next time he turns up, call me."

'I did, too. I said, "Remember I told you about that black guy? He's here again."

' "Hmm, give me ten minutes then send him up," she said.

'I asked the guy, "Would you like to meet Miss West?" and I thought he was going to faint. He was absolutely speechless. I had to push him in the elevator and push the button for him. I told him to turn left when he got to the sixth floor, and ring the bell at 611.

'He was up there for about an hour and a half, and then he came back down again. I don't know what went on up there, but he came to me looking completely dazed. He simply said, "I will never forget you, and what you've done for me, for the rest of my life." He didn't walk out, he floated.'

She was probably telling him how she saved Paramount singlehandedly.

In June 1979 *Sextette* was given a block booking throughout the Manhattan and East Hampton areas. Now the reviews echoed *Playboy's* original spiteful attack, notably Rex Reed's: 'Most pathetic is seeing her enter in full bridal regalia, the groom at her side. He looks twenty-five, she looks like something they found in the basement of a pyramid. "How do you like it here in London?" a reporter asks. "Oh, I like it anywhere," she drools, her left eye involuntarily taking a look at her right eye . . .'

Happily, it seems unlikely Mae ever read those sentences and the rest of the article from which they are extracted; bad reviews upset her and were, quite sensibly, kept from her. What, if anything, could be gained by upsetting an old lady of eight-six, now incapable of defending herself? And that is what she had become. By now, even she must have realized her filming and stage days were over.

But Mae still wanted to be beautiful. Hollywood leading lady Ann Rutherford, who had starred as a teenager with Mickey Rooney in the Andy Hardy films plus numerous others, including *Pride and Prejudice* and *Gone with the Wind*, recalls meeting her at a dinner party.

Mae, as always, arrived just late enough to make a good entrance. 'In came this darling little lady,' says Miss Rutherford, 'on her high platform shoes, propped up by two strong young men. Great eyelashes, an inch long. She could barely walk, but she took little, mincing steps. She was dressed all in white, dripping with furs and, oh, my dear, the diamonds.

'She was a legend in Hollywood. Your day was made if you saw her, it was like being in New York and coming across Garbo in Bloomingdales. If you ever saw her about you would rush home and scream "I've just seen Mae West!"'

'And she was still the prettiest one there. Her face was so smooth, and she said everything for effect. All her lines were drawn out, and she was really giving a performance. She took herself very seriously and did, indeed, become a caricature of what she'd been.

'The only mistake she had made was with her hair. She wore it down, as though she was about fourteen. She had arranged it in a lift, pulled it tight so that it pulled the face taut, but it was very thin on top, and as I passed her chair I could see these little silken threads pulled across and her scalp underneath. But she remained young, in her own mind, until the day she died.'

Mae seemed to mellow after *Sextette*: an aura of serenity and gentleness that had always been there but had so often been masked by shrewd business talk and the need to ensure she was not being ripped off now surrounded her. Chris Basinger was set upon and beaten up just before Christmas 1979 and she was very solicitous about his welfare. 'My jaw was broken,' he reports, 'but I had just got out of hospital and was back at the Ravenswood. It was Christmas Eve and I saw the limo drive up and she came to me at the desk. "Oh, dear," she said. "I hear you was beat up? Would you like to have Christmas Eve dinner with us?"

'We went to a Chinese restaurant she liked and some old bum was stumbling down the street. Paul was just helping her from the limousine and the bum yelled out, "Hey, you're looking good, Mae!" "Oh, er, thank you, dear," she replied. She was fazed, but instinctively good mannered.'

The New Year saw her suffer further bouts of disorientation. There were times when it was clear her mind had fled 1980 and withdrawn to the past. She would talk of Tillie and say she had to go to meet her. She still saw her friends, but spent most of her time with Paul, and as always Beverly was a regular visitor. Paul nursed her, gave her injections, dressed and even bleached her hair when she was too tired to see a hairdresser. He cooked for her, sometimes spoiling her with her favourite dish, rack of lamb.

Robert Duran visited in July and they made arrangements to meet on her birthday, the 17th of August. Unfortunately, only a few weeks went by before Paul telephoned him with the sad news that Mae had been taken to hospital. She had fallen out of bed and was suffering from a concussion. A doctor had examined her and found she could neither speak coherently nor synchronize her hand movements – the classic symptoms of a stroke.

She had not wanted to go to hospital, but was admitted to the Good Samaritan the next day. Paul went with her and stayed

in an adjoining room. They registered under the names of Mr
and Mrs Drake. Paul kept this secret well, just as he had kept
her many secrets. Friends thought she may have gone to
hospital for a face tuck or something similar. Such an operation
would have been veiled with just as much secrecy. However the
news leaked, as it inevitably would, and radio and television
stations blared the fact she had had a stroke. Nonetheless
reporters still did not have the full story – Paul let it be known
she had fallen out of bed after dreaming of Burt Reynolds – and
the hospital, well used to looking after movie stars, kept the real
reason for her hospitalization under wraps.

Because of her stroke Mae could not move her tongue; she
was fed through a tube inserted into her nostril. Dolly
Dempsey, a fan of Mae's since the 1930s, helped Paul nurse
her. But Mae was not finished yet. Amazingly she regained
strength, took a few brief walks around the room and was able
to sit in a chair. She attempted to communicate with the spirit
world in the hope its denizens could help her. Incense was
burnt, which did not please the hospital authorities, as the
fumes were not considered helpful to an invalid.

Her gramophone records were played to her and a film pro-
jector was installed in her room. The only films shown, of
course, were her own. Sitting in this hospital room fighting for
her life, the eighty-seven-year-old sex symbol tapped her foot to
her own music and turned her face in the direction of a screen
upon which the virile Mae West strutted her stuff. She had
been absorbed in that image all her life; why, near death,
should the pattern change?

Mae rallied and was taken for an occasional drive. However,
she suffered a relapse and her right arm and leg became
paralysed. Messages and tokens of support came from all over
the world. The stars sent flowers; conspicuous among them was
a huge bouquet from Elizabeth Taylor. A psychic intoned some
mantras and set up a device which streamed coloured lights
about her. Beyond this there was not a great deal anyone could
do and the decision was taken to bring her home where she
would receive constant attention from Paul, supported by a
team of nurses.

The great canopied bed with its mirrored ceiling, in which she had been photographed countless times, was stored in the basement and a hospital bed took its place. There Mae received the best care possible. Some days she was better than on others. One good day, it was thought it might cheer her if she had her hair set, so a hairdresser was summoned. This was not a success, as the hairdresser burst into tears as soon as he saw her and had to be helped from the room. But by that time Mae had again slipped into unconsciousness.

She died on 22 November, having received the last rites from a Catholic priest. This was no deathbed conversion, nor need to be re-admitted into the Catholic Church – simply Paul looking after her and doing what he believed she would like. The presence of an ordained man of God did, indeed, seem to comfort her.

chapter twenty-nine

AFTERMATH

Chaos broke out after her death. The news flashed all over the world, to be immediately followed by lengthy and liberally illustrated obituaries. The staff of the Ravenswood switchboard – her friends – were driven insane by the barrage of calls from those who wanted to know the funeral arrangements.

A universal feeling of shock swept Hollywood. Mae was the movies' most enduring sex symbol: the demise of any institution leaves a vacuum. Within two days of her death George Raft, the man who had given her her break, also died.

'I want to give her the greatest Hollywood funeral ever,' Paul announced. Her funeral was to be Mae West's final public appearance before her fans. She had been delighted with the furore caused by her appearance at the première of *Myra Breckinridge* and would have expected her funeral to provoke no less excitement. But as too often happens when someone dies, others intervened and suggested that a small service, attended by a select few, would be more appropriate. This decision was upheld by her publicist Stanley Musgrove. Eventually Paul agreed.

It is a sad comment on the state of the modern movie industry that this view was not opposed. Such giants as L. B. Mayer, Jack Warner, or even Harry Cohn, would never have countenanced such a breach of showbiz etiquette. Under the administration of any one of these men, Mae's last public appearance would have been a carnival. Movie stars feed on publicity; what have they to do with quiet funerals?

Restraint was not entirely prompted by concern for Mae's dignity but rather from fear that there might be too large a crowd at the cemetery. For this reason Mae was denied her last gala appearance. This po-faced course of action (which Mae would have abhorred) was agreed and the service took place at 3 p.m. on 25 November 1980 at the replica of the Old North Church, Forest Lawn Cemetery, Hollywood Hills.

It was planned to have Mae laid to rest in a closed coffin on the grounds that the stroke may have disfigured her looks and she would have hated to have appeared ugly. In death, however, Mae was beautiful – and even more so after the embalmers had finished with her. The peach-pink smile curved her lips, the eyelashes fanned her cheekbones and her face was free of wrinkles. A beautifully dressed platinum wig topped her head and her hands were folded on her bosom. Her hands were so dainty, and the skin which clothed them (of which she had always been so justly proud) remained so soft, they might have belonged to a child. She was dressed in the long white gown she had worn in *Sextette*, but the marabou hem had been removed and draped around her neck to frame her face. Because she was so lovely the coffin was left open and banks of white roses were placed about her. She looked truly angelic.

The eulogy was given by director Ross Hunter; Lloyd Ogilvie of the Hollywood Presbyterian Church delivered the sermon. During his address the minister gave a twist to her famous aphorism by announcing, 'Goodness had everything to do with it, she was a profound woman and distinguished by goodness. Behind the caricature was character and a good woman.'

As mourners filed past the coffin, an organ played a medley of her songs gently in the background: 'Frankie and Johnny', 'Easy Rider' and 'After You've Gone'. Paul was the last to visit the coffin. Among those present was George Eiferman, one of her many musclemen. Several of the other boys came to pay their respects.

Beverly was present, but unable to enter the church; she was too stunned to take in the news and veered between grief at her sister's death, fury at Mae for dying and leaving her, and a refusal to accept she had died at all. She sat outside in a limousine, fortifying herself with sips of champagne from a bottle she had prudently brought with her.

Shortly after the service Mae, accompanied by Paul and Dolly Dempsey, was flown to New York where she was interred in the Abbey of Cypress Hills Cemetery, atop a small pile of marble containers housing the remains of Tillie, Battling Jack and her brother John. Mae lies there to this day, protecting her brood just as she did when alive (Beverly is now with her). It is a silent, tasteful place, redolent of prosperity. Her casket bears the straightforward inscription 'Mae West'. No prayer, no motto, no cant.

Mae's will was filed for probate in Santa Monica Superior Court on 16 January 1981. Beverly was left $25,000, her limousine, personal jewellery and belongings; Mae's nephew, John, was left $15,000; Paul and her secretary, Larry Lee, who had so greatly assisted with her writing, were left $10,000 each. $3500 was left to the Mae West Fan Club in Ontario, Canada, while smaller bequests were left to other friends and relatives.

Many had expected Mae to leave more, probably as a result of the publicity she had encouraged concerning her alleged wealth. But if the amount of money she received for both *Myra Breckinridge* and *Sextette* are deducted from her assets, then Mae's return in advanced age to the movies takes on a starker meaning. For all the advice of her psychics and her belief in her own infallibility, it suggests that perhaps Mae had found herself getting hard up. She had either to make more movies or face a life of unacceptable economy. The beach house had already been sold and the ranch was in a state of decomposition.

Many were also surprised at the smallness of Paul's legacy. He had been her constant companion for twenty-five years and, towards the end, she would have been unable to function without him. A more generous settlement was finally agreed.

Beverly was also in trouble. The elderly limousine Mae had bequeathed her had been purchased in 1966, and Mae's will predated its purchase by two years. To whom, then, did the car now belong? The matter, largely a technicality, was complicated in that the car had been registered in the name of a company Mae had formed and which now no longer appeared to be trading.

Further problems confronted Beverly had she been in a fit

state to recognize them. But shortly after Mae's death, her own frail grip on reality abandoned her and she entered a nursing home where she could be properly cared for. Mercifully she died in March 1982 after a period of increasing bewilderment.

The ranch was left unoccupied. It did not take looters long to move in and they systematically relieved the place of its valuables. The trunks of props and costumes which Mae had preserved were forced open, the contents strewn about, removed or destroyed. Mae West memorabilia began to turn up at various sales throughout America as the stolen goods were disposed of. The movie star ranch became derelict, with just a ghostly wind howling about it, rattling the shutters of the empty rooms. The old drawing room with its white grand piano became a defiled and foul-smelling mausoleum; the piano remained in position but obscene glutinous material was poured over it.

chapter thirty

THE LEGEND LIVES ON

Most stars are as tough as old boots and so, to some degree, was Mae, yet her toughness masked a lethal insecurity. As a child she never knew emotional stability and she spent her life in pursuit of it. She was dragged from stock company to stock company by her mother, to play whatever role was required. Out of this experience came 'Mae West'. That shimmering, audacious figure illuminating motion picture screens around the world became symbolic of mother and father to Mae the woman, embodying characteristics pleasing to the memory of both. Mae West's sexual allure was a tribute to her mother and her pugnaciousness a recognition of the debt she owed her father.

Mae, the bane of the film censors on the one hand, was the epitome of convention on the other. True, she became hooked on sex – it would be the mighty panacea with which she remedied her life – but nonetheless she remained a quintessential product of the Victorian morals instilled in her in childhood.

Stardom provided Mae's security. Men all over the world desired her screen image, reassuring her that she would never experience the emotional isolation her mother had known. Tillie never lived to see Mae become a movie star, but she had drummed into her daughter that stardom was the only worthwhile goal in life. This was a dictum baby Mary Jane quickly absorbed, and never forgot.

Hollywood never beckoned Mae, she arrived there by accident, and as a character actress, not as a star. At the time she was nearly forty years old, overweight and – after years in vaudeville – a Broadway disaster. Her story might have ended there but for her remarkable belief in herself. Such was her determination for the Mae West character to survive that she literally took on the movie moguls singlehandedly.

With Texas Guinan as her inspiration she floored Hollywood with her panache and irreverence, and the film-going public could not get enough of her. Typically she also challenged the taboos of the day and groups of the outraged, mostly religious, some political, massed to silence her. She gave her all to the movies, as she had given her all to creating the Mae West legend on stage, and for the narrow-minded her all was far too much. Censorship killed off Mae's first Hollywood incarnation. But morals change, and Mae might well congratulate herself, if she were alive today, for making acceptable what she fought so hard to have recognized.

Stardom fuelled Mae's existence; it was her meat and drink. When Hollywood turned its back on her in 1943, her defeat seemed total. However, she did not buckle under, although she did not know at the time she would not make another film for twenty-six years. Such was the power of her own commitment to her 'Mae West' creation, she remained loyal to herself. She never ceased to be a star throughout that bleak period when she found herself out in the wilderness playing stock in backwater towns. Audiences everywhere were always aware they were in the presence of someone special. She was uniquely Mae West.

Personal happiness is sacrificed by most long-term movie stars. Being a star is a full-time job and every moment must be devoted to ensuring success. Lovers and friends take second place and only the toughest get to the top. It's a lonesome occupation as most prospective partners of a star cannot stand the competition and drop out. Those who put their careers above all else wind up isolated with just a press-cuttings book to keep them company in old age.

Mae knew the price to be paid and thought the deal fair. Not for her the alcoholic excesses, drugged oblivion or suicide attempts of some of her Hollywood contemporaries. And she was able to run rings round the hardened entertainment people who induce nervous breakdowns.

She was, in her own overweight and mature way, an original: the prototype wisecracking, hand-on-hip, platinum sex symbol. Only Jean Harlow, who hit the movies several years before Mae, made such an impact. Those who came after Mae – Judy Holliday, Jayne Mansfield and Marilyn Monroe – owe her a large debt. The caricatured walk, the gestures, the grooming and the salutary good-natured vulgarity were all gifts bestowed by Mae. She alone, however, dared to express that undisguised and irredeemable carnal lust that has made her an icon of the twentieth century. Her honest, upfront delight in sex is one of her finest legacies.

Yet she did not achieve quite the fulsome style of immortality she was looking for. She expected to be remembered as the greatest sex symbol of them all, the peerless beauty, but Marilyn Monroe wears that crown. Today, the young know Mae West less as the 'Empress of Sex' than as a comedienne. When her films are shown it is her singular gift for comedy that is applauded, not her sexual allure nor how she set about satisfying her desires.

Mae's true fibre really came to the fore after 1943; she had been spat on by Hollywood but refused to be beaten. In retaliation she did not so much fight the system as ignore it, continuing relentlessly to be Mae West, her chosen vocation.

Most of Mae's career strategy was worked out in apartment 611 at the Ravenswood, in the heart of Hollywood. Tough-talking agents and producers were seldom present when these discussions took place. The *ménage*, headed by Mae herself, consisted of her lawyer Jim Timony, very much the worse for wear by the time Mae went into the movies, and her sister Beverly. That ill-assorted, some might say disreputable, trio masterminded one of the world's great film careers. Mae, of course, made all the decisions herself. The others were catalysts, merely helping her to focus her mind and agreeing with whatever decision she took.

Mae booked her club act into Las Vegas in 1954 at the age of sixty-one. She had not made a film for eleven years and her last one had been a disaster. Still she knew herself to be a star. She surrounded herself on stage with the cream of American manhood and triumphed. Her undiminished sexual appetite stood her in good stead: she did not have to fake her sentiments on stage – lust sustained her. Her determination to enjoy as many attractive men as possible was the standard she set for herself and followed. The difference between Mae and others was her downright honesty. Again, her desires were sometimes too strong for her times, and might well be too strong today, and she had to pretend they were just part of her act. Her little curtain speeches, ending each show, were one device she used to cover her tracks.

Real fortitude was needed when Mae accepted her role in *Myra Breckinridge*. She was aware that the spotlight of the world was upon her. There was great curiosity about her return to the screen after such a prolonged absence, particularly in the role of the sex-obsessed Leticia van Allen. At seventy-six Mae never wavered, and never considered turning down the part, or reducing the character's sexual voraciousness. With a little help from her plastic surgeon, she walked away with the show.

Eight years later, however, when she made *Sextette* the vicious effects of age could no longer be held at bay. Her mental faculties began to fail her. Her brain, which had so carefully honed her jokes and masterminded each step in her extraordinary career, could no longer cope with learning a simple line of dialogue. Periods of disorientation blotted out reality and in her mind she was back in vaudeville. Only a performer with great guts could possibly have completed the picture.

Mae was brought up in vaudeville. It was the basis of her training and she remained true to it. The movies were always upstarts to Mae: in her eyes vaudeville was where real art lay. Every inch the professional, she nonetheless learnt the film business easily and quickly, mastering the medium from the first to capture immediately its illusional nature.

As a human being Mae was brave, but she was far from fearless, which made her bravery so much greater – if fear is not felt then there is no need for courage. She was a mass of insecurity as the stream of lovers, the intransigence, the tantrums and the reclusiveness demonstrate; when not threatened, however, her genuine good nature floated to the surface. Then she was usually warm and kind. She was never a bully and only ever attacked those who sought to diminish the Mae West image. Underneath she was the softest touch in Hollywood as the continuous parade of losers, who came to her door and never left without a spontaneous cash gift, demonstrate.

Mae never fully trusted people but then who would have done otherwise given a similar background? She had been a child actress, played vaudeville until middle age, stormed Hollywood, starred in Las Vegas cabaret and returned – in her own way triumphant – to the movies. Before she was a star she was despised and discarded; when she became a star everyone tried to make a fast buck out of her. She had known hostility, rejection and the dilution of her talent, but she had also known the unique thrill of unquestioned stardom and the public's heartfelt appreciation of her great art. She was truly touched with genius.

Among the many things she taught her fans was that thinness is not an essential aspect of female desirability, and that sex is not the sole prerogative of the young. Above all she preached the lesson, still not learned, that sex should be uncomplicatedly enjoyed and not fretted over. She made a lot of money and had the companionship of two loyal men. Most of us get far less out of life, but then most of us put far less into it than Mae West.

Mae West was a great lady and we will not see her like again.

INDEX